Research Series on the Chinese Dream and China's Development Path

Drawing on a large body of empirical studies done over the last two decades, this Series provides its readers with in-depth analyses of the past and present and forecasts for the future course of China's development. It contains the latest research results made by members of the Chinese Academy of Social Sciences. This series is an invaluable companion to every researcher who is trying to gain a deeper understanding of the development model, path and experience unique to China. Thanks to the adoption of Socialism with Chinese characteristics, and the implementation of comprehensive reform and opening-up, China has made tremendous achievements in areas such as political reform, economic development, and social construction, and is making great strides towards the realization of the Chinese dream of national rejuvenation. In addition to presenting a detailed account of many of these achievements, the authors also discuss what lessons other countries can learn from China's experience.

More information about this series at http://www.springer.com/series/13571

Yingqiu Liu
Editor

New Interpretations on the Development of China's Non-Governmental Enterprises

SSAP

Springer

Editor
Yingqiu Liu
Center for Private Economic Studies
Chinese Academy of Social Sciences
Beijing, China

Translated by CHEN Fuyu, CAO Shunfa;
Sponsored by the Chinese Fund For the Humanities and Social Sciences

ISSN 2363-6866 ISSN 2363-6874 (electronic)
Research Series on the Chinese Dream and China's Development Path
ISBN 978-981-10-3870-9 ISBN 978-981-10-3872-3 (eBook)
DOI 10.1007/978-981-10-3872-3

Library of Congress Control Number: 2017940485

Printed on acid-free paper

This Springer imprint is published by Springer Nature
The registered company is Springer Nature Singapore Pte Ltd.
The registered company address is: 152 Beach Road, #21-01/04 Gateway East, Singapore 189721, Singapore

- Key Research Project of Chinese Academy of Social Sciences, 2009
- Program of National Social Science Fund of China, 2009

Authors

(In order of task undertaken)
Liu Yingqiu, Zhang Jun, Liu Xiahui, Li Mengjuan, Ju Jinwen, Lü Fengyong, Xue Bai, Xu Haoqing, Zhao Lei, Liu Jianxiong, Zhu Xiongbing, Wu Yanbing, Wang Hongling, Gu Qiang, Dong Ruiqing, Zhao Sanying, Zhang Liang, Xia Xianliang

Abstract

Following the shadow of the international financial crisis and its indelible impact on China's non-governmental enterprises (NGEs), this book investigates and analyzes the problems in and challenges to NGEs' development in the new stage of China's economic and social development, following its entry into the WTO. It elaborates on and demonstrates the necessity, urgency, and inevitability of China's NGEs to vigorously promote their organizational, technological, and managerial innovation at the present stage, and suggests some strategic options for further development.

This book consists of twelve chapters. Chapter 1 reveals and analyzes the new challenges, choices, and countermeasures available for the new development of China's NGEs. Based on the effect principles, Chap. 2 describes the dynamic process of NGEs' development and, using human resource management models, illustrates the positive role they play in China's economic growth. Chapter 3 reveals that China's NGEs are still concentrated in low-end industries and fields, and points out that, in the process of industrial transformation and upgrading, NGEs should not blindly discard traditional industries, but should instead focus on integrated innovation and innovative development in order to push forward the integration of industrial chains and regional industrial transfer. Through an empirical analysis of the barriers to NGEs' entry into monopolized industries, Chap. 4 explores the origin of monopoly barriers and proposes feasible measures for better and more rapid development of China's national economy. Chapter 5 is an in-depth analysis of the governance structure and mechanisms of China's NGEs as well as the problems therein. Chapter 6 teases out the new characteristics and trends of NGEs' expansion and improvements to their efficiency, analyzes the relationship between scale, efficiency, and growth, and lays out several reasonable paths for NGEs' growth and development. Chapter 7 focuses on the labor-capital distributive relationship and its development within China's NGEs and tests it empirically by using the C-D production function. Chapter 8 studies the arrival of the Lewis Turning Point, the disappearing advantage of cheap labor, and new changes in labor supply and demand as China enters a new stage of economic transformation, while empirically concluding that only by increasing their competitiveness can NGEs obtain sustainable and sound development. Chapter 9 starts with the status and efficiency of NGEs' technological innovation and illuminates the paths to and realization of potential technological innovations. Against the background of SMEs' (small- and medium-sized enterprises') financing difficulties, Chap. 10 explores and expounds upon the special significance of developing micro finance institutions with an eye towards the long-term, sustainable, and healthy development of China's economy. Based on NGEs' development in high-tech industries, Chap. 11 reveals the driving role high-tech industries play in the development of China's NGEs by using the Coordination Degree Model and a quantitative analysis of ridge regression. Finally, Chap. 12, while stressing the fact that China's NGEs are entering a new stage of transnational development, centers around the internationalization of the RMB and focuses on the new environments, problems, and challenges facing NGEs' transnational operation from the perspective of global economic adjustment and rebalancing in the post-crisis era.

Series Preface

Since China's reform and opening began in 1978, the country has come a long way on the path of socialism with Chinese characteristics, under the leadership of the Communist Party of China. Over 30 years of reform efforts and sustained spectacular economic growth have turned China into the world's second largest economy, and wrought many profound changes in the Chinese society. These historically significant developments have been garnering increasing attention from scholars, governments, and the general public alike around the world since the 1990s, when the newest wave of China studies began to gather steam. Some of the hottest topics have included the so-called China miracle, Chinese phenomenon, Chinese experience, Chinese path, and the Chinese model. Homegrown researchers have soon followed suit. Already hugely productive, this vibrant field is putting out a large number of books each year, with Social Sciences Academic Press alone having published hundreds of titles on a wide range of subjects.

Because most of these books have been written and published in Chinese, however, readership has been limited outside China—even among many who study China—for whom English is still the lingua franca. This language barrier has been an impediment to efforts by academia, business communities, and policy-makers in other countries to form a thorough understanding of contemporary China, of what is distinct about China's past and present may mean not only for her future but also for the future of the world. The need to remove such an impediment is both real and urgent, and the *Research Series on the Chinese Dream and China's Development Path* is my answer to the call.

This series features some of the most notable achievements from the last 20 years by scholars in China in a variety of research topics related to reform and opening. They include both theoretical explorations and empirical studies, and cover economy, society, politics, law, culture, and ecology, the six areas in which reform and opening policies have had the deepest impact and farthest-reaching consequences for the country. Authors for the series have also tried to articulate their visions of the "Chinese dream" and how the country can realize it in these fields and beyond.

All of the editors and authors for the *Research Series on the Chinese Dream and China's Development Path* are both longtime students of reform and opening and recognized authorities in their respective academic fields. Their credentials and expertise lend credibility to these books, each of which having been subject to a rigorous peer review process for inclusion in the series. As part of the Reform and Development Program under the State Administration of Press, Publication, Radio, Film and Television of the People's Republic of China, the series is published by Springer, a Germany-based academic publisher of international repute, and distributed overseas. I am confident that it will help fill a lacuna in studies of China in the era of reform and opening.

Xie Shouguang

Acknowledgments

After a relatively short gestation period, the *Research Series on the Chinese Dream and China's Development Path* has started to bear fruits. We have, first and foremost, the books' authors and editors to thank for making this possible. And it was the hard work by many people at Social Sciences Academic Press and Springer, the two collaborating publishers, that made it a reality. We are deeply grateful to all of them.

Mr. Xie Shouguang, president of Social Sciences Academic Press (SSAP), is the mastermind behind the project. In addition to defining the key missions to be accomplished by it and setting down the basic parameters for the project's execution, as the work has unfolded, Mr. Xie has provided critical input pertaining to its every aspect and at every step of the way. Thanks to the deft coordination by Ms. Li Yanling, all the constantly moving parts of the project, especially those on the SSAP side, are securely held together, and as well synchronized as is feasible for a project of this scale. Ms. Gao Jing, unfailingly diligent and meticulous, makes sure every aspect of each Chinese manuscript meets the highest standards for both publishers, something of critical importance to all subsequent steps in the publishing process. That high-quality if also at times stylistically as well as technically challenging scholarly writing in Chinese has turned into decent, readable English that readers see on these pages is largely thanks to Ms. Liang Fan, who oversees translator recruitment and translation quality control.

Ten other members of the SSAP staff have been intimately involved, primarily in the capacity of in-house editor, in the preparation of the Chinese manuscripts. It is time-consuming work that requires attention to details, and each of them has done this, and is continuing to do this with superb skills. They are, in alphabetical order: Mr. Cai Jihui, Ms. Liu Xiaojun, Mr. Ren Wenwu, Ms. Shi Xiaolin, Ms. Song Yuehua, Mr. Tong Genxing, Ms. Wu Dan, Ms. Yao Dongmei, Ms. Yun Wei and Ms. Zhou Qiong. In addition, Xie Shouguang and Li Yanling have also taken part in this work.

Ms. Yun Wei is the SSAP in-house editor for the current volume.

Our appreciation is also owed to Ms. Li Yan, Mr. Chai Ning, Ms. Wang Lei and Ms. Xu Yi from Springer's Beijing Representative Office. Their strong support for the SSAP team in various aspects of the project helped to make the latter's work that much easier than it would have otherwise been.

We thank associate professor Chen Fuyu and professor Cao Shunfa for translating this book and Ms. Virginia L. Conn. for her work as the polisher. We thank everyone involved for their hard work.

Last, but certainly not least, it must be mentioned that funding for this project comes from the Ministry of Finance of the People's Republic of China. Our profound gratitude, if we can be forgiven for a bit of apophasis, goes without saying.

Social Sciences Academic Press
Springer

Contents

List of Figures

List of Tables

Chapter 1
Problems and Challenges for NGEs in the New Stage

Yingqiu Liu and Jun Zhang

1.1 China's Increasingly Prominent Role in the World Economy

When we take the powerful growth of China's economy—even under the influence of the recent global financial crisis—in combination with the country's ongoing process of industrialization and urbanization, the shift in economic development models, and policies for the promotion and advancement of science and technology (especially those marked by encouraging new energy sources and materials), one thing is clear: China's economy has already entered a new stage of development, completely different from anything previously seen in the past.

1.1.1 A More Important Position for China in Global Economic Development

In August of 2010, the Chinese National Bureau of Statistics (NBS) released information on the second quarter of the national economy in that year. China's Gross Domestic Product (GDP) had already exceeded that of Japan, ranking second in the world; China had grown into the second largest global economy, second only to the U.S. When the world economy was still suffering from the US subprime mortgage

Y. Liu (✉)
Center for Private Economic Studies, Chinese Academy of Social Sciences, Beijing, China
e-mail: liuyq@cass.org.cn

J. Zhang
Chinese Academy of Social Sciences, Beijing, China

Y. Liu (ed.), *New Interpretations on the Development of China's Non-Governmental Enterprises*, Research Series on the Chinese Dream and China's Development Path, DOI 10.1007/978-981-10-3872-3_1

market meltdown and the world's major economies were undergoing apparent recessions, China was maintaining a relatively high rate of growth, despite internal and external interferences, and was expected to lead the world economy out of the mire of recession. This situation was unprecedented and attributable not only to China's increasing economic capacity and enhanced overall national strength, but also to the special advantages inherent in China's present economic system. The world economy needs China, and vice versa. China is now entering a brand new economic stage—one characterized by the co-existence of the country's unique features and economic openness on the one hand and greater integration with the rest of the world in terms of economic operations and institutional frameworks on the other.

Since the beginning of its period of reform and opening up, China has made significant achievements in the development of its national economy, and—with its improved comprehensive national strength—its status within the world economy has greatly improved as well. In 1978, China's gross national product (GNP) was only RMB 354.6 billion; while in 2009, it was RMB 34.051 trillion. Calculated at current prices, it increased 96.03 times with a nominal annual rate of growth of 15.9%. Calculated according to constant prices, China's GDP increased by an average of 9.87% annually over the 30 year period of its reform and opening up. Both the speed and time span of its growth far surpassed those of South Korea and Japan, a feat that has often been billed a "miracle." During this time, China's per capita GNP also increased from RMB 381 in 1978 to RMB 37,055 (approximately USD 3729.8) in 2009, achieving the level of comparable middle-income countries. In terms of a country's position in the world economy as reflected by GDP, China rose from the 10th in 1978 to the 3rd in 2007 and the 2nd in 2010. The share of China's GNP in the world economy also rose from 1.6% in 1978 to around 10% in 2010.

In regards to trade relations, China's status is continuously rising, and its role as the engine behind the world's economic growth is becoming increasingly prominent. China's total volume of imports and exports was merely USD 20.64 billion at the end of 1978 and its foreign trade accounted for only a very small part of global trade, with a practically nonexistent record of foreign investment in China and a foreign exchange reserve of only USD 167 million. Over 30 years of reform and opening up, China has made remarkable progress in imports and exports, the attraction of foreign investment, and its foreign exchange reserve. In 2008, the total volume of the country's imports and exports was USD 2.563263 trillion, 124.19 times the size of 1978; its proportion of world trade had risen from 0.8% to 7.87%; and its ranking had shot up from the 29th to 3rd in the world in terms of the total volume of imports and exports. With such a development in China's foreign trade, the country is attracting an ever-increasing amount of foreign investment. By the end of 2008, foreign investment in China totaled USD 1.0398 trillion, making China one of the most attractive countries for global investment. Meanwhile, as a result of its foreign trade and foreign-funded investments, China's foreign exchange reserve began soaring. In 2008, China's foreign exchange reserve was USD 1.946 trillion, an increase of 11,652.69 times compared to USD 167 million in 1978. By the end of 2010, its foreign exchange reserve had approximated USD 3 trillion, the largest throughout the world.

Since 2008, the international financial crisis, in weakening the leading role of the U.S. in global economic development, has reminded the world of the necessity of restructuring the international monetary system and giving emerging countries a greater role. Judging by its economic development in the first two quarters, China would again achieve a growth of over 9% in 2010, when the international financial crisis was still affecting the world and recessions were sweeping industrial countries, as represented by the U.S. This reveals once again China's strong capacity for growth and its huge role in stabilizing the global economy. On the other hand, China's growing share in the world economy highlights the position and role of the RMB (*Renminbi*) in the international monetary system. China has become an indispensible part of the world economy. For example, according to a survey published by the IMF early in 2011, if China's GDP decreases by 1%, the rest of the world will suffer a decrease of about 0.5% or greater.[1]

China has also made significant breakthroughs in certain fields of economic development as well as preparations for full integration into the world economy. For example, over 30 years of development, it has comprehensively improved the country's transportation and communications infrastructure; it is the second in the world in length of expressways open to traffic (next only to the U.S.); it has made great breakthroughs in petascale computers—in fact, the secondary system of China's Tianhe-1 (TH-1) has replaced the Jaguar supercomputer system of the U. S.—and it ranks first in all supercomputers worldwide for the first time; in aerospace, China has succeeded in manned spaceflights and is making preparations for a moon landing; and so forth.

Its growing comprehensive economic strength and active participation in regional and international economic affairs—along with the confidence gained from its reform and opening up—have won due respect in the world economy and an unprecedented improvement of its discursive power on the global stage. This shows that China's image as a responsible country with a large economy and its own political power has been widely acknowledged and accepted by the international community. China has not only grown from a weak economy into a large economy, but has also started its historical process towards becoming an economic superpower.

1.1.2 Favorable Conditions for the Sustained, Steady, and Rapid Growth of China's Economy

At present, profound changes have taken and are still taking place among global political and economic patterns, new adjustments have been and are being made

[1]Neil, Hume. (Jan. 21, 2011). What happens in China matters in London. *Financial Times* online (FT.com). Briefly introduced in World Markets Begin Responding to China's Economy. (Jan. 23, 2011). *News for Reference*, p. 4.

among different political forces, and new divisions and alliances have occurred and are still occurring among various interest groups within the international community. A new and profound revolution is occurring in terms of global production, people's lives, and the existing economic growth models. These drastic adjustments and changes to international political and economic relations have provided a new historical opportunity for China to rise to the top of the world economy. This requires us, after leaving Japan behind, to make clear-minded analyses and rational judgments concerning the external and internal environments and conditions for overtaking the U.S., and also to consider objectively, reasonably, and strategically how to realize the more significant historical goal of developing China into the world's largest economy and an economic power in the realest sense.

A fundamental premise on which China bases its objective of overtaking the U.S. in coming years and, in doing so, becoming the largest economy in the world is the subjective and objective conditions necessary for sustaining the steady and rapid growth of the country's economy. In addition, the country must consider the question of whether or not China will be able to maintain a steady and rapid economic growth rate over the next 10–20 years (or even longer), as well as take into account the uniqueness of its system and mechanisms of economic and social development. The aforementioned subjective conditions mainly refer to the internal conditions of China's economy that will support a sustained, steady, and rapid development in the long run, including those driving forces and marketing factors for such growth, the establishment and improvement of economic development, and its self-modifying functions. The objective conditions, on the other hand, refer to the external conditions for a steady and rapid growth of China's economy—that is, whether the global economic and political environment can provide China with an opportunity for long-term stable development.

Leaving the international environment and conditions aside, we believe that, on the basis of the domestic environment alone, China has all the prerequisite conditions necessary for a steady and rapid growth over the next 10–20 years—or even longer—in the future.

1.1.2.1 China in the Mid-to-Late Stage of Industrialization

According to internationally-accepted theories of the stages of industrialization, along with the rise of per capita income, the proportion of added industrial value generally follows an inverted U shape. When the per capita GDP is below USD 300, industrialization can be considered to beat the early stage, with the proportion of added industrial value tending to increase constantly; when the per capita GDP is between USD 2000 and 5000, industrialization is at the middle stage and the proportion of added industrial value remains generally stable; when the per capita GDP is over USD 5000, industrialization is in the late stage of development, and the proportion of added industrial value tends to decline (Table 1.1).

In 2008, China's per capita income was over USD 3000, and the ratio of the primary, secondary, and tertiary industries to per capita income overall was 11.3:

Table 1.1 Standards in the different stages of industrialization

	Pre-industrialization	Stages of industrialization			Post-industrialization
		Early	Middle	Late	
1. Per capita GDP (1) USD in 1970 (2) USD in 1996	140 ~ 280 620 ~ 1240	280 ~ 560 1240 ~ 2480	560 ~ 1120 2480 ~ 4960	1120 ~ 2100 4960 ~ 9300	Over 2100 Over 9300
2. Industry structure	Primary industry dominates; S < 20%	P > 20%; S > 20% though small	P < 20%; S > T, largest in GDP	P < 10%; S at highest level	S stable or down; T > S
3. Proportion of agricultural population to overall employment	Over 60%	45 ~ 60%	30 ~ 45%	10 ~ 30%	Below 10%
4. Structure of industrialization	–	Heavy-industry stage, focus on resources	High-processing stage, focus on processing and assembling	Technologically intensive stage	–

Note: P, S, and T represent the proportion of the primary, secondary, and tertiary industries, respectively, to the overall GDP

48.6: 40.1. Viewed in this light, generally speaking, China is now at the mid-to-late stage of industrialization in which its proportion of added industrial value is further increasing; its industrialization—as represented by the heavy and chemical industries—is also accelerating. This conforms to the regularity of industrialization in an inverted U shape that is found in other countries. According to a study on the major factors and drives behind China's sustainable rapid economic growth (by Chen Jia-gui, Huang Qun-hui, and Zhang Tao with the Chinese Academy of Social Sciences (CASS)), China is now at the mid-to-late stage of accelerating industrialization. In other words, it has not yet fully accomplished the tasks of industrialization and is continuing in the industrialization process. The huge demands of the domestic market, together with changes in the production gradients and the effect of industrial upgrading, will enable China to maintain a relatively rapid growth rate for the foreseeable future.[2]

Since the beginning of the twenty-first century, especially after China's entry into the WTO, the robust growth of the demand for automobiles, houses, infrastructure construction, and so forth., has caused a rapid increase in the demand and production of intermediate products such as steel, machines, building materials, and chemicals, which, in turn, has led to a huge rise in the demand for energy sources such as coal, oil, and electricity. This has given rise to a number of dominant industrial clusters that have integrated capital and technology and are driving the country's rapid economic growth. Such a developmental situation is likely to become a solid foundation for the sustainable and potent growth of China's economy within the foreseeable future.[3]

1.1.2.2 China's Quickening Urbanization

In 1975, American urban geographer Ray. M. Northam posited the curve of urbanization. According to what is now known as Northam's curve, urbanization is considered to be proceeding at a low speed and within the initial stage of development when the urban population accounts for less than 30% of the total population. It accelerates and enters the central/acceleration stage when the urban population accounts for 30–70% of the total population. When the urban population accounts for over 70% of the total population, urbanization slows and enters the terminal stage of development. This curve of urbanization process is S-shaped, with the two ends slightly flattened (Fig. 1.1). By 2008, China's urbanization had reached 45.68%. Measured by Northam's curve of the urbanization process, China had already entered the central stage of urbanization. This means that, on the one hand, China is accelerating its urbanization, and on the other hand, it

---

[2]Chen Jiagui, Huang Qunhui, & Zhang Tao. (2008). From Rapid Growth to Harmonious Development: China Economy Retrospect and Prospect. In *China Economic Research Report (2007–2008)*. Beijing: Economy & Management Publishing House, p. 3.

[3]Ibid.

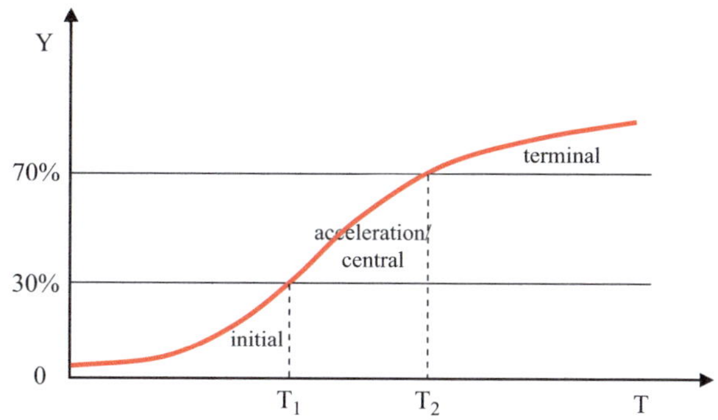

Fig. 1.1 Northam's curve *of* urbanization

continues to remain an important task for China to focus on its urbanization level within the framework of its economic and social development in the future.

1.2 New Problems Facing NGEs' Development in the New Economic Stage

Observation of China's economic development in terms of it being considered a rising power leads to the undeniable fact that, with the recent increase in its comprehensive national strength, China has become (or is becoming)one of the most important economies in global economic development as a whole, and has already entered a new stage of its own economic development. At the same time, there are many problems China will have to face if it is to further develop its economy. For example, at the particular stage in which China has grown from a lower-middle income country to an upper-middle level—and is continuing to move towards a position as a high income country—challenges remain severe in several aspects, such as incomplete structures and institutions (e.g., the income gaps between social classes, between urban and rural areas, and between regions), insufficient technological innovation capacity, and a ubiquitous shortage of resources. In particular, non-governmental enterprises (NGEs), as an important part of China's economy, are faced with many difficulties and problems during the period of structural transformation and industrial upgrading. These difficulties and problems come from either the systems and markets or from inside the enterprises themselves (e.g., weak independent innovation capacity, the adjustment of enterprises' spatial distribution, the promotion of market competitiveness, their relatively low level of internationalization, and so forth.). To fully overcome such difficulties and effectively solve such problems will be to contribute to the rapid, sound, and sustainable development of both Chinese NGEs and China's economy, specifically, as well as the realization of its great-nation strategy.

1.2.1 Institutional Restraints and Marketing Hardships in Structural Transformation and Industrial Upgrading

Never before has China received such wide attention on its economy and such wide space for its economic development. But to Chinese enterprises, in particular NGEs, tough challenges remain. Judging by their current development, those Chinese NGEs entering a new stage of development are confronted with unprecedented institutional and marketing difficulties during their structure transformation and industrial upgrading process, especially considering they are yet to be completely free from the influence of the international economic recession.

By 2009, China had already grown from a low-income country into a medium-income country as measured by per capita GDP. Consequently, changes in the structure of its domestic consumption are not only accelerating the country's industrial upgrading and the structural transformation of China's national economy, but are also bringing new challenges to all the market participants in the new development game (including NGEs, SOEs, individual and private enterprises, and large, medium, and small enterprises).

Over its more than 30 years of market-oriented reform, China has made unprecedented achievements and established an institutional framework for a market economy and market transaction system, but there are undeniably still many deep-seated contradictions and problems in the marketing process, which tend to become more intractable over time. As one of the interested parties, the state-owned sectors of the economy are continuously exerting their influence on and even determining governmental policy-making; meanwhile, based on the huge economic resources controlled by the government, they are actually having a crowding-out effect on the development of NGEs. Thus, for NGEs in the process of industrial upgrading and structural transformation, it has become an inevitable choice and an important path of development to shift from the lower end to the middle and high end of the production price curve and from labor-intensive industries to capital- and technology-intensive industries. In making such a choice and shift, they will have to compete with SOEs, which is bound to affect their vested interests and invite their resistance. If this game of interest is played in an arena of full market competition, the result would most likely be a win-win (or all-win) situation; otherwise, it would probably become a zero-sum game that will bring no improvement to the well-being of the country or the people.

Whether win-win or a zero-sum game ultimately depends on the market system and the institutions and mechanisms of governmental policies and economic administration. As early as 2005, the State Council had already issued the 36 Provisions ("三十六条") that encourage, support and guide the sustainable and sound development of the non-governmental sectors of the economy. On August 19, 2009, aiming at lowering the threshold for market access, the State Council unveiled a further six policies promoting the development of small- and medium-sized enterprises (SMEs) while emphasizing its encouragement and support for the participation of non-governmental capital in those economic fields previously characterized by an apparent administrative monopoly (such as oil, the railways, electricity, telecommunications, public facilities, and infrastructure). At the same time, it offered supporting policies concerning taxation, loans, and credits. On May 7, 2010, the State Council issued *Several Opinions on Encouraging and Guiding the Sound Development of Non-Governmental Investment*, once again expanding the scope of non-governmental investment, emphasizing the equal treatment of different types of investment entities, and prohibiting secondary conditions imposed solely on non-governmental capital alone. The *Opinions* highlighted the guidance of non-governmental capital into such areas as basic industries and infrastructure, municipal utilities, policy-based housing, social undertakings, financial services, commercial circulation, and national defense industries, among others. Moreover, it stressed the government's support for non-governmental capital to engage in the alliance and restructuring of enterprises, as well as the reform, reorganization, and renovation of SOEs. It emphasized the implementation of policies that would create a fair and standardized market environment for NGEs' development. As shown by extant economic practice and development, however, NGEs are still confronted with formidable institutional barriers to their structural transformation and industrial upgrading, as well as their entry into the above-mentioned areas. From the Tieben Event (in which a 10-billion project of the private Tieben Iron & Steel was halted by the government, resulting in huge losses of farmers, banks, and other investors) in the beginning of the twenty-first century to the withdrawal of a local oil corporation founded by several NGEs in Shaanxi Province, from the merger of the highly profitable Rizhao Iron & Steel Factory by the then loss-incurring Shandong Iron & Steel Factory, to COFCO's control of Mengniu Dairy Group, from the "nationalization" wave among the coal corporations in Shanxi Province to the crowding out of NGEs during the international financial crisis, these phenomena reflect different aspects of the numerous restrictions on the market access of non-governmental capital and its free flow from one industry to another. For all the policies introduced by the State Council to encourage the development of a non-governmental economy and to support and guide private investment, non-governmental investors are still faced with various difficulties in their entry into those high-profit, high-benefit industries originally monopolized by SOEs, or the economic sectors under governmental control, or in their participation in the restructuring, renovation, and reform of SOEs (characterized by such serious problems as the "glass-door" and "spring-door" situations). Under such circumstances, to avoid involvement in the over-capacity of low-level industries/sectors, non-governmental investors are forced into unfamiliar fields or industries, where competition is just as fierce as in their primary industries. The consequence is that they are then, inevitably, trapped in new and unfamiliar developmental hardships. The most typical examples of this are the failure of the Wenzhou Bali Group to participate in resource-based industries and of the Taizhou Feiyue Group to enter the real estate and hotel industries. The structural upgrading and industrial transformation of NGEs generally seek new opportunities for development, but often the reality and results are the opposite of those sought. New risks often arrive one after another before the original is dealt with effectively.

Such are the institutional and marketing difficulties NGEs are confronted with during their structural transformation and industrial upgrading.

1.2.2 *Challenges in the Replacement of Labor by Technology*

For NGEs to shift from the lower end to the medium and higher end of the value chain through restructuring, upgrading, and/or transformation, it is most crucial to specialize their production and management and upgrade their technology. The principal means for effecting this is to update their technology on large scale and to carry out technological innovation. Technological innovation is of particular significance to NGEs, particularly in the vein of the following three modes: the introduction-absorption-renovation mode, the integration-innovation mode, and the independent innovation mode. López-Rodríguez and García-Rodríguez have described,[4] from the perspective of resources, the paths and mechanisms by which enterprises may achieve cost competitiveness and a product-diversity advantage by increasing both the supply and innovation of their technological resources. As intangible assets such as technological resources are knowledge-intensive, any increase in their supply will help enterprises create and maintain a doubly-competitive advantage, that is, cost competitiveness will be newly gained by increasing the supply of technological resources and promoting the development of efficient production technologies, and at the same time, a larger product-diversity advantage will be achieved through product innovation such as product diversification and quality promotion. With the increasing level of market specialization and diversity-based competition among NGEs, the diversified demand of customers is also growing. Hence, those enterprises with cutting-edge technologies are entitled to more competitiveness in the market (Fig. 1.2).

Cassiman and Veugelers once pointed out that the competitive advantage resulting from innovation will further stimulate enterprises to enter the international market, promote their market performance, and enhance their international competitiveness.[5] In such a market economy, innovation has become an increasingly important basis for and pre-condition to enterprises sustaining and promoting their competitiveness. Since there are various types of enterprises, however, which may vary in their attitudes towards innovation and innovative practices, a universal conclusion regarding the relative advantages of innovation is impractical and unrealistic. As Joseph A. Schumpeter mentioned, larger enterprises with market monopoly power are endowed with greater innovative advantages compared with

---

[4]López-Rodríguez, J., & García-Rodríguez, R. (2005). Technology and Export Behaviour: A Resource-Based View Approach. *International Business Review*, 14(5), 539–557.

[5]Cassiman, B., & Veugelers, R. (2002). Complementarity in the Innovation Strategy: Internal R&D, External Technology Acquisition and Cooperation. Working paper, available at http://search.epnet.com/login.aspx?direct=true&db=ecn&an=0694553.

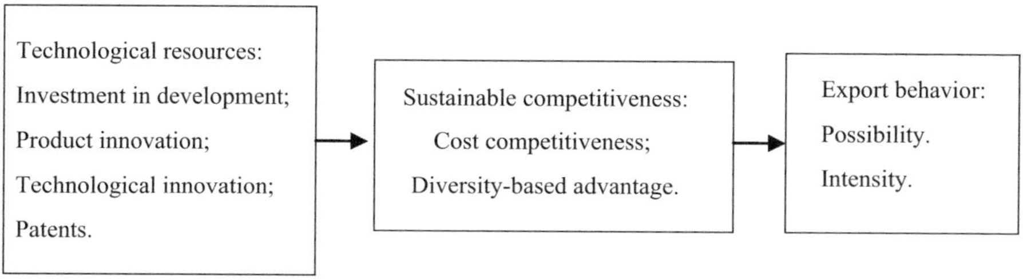

Fig. 1.2 The conceptual modeling of competitiveness in technological resources & export behavior (Source: López-Rodríguez and García-Rodríguez 2005)

smaller enterprises.[6] But SMEs, in particular small enterprises, are no less capable of innovation than large enterprises, as has been proved in different countries.[7] Currently, over 97% of Chinese enterprises are NGEs, including both large-sized and micro-enterprises, but their level of and capacity for independent innovation are far from satisfactory, be they large, small, or micro. The result of a survey on the independent innovation of China's NGEs shows that they have a relatively weak will and capacity for independent innovation.[8] The reasons for this lie in the following four aspects.

First of all, China's labor force—characterized by low costs and a seemingly infinite supply—is having a negative effect on NGEs' will to independent innovation. As a general law of global industrial development, a country's industry usually develops along a fairly set path from traditional industries to modern industries. The course starts with factor-input industries (labor- or resource-intensive), which are gradually upgraded into capital-intensive industries; these industries are then further upgraded into technology-intensive industries. The course ends with knowledge-intensive industries. Industrial regeneration, upgrading, and advancement, as well as the length of this process, depends largely on the supply and development of a low-cost labor force. With an abundant supply of low-cost labor, enterprises are naturally inclined to use more labor than technology. Only when there is a sharp rise in labor costs and a large potential comparative profit would they then feel an incentive to use more technology. In China, with the labor supply reaching the Lewis Turning Point, it is a rising and inevitable trend that technology will replace labor; yet until such conditions have matured, Chinese enterprises, especially NGEs, still lack the will for independent innovation.

Secondly, existing diversity in the demand structure has provided NGEs with a relative level of competitive advantages and ensured enough space for their survival

[6]Liu Yingqiu., & Xu Zhixiang. (2006). *Report on Chinese Non-Governmental Enterprise Competitiveness No. 3, Indexes of Independent Innovation and Competitiveness*. Beijing: Social Sciences Academic Press. P. 24.

[7]Kamien, M. I., & Schwartz, N. L. (1982). *Market Structure and Innovation*, Cambridge University Press.

[8]CASS Division of Economics. (2008). *China Economic Research Report (2007–2008)*. Beijing: Economy & Management Publishing House, p. 280.

and growth, but it is at the same time hampering their willingness to innovate. In China, the country's relatively large income gap has given rise to different income groups; accordingly, a hierarchy and a diversity at the level of its demand structure are evident. There are always certain volumes and scales of market demand for all grades of products, be they low- or high-end, necessities or luxuries, which contributes to the long-term survival and parallel development of enterprises of various sizes and technological levels. In this case, earlier engagement in technological innovation does not necessarily mean greater profits, even when the income growth of urban and rural citizens has led to higher consumer demands, which require more diversified products of higher quality and technology. This has caused a certain degree of "hesitation" among enterprises, in particular NGEs, in coping with complex market demand—a dilemma as to whether or not they are to renew and/or upgrade their industrial structure and what technology will be used to enhance their competitiveness. As a result, their technological innovation is hampered.

Thirdly, NGEs are not particularly capable of integrating innovative resources, which stymies their independent innovation to some degree. At present, the main resources of technological innovation in China (including research teams, high-tech laboratories, and research funding) are mostly in the hands of the state-run research institutions, universities, and SOEs. Due to the current state of the institution, NGEs have very few such innovative resources, nor do they have convenient access to those they do possess. As resources are allocated primarily by the government, market-based allocation and the integration of innovative resources is rather difficult. Under these circumstances, without a doubt, it is indeed difficult for NGEs to acquire more innovative resources through the market and to then exercise independent innovation. For example, Chery, a non-governmental automobile manufacturer, has made remarkable achievements in its independent innovation of car engines and has grown into the first and only domestic car-engine manufacturer with independent intellectual property rights. This is, to a certain degree, because the Ministry of Science and Technology has provided it with great support and more innovative resources. But for many small- and medium-sized NGEs without enough national support, it is indeed very difficult for them to obtain innovative resources because of high costs, and thus they can hardly be expected to carry out independent innovation while relying on state-owned innovative resources—although there are some so-called innovative resources like the SMEs' Innovation Fund, which can be considered part of the so-called "desktop policies" ("桌面政策", zhuōmiàn zhèngcè).

Finally, NGEs' independent innovation is also greatly limited by the lack of a risk-sharing mechanism. Large or small, NGEs should be able to tolerate the risks if they are to innovate independently. Otherwise, they will fall into a debt crisis or even be forced to face bankruptcy if they unfortunately fail in their attempts at innovation. On the other hand, the fruits of enterprises' innovation (such as intellectual property rights) are still far from having effective legal protection in China at present. Especially with the prevailing local protectionism, infringement of intellectual property rights is rarely punished in a timely manner, but, to the contrary, tends to be secretly encouraged in some places. Over the past 2 years, rising labor prices have been driving the technological innovation of enterprises, but NGEs' independent innovation is bound to remain in a difficult infancy, since there is no adequate market mechanism to protect the fruits of technological innovation. Furthermore, the creation and management of various venture investment remains at the threshold, while a sharing and transfer mechanism of innovative risks is yet to be established.

1.2.3 Time Needed for Adjustments to the Geographical Distribution and Cultivation of Comprehensive Regional Competitiveness Among NGEs

In terms of their origins, China's NGEs mainly fall into two categories: grass-root NGEs that have grown over a period of time from individual businesses into NGEs of a certain scale under the guidance of state policies, and those born out of township enterprises through leasing management or bankruptcy auctions. In the mid- to late-1990s, inefficient township enterprises were generally transformed into NGEs after the central government proposed a strategy for "invigorating large enterprises and relaxing control over small ones." Therefore, compared with grass-root NGEs, far more were transformed from township enterprises. Both types of NGEs are basically distributed at or below the county level due to their historical backgrounds, however, be they of the transformed type or grass-rooted. Due to their need for survival and development based on specialized division, NGEs usually gather in specific areas and form a large number of industrial clusters, which are typical of their demand for internal collaboration and desire for external competition, such as the textile printing and dyeing cluster in Shaoxing of Zhejiang Province, the sports-leisure product cluster in Xiamen, Zhangzhou, and Quanzhou of Fujian Province, the appliance and toy clusters in Dongguan of Guangdong Province, and so forth. Such industrial clusters have, to some degree, strengthened the competitiveness of the involved NGEs in foreign markets.

Since the beginning of the twenty-first century, with the rapid rise in industrial upgrading and the growing demand for regional economic restructuring and transformation, the central cities and their functions have been re-designed in the Yangtze River Delta, the Pearl River Delta, and the Bohai Rim areas. This marks the kick-off of geographical distribution adjustments and enterprise restructuring within the Chinese economy. The goal is to integrate the resources of economic and social development, to bring into full play comparative regional advantages, and to cultivate new comprehensive regional competitiveness along with the capacity for national economic development. In the course of this process, the functional adjustment of the central cities in these regions is an important prerequisite for the reasonable re-arrangement of NGEs' geographical distribution, which is itself an internal requirement of the market economy. As part of this process, governmental policies are of special significance. As surveys have shown, however, institutional differences and policy sluggishness are, to a large extent, still preventing the reasonable adjustment of NGEs' geographical distribution and their cultivation of comprehensive regional competitiveness.

1.2.3.1 Regional Differences in Market Systems

Currently, urban transformation and industrial structural upgrading are new trends in the industrialization and urbanization of China's developed coastal areas. For example, Shanghai used to be a city of manufacturing and processing industries with relatively developed financial services. With the development of the market economy and the deepening of industrial structural adjustments, modern service industries such as logistics, commerce and trade, finance, and consultation have also gradually developed in Shanghai. Some manufacturers gathered in Shanghai and the Yangtze River Delta, especially private manufacturing SMEs with decreasing marginal incomes, have begun relocating to the outlying areas of the delta or even farther. At the same time, Shanghai has greatly improved its own position as a shipping and financial center and accelerated its geographical shift of the industries. This not only means a denial of its original geographical arrangement of industries as well as the loss of its traditional competitiveness, but indicates the formation of a new comprehensive regional competitiveness. In this process, government input is still important, but the construction of regional market systems and government policies are beginning to play an increasingly decisive role. The Mezzogiorno phenomenon[9] in Italy reflects this from one aspect, that is, regional institutional differences have great influences on and even determine enterprises' rational adjustment of industrial distribution and the formation of comprehensive regional competitiveness during their industrial restructuring and geographical shift.

The same is true for China's NGEs. Their regional shift and adjustment of geographical distribution, especially their movement from the coastal areas to the central and western regions, are also challenged by differences in market systems between the eastern and western areas. If the east-west differences in the systems and system construction are not closely monitored or, worse, neglected, it is possible for the Mezzogiorno phenomenon to occur during China's industrial shift. If we observe the geographical adjustments of industrial distribution throughout the world, especially those occurring over the past half century, we may find that it is more or less because of institutional support and government participation that they turn out to be successful. There are two primary forms of institutional

[9]Mezzogiorno" in Italian means Midday. Here, it refers to the phenomenon of a widened income gap against the overall economic growth in the south of Italy, a result of the lagging system and mechanistic construction as well as the influence of government policies in the transition from the dual structure of an agrarian economy to a modern economy (See the full meaning of this concept in Cai Fang's blog post "Beware of the 'Mezzogiorno Trap' in the Central and Western Parts" at http://www.pinggu.org/bbs/thread-674987-1-1.html).

support and government participation. One is to eliminate regional differences in systems and institutions by improving institutional stipulations and institutional structures, and the other is to make specific guidelines and policies that encourage and guide industrial distribution and adjustment according to the requirement of market development laws while promoting reasonable geographical distribution and adjustment of industries. However, until this point, most regional governments in China have continued to pay too much attention to preferential policies for introducing investment and attracting investors, but very little to the institutional construction that will benefit the in-depth development of industries. The consequence is shortsighted behavior on the part of enterprises and negative impact on the reasonable adjustment of NGEs' geographical distribution, as well as a rise in the costs of industrial distribution and adjustment, which hamper the promotion of comprehensive regional competitiveness.

1.2.3.2 Lack of a Supporting System for Overall Industrial Distribution

The formation and promotion of regional industrial competitiveness is closely related to the formation and development of regional industrial clusters. A study by the CASS Center for Private Economic Studies points out that the formation of industrial clusters has a profound influence on the capacity of NGEs for independent innovation, brand competitiveness, human-capital level, and international competitiveness.[10] The development of NGE clusters in Zhejiang Province (locally called a "massive economy") shows that the formation and development of regional industrial clusters have direct and qualitative influences on individual enterprises, especially SMEs. Such influences manifest themselves as both the price advantages of production factors and the production and sales advantages of the enterprises in question. According to the theory of new economic geography, the formation and development of industrial clusters in a region not only contributes to sustaining that region's competitive advantages, but also to diversified development within the region so that enterprises from other regions can hardly compete with those already in such industrial clusters. At the same time, however, this brings a corresponding problem; that is, if the enterprises in the industrial clusters are to move elsewhere, they will have to risk losing the cluster support they used to enjoy. Therefore, enterprises within a cluster are generally unwilling to relocate to other areas unless their relative advantages vis-à-vis production factor prices are obviously smaller than the comparative costs. In other words, only when the marginal return exceeds the cost of enterprise movement, or when the new competitiveness and returns are greater than the original, will these enterprises choose to move. The adjustment of

[10]For the above conclusions on the relationship between industrial clusters and NGEs' competitiveness, refer to Liu Yingqiu & Xu Zhixiang. (2005, 2006, 2007, 2008). *Report on Chinese Non-Governmental Enterprise Competitiveness No. 2–5*. Beijing: Social Sciences Academic Press.

the geographical distribution of China's NGEs is basically the independent behavior of individual enterprises, rather than the adjustment of the overall distribution of the industrial supporting system. The question of how to raise the spontaneous adjustment level of individual enterprises to the overall adjustment level of the surrounding industrial supporting system (so as to integrate the clustered development and geographical distribution of industries within the whole) is significant not only to the whole country but also to the issue of NGEs' industrial shift and the promotion of their comprehensive regional competitiveness. The proposal of the CPC Central Committee during the 12th Five Year Plan explicitly pointed out that great efforts should be made to "develop a modern industrial system and promote the core competitiveness of industries" and to "properly guide enterprise mergers and restructuring, as well as to improve industrial concentration".[11] These requirements are especially important to guiding enterprise shifts and industrial adjustment in the sense of the overall distribution of China's industrial supporting system, and to the promotion of NGEs' core competitiveness and the comprehensive competitiveness of regional economic development overall.

1.2.4 Further Improvement of the Environment and the Conditions Necessary for Full Integration into the International Economy

To Chinese enterprises, it has already become a trend to "Go Global" for their greater development. From 2002 to 2008, the overseas investment of Chinese enterprises had increased from USD 2.7 billion to about USD 56 billion, a growth of 66% annually. By the end of 2008, the stock of overseas investment by China-funded enterprises was USD 184 billion, and their total assets abroad were over USD1 trillion.[12] In the process of Chinese enterprises' going global, NGEs have played a pioneering role. Though no authoritative statistics have been published, this judgment is supported by partial observation. For example, in Taizhou City of Zhenjiang Province—where NGEs are developing in large concentrations—the number of NGEs going global increased from 11 in 2000 to 251 in 2007, up by an annual rate of 56.4%; meanwhile, the overseas investment of Taizhou's NGEs was growing by 97.75% annually.[13] The 2008 international financial crisis has not delayed or stopped the going-global of Chinese enterprises. On the contrary,

[11]The Proposal of the CPC Central Committee for Formulating the Twelfth Five-Year Plan for National Economic and Social Development. *People's Daily*, Oct. 28, 2010.

[12](Nov. 4, 2009). The Assets Abroad of China-Funded Enterprises Exceed USD1 Trillion. *CPPCC Newspaper* (*Renmin Zhengxie Bao*).

[13]Liu Yingqiu & Xu Zhixiang. (2008). *Report on Chinese Non-Governmental Enterprise Competitiveness No. 5, Index of Going Global and Competitiveness*. Beijing: Social Sciences Academic Press, p. 12.

powered by an improving domestic economy, their overseas mergers and acquisitions and investments are, rather, growing steadily. In the first three quarters of 2009, there was a sharp rise in the number of overseas mergers and acquisitions by Chinese enterprises, including 61 overseas acquisitions totaling USD 20.1 billion, with the largest single purchase amounting to USD 2.6 billion.[14]

Up to the end of 2006 since China's entry into the WTO, 32 countries/regions had initiated 288 investigations against China to the tune of USD 7.1 billion, concerning anti-dumping, anti-subsidy, safeguarding, and special safeguarding measures. China has been involved in the most trade frictions throughout the world for 11 years in succession.[15] To avoid further losses caused by such setbacks to their development, Chinese enterprises would naturally choose to go global at a larger scale and more rapid pace. According to the classical theories of international trade, the overseas mergers and acquisitions of a country's enterprises usually grow out of the desire to avoid trade sanctions by the target country, to break the tariff barrier and lower their trade costs, or to promote their sales in the international market. For Chinese enterprises, in addition to the above-mentioned motives, another important reason is to expand their market share. As is widely known, the competitiveness of Chinese enterprises in the international market is generally based on the low-cost factor input, so they are naturally inclined to expand their market capacity and share at a higher speed and at a larger scale.[16] Through overseas mergers and acquisitions or direct investment in new factory construction, enterprises going global can acquire not only new production factors but also attain new and greater market capacity. According to the statistics provided by Deloitte in a report entitled, *Rise of China: New Fields of Overseas Mergers and Acquisitions*, energy and mineral resources are the major fields of overseas mergers and acquisitions by Chinese enterprises going global. From 2003 to the third quarter of 2009, as the primary focus of overseas mergers and acquisitions by Chinese enterprises, energy, mining, and public utilities comprised 29% of the total number and 66% of the value of the total transactions, while during the same period, industrial product transactions comprised only 19% and 6% of the same values, respectively, and the industries of science and technology and media and telecommunication, only 16% and 7%, respectively.[17] The Deloitte report has pointed out the encouragement and support of the Chinese government for the overseas mergers and acquisitions of Chinese enterprises, but they have neglected the difference in its support for the "Going-Global" initiative of SOEs and NGEs.

---

[14]Chen Qinghua. (Nov. 10, 2009). Chinese Enterprises Quickening Overseas Mergers and Acquisitions. *China Financial & Economic News*.

[15]Liu Yingqiu & Xu Zhixiang. (2008). *Report on Chinese Non-governmental Enterprise Competitiveness No. 5, Index of Going Global and Competitiveness*. Beijing: Social Sciences Academic Press, p. 3.

[16]Wu Jinglian, et al. (Nov. 26, 2009). Four Warnings for China's Economy, *China Financial & Economic News*.

[17]Chen Qinghua. (Nov. 10, 2009). Chinese Enterprises Quickening Overseas Mergers and Acquisitions. *China Financial & Economic News*.

Policy support is one of the key elements for the success of enterprises going global. For more than half a century, enterprises from different parts of the world, especially Southeast Asia, have succeeded in going global. Their experiences show that governmental policy and financial support is a significant driving force for the going-global of SMEs. Up till now, the Chinese authorities have issued many policies that encourage and support enterprises to go global. But as analyses have suggested, there remain many problems open to further study concerning these policies. The main problems are divided policies from various sources in the formulation and implementation, inefficient support, and even the constraints of some policies, which have weakened the effect of policies overall and their support for enterprises to successfully go global in particular. Moreover, it is important to notice that many policies beneficial to SOEs' "Go-Global" strategy may be of no help and may even present an obstacle to NGEs' going global. That is to say, so far, Chinese enterprises are still faced with the difficulty of mismatching policies and environment if they are to go international.

Apart from the above, Chinese enterprises, especially NGEs, are faced with many challenges in the improvement of their own qualities. Whether NGEs can successfully go global and integrate into the international economy depends on their own structure of governance and institutional arrangement, as well as the number and quality of their internationalized personnel stocks, which are of equal importance to the other mitigating conditions. China's NGEs still largely have the problem of a small and low-level pool of personnel as well as a severe shortage of managerial, productive, and operational talents with a broad international vision. Despite the fact that some enterprises of considerable scale and competence have already started going global, they have neither established their talent cultivation system for internationalized production and sales, nor have they formulated the mechanisms and institutions of the discovery, employment, management, and utilization of internationalized talents. Most enterprises still lack an advanced and specialized team that meets the demands of their international integration and development.

In summary, in light of the supporting policies of the Chinese government and NGEs' development, China must make greater efforts to improve the policy environment and quality of enterprises for its full integration into the international economy, even though there is a rapid increase and development of overseas mergers and acquisitions by Chinese enterprises going global.

1.3 Choices for NGEs' Greater Development in the New Stage

It is now widely acknowledged that NGEs are increasingly important to and playing a bigger role in China's economic development. At this stage, an urgently important task is to create conditions that further encourage, support, and guide NGEs' greater development while maintaining public ownership as the mainstay, so as to guarantee the successful navigation of China's economy past the potential "middle income trap," to accomplish the transformation from a large economy into a global economic powerhouse, and to realize the great rejuvenation of the Chinese nation.

1.3.1 Correctly Recognizing NGEs' Nature and Overcoming Ideological Obstructions for the Great Development of NGEs

Deepening the understanding of NGEs' essential attributes has already become an issue that directly influences not only the development of NGEs themselves, but also the overall development of the national economy. Although it is now commonly recognized that non-governmental sectors and NGEs are important parts of China's socialist market economy, various viewpoints differ as to the nature of a non-governmental economy, that is, whether it belongs to socialism with Chinese characteristics or whether it is of a purely capitalist nature. One opinion is that the current non-governmental economy and NGEs are "private" and capitalist in nature. Accordingly, this recognition has led to a so-called concern that the predominant status of the public ownership sectors would be weakened by the continuously-rising proportion of non-governmental sectors in the national economy, as well as concerns that the safety of the national economy would be threatened by the entry of NGEs into monopolized industries such as electricity, oil, and coal. Some people even boldly claim that to develop a non-governmental economy is to develop capitalism and to shake off the economic basis of socialism altogether. It is exactly the existence of such opinions that inevitably gives rise to worry and fear among Chinese enterprises and Chinese society, which are worth deliberation. That is, the question of whether there is going to be another "socialist transformation" of the privately-run non-governmental sectors and NGEs, once the task of economic development in the primary stage of socialism has been basically completed and the socialized level of production has been further raised is, along with other related issues, a legitimate avenue of inquiry.

Obviously, whether or not we can correctly recognize and scientifically understand the nature of China's NGEs is a matter directly related to not only the development of NGEs and the growth of non-governmental investment, but also to the sound and sustainable long-term development of the national economy, as well as to the great rejuvenation of the Chinese nation. Such questions are coming into sharper and more prominent focus at present, particularly as China's systemic economic reform enters a critical period, bringing with it an urgent demand for the transformation of the existing models of economic development. Why have many private entrepreneurs begun to give up long-term productive operations and re-investments only to turn to speculative investments? Or to sell their assets through auctions and act as renters? Or even to directly move their enterprise assets abroad? Is this a phenomenon of early degeneration? Can we turn a deaf ear or a blind eye to it? Definitely not. It is therefore urgent but practical that we research the nature and essential attributes of NGEs. We should, through more profound studies and explorations, objectively analyze and state the new problems occurring and met with in the development of NGEs, and demonstrate scientifically that NGEs are no longer the traditional private sectors of the economy, that private entrepreneurs are no longer the traditional "capitalists," and that the capital accumulated by NGEs—especially large-sized NGEs—is of a distinct social quality or a socialized quality in the broad sense. We should also realize that the non-governmental economy is an important part not only of the socialist market economy, but also the socialist economy with Chinese characteristics; that essential changes have taken and are still taking place altering its very nature; and that it goes against the reality of China's economic development and system construction to equate it simply with capitalism.

First of all, China's non-governmental economy and NGEs are subordinated to China's basic economic and social systems. This seems to be a "paradox of philosophy"—the basic economic and social systems are naturally determined by both the economic base and the superstructure, and the economic base makes up the first decisive role; how, then, can the non-governmental economy and NGEs, which formerly belong to the economic base, be regarded as subordinated to the country's basic economic system? To clarify this paradox, it is necessary to dissect the connotations of what is meant by the economic base and basic economic system, respectively. On the one hand, the relationship of production as reflected by the non-governmental economy and NGEs is undoubtedly an essential part—though not the whole of—China's economic base. If the role of the non-governmental economy and NGEs in the overall national economy is subordinate rather than dominant, they are surely subordinate in nature as well. On the other hand, the basic economic system is determined by the ownership of society as a whole, but is meanwhile restricted by a particular type of superstructure. The basic system in China is the people's democratic sovereignty based on the worker-peasant alliance, which is socialist in nature, rather than capitalist. Laborers—in the form of workers and peasants—are the principal component of this social system, whose interests and demands and their realization are the basic orientation of both policy and legal requirements, both of which are necessary and essential to such a social system. This situation objectively determines that all forms of non-governmental economy, in particular NGEs, should regard the realization of the laborers' fundamental interests as one of their basic goals in the production and management activities, rather than the contrary. Once an enterprise neglects its employees' demands for their fundamental interests or even attempts to pursue excess profits at the expense of harming the fundamental interests of its employees, it is bound to be restricted, controlled, and even punished by the basic economic system and legal system. The above two points make it clear that, in terms of their behavioral characteristics, the non-governmental economy and non-governmental enterprises have to be subordinated to, rather than exceptional to, the basic economic system and social system at the current stage, no matter how their activities and operational strategies may vary.

The operation of a country's economy and society is a complex system and process, never as simple or direct as what is described in theories. Therefore, this seemingly paradoxical phenomenon is consistent with and corresponds to existing practice; that is to say, there never exists an impassable gulf between a single enterprise and the economic system of society as a whole. This is probably the first prerequisite and an important basic point for our full understanding and recognition of the nature of China's NGEs in the current period.

Secondly, it is impossible for China's NGEs to be of a purely capitalist nature at the present stage. Capitalism didn't emerge in China until the founding of the People's Republic of China. As Mao Zedong identified and pointed out, "the invasion of China by the imperialist powers is never targeted at turning the feudal China into a capitalist China."[18] Hence, China's NGEs and national enterprises mostly adhered to the economic subjects of feudalism or comprador capitalism at that time, and were hardly characterized by capitalist qualities. After the founding of the People's Republic, China went through a new democratic stage, but still there was no emergence of real capitalism. From the perspective of the superstructure, this is because China had chosen the new democratic system or the later socialist system, which are quite different from capitalism. Such a system is, in fact, an attempt to directly bring China up from a semi-colonial and semi-feudal society into a brand-new one, instead of merely recreating a capitalist society. As the country's economic system was founded based on the Stalin model, there were certain disadvantages, such as over-centralized power, excessive public ownership, the low efficiency of enterprise operation, and so forth., which had stymied the due development of productive forces and finally led China onto the inevitable road to reform and opening up. But China's social system, since the implementation of its reform and opening up, is a socialist system with Chinese characteristics, which is also different from capitalism. The country's NGEs and the non-governmental sectors of the economy that have emerged in the process of reform and opening up, whether individual or private, are neither of a purely capitalist nature nor of a purely (or traditionally) socialist nature, but are attached to the dominant public ownership and are characterized by socialism with Chinese characteristics. In other words, the non-governmental economy is not exogenous, external, or dissident, but inversely, endogenous, internal, and conforming to the strength of socialism with Chinese characteristics. Moreover, the more than 30 years' practice of reform and opening up indicates that the ultimate result of NGEs' development in China is very likely to be a new type of "management-labor interest community,"[19] instead of a "new variety of capitalism." Though we can still see some isolated cases of delinquent business owners violating laws, rules, or others' interests, they are neither within the mainstream of NGEs' development nor a common social phenomenon; in addition, they would never be allowed to develop at will or be exempt

[18]Mao Zedong. 1991. *Selected Works of Mao Zedong*. Beijing: People's Publishing House, p. 628.

[19]Wang Huimin and Jiang Nan. Harmony Between Management and Labor in Zhejiang, *People's Daily*, Jan. 31, 2011, pp. 1 & 10.

from restriction and control, but would ultimately be constrained by China's basic social system and punished by the laws. Therefore, when we judge the nature of China's NGEs at present, we should not be blinded by a single leaf before our eyes and regard such misconducts or violations of individual business owners as the very basis of our judgment.

Finally, from the perspective of consolidating the basic economic system of socialism with Chinese characteristics, it is necessary to further vigorously develop the country's non-governmental economy and NGEs at the present stage. For over 30 years, since the implementation of reform and opening up, NGEs have been playing an increasingly important role in the national economy and in life in general. On one hand, NGEs have become the country's main employers and have accepted an increasingly larger share of the labor force. Up until now, more than 70% of the labor force has been employed in non-governmental economic organizations, such as NGEs and private industrial and commercial households, while employment in SOEs is continuously declining, no matter whether we use a metric of relative quantity or absolute quantity. What's more, NGEs have grown into an important subject of taxation. Although the total amount paid by NGEs has just approximated half the tax revenues of society as a whole so far, this proportion is continuously rising, and their role is becoming increasingly powerful. NGEs are making an increasingly evident contribution to China's fiscal income. As illustrated previously, through the country's transformation from a large economy to an economic global superpower, China will have to face many challenges in its development, one of the greatest being the bottleneck of resources and technology. As such, it is a must to implement the "Going Global" strategy and thus to obtain more international economic techniques and resources as an economic support. In the process of the implementation of "Going Global," however, due to the rules of the internationally-competitive market and the limitations of the system, it is probably the NGEs, rather than the SOEs, that will play a greater role. This has been proven and will continue to be proven by practice. Under these circumstances, to unswervingly encourage, support, and guide the development of NGEs and their going-global is no longer simply a matter of technology or ownership structure, but will, instead, decide whether China's great-nation strategy can be effectively implemented and finally realized. Accordingly, all our analyses, judgments, and practice should start from this new perspective and level.

To sum up, the formation of the above-three common theoretical understandings and the establishment of the above-three policy orientations can help not only to eliminate all sorts of worries or doubts among the people, but to fundamentally solve the short-term inclination of NGEs' production and investments. What's more, they will also contribute to accelerating the modal transformation of China's economic development and to emancipating and boosting China's productive forces towards greater development, and will ultimately contribute to an earlier realization of the great rejuvenation of the Chinese nation.

1.3.2 Mechanisms for Deepening Economic System Reforms and Solving the Institutional Problems Facing NGEs' Greater Development

An important goal for furthering the reform of the economic system and associated mechanisms is to establish a self-correcting and self-adaptive set of systems and mechanisms that will benefit the sound development of the economy and society. Whether the economic and social system of a country is advanced should be judged at its most fundamental level by whether it contributes to the emancipation and development of productive forces. An economic and social system that contributes to the emancipation and development of these productive forces includes not only those stipulations and regulations beneficial to the promotion of their development, but also the systems and mechanisms that are capable of self-adjustment, self-repair, and self-improvement so as to meet the demands of and boost the development of the productive forces in and of themselves. That is, an excellent system must be in line with the improvements and further perfection of the systems and mechanisms that contribute to the sound development of productive forces, the economy, and society. The continuous improvement of the systems and mechanisms involved is an internal requirement of the development of these productive forces, and a result of the mechanism design and transformation in which the representatives of advanced productive forces take part. In more than 30 years of reform and opening up, one of our most important jobs has been improving and perfecting China's systemic design and functioning mechanisms under the guiding premise that the system of government remains unchanged. After over 30 years of exploration, the present systems and mechanisms are completely different from those that existed before the reform and opening up, and their efficiency is incomparable to those of the past. With the rapid social development and increasing complication seen in China's market economy relations, however, those systems and mechanisms newly-established in the process of reform and opening up are gradually becoming "old-fashioned," themselves, and their effectiveness in boosting the development of the productive forces has started decreasing correspondingly. This is caused, on the one hand, by the revolutionary property of the country's productive forces, and, on the other hand, by the fact that economic and social changes cannot keep up with the demands of the rapidly-developing productive forces. Therefore, further deepening of the reform of the economic systems and mechanisms is a prerequisite for overcoming the institutional difficulty inherent in the great development of NGEs.

We must further deepen the reform of the country's economic management, as well as its economic systems and mechanisms, in order to effectively solve NGEs' financial difficulties. Since most NGEs are small- and medium-sized, and, further, a great majority of them are micro-sized, it is generally difficult for such enterprises to raise funds because of their low level credibility and weak mortgage capacity, particularly the micro-sized enterprises. Such financial difficulties among SMEs also exist in the West, rather than being a special case in China. But what seems to be an insoluble problem in the West may find its way out in China, because China's market economy is quite different from that of the West. The market economy of China is "an economic management under the macro regulation and control of the state, in which the market plays a fundamental role in the allocation of resources."[20] That the market plays a fundamental role in the allocation of resources within the country's institutional framework is similar to the practice in the West. The Western countries with market economies do not, however, often exercise regular macro regulation and control of the market, nor do they regularly use the economic management method of direct participation of SOEs in market competitions. In China there is surely some solution to the problem of NGEs' financing difficulty that can be found either in the policy of socialism with Chinese characteristics and its fundamental attendant economic system or in the economic management unique to China. The central principle of socialism with Chinese characteristics is to focus on the people and to guarantee and improve their well-being, while recognizing that employment is the source of the people's livelihood. To guarantee and improve their well-being, it is of prime importance to ensure the survival and development of NGEs, the major carriers of China's employment. To this end, we must effectively solve NGEs' financing difficulties through institutional reform. We must integrate our civil finances and open the small- and medium-sized financial markets through institutional design and systemic improvement and facilitate the establishment and development of small- and medium-sized banks at the county, community, and township levels, so as to set up those institutions and mechanisms most convenient for the financing of NGEs, especially SMEs. Meanwhile, we should develop guaranteed funds with governmental financial support for SME loans by using the full force of the nation's financial strength, encourage NGOs' participation in NGE credit guarantee, lower the threshold of NGEs' mortgaged or/and guaranteed loans, and improve the competence of mortgage guarantees; in such a way, we can bring greater convenience to NGEs' financial situation and create new institutions and mechanisms with Chinese characteristics, which are appropriate to the financing of SMEs.

Since the promulgation of the 36 Provisions regulating non-public sectors of the economy, i.e., the *Opinions of the State Council on Encouraging, Supporting, and Guiding the Development of Individual, Private, and Other Non-Public Sectors of the Economy* in 2005, it has been commonly understood that non-prohibition means permission, but, in practice, obstacles facing the entry of NGEs into monopolized sectors or industries have not yet been overcome. What's worse, there came into being the so-called "glass door," which is seemingly accessible but impossible to enter, and the "swinging door," which would toss NGEs out even if they enter it. The result is the so-called "advance of SOEs and retreat of NGEs" that turned up during the global financial storm since 2007.

Since the financial storm started in the US in 2007, the easy monetary policy of the Chinese government to stimulate the economy has, to a certain degree, softened

[20]Hu Jintao. (Dec. 19, 2008). Speech at the Convention to Commemorate the 30th Anniversary of the 3rd Plenary Session of The 11th CPC Central Committee, *People's Daily*, p. 1.

the impact of the global financial storm on China's economy and boosted the country's steady economic growth. We should also notice, however, that most newly–released money has flooded into the hand of SOEs through governmental channels; these SOEs have not invested the money rationally in infrastructure construction as required, but have poured it into more profitable industries such as real estate and the stock and bond markets, which has given rise to a new wave of soaring property prices. Worse, it has also led to a phenomenon known as the "advance of SOEs and retreat of NGEs" in certain industries. The "advance of SOEs and retreat of NGEs" can be regarded as the product of a particular stage of development, but it just goes to show how urgent it is to reform the economic management system and practically solve the institutionalized difficulties of NGEs' industrial entry and development. The new 36 Provisions (*Several Opinions of the State Council on Encouraging and Guiding the Sound Development of Non-Governmental Investment*), released in 2010 as a supplement to the aforementioned 36 Provisions on non-public sectors of the economy, intends to break industrial monopolies and provide increased support for private investment and NGEs' development. The difficulty of NGEs' industrial entry remains unsolved, however. Why? The major resistance to it is the interests of special interest groups, in particular the personal interests of departments or sectors. The departmentalized interests are a particular form of, as well as characteristic of, China's interest relations at the current stage. In addition, industrial monopolies are a benefit given by the state administrative power and the product of the alliance between capital and power.[21] We should keep an open mind regarding this point. Otherwise, it would be difficult to understand why NGEs cannot actually gain access to certain industries, regardless of the fact that the CPC Central Committee and the State Council have repeatedly emphasized that NGEs are entitled entry into all economic and social fields except for those involving national economic security and those without an effective allocation of resources by the market. From this perspective, further reform of the economic management system should establish an institutional mechanism that includes all industries and sectors, except the above-mentioned three industries prohibited by law, in an industrial- or sector-based management, rather than the ownership- or department-based management seen in the past. Take, for example, the management of railways, highways, aviation, water transportation, and the ocean transportation industries. As they all belong to transportation, it is advisable to end the traditional management system based on specialized sectors and to adopt a centralized administration by the Ministry/Commission of Transportation directly under the State Council. All the operational divisions of railways, highways, aviation, water transportation, and ocean transportation should, without exception, be transformed into enterprises. Such enterprises may be classified according to their ownership as necessary for clear administrative division; they can also set up non-governmental industrial organizations that will

---

[21]Chen Jiagui. (Nov. 19, 2009). Properly Handle the Relationship Between Keeping Growth and Adjusting Industrial Organizations and Structures. *China Social Sciences Today*.

conduct the self-regulation and management of such enterprises. The general principle is that all the operational enterprises are equal parts of the transportation market and should return to it without exception, be they large or small. On behalf of the state, the Ministry of Transportation under the State Council merely exercises the administration of and policy adjustment for industrial and sector operations, and provides policy directions for the above-mentioned transport enterprises, as well as executes macro control and management of them. We must establish and improve the institutional mechanism of the economy based on equal competition and efficiency by allowing enterprises under different types of ownership to choose and engage themselves in the production and operational activities of various industries, which is in accordance with the inherent law of the movement of capital. It will contribute to the further improvement of the efficiency of resource allocation and utilization, and enable China's NGEs to achieve healthier and more sustainable development. In this way, the transformation of the economic development model will turn from a theoretical discussion into reality all the sooner, and China's national economy will maintain a more stable and rapid growth over the long term.

Undoubtedly, there are far more institutional difficulties in the developmental process of NGEs than just these listed, but the aforementioned three aspects are the most critical. If they are handled properly together with improvements of other aspects, China's NGEs will be able to achieve a greater development on the new economic stage, and China's economic development will reach new heights.

1.3.3 Strengthening the Capacity for Independent Innovation and Extricating NGEs from Their Current Market Plight

As a study by Paul Krugman shows, the short-term monopoly of the market resulting from technological advancement not only contributes to the economic and social development of a country, but also increases those profits gained from the economic globalization.[22] It is exactly in the pursuit of such profits that enterprises tend to be active in technological innovation in order to improve their products or production techniques, so as to promote their competitiveness, change their conditions in the market, and to gain extra profits for the enterprises. The above-mentioned conclusion of Krugman coincides with the viewpoint of Schumpeter that an enterprise's inclination to invest in new knowledge and technological innovation, which may enable it to acquire a monopoly and earn monopoly profits, contributes to the continuous development of the national economy.[23] We must be aware, however, that their discussion is about the behavior of

[22]Krugman, Paul. (2001). *Rethinking International Trade*. Beijing: China Social Sciences Press, p. 176.

[23]Schumpeter, J. (1942). *Capitalism, Socialism and Democracy*, New York: Harper & Row.

enterprises only in the general sense, while in reality, not all enterprises are capable of technological innovation. A report by the CASS Center for Private Economic Studies points out that NGEs of different industries and scales may choose different forms of and paths to innovation. For China's NGEs, in particular those of small and medium size, imitation is likely to be a more effective way of improving a given enterprise's technology. The report also points out that the environment for technological innovation among NGEs is still currently lacking in China, which limits their technological innovation and choice of innovative forms.[24] The environment for innovation mentioned here is actually, in Krugman's terms, the influences of governmental institutions and taxation on enterprises' technological innovation.[25] At present, the prices of production factors are going through obvious relative variations in China, a change in direction that favors NGEs' technological innovation. To extricate NGEs from the difficulty of inadequate technological innovation and the overall market plight of their increased development, we must pay attention to and strengthen the following aspects.

First of all, we must strengthen the construction of institutions that further encourage and support NGEs' independent innovation. This means to strengthen the construction of related national rules and regulations, as NGEs' technological innovation requires the support of related national institutions and policies. The modification and improvement of the rules and regulations, which would better encourage and support NGEs' independent innovation, indicates not only China's policy orientation but related national development goals. The promulgation of more and better rules, regulations, and policies conducive to the independent innovation of NGEs will contribute not only to lowering the cost of technological innovation—especially small- and medium-sized NGEs—but to the normalization of their technological innovation and sustainable development. At present, in order to strengthen an institutional structure that meets the demands of market economy operations and effectively promotes independent innovation on the part of NGEs, it is critical to focus on NGEs' technological innovation within the national system of innovation, and, on that basis, formulate and establish a system of entrepreneurial technological innovation directly correlated with the country's emerging industries and strategic industries. We should also provide more conveniences for NGEs' technological innovation in such aspects as finance and taxation support, the technical renovation of program initialization, new product applications, and trial-production, so as to better promote NGEs' technological innovation and enhance their long-term market competitiveness.

Secondly, we must strengthen the construction of the existing service platform supporting NGEs' innovation and effectively integrate the necessary resources for

[24]Liu Yingqiu & Xu Zhixiang. (2006). *Report on Chinese Non-Governmental Enterprise Competitiveness, No. 3*. Beijing: Social Sciences Academic Press, pp. 7–14.

[25]Krugman, Paul. (2001). *Rethinking International Trade*. Beijing: China Social Sciences Press, p. 158.

NGEs' further innovation. Generally speaking, as large-sized NGEs are stronger, they are much more competent than the small- and medium-sized ones at integrating innovative resources through the market, and are more capable of larger-scale independent innovation. Seen this way, it is both reasonable and realistic to promote the independent innovation of large-sized NGEs through the application of market rules. Small- or medium-sized NGEs are less capable of integrating the appropriate resources for innovation, since they are smaller in scale and insufficient in capital strength and human capital accumulation. Considering this circumstance, it is probably impractical to guide such enterprises towards carrying out more independent innovation through the market and market regulation. This requires our government to build up a platform for innovation services that both meets the demands of the rules of market innovation and accommodates the characteristics of small- and medium-sized NGEs, while also effectively integrating the innovative resources of NGEs and promoting more rapid, quality development of the enterprises in question. The construction of this platform for innovation may start with the following two respects. One is the alliance between research institutions and enterprises and the establishment of a mechanism for the effective and rapid combination of research and application, which will accelerate the conversion of research achievements into practical production. The other is the establishment of an industrial innovation coalition, by which the innovative resources can be integrated and more services can be provided for NGEs' own innovation. We must rely on the functions of market mechanisms and follow the inherent laws of market development, and, on the basis of enterprises' development demands, integrate the specialized research of those enterprises, universities, and institutes that are of high industrial relevancy, so that we can build up such a platform for innovation, formulate the proposed innovation coalition, launch joint breakthroughs in scientific research, and promote greater development of the independent innovation of China's NGEs.

Thirdly, we must strengthen the construction of the legal system so that it effectively protects NGEs' fruits of innovation. As several theoretical studies shows, having the initiative in technological innovation depends on the innovator's return expectations under the condition of a short-term technological monopoly.[26] Therefore, it is an understood institutional premise for the active engagement of enterprises in technological innovation to effectively protect their fruits of innovation and enable the innovators to maximize their returns in the form of short-term monopolistic profits on the market. The first key step to and the ideological core of the effective protection of innovative results that must be undertaken by the government is to prolong their payback period and to protect them from free-riding action by other enterprises. In this regard, it is the duty of the government to strengthen protections over intellectual property rights and to reward innovation by enterprises. The key to intellectual property

[26]Krugman, Paul. (2001). *Rethinking International Trade*. Beijing: China Social Sciences Press, p. 159.

protection is to intensify the struggle against the espionage of technological innovation by other organizations, to completely remove the local protectionism that encourages such free-riding behavior, and to strengthen and perfect the legislation surrounding intellectual property rights and the accompanying relevant legal codes.

Fourthly, we must formulate a development plan for the independent innovation of small- and medium-sized NGEs and incorporate them in the national system of innovation. Innovation requires input, which is an experience correlating with development in many countries. But those that dare to venture and innovate are usually SMEs with insufficient financial strength. This gives rise to the question of how to better encourage and stimulate NGEs to become involved in independent innovation and, further, how to enhance their technological innovative competence? It would be sensible and effective for the state to formulate and include in the national innovation system a developmental plan that encourages the independent innovation of NGEs, in particular small- and medium-sized NGEs. A long withstanding serious problem has existed among the repeated entry-level attempts of NGEs into certain industries, as well as vicious competition between them, both of which are problems that have hindered NGEs' independent innovation and hampered their due development. Thus, from the perspective of transforming the economic development model and adjusting the economic growth structure, it is necessary to promote the independent innovation and development of small- and medium-sized NGEs to the level of a state strategy, formulate concrete plans for them, and include such plans in the national innovation system. Only in this way can we establish a long-term mechanism for the independent innovation of small- and medium-sized NGEs, raise the level of the independent innovation and the development of small- and medium-sized NGEs to a new plane, and lay a solid business foundation for the greater development of China's economy and society.

1.3.4 Improving Industrial Shift Policies to Form Newly Competitive NGEs

Experience shows that the development of industrial clusters has a special output effect. On the one hand, the development of industrial clusters does not exclude competition between similar enterprises or different enterprises within such clusters, and thus contributes to strengthening the complementation and cooperation between enterprises within the clusters, to forming a synergistic effect on the part of the clusters, and to creating the advantages of lowered production costs, product diversity on the basis of higher quality, and sales advantages in the regional market. On the other hand, the development of industrial clusters helps establish new regional systems of industrial innovation through the interaction between administrative institutions and enterprises, and contributes to substantially promoting the collaborative innovation competences of various enterprises in such industrial clusters.[27] As the formation of industrial clusters is closely correlated to regional industrial clusters and the geographical agglomeration of industries, the development of industrial clusters can not only benefit enterprises' competitiveness, but also the continuation and extension of the industries in these clusters.[28]

We must also notice, however, that there is a boundary circumscribing industrial cluster development. The scholars Low and Abrahamson have studied the evolution of industrial clusters and drawn the significant conclusion that, when industrial clusters have developed for a certain period—especially when they have reached maturity—they will automatically enter into a stage of adjustment. If they do not, it will result in the decline of industrial agglomeration. If such an economic phenomenon cannot be overcome through technological innovation, the over-expansion of industrial clusters will lead to an industrial decline and perhaps even destruction.[29] If this occurs, the enterprises in such industrial clusters will choose to move out, that is, to move their output capacity to other regions where they can better improve their competitiveness, or, in the same vein, to join new industrial clusters. In recent years, there has been a certain degree of shifting among enterprises in China, in particular the shift of small- and medium-sized NGEs. This type of regional movement of enterprises from east to west or from south to north is indeed a major geographical adjustment of industrial clusters. Whether or not such adjustments can bring about strong and sustained competitive advantages[30] depends on two factors: one is the cycle length from enterprise shift to the formation of enterprise competitiveness, and the other is the promotion of related state policies and their strength. To meet the demands of China's greater development after it became the world's second largest economy, as well as to encourage and support the rational geographical distribution of industries and effectively promote enterprises' market competitiveness by means of industrial clusters, it is obligatory that we focus on the following aspects.

First of all, we must formulate a plan at the state level for NGEs' industrial shift that conforms to the requirements of China's developmental strategy as a large and populous country. In light of China's economic development, the structural and geographical adjustment of enterprise distribution—which is a result of the industrial upgrading—mainly reflects the central-westward and northward movements of enterprises in the eastern coastal regions, which are subjected to decreasing comparative labor production rates and market competitiveness. In the course of this shift, the approval and establishment of Wanjiang City Group (which functions as

[27]Wei Shouhua, & Shi Bihua. (2002). On the Competitve Advantages of Industrial Clusters. *China Industrial Economics*, (1): 59–65.

[28]Wei Houkai. (2006). *Modern Regional Economics*. Beijing: Economy & Management Publishing House, p. 172.

[29]Low, M., & Abrahamson, E. (1997). Movements, Bandwagons and Clones: Industry Evolution and the Entrepreneurial Process. *Journal of Business Venturing* 12 (6): 435–457.

[30]Poter, M. E. (1998). Clusters and New Economics Competition. *Harvard Business Review,* (11).

an experimental area accepting the industrial shift from the Yangtze River Delta), is a new attempt by the Chinese government to push forward the geographical shift of industries in the east to the central and western regions. This impulse stems from the strategic standpoint of economic development and is of a strong demonstrative effect and profound significance. This emphasis on cross-regional shift is a choice made on the part of enterprises and guided by the market, but experience shows that, even in mature market economies, cross-regional shift or the wide-ranging adjustment of the geographical distribution of enterprises cannot be accomplished without the guidance and political support of the government. This is a firm requirement for the increasingly complicated development of the modern market economy, as well as a symbol of the new improvements being made in the quality of the geographical adjustment of industrial distribution in China. On this account, it is of profound strategic and practical significance to formulate a national plan for industrial shift that is in line with the inherent laws of market economic development and in the interest of those NGEs involved in the aforementioned industrial shift, in order to raise the level of enterprising industrial shift to the level of the nationally-regulated regional development plan and to provide strong guidance and policy support for it, as well as to combine it with the construction and development of the country's major functional areas. The development of a national plan outlining the industrial shift of NGEs will help not only to greatly improve the efficiency of their shift itself, but also to greatly increase the economic returns and enhance the overall competitiveness of the national economy. Thus, we must make great efforts to push forward and fulfill such a significant mission.

Secondly, it is necessary to encourage pattern innovations within NGEs' industrial shift. In China, there are already signs of cross-regional industrial shift, but there is neither existing experience nor a ready pattern for Chinese enterprises to follow. This means that our enterprises, especially NGEs, must learn from the cross-regional industrial shift that already exists in developed countries, localize such experiences, and integrate it with the actual situation in China, so as to create a new experience of cross-regional industrial shift that accords with the realities of China and that will form new patterns of cross-regional industrial shift with Chinese characteristics. To achieve this goal, we must further open our minds. Moreover, we must pay special attention to and learn from the experiences and lessons of different regions in the process of cross-regional industrial shift. More importantly, we must allow for frustrations and failures to occur in the experimental areas without becoming discouraged. Meanwhile, we must also bring an end to the ongoing developmental process and establish a policy-supporting system for the effective cross-regional shift of industries, so that we can successfully relocate industries to the central, western, or northern regions, that—while normally in the eastern coastal regions—have historically been subjected to a lowering of comparative labor production rates and market competitiveness, which will then revitalize the originally competitive enterprises and effectively promote their market competitiveness.

One issue to be further discussed here is the reason behind why enterprises in the eastern coastal regions with decreasing comparative labor production rates and market competitiveness move to regions with less developed economies. Is it because they have lost their market competitiveness, or is it due to their desire to improve their technology and market innovation capabilities? As experience suggests, those enterprises able to afford the shift from the eastern coastal regions to the central, western, or northern regions were generally of very high, rather than low, competitiveness in the eastern regions. That is to say, the geographical shift of such enterprises is never a movement or clearance of the backward production forces evident in the east to the central, western, or northern regions, but rather the continuation and advancement of the innovation taking place in the country's eastern coastal regions. Therefore, the shift of NGEs from the eastern coastal regions to the central, western, or northern regions is not only an innovative process of industrial shift patterns, but also an innovative process of enterprise organization, technology, and participation in the system of market competition.

Thirdly, we must subsidize the country's NGEs, thus enforcing industrial shift. The shift of NGEs from the eastern coastal regions to the central, western, and northern regions is a necessary requirement of the rational distribution of China's industries and the greater development of the country's production forces. As China has surpassed Japan in gross national product (GDP) and is currently the second largest economy in the world, a new and significant change is taking place in the world's developmental pattern—i.e., the historical course of China catching up with and surpassing the U.S. in GDP. In this process, given that all the other conditions remain unchanged, the decisive factor would be whether or not China is able to gain a higher rate of labor production. This gives rise to another question: where does the higher rate of China's labor production come from? While there are various sources, one important source is NGEs' shift from the eastern coastal regions to the central, western, or northern regions. As stated previously, this type of shift would enable such enterprises to obtain higher comparative labor production rates and market competitiveness, and even to create new market competitiveness among enterprises and bring about new social productive forces. Accordingly, it is necessary and in line with China's conditions for the government to subsidize those enterprises inclined towards an industrial shift, especially small- and medium-sized NGEs, because industrial shift inevitably involves input cost, which is to be borne by the enterprises themselves. With these features of the external economy, however, the industrial shift from the eastern coastal regions will not only create new jobs in the central, western, and northern regions, but will bring new fiscal revenues and other forms of prosperity to these areas. Thus it will contribute to both the promotion of the economic and social development in the central, western, and northern regions and to the realization of China's great-nation strategy. Therefore, it is necessary to offer a certain amount of financial subsidies to the enterprises that are carrying out or have already finished an industrial shift, so as to better push forward this process and, on this basis, accomplish the strategic adjustment of China's productive force distribution, the great improvement of the market competitiveness of various enterprises (especially NGEs), and the strategic development of China's overall national economy.

1.3.5 Formulating a Package of Supporting Policies for NGEs' Going-Global

According to a new theory on international trade, trade is not necessarily the inevitable outcome of differences between countries in terms of technical levels or the natural endowment of production factors. On the contrary, it is very likely that trade is an important new approach to expanding the target market and developing economies of scale. Under the condition of increasing wages, each country tends to export products that are of higher market competitiveness or enjoy a larger market.[31] Since trade can benefit the market expansion of a country's enterprises and their products—as well as the development of its international trading and long-term economic growth—policy intervention in trade and political support for the transnational investment of domestic enterprises are indispensable and fundamental to intervention in and the promotion of national economic development.

From the perspectives of China's long-term development and great-nation strategy, it is bound to remain a large industrial producer for a long time, and, as a result, still has to go through a long process before it grows into a great country of technological innovation. Because of this, the bondage of resource problems will become all the more evident, and the supply of productive resources—and in particular raw materials—will become an enormous bottleneck to economic development. In this circumstance, when we mention the importance of expanding foreign trade, it is more accurate to emphasize the importance of strengthening overseas investment, especially investment in overseas resources and their development and production. It is a significant choice for the achievement of China's long-term development and its great-nation strategy to encourage the going global of China's enterprises, in particular NGEs, and to fully develop and utilize available overseas resources.

The going global of China's NGEs first appeared in the form of merchandise sales, and later evolved into product purchasing by Chinese enterprises in overseas concentrations of resources. In recent years, the form of going global has been further upgraded, as there have been the acquisitions of technological products, in particular production technology, in these gathering places. In this process, the overseas mergers and acquisitions, as well as the direct development and production of productive resources by Chinese enterprises, especially NGEs, are of a greater "Going-Global" significance contemporarily. While further expanding China's foreign trade, the going global of these enterprises, especially NGEs, strengthens the country's foreign investment, focuses on the development and production of productive resources, and meets the needs of the domestic industrial production for a larger scale of production and a higher quality of goods. It is already a call to the times and a historical necessity.

---

[31]Krugman, Paul. (2001). *Rethinking International Trade*. Beijing: China Social Sciences Press, pp. 13 & 29.

Chinese enterprises have already taken steady steps towards going global, but they are still faced with many difficulties and challenges in realizing this goal, due to both subjective and objective limitations, and thus require more legal protections, policy support, and the assistance of the Chinese government.

First of all, we must quickly enact the law on the promotion of the overseas investment of Chinese enterprises. Such legislation will, in the first place, make clear the legal basis of the "Going Global" of Chinese enterprises and help them decide on effective methods of going global and corresponding investment arrangements according to the law. In the second place, it will help properly and legally approach the matter of the equal status of various types of enterprises engaged in overseas investment, and change the presently ubiquitous inequality in status and treatment that exists between NGEs and SOEs in terms of fiscal support, bank loans, and funding, and personnel entry-exit management. In the third place, it will help improve the government's macroscopic management of enterprises' going global, create an effective policy environment for NGEs' overseas investment, and promote the efficiency of enterprises' going global. Lastly, it will help change the current situation of there being no law to protect the interests and rights of the enterprises engaged in overseas investment, as well as create a favorable legal environment for protecting NGEs' interests and rights in their going global, while also encouraging Chinese enterprises to better realize the goal of "Going Global." Therefore, we must waste no time in researching and enacting laws on the promotion of the overseas investment of Chinese enterprises.

Secondly, we must implement policies that support and encourage the going global of Chinese enterprises. We should duly release such policies in accordance with the existing developmental stage of China's economy. For example, as a countermeasure to the fact that China, currently a large industrial processer, is faced with an increasingly severe shortage of domestic productive resources, we must provide preferential policies for those enterprises going global in regards to the production and development of resources, such as simpler examination and approval procedures, more conveniences in fund procurement and finance, more tax preferences, easier personnel entry and exit, more effective support for the protection of enterprises' interests and rights, and so forth. But when China's economy further develops into a combination of industrial processes and technological innovation (a process which is gradually dominating its industries), we should make timely adjustments to the governmental policies that support and encourage enterprises to go global in the first place, that is, to convert those policies that encourage the production and development of resources abroad to support the domestic industrial production into those that are more likely to encourage and support enterprises to obtain more and better high and new technology abroad. The core of the government policies that support and encourage China's enterprises going global is to balance the domestic and international markets and domestic and foreign resources, as well as to guarantee the sound, sustainable, and rapid long-term development of China's economy.

Thirdly, we must construct supportive platforms for comprehensive services, including credit, insurance, collective brand promotion, and so forth., all of which will better support Chinese enterprises' going global. Credit and insurance play a very important role in protecting the enterprises participating in international trade and investment. To better serve these enterprises' going global, the government must consider the immediate construction of a brand-new supportive platform for comprehensive services, which absorbs and benefits from successful foreign experiences and is more efficient than domestic credit and insurance operations. We must accelerate the internationalization of Chinese commercial banks, encourage and push forward the establishment of international financial branches, support their mergers and the acquisitions of international financial institutions, and improve their professional competence in import-export credits and international credit investment; furthermore, we must guide them to carry out transnational relocation following Chinese enterprises going global and to provide more excellent, more timely, and more effective financial services for the going global of such enterprises. We must strengthen the construction of the insurance system and institutions for the overseas investment of Chinese enterprises, develop new insurance products to meet the needs of development, provide more and better insurance services for the going global of Chinese enterprises, reduce their risk in overseas investment, and improve their success rate when they do decide to go global. We must project and construct a service and support platform for the collective promotion of Chinese brands, formulate a collective promotion institution of Chinese brands that integrates both government domination and enterprise participation, raise the international popularity and influence of Chinese brands, and create productive forces behind Chinese brands.

Fourthly, we must encourage the clustered going-overseas of Chinese enterprises. The clustered going-overseas of Chinese enterprises (and in particular NGEs, especially those of complementary industries) will not only improve the industrial coordination capacity of such enterprises and lower their cost of overseas production, but also serve as an effective solution to certain problems in the process of their going global, such as unfamiliarity with local policies and regulations, the lack of human resources and market information, and so on. In spite of the fact that China's GDP has ranked second in the world since the end of 2010, Chinese enterprises, particularly NGEs, are still weak in terms of business scale, capital strength, and market competitiveness. Even some NGEs of considerable scale in the domestic market are generally weak and small compared with other large foreign enterprises. Therefore, to encourage and support Chinese enterprises, especially NGEs, going global, one feasible option is to encourage and support the clustered going-overseas of such enterprises and guide them to go overseas gathered, united, and allied. To this end, when the government formulates related polices to encourage and support Chinese enterprises going global, we must regard it as one important part of encouraging, supporting, guiding, and facilitating the clustered going-overseas of Chinese enterprises, especially NGEs, and place it in a prominent position, so that we can better promote the industry, personnel, and information complementation between Chinese enterprises, the faster formation of joint forces within the clusters, the successful entry into overseas markets along with the acquisition of more overseas resources, and the creation of higher economic benefits, all of which serve to boost the great development of China's economy.

1.3.6 Guarding Against External Risks and Guaranteeing the Quality and Security of Chinese Enterprises' Going Global[32]

With the growing national economic power and the expanding foreign trade of China, there are more and more external threats bringing increasingly great risks. They present themselves mainly in the following forms:

First, the threat and risk of intellectual theft by foreign governments. This falls into two categories. One is the overt risk of intellectual theft, such as the pressure on China to revalue the *Renminbi* by some countries and regions in Europe and America; the other is the covert risk of intellectual theft, such as the export damping imposed on Chinese enterprises by some Western countries suffering an economic slowdown during the international financial crisis.

Second, the threat and risk of policymaking interference is an external threat. This mainly results from certain influences exerted on the formulating organizations and key personnel behind China's laws, regulations, and policies by international interest groups. The consequence is that the new policies are made in the better interest of these groups but are likely to bring economic losses to Chinese enterprises themselves. Take the Monsanto Company of the U.S., for example. It is a transnational agricultural biotechnology corporation headquartered in Missouri. To occupy the American agricultural market with its genetically modified products, Monsanto first lobbied the U.S. Congress to enact a bill that newly-invented biological species belonged to the inventor. Then it developed genetically modified species (corn, soybean, and so forth.), which perform better than traditional crops in terms of output, insect resistance, and production cost. Finally, by selling genetically modified seeds to farmers for mass production, it has gained control over 90% of the genetically modified crops in the U.S. market and earned more profits thereby. Such behavior as this has completely changed the production mode of U.S. agriculture. The farmers are just like workers in factories, while Monsanto firmly controls the key elements on the production chain of U.S. agriculture. In recent years, Monsanto has turned to China in an attempt to realize its business interests through interference in China's policy formulation. Not only should the Chinese government pay close attention to such risks, but Chinese enterprises should also guard against them cautiously.

Third, the threat and risk of advantage-based fraud. This mainly refers to the threat and risk brought about by some combinations of international interest groups.

[32]This part borrows some contents from *Prominent Problems in China's National Interest and Economic Security and the Countermeasures* by Dr. Shui Rundong and Prof. Liu Yingqiu.

They take advantage of their international market information and the fact that many Chinese people are still blindly worshiping foreign products and fawning on foreigners, and use it to release some information about their services or products, which is partially or completely false and misleads Chinese enterprises. Typical examples of this type of threat and risk are the huge loss of a large-sized Chinese SOE in the investment in the Blackstone Group, the significant failure of large-sized Chinese enterprises in the investment in overseas derivatives markets, and the repeated frustrations of Chinese enterprises in iron-ore import negotiations.

Obviously, it is high time that we place the management of external threats and risks on the agenda when Chinese enterprises are in the process of going global.

In order to do so, firstly, we should prevent unnecessary losses posed to Chinese enterprises in their going global by responding to potential threats and the risk of policy kidnapping and policy-making interference by foreign governments. In this respect, we should make investigations into the issue and form special think tanks as soon as possible, which are made up of persons from governments, enterprises, and research institutes, and establish strict mechanisms of program identification. The establishment of such organizations and mechanisms will help correctly formulate and implement preventive and countermeasures, and quickly recognize the intentions of foreign interest groups for improper benefits and other potential threats to Chinese enterprises going global.

Secondly, with regard to potential market threats and risks in the going global of our national enterprises, we should enforce more rigid rules of leader comprehension and independent Chinese intermediary institutions for major investment projects. All the examiners, approvers, and signers of major overseas investment projects should fully understand the concepts surrounding optimum profit, the highest risk, and other possible losses such a project may bring about. It is necessary to emphasize that, among the intermediary organizations and the relations between their intermediary acts, there should be at least one Chinese institution that is completely independent from the foreign or target corporation and is qualified to independently issue a consultation and assessment report, and which should make clear the possibilities and boundaries of the risks, benefits, and losses posed by such major investment projects. It is obligatory that we strictly guard against giving too much say to foreign intermediary institutions.

Thirdly, we should establish a rigid process-supervising and information-tracing mechanism to solve the difficulty and problem of risk responsibility confirmation in foreign-related economic activities. In the process of Chinese enterprises' going global, once a major investment project is initiated, all the involved personnel should be listed, classified, and kept on file. Meanwhile, they should be required to make quarterly reports about their personal information, close relatives, and family possessions, all of which should be verified and confirmed quarterly. Furthermore, we should establish a responsibility-confirming and -tracing mechanism outlining significant consequences and a mechanism for the investigation, study, and judgment of major investment projects that have failed.

In summary, the going global of Chinese enterprises is a new phenomenon taking place in a special period of time. As an answer to the process of economic globalization, it is bound to meet many challenges as well as opportunities. We must start from the great development of China's economy, make a correct assessment of the situation, cope with all challenges, and seize all opportunities sober-mindedly, all in order to facilitate Chinese enterprises going global more successfully.

1.4 Conclusions

Through the above analysis, we can draw the following conclusions:

First, China's NGEs have made and are continuing to make great contributions to China's economic development and require us to continuously improve the environment and conditions for their future development through the deepening of political and economic reforms. The development of China's NGEs has made significant contributions to the sustained growth and development of China's national economy as a whole. In order to promote NGEs' role in boosting the sustainable, sound, and rapid long-term development of China's national economy, however, we must continuously deepen the country's institutional and mechanistic reforms and improve both the internal and external environments surrounding their development. In terms of the external environment, NGEs have lately met with marketing hardships and institutional and mechanistic difficulties at the macro management level, a problem which requires close attention from the government. The government should continuously deepen the institutional and mechanistic reforms leveraged to solve such problems as the high threshold for NGEs' entry into certain industries, the difficulty of small and micro NGEs in obtaining loans, the shortage of innovative support for NGEs, and the uncoordinated supporting policies for NGEs' going global, and, in doing so, create more and better external conditions for the better, faster, and healthier development of China's non-governmental economy. In terms of the internal environment surrounding NGEs' development, they must abandon the diversified, extensive, and low value-added model of development they have used for years, and turn to the specialization-based model of development that appropriately integrates scaled expansion and institutional and technological innovation, as well as meets the demands of urbanization, so as to effectively and greatly promote their industrial upgrading, structural optimization, and market competitiveness.

Second, technological innovation and market innovation are the keys to the promotion of NGEs' competitiveness. To avoid the marketing difficulties facing them during the transformation of their development models, NGEs must not only transform their industry and upgrade their technology, but also, through market innovation, make clear the goals of their industrial transformation and technological upgrading as well as the system, organization, and goals behind their development. We must appropriately handle the following relationships:

First of all, the relationship between the innovation of SOEs and that of NGEs. The state should scientifically guide the technological innovation of enterprises in terms of classifications, and divide SOEs and NGEs by the different emphases in their technological innovation. That is, we should guide SOEs to undertake more innovation regarding the strategic and fundamental technology that concerns the lifeline of the country's national security and economic development, while NGEs should be prompted to exercise more innovation in terms of practical technology.

Secondly, we should pay attention to the relationship between traditional technology and high technology in the development of enterprises. When judged by the present situation of development, most enterprises still have to rely on the traditional industries for survival and development. Therefore, they have to adopt traditional production technology and, on that basis, gradually increase the added value of their products and their enterprise competitiveness through the moderate innovation of their products and the consummation and integration of their value chains.

Thirdly, the relationship between different regions that may vary in innovation capacities should be attended to. On the basis of the evident differences between regions in technological innovation, the considerable difference in the patterns of technological innovation between industries, and the difference in technological innovative benefits between enterprises, the state should act in accordance with local conditions, make full use of favorable circumstances, make distinctions between different enterprises to decide their particular emphases, and actively boost innovation and promote the innovative capacities of different regions, industries, and enterprises, so as to improve the overall level of innovation of the country.

Third, the promotion of human-capital investment is the basis for the long-term development of NGEs. That China's economic transformation has entered a new stage indicates that it is of directional significance to the country to raise the levels of total-factor productivity. Only when NGEs increase their investment in human capital can they raise their level of total-factor productivity. With the structural change of China's population and the arrival of the Lewis Turning Point, the advantage of an infinite supply of cheap labor—which used to play an important role in the country's economy—will rapidly disappear; the reliance of NGEs on the traditional path of growth and development will also disappear gradually, and, eventually, completely. This reality requires that China's NGEs adapt themselves to the changing situation, increase their investment in human capital, and constantly upgrade their comparative advantages, so that they can promote their market competitiveness effectively.

Fourth, NGEs' going global is a natural trend of development. From the perspective of the top-level design, the state must formulate a package of policies and measures for the going global of Chinese enterprises (including NGEs), and accelerate NGEs' going global. Currently, the global economy is experiencing a period of structural adjustment and a revolution in its management mechanisms, and is at the incubation stage of technological innovation and industrial transformation; meanwhile, the power of the emerging market countries is on the rise. Such is the macroscopic situation of the world's economic development. For the greater development of China's NGEs, this is not only a period promising important strategic opportunities, but also a critically-difficult period for transforming their development models. China cannot separate from the rest of the world, and the world cannot live without China. As a call for the immediate reform of the international monetary system has been made, and the demand of many countries for the *Renminbi* keeps rising, the internationalization of the *Renminbi* is becoming an irresistible tide in history. In this new context of development, the proportion of NGEs' foreign trade and overseas investment is rising yearly; NGEs' competence in participating in the international division of labor is growing stronger; the proportions of FDI (foreign direct investment) stock and FDI subjects have experienced a measurable rise; transnational investment and the operation of NGEs have stepped into a new stage in history. For their greater development, it is an urgent requirement that China's NGEs should form transnational strategic alliances, and that China's enterprises, especially NGEs, should cultivate their competitiveness in the international market through direct or indirect overseas investment, overseas listing, and going overseas clustered. Therefore, the state must start from a higher standpoint and formulate a package of top-level policies and measures such as overseas investment, credit loans, use of foreign currency, insurance, personnel training, and more, all in support of the going global of China's NGEs.

Bibliography

Baidu Encyclopedia China's urbanization process. http://baike.baidu.com/view/2418751.htm?fr=ala0_1_1. Accessed 18 Mar 2009

Cai F, How to sustain China's economic growth in the 21st century? http://www.stockstar.com. Accessed 8 Nov 2006

Cai F (2006) How can China's economy grow without labor force advantage? China Education Daily, 14 Oct

Cai F (2008) A long-term perspective of China's macro economic stabilization. In: China economic research report (2007–2008). Economy & Management Publishing House, Beijing

Cassiman B, Veugelers R (2002) Complementarity in the innovation strategy: internal R&D, external technology acquisition and cooperation. http://search.epnet.com/login.aspx?direct=true&db=ecn&an=0694553. Accessed 20 July 2009

Chen J (2009a) Properly handle the relationship between keeping growth and adjusting industrial organizations and structures. China Social Sciences Today, 19 Nov

Chen Q (2009b) Chinese enterprises quickening overseas mergers and acquisitions. China Financial & Economic News, 10 Nov

Chen J, Huang Q, Zhang T (2008) From rapid growth to harmonious development: China economy retrospect and prospect. In: China economic research report (2007–2008). Economy & Management Publishing House, Beijing

China National Bureau of Statistics (2007) Statistical and monitoring report on the process of China's construction of a well-off society in an all-round way. Beijing, China

Kamien MI, Schwartz NL (1982) Market structure and innovation. Cambridge University Press, Cambridge

Krugman P (2001) Rethinking international trade. China Social Sciences Press, Beijing

Kuznets S (1989) Modern economic growth (Chinese version). Beijing Economics College Press, Beijing

Liu Y, Xu Z (2005) Reports on Chinese non-governmental enterprise competitiveness, (no. 2, 4, 5). Social Sciences Academic Press, Beijing
Liu Y, Xu Z (2006) Report on Chinese non-governmental enterprise competitiveness. (no. 3). Social Sciences Academic Press, Beijing
Liu Y, Xu Z (2007) Reports on Chinese non-governmental enterprise competitiveness, (no. 2, 4, 5). Social Sciences Academic Press, Beijing
Liu Y, Xu Z (2008) Reports on Chinese non-governmental enterprise competitiveness, (no. 2, 4, 5). Social Sciences Academic Press, Beijing
López-Rodríguez J, García-Rodríguez R (2005) Technology and export behaviour: a resource-based view approach. Int Bus Rev 14(5):539–557
Low M, Abrahamson E (1997) Movements, bandwagons, and clones: industry evolution and the entrepreneurial process. J Bus Ventur 12(6):435–457
Poter ME (1998) Clusters and new economics competition. Harv Bus Rev 11:77–90
Schumpeter J (1942) Capitalism, socialism and democracy. Harper & Row, New York
Schumpeter J (1990) Theories on economic development (Chinese version). The Commercial Press, Beijing
Schumpeter J (1994) Cycles of economy (Chinese version). The Commercial Press, Beijing
Schumpeter J (1999) Capitalism, socialism and democracy (Chinese version). The Commercial Press, Beijing. http://www.npc.gov.cn/npc/xinwen/fztd/yfxz/2008-12/19/content_1462768.htm. Accessed 20 June 2009
UNDP (2007/2008) Human development report. http://hdrstats.undp.org/indicators/147.html. Accessed 13 June 2009
Wartzel J (2007) China: optimal models of growth. In: Li B (ed) Rise?! Two possibilities of China's economic development in 10 years. Social Sciences Academic Press, Beijing
Wei S, Shi B (2002) On the competition advantages of industrial clusters. China Ind Econ 1:59–65
Wu J et al (2009) Four warnings for China's economy. China Financial & Economic News, 26 Nov
Xinhua News Agency (2009) The assets abroad of Chinese enterprises exceed USD 1 Trillion. CPPCC Newspaper (Renmin Zhengxie Bao), 4 Nov, p 4
Zheng H (2009) Real estate market crisis: seek help or self help? People's Daily Overseas Edition, 17 Feb

Chapter 2
The Post-WTO Era: NGEs' New Development and the Sustained Rapid Growth of China's Economy

Xiahui Liu

2.1 The Roles of NGEs' Development in China's Economic Growth

A non-governmental economy is essentially one in which economic activities and investments are made, benefits are enjoyed, and risks are taken by the citizens; or, in more common language, it refers to the economic activities that involve private investment, private benefits, and private risk-taking. Strictly speaking, such an economy should be better named a "civilian economy" or "private sector of the economy".

There were two types of private sectors within the economy in China before 1949. One consisted of the bureaucrat-capitalist enterprises, while the other was the national bourgeoisie enterprises. The bureaucrat-capitalist class was born out of the Westernization Movement in the late Qing Dynasty. By 1949, a total of 2858 bureaucrat-capitalist enterprises were confiscated, consisting of only 750,000 production workers, but they also accounted for 80% of the fixed assets of the industry, traffic, and transportation at that time. On the other hand, the national bourgeoisie enterprises, which consisted of three parts, had a short history of less than 100 years. The first part were grown gradually out of manufacturing workshops alongside the introduction of new machines. The second part consisted of some private-run government-sponsored or government-monitored enterprises that emerged along with the Westernization Movement in the nineteenth century. And the third part was a new form of capitalist industry and commerce initiated by landlords and officials at that time.

X. Liu (✉)
Chinese Academy of Social Sciences, Beijing, China

Y. Liu (ed.), *New Interpretations on the Development of China's Non-Governmental Enterprises*, Research Series on the Chinese Dream and China's Development Path, DOI 10.1007/978-981-10-3872-3_2

The "nationalization of private industry" was one of China's goals[1] when the People's Republic of China was founded. Soon after its founding, the government acquired the monopoly on foreign trade and obtained considerable capacity for the constraint of capitalist industry and commerce through taxation, credit loans, and industrial relations. Through the campaign against the "three evils" (corruption, waste, and bureaucracy) and the struggle against the "five evils" (capitalist bribery of government workers, tax evasion, theft of state property, cheating on government contracts, and stealing economic information for private industrial and commercial enterprises), the social reputation and status of the capitalist class declined rapidly in China. Meanwhile, "capital exposure" and "democratic appraisal" activities caused the loss of integrity in the authoritative relations between private enterprises. With the growth of state-owned industry and commerce and the consequent thriving of agricultural cooperatives, it had become a significant and feasible method of "nationalization" to realize "the socialist transformation of capitalist industry and commerce" and to further incorporate them into the national program through "national capitalism" by means of processing, ordering, central purchasing, exclusive selling, and joint state-private management.[2]

After the general proposed transitional period put forward by the Party, the central purchasing and selling of farm products, the common establishment of agricultural cooperation, and the exclusion of private wholesalers further squeezed the margin for decision-making insofar as private capitalist industry and commerce was concerned. Hence, the government at that time was able to considerably push forward the joint state-private management through the "Four Horses Dividing Fruits" (四马分肥, sì mǎ fēn féi)[3] movement in terms of profit allocation and the "Championship of Advanced Capitalists" ("先进资本家"的"锦标赛", "xiān jìn zī

[1]See Address of Mao Zedong at the Closing Ceremony of 2nd Session of 1st CPPCC, June 23, 1950. In Mao Zedong. (1999). *Works of Mao Zedong*. Beijing: People's Publishing House, p. 80.

[2]Article 31 of the *Common Program* stipulates, "Enterprises jointly operated by state and private capital are enterprises of a state-capitalist character. When necessary and possible, private capital should be encouraged to develop into national capitalism, e.g., processing for the SOEs, jointly operating with the state, operating SOEs on loan, developing the state resources, and so forth." By then, it had not been recognized that national capitalism is a path towards the transformation of private-owned capitalist industry and commerce.

[3]On Sept. 7, 1953, Mao Zedong invited and had a talk with Chen Shutong and nine other people outside the Party at the Hall of Health and Longevity. According to the talk, "Four Horses Dividing Fruits" means that in the profit allocation of national capitalist enterprises (namely, enterprises of joint state-private management), the income tax accounted for 34.5%, the welfare fund for 15%, the reserve fund for 30%, and the capitalists' dividend for the rest, or 20.5%..

běn jiā" dē "jǐn biāo sài")[4,5]. After the high tide of the country's agricultural cooperation, the capitalist class in China was completely isolated. Through the "persuasion" and "education" of the capitalists on the prospects of socialism and their own future, there came the climax of joint state-private management across all domestic industries.[6] Finally, the government completely bought out control from the enterprise capitalists by means of fixed interests and succeeded in a socialist transformation of the capitalist industry and commerce, that is, the conversion from divided, personal decision-making to centralized, public decision-making on questions of national production and management.

By 1956, China had finished the socialist transformation of 123,000 industrial units with 1.64 million workers and 4.02 million commercial units with 6.62 million employees. By then, private enterprises had completely disappeared in China. At that time, 860,000 individuals were identified as national capitalists; however, 700,000 of them were re-identified as merchants and peddlers after the 3rd Session of the 12th CPC Central Committee. Therefore, only 160,000 of the original remained national capitalists.

With the deepening of the country's reform and opening up, the non-governmental sectors of the economy have made great developments and are becoming increasingly important, after having gone through the long process of growing out of nothing, developing from small to large, and from being restricted to being encouraged and inspired by the government. Their importance mainly shows itself as a new growth point within the national economy. Though the large-sized SOEs or state-holding enterprises are the guarantee of national security and the anchor of national economy and industrial development, as well as representing the country's technological and economic power, it should not be neglected to note that non-governmental economy is also an important point of economic strength and a fresh force within the national economy. The proportion of non-governmental

[4]At the General Assembly of the All China Federation of Industry & Commerce (ACFIC) on Oct. 11, 1953, many people recognized that "socialism is an irresistible trend everyone should follow." Some proposed to "actively run their business, endeavor to play their roles, keep away from the five evils, receive the restrictions, reinforce learning, and welcome the transformation." See Pang Xianzhi, & Jin Chongji. (2003). *Biography of Mao Zedong* (1949–1976), (1st ed.). Beijing: Central Committee Documents Publishing House, p. 435.

[5]In 1954, the government adopted the "apple-biting" or the one-by-one model, and realized the joint state-private management of 793 industrial enterprises, all of which were relatively large and concerned the national interest and people's livelihood. Their output of that year was valued at RMB 2.56 billion, more than the totaled output of all the jointly-managed enterprises in the previous several years. See Pang Xianzhi, & Jin Chongji. (2003). *Biography of Mao Zedong* (1949–1976), (1st ed.). Beijing: Central Committee Documents Publishing House, p. 437.

[6]Towards the bourgeoisie, it was pointed out in the *Resolution of the Central Committee of the Communist Party of China on the Transformation of Capitalist Industry and Commerce* that, firstly, we should change the capitalist ownership by ways of buyout and state capitalism gradually rather than abruptly, with compensation rather than without compensation; secondly, we should arrange their work as necessary while conducting the transformation, and; third, we should not disfranchise them of the right to vote, but must make appropriate political arrangements for the representatives of those who have vigorously supported and contributed to the socialist transformation.

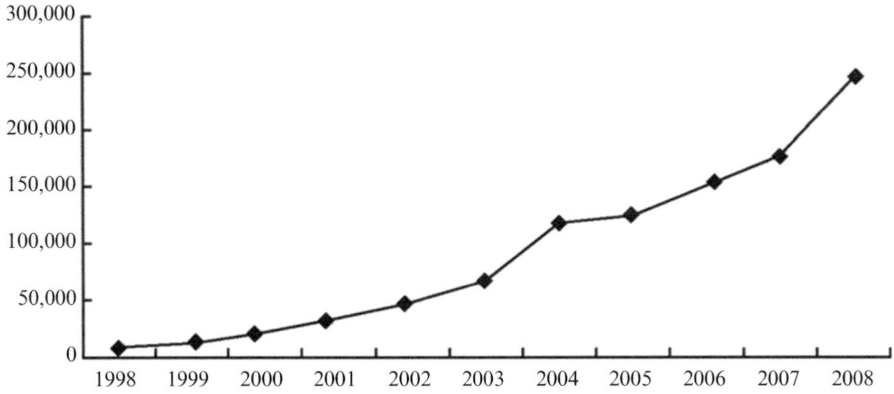

Fig. 2.1 Numbers of NGEs (Source: *China Statistical Yearbook 2009*)

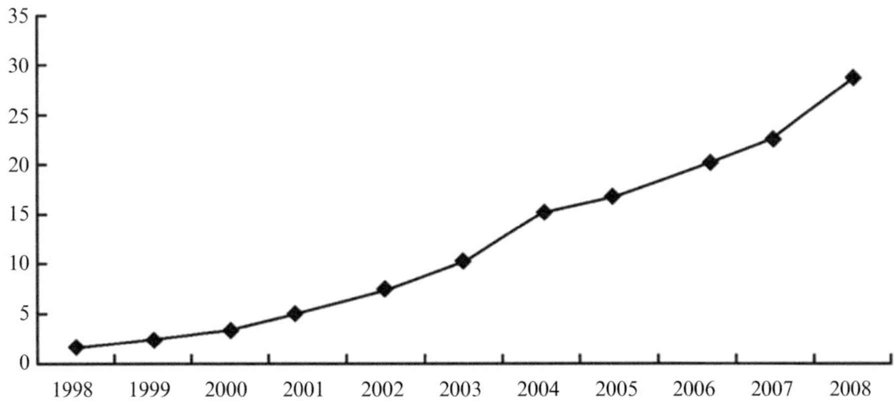

Fig. 2.2 Employees in industrial NGEs (million) (Source: *China Statistical Yearbook 2009*)

economy is continuously rising in China. Since 1980, the output value of non-governmental sectors of the economy has maintained an annual growth of about 30%, which has made a prominent contribution to China's economic growth.

1. The number of NGEs keeps growing. Take industrial NGEs for example. From 1998 to 2009, the scale of industrial NGEs had increased from around 10,000 to about 250,000 (See Fig. 2.1). Certainly, other types of NGEs were developing at a very rapid pace as well. Moreover, non-governmental sectors of the economy had also gained rapid development in the primary and the service industry and were playing an increasingly important role.
2. Employment in NGEs keeps expanding. From 1998 to 2009, the employees associated with industrial NGEs had increased from 1.06 million to over 30 million (Fig. 2.2), or nearly 30 times, which proves the enormous capacity of NGEs to absorb and accept the national labor force. Employment in NGEs has already become a significant means to raise the employment rate of society as a whole, to

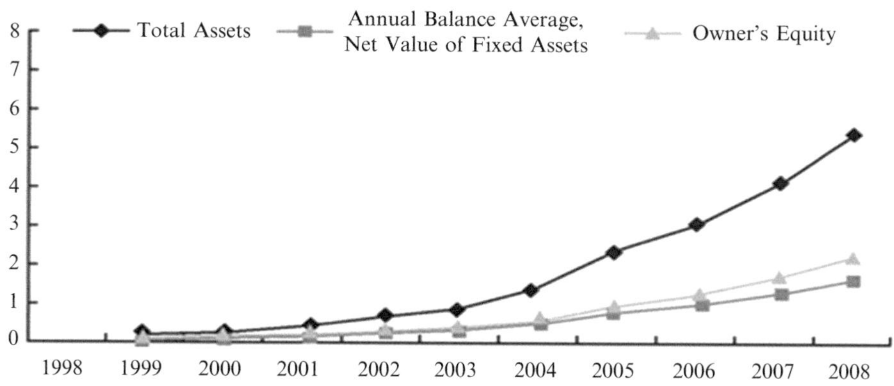

Fig. 2.3 Condition of assets in industrial NGEs (trillion yuan) (Source: *China Statistical Yearbook 2009*)

(trillion RMB)

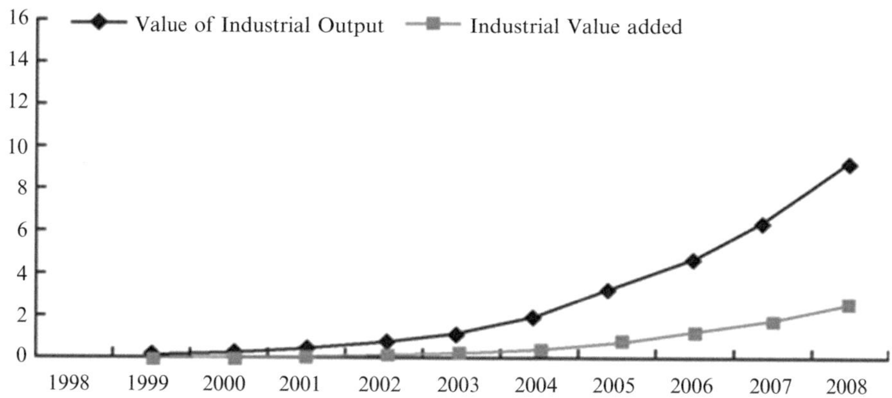

Fig. 2.4 Value of industrial output and industrial value added, industrial NGEs (Source: *China Statistical Yearbook 2009*)

relieve the employment pressure of urban populations, and to shift the surplus labor force from the rural areas. It is safe to say that non-governmental sectors of the economy are the major employment channel in China if we take into consideration the employees in the service industry and the primary industry.

3. The capital of NGEs keeps growing. From 1998 to 2008, the paid-in capital of industrial NGEs had increased from RMB 148.7 billion to over RMB 8 trillion, and owners' equity from RMB 57.7 billion to RMB 4 trillion, both of which prove that NGEs have become an important part of China's industrial enterprises. NGEs also play an important role in the service industry (Fig. 2.3).
4. The production of NGEs keeps expanding and their income continues to grow rapidly. From 1998 to 2008, the value of industrial output of industrial NGEs had increased by 6.8 times and from RMB 208.3 billion to RMB 13.634 trillion; their industrial value added had increased from RMB 51 billion to RMB 2.6382 trillion (Fig. 2.4); their income from major business had increased from RMB

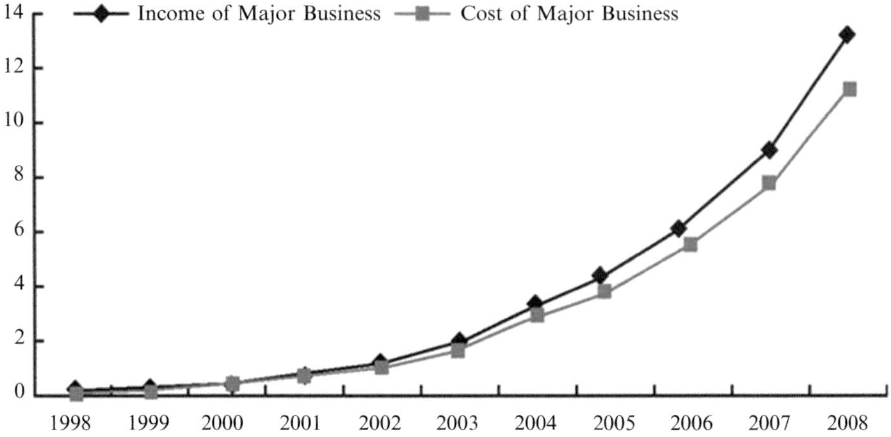

Fig. 2.5 Income and cost of major business, industrial NGEs (trillion RMB) (Source: *China Statistical Yearbook 2009*)

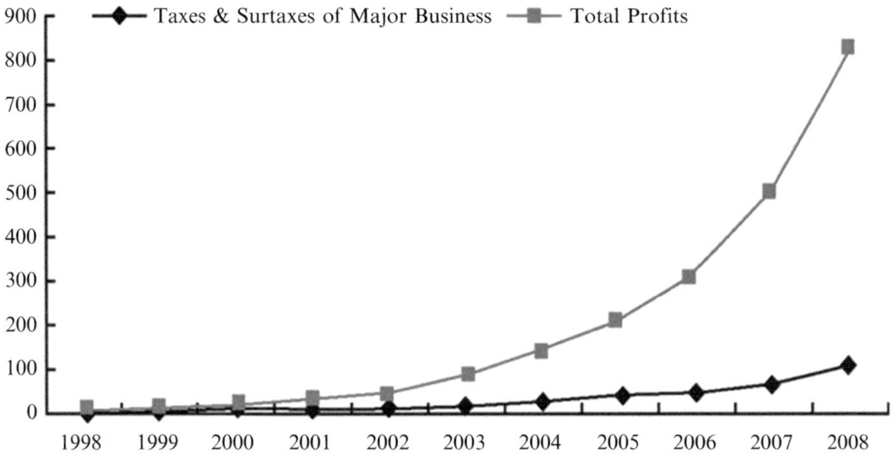

Fig. 2.6 Total profits and taxes, industrial NGEs (billion yuan) (Source: *China Statistical Yearbook 2009*)

184.6 billion to RMB 13.1525 trillion (Fig. 2.5); their total profits had increased from RMB 6.7 billion to RMB 830.2 billion; and their taxes and surtaxes had increased from RMB 2.1 billion to RMB 112.3 billion (Fig. 2.6). In short, NGEs have already made a great contribution to society.

In addition to directly driving the national economic growth and providing social employment, the non-governmental sectors of the economy are also playing a prominent role in solving many other problems in the country's economic development. With the formation of the mixed-subject economy, the non-governmental sectors of the economy are bound to play an increasingly important role in the cultivation of market players and the furtherance of market growth.

2.2 Characteristics of NGEs' Development in the New Economic Stage

Currently the non-governmental sectors of the economy have finished their primitive accumulation and are of a rather considerable scale. They are playing an important role in employment, investment, taxation, foreign exchange earnings, and the development of science and technology. NGEs are growing in terms of average capital scale and strength, and a number of them are developing towards economies of scale. Specifically, the characteristics of China's non-governmental economy are as follows.

2.2.1 Secondary Industry: The Major Domain of NGEs

As statistics from some parties show, the secondary industry is where NGEs are mainly concentrated. For example, the statistics provided by the Enterprise Census in 2001 indicate that the secondary industry is the highest among three of the four indicators (enterprise numbers, employment numbers, paid-in capital, and operating income), excluding only paid-in capital. In 2001, 720,000 NGEs were engaged in the secondary industry, accounting for 54.3% of the total number of NGEs; more than 24 million people were employed in the secondary industry, accounting for 76.7% of all NGE employees; NGEs' operating income in the secondary industry was RMB 1.8625 trillion, or 58.4% of the total income of all NGEs. In light of the average scale, NGEs of the secondary industry are the largest in terms of the average number of employees (33.9 persons) and the smallest in their average paid-in capital (RMB 937,000). In contrast, NGEs of the tertiary industry are the smallest in the average number of employees (12.1 persons) but the largest in their average paid-in capital (RMB 1.209 million). At present, the general tendency of industrial structural change among non-governmental sectors of economy is that the secondary industry is gradually declining in its proportion to the whole, while the tertiary industry is rising steadily in its proportion, but is not yet in a dominant position. The reasons are as follows. Firstly, the primary and secondary industries have not yet developed fully, which delays the formation of a huge market demand for the tertiary industry and impedes any kind of powerful financial and technological support for the tertiary industry. Secondly, there are currently strong barriers to entry into the tertiary industry in China. NGEs can only access some traditional trades, such as the wholesale and retail trade, the catering trade, and the social services trade, while they find it rather difficult to enter the modern trades of the tertiary industry like communication, air transportation, finance, and insurance.

Calculations performed using the enterprise database of China's National Bureau of Statistics shows that the industries/sectors in descending order of NGEs' proportion in the total assets of each industry/sector in 2008 are: smelting and the pressing of ferrous metals; the textile industry; electromechanical and equipment manufacturing; chemical materials and products manufacturing; the manufacture of non-metallic mineral products; the manufacture of general purpose machinery; transportation equipment manufacturing; agricultural and sideline products processing; metal products manufacturing; communications equipment, computer and other electronic equipment manufacturing; medical and pharmaceutical products manufacturing; special purpose equipment manufacturing; papermaking and paper products manufacturing; petroleum processing, coking, and nuclear fuel processing; plastic products manufacturing; the manufacture of clothing, footwear, and headgear; coal mining and dressing; food manufacturing; chemical fiber manufacturing; beverage manufacturing; the production and distribution of electricity and heat; rubber products manufacturing; the manufacture of leather, furs, down, and related products; the printing and replication of recording media; mining and dressing of ferrous metals; wood processing and manufacturing of wood, bamboo, rattan, palm coir, and straw products; the manufacture of handicrafts and other products; furniture manufacturing; the manufacture of cultural, educational, and sports products; the mining and dressing of non-metallic minerals; the production and distribution of water; the production and distribution of gas; the extraction of petroleum and natural gas; recycling and the processing of discarded resources and materials; tobacco manufacturing; and the mining of other minerals. Sequencing of NGEs' proportions in terms of major business income, total profits, industrial value added, or industrial sales value of each industry/sector produces similar results (See Tables 2.1 and 2.2).

2.2.2 SMEs: Major Types of NGEs

Among the 93,579 NGEs surveyed in 2008, only 507 were large-sized, accounting for 0.54% of the total number of NGEs; 9916 were medium-sized, accounting for 10.60%; and 83,156 were small-sized, accounting for 88.86% (Fig. 2.7). The average assets of large-sized NGEs were RMB 3,032,009.71, the average assets of medium-sized NGEs were RMB 2,446,776.68, the average assets of small-sized NGEs were RMB 31,919.73.

The average major business income of large-, medium-, and small-sized NGEs are:olarge-sized NGEs RMB 4,025,441.18, medium-sized NGEs RMB 325,839.74 and small-sized NGEs RMB 56,800.74, respectively. The average industrial output value of large-, medium-, and small-sized NGEs are:large-sized NGEs RMB 4,096,592.39, medium-sized NGEs RMB 339,201.60 and small-sized NGEs RMB 58,808.24, respectively (Table 2.3).

The average industrial sales value of large-, medium-, and small-sized NGEs are:large-sized NGEs RMB 4,029,466.39, medium-sized NGEs RMB 328,829.57 and small-sized NGEs RMB 57,287.84, respectively. The total profit of NGEs was RMB 634,403,480, in which that of large-sized NGEs accounted for 21.31% (RMB 135,160,129), that of medium-sized NGEs for 33.82% (RMB 214,577,938), and that of small-sized NGEs for 44.87% (RMB 284,665,413).

Table 2.1 NGEs' proportions of assets, output value, and employment by industry 2008 (%)

Industry/Sector	Assets	Major business income	Profits	Industrial output value	Industrial sales value	Export delivery value	Employees	Legal entities
Coal mining and dressing	2.02	1.68	4.65	1.63	1.65	0.03	2.51	1.70
Extraction of petroleum and natural gas	0.09	0.05	0.11	0.04	0.05	0.00	0.04	0.04
Mining and dressing of ferrous metals	0.94	0.89	3.35	0.90	0.89	0.01	0.69	0.73
Mining and dressing of non-metallic minerals	0.38	0.48	0.61	0.48	0.48	0.10	0.63	0.79
Mining of other minerals	0.00	0.00	0.00	0.00	0.00	0.00	0.00	0.00
Agricultural and sideline products processing	4.78	7.20	5.86	7.18	7.18	4.05	4.73	5.66
Food manufacturing	1.82	1.94	1.87	1.96	1.95	1.57	2.12	1.87
Beverage manufacturing	1.47	1.20	1.39	1.24	1.23	0.27	1.19	1.18
Tobacco manufacturing	0.02	0.01	0.02	0.01	0.01	0.00	0.03	0.02
Textile industry	8.89	8.70	6.95	8.70	8.73	11.98	12.13	10.09
Manufacture of clothing, footwear and headgear	2.45	2.67	2.54	2.72	2.71	7.16	5.12	3.97
Manufacture of leather, furs, down and related products	1.13	1.52	1.55	1.52	1.53	3.72	2.68	2.12
Wood processing and manufacturing of wood, bamboo, rattan, palm coir, and straw products	0.93	1.23	1.26	1.23	1.23	1.20	1.49	1.91
Furniture manufacturing	0.70	0.72	0.59	0.72	0.72	1.80	1.10	1.01
Papermaking and paper products manufacturing	2.70	2.47	2.36	2.49	2.49	0.40	2.57	3.28
Printing and replication of recording media	1.02	0.72	0.72	0.72	0.73	0.22	1.04	1.84
Manufacture of cultural, educational and sports products	0.49	0.50	0.39	0.50	0.50	1.85	0.97	1.02
Petroleum processing, coking and nuclear fuel processing	2.59	2.55	2.00	2.47	2.47	0.38	0.96	0.66
Chemical materials and products manufacturing	7.46	8.15	8.79	8.15	8.14	4.99	8.96	7.71
Medical and pharmaceutical products manufacturing	3.46	2.34	3.98	2.47	2.42	1.88	2.38	1.99

(continued)

Table 2.1 (continued)

Industry/Sector	Assets	Major business income	Profits	Industrial output value	Industrial sales value	Export delivery value	Employees	Legal entities
Chemical fiber manufacturing	1.54	1.50	0.77	1.49	1.50	1.32	0.65	0.60
Rubber products manufacturing	1.18	1.26	1.20	1.27	1.28	1.60	1.30	1.25
Plastic products manufacturing	2.53	2.59	2.32	2.58	2.58	2.43	2.85	4.72
Manufacture of non-metallic mineral products	7.44	6.76	8.01	6.83	6.80	3.71	8.67	8.73
Smelting and pressing of ferrous metals	9.73	11.23	9.00	10.98	11.10	4.82	3.93	2.46
Metal products manufacturing	4.04	4.37	3.70	4.37	4.35	5.91	5.02	6.02
Manufacture of general purpose machinery	6.51	6.40	6.51	6.49	6.45	6.14	7.12	9.36
Special purpose equipment manufacturing	3.31	2.89	3.32	2.96	2.92	1.84	3.14	3.81
Transportation equipment manufacturing	5.20	4.69	4.36	4.73	4.71	6.05	4.65	4.31
Electromechanical and equipment manufacturing	8.86	8.87	8.18	8.85	8.88	11.21	6.66	6.69
Communication equipment, computer and other electronic equipment manufacturing	3.57	2.69	2.11	2.58	2.60	10.00	2.49	1.82
Manufacture of handicrafts and other products	0.80	1.02	0.83	1.03	1.03	3.36	1.54	1.65
Recycling and processing of discarded resources and materials	0.08	0.15	0.12	0.15	0.15	0.01	0.09	0.14
Production and distribution of electricity and heat	1.43	0.41	0.39	0.41	0.41	0.00	0.39	0.58
Production and distribution of gas	0.13	0.08	0.12	0.07	0.07	0.00	0.04	0.08
Production and distribution of water	0.29	0.07	0.07	0.07	0.07	0.00	0.09	0.19

Source: Enterprise database of China National Bureau of Statistics

Table 2.2 NGEs' assets, output value and employment by industry 2008

Industry/Sector	Assets (RMB mn)	Major business income (RMB mn)	Profits (RMB mn)	Industrial output value (RMB mn)	Industrial sales value (RMB mn)	Export delivery value (RMB mn)	Employees	Legal entities
Coal mining and dressing	131.92	166.00	29.24	166.65	165.06	0.33	502,042	1566
Extraction of petroleum and natural gas	5.81	4.46	0.68	4.57	4.57	0	87,560	35
Mining and dressing of ferrous metals	61.34	88.31	21.06	92.51	89.00	0.17	138,827	674
Mining and dressing of non-metallic minerals	24.65	47.31	3.83	49.11	48.11	1.13	126,003	733
Mining of other minerals	0.05	0.24	0.02	0.23	0.23	0.01	612	3
Agricultural and sideline products processing	312.18	713.18	36.80	735.16	716.14	48.13	945,919	5228
Food manufacturing	118.60	191.71	11.74	200.81	194.36	18.73	423,104	1730
Beverage manufacturing	95.97	119.03	8.75	127.46	122.61	3.21	237,500	1089
Tobacco manufacturing	1.53	1.43	0.14	1.41	1.41	0.02	5632	19
Textile industry	581.03	861.55	43.64	890.61	870.69	142.47	2E + 06	9323
Manufacture of clothing, footwear and headgear	160.12	264.70	15.960	27.892	270.03	85.190	1E + 06	3669
Manufacture of leather, furs, down and related products	73.90	150.74	9.75	155.56	152.43	44.21	536,314	1959
Wood processing and manufacturing of wood, bamboo, rattan, palm coir, and straw products	60.65	122.16	7.93	125.78	122.45	14.26	298,709	1764
Furniture manufacturing	45.96	71.31	3.69	73.31	71.78	21.37	219,577	930
Papermaking and paper products manufacturing	176.42	245.00	14.83	254.67	248.56	4.76	513,172	3029
Printing and replication of recording media	66.38	71.67	4.51	74.20	73.11	2.58	207,442	1699
Manufacture of cultural, educational and sports products	32.04	49.75	2.45	51.08	49.61	22.04	194,656	943
Petroleum processing, coking and nuclear fuel processing	169.49	252.88	12.55	252.89	246.82	4.52	190,944	614
Chemical materials and products manufacturing	487.57	806.94	55.20	834.06	812.43	59.39	2E + 06	7123

(continued)

Table 2.2 (continued)

Industry/Sector	Assets (RMB mn)	Major business income (RMB mn)	Profits (RMB mn)	Industrial output value (RMB mn)	Industrial sales value (RMB mn)	Export delivery value (RMB mn)	Employees	Legal entities
Medical and pharmaceutical products manufacturing	226.25	231.98	24.99	253.15	241.36	22.38	475,130	1835
Chemical fiber manufacturing	100.93	148.31	4.81	152.30	149.48	15.72	129,818	554
Rubber products manufacturing	77.08	125.04	7.53	130.18	127.24	18.99	260,836	1158
Plastic products manufacturing	165.52	256.69	14.56	264.27	257.34	28.90	570,343	4358
Manufacture of non-metallic mineral products	486.04	669.25	50.35	699.21	678.64	44.08	2E + 06	8061
Smelting and pressing of ferrous metals	635.54	1111.87	56.56	1124.19	1107.14	57.35	785,721	2270
Metal products manufacturing	264.13	432.51	23.27	447.38	434.50	70.28	1E + 06	5560
Manufacture of general purpose machinery	425.55	634.20	40.89	664.67	643.99	72.98	1E + 06	8644
Special purpose equipment manufacturing	216.11	286.61	20.84	302.59	291.36	21.89	627,798	3515
Transportation equipment manufacturing	339.69	464.51	27.39	484.63	470.19	71.93	929,335	3980
Electromechanical and equipment manufacturing	579.17	878.24	51.39	905.91	886.10	133.32	1E + 06	6177
Communication equipment, computer and other electronic equipment manufacturing	233.34	266.18	13.25	264.38	259.28	118.91	498,614	1677
Manufacture of handicrafts and other product	52.28	101.41	5.25	105.02	102.42	39.96	308,553	1528
Recycling and processing of discarded resources and materials	5.06	14.39	0.75	14.98	14.75	0.17	18,686	126
Production and distribution of electricity and heat	93.48	40.97	2.47	41.61	40.46	0.01	78,953	538
Production and distribution of gas	8.49	7.58	0.75	7.08	7.06	0	8380	74
Production and distribution of water	19.15	6.57	0.43	6.92	6.76	0	18,976	178

Source: Enterprise database of China National Bureau of Statistics

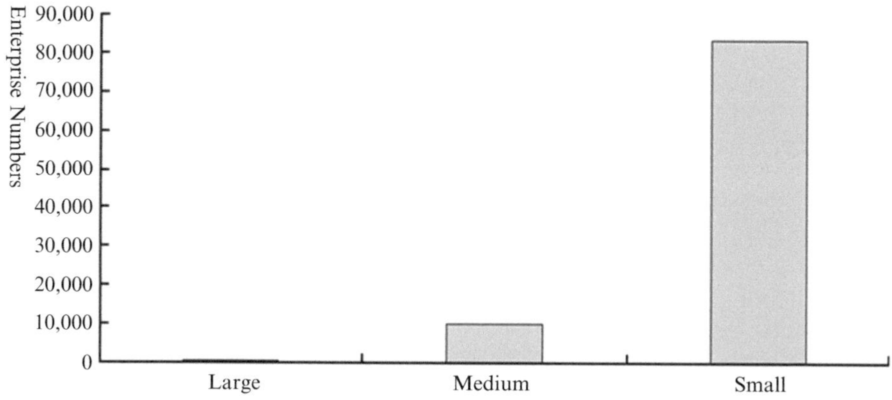

Fig. 2.7 Sizes and numbers of NGEs 2008 (Source: Enterprise database of China National Bureau of Statistics)

The average export delivery value of large-, medium-, and small-sized NGEs are: large-sized NGEs RMB 4,029,466.39, medium-sized NGEs RMB 328,829.57 and small-sized NGEs RMB 5095.5, respectively.

2.2.3 *Most NGEs Founded After 1992*

A survey from 2008 shows that China's NGEs have achieved great levels of development since the implementation of the country's reform and opening up, but this can only be measured after the establishment of the socialist market economy at the 14th National Congress of CPC. From 1978 to 1991, newly founded NGEs numbered fewer than 1000 each year. From 1992 to 2004, however, over 2000 NGEs were founded each year. The year 2002 witnessed the climax of NGEs' founding, when 10,947 were established. From 2005 to 2008, the number of newly-founded NGEs declined from 1120 to 142. Figure 2.8 shows the years and annual numbers of newly founded NGEs, most of which were founded between 1992 and 2004.

2.2.4 *NGEs' Uneven Regional Distribution*

In 2008, the average total assets of NGEs nationwide was RMB 213,476,119. It was RMB 435,515,401, RMB 134,897,243 and RMB 62,326,027 in the eastern, central, and western regions, respectively. The eastern region was 222.85% and 598.77% larger than the central and western regions, respectively, in the average total assets of NGEs, while the central region was 116.44% larger than the western region in the average total assets of NGEs.

Table 2.3 Sizes, assets, values, and employment of NGEs 2008

Size	Number	Average assets (mn RMB)	Average major business income (mn RMB)	Total profit (mn RMB)	Average industrial output value totaled (mn RMB)	Average industrial sales value (mn RMB)	Average export delivery value (mn RMB)	Employees totaled (mn)
Large	507	3.032	4.025	135.16	4.097	4.03	0.712	2.432
Medium	9916	0.245	0.326	214.578	0.339	0.329	0.043	7.424
Small	83,156	0.032	0.057	284.665	0.059	0.057	0.005	10.361
Total	93,579	3.309	4.408	634.404	4.495	4.416	0.76	20.217

Source: Enterprise database of China National Bureau of Statistics

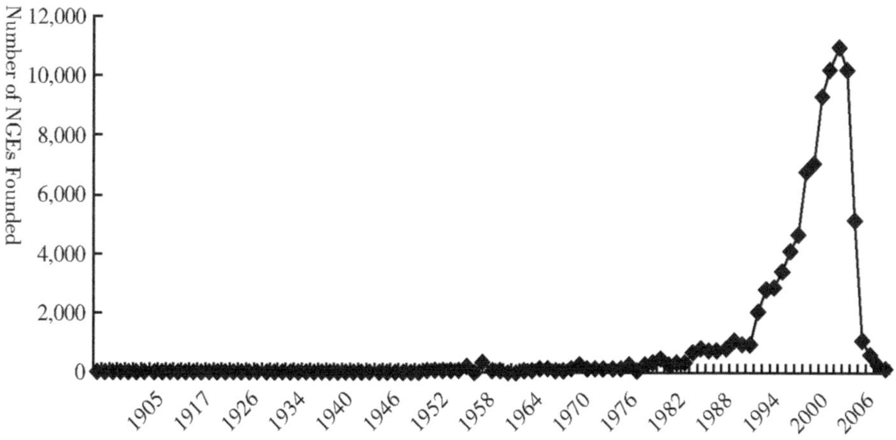

Fig. 2.8 Years and numbers of NGEs founded (Source: Enterprise database of China National Bureau of Statistics)

The average major business income of NGEs nationwide was RMB 322,427,363. It was RMB 667,953,335, RMB 219,596,979, and RMB 74,248,812 in the eastern, central, and western regions, respectively. The eastern region was 204.17% and 799.61% larger than the central and western regions, respectively, in the average major business income of NGEs. The central region was 195.76% larger than the western region in the average major business income of NGEs.

The average total profit of NGEs nationwide was RMB 20,464,628. It was RMB 39,211,118, RMB 17,661,717, and RMB 5,148,953 in the eastern, central, and western regions, respectively. The eastern region was 122.01% and 661.54% larger than the central and western regions, respectively, in the average total profit of NGEs. The central region was 243.02% larger than the western region in the average total profit of NGEs.

The average industrial output value of NGEs nationwide was RMB 333,250,104. It was RMB 686,579,835, RMB 229,808,143, and RMB 78,325,826 in the eastern, central, and western regions, respectively. The eastern region was 198.76% and 776.57% larger than the central and western regions, respectively, in the average industrial output value of NGEs. The central region was 193.40% larger than the western region in the average industrial output value of NGEs.

The average industrial sales value of NGEs nationwide was RMB 324,756,169. It was RMB 670,487,838, RMB 224,176,340, and RMB 74,888,693 in the eastern, central, and western regions, respectively. The eastern region was 199.09% and 795.31% larger than the central and western regions, respectively, in the average industrial sales value of NGEs. The central region was 199.35% larger than the western region in the average industrial sales value of NGEs.

The average export delivery value of NGEs nationwide was RMB 38,902,964. It was RMB 99,764,632, RMB 9,296,916, and RMB 2,850,467 in the eastern, central, and western regions, respectively. The eastern region was 973.09% and 3399.94%

larger than the central and western regions, respectively, in the average export delivery value of NGEs. The central region was 226.15% larger than the western region in the average export delivery value of NGEs.

The average employees of NGEs nationwide totaled 652,151 persons. It was 1,262,426 persons, 526,384 persons, and 176,576 persons in the eastern, central, and western regions, respectively. The eastern region was 139.83% and 614.95% larger than the central and western regions, respectively, in the average number of employees of NGEs. The central region was 198.11% larger than the western region in terms of the average employees of NGEs.

The average legal entities of NGEs nationwide numbered 3019. It was 6315 in the eastern region, 1929 in the central region, and 724 in the western region, respectively. The eastern region was 227.35% and 772.29% larger than the central and western regions, respectively, in the number of average legal entities of NGEs. The central region was 166.47% larger than the western region in the average legal entities of NGEs (Table 2.4).

2.3 NGEs' Development Models and Their Influence on China's Economic Growth

Developing on the margins of SOEs, China's NGEs have their own particular advantages, in that they are close to the actual situation of China insofar as they appropriately meet the existing market demands and that they are small in size and flexible in operation. Such advantages have enabled the number of NGEs to bloom throughout the country during the period of their rapid development. But it should also be noted that it is not easy for NGEs to maintain a long life or to form sustainable competitiveness simply based on their being small, quick, and flexible. This disadvantage is all the more evident once NGEs have grown to a certain scale.

After nearly 20 years of rapid development, China's NGEs have entered a new stage of development beginning with the dawn of the twenty-first century. As we can infer from the above analysis, the effect of NGEs' reformation (or transformation) has already disappeared in China. China's entry into the WTO has provided new power and new platforms for NGEs' development, which has led to the acceleration of their growth. On the other hand, the resurgence of SOEs, while bringing certain opportunities, has also brought more pressure to bear on the development of NGEs—their space for development is being compressed in some fields, and they have few opportunities to capitalize on the process of urbanization. What's worse, NGEs have suffered greatly under the impact of the global economic crisis starting in 2008 and are currently experiencing differentiation in their development as a result. In the particular stage and context of China's economic development, the NGEs have been attempting to develop in the crevices of the economy. With the country's relatively unreasonable enterprise formation and industrial structure and distribution, we may say that most NGEs adopt a short

Table 2.4 NGEs' assets, values and employment by region 2008

Region	Total assets (RMB mn)	Major business income (RMB mn)	Total profit (RMB mn)	Industrial output value (RMB mn)	Industrial sales value (RMB mn)	Export delivery value (RMB mn)	Employees (mn)	Legal entities
Beijing	100.722	91.827	3.86	87.329	86.24	6.318	0.23	1835
Tianjin	72,646	122.668	3.59	124.098	122.539	10.122	0.171	1234
Hebei	331.437	613.283	44.075	639.578	622.87	27.829	0.925	3655
Liaoning	218.761	308.66	20.157	328.803	314.40	26.10.3	0.571	3376
Shanghai	164.322	189.647	8.965	192.281	188.353	22.133	0.476	4004
Jiangsu	932,523	1520,166	105,557	1556.627	1525.39	187.568	2.475	12,540
Zhejiang	1265.057	1429.90	66.354	1484.755	1442.315	379.018	3.423	20,587
Fujian	175.08	286.021	17.552	295.147	287.387	54.312	0.83	3882
Shandong	964.02	1879.807	116.836	1921.473	1884.986	157.026	2.73	9554
Guangdong	552.618	893.879	43.609	910.111	889.339	225.874	2.032	8679
Hainan	13.486	11.628	0.77	12.178	11.548	1.109	0.024	115
Eastern average	**435.515**	**667.953**	**39.211**	**686.58**	**670.488**	**99.765**	**1.262**	**6315**
Shanxi	243.233	248.391	14.731	250.918	243.376	7.576	0.461	1278
Jilin	80.621	105.015	4.964	113.485	109.584	2.685	0.192	920
Heilongjiang	51.524	61.307	3.526	60.688	59.176	0.981	0.174	787
Anhui	113.725	169.898	12.204	183.207	175.125	17.499	1.038	1963
Jiangxi	83.076	147.394	9.813	148.782	146.294	10.669	0.344	1402
Henan	268.857	628.495	71.332	664.516	653.319	14.319	0.984	4215
Hubei	139.085	187.931	11.574	201.074	194.565	11.116	0.505	2212
Hunan	99.057	208.345	13.15	215.794	211.971	9.531	0.513	2655
Central average	**134.897**	**219.597**	**17.662**	**229.808**	**224.176**	**9.297**	**0.526**	**1929**

(continued)

Table 2.4 (continued)

Region	Total assets (RMB mn)	Major business income (RMB mn)	Total profit (RMB mn)	Industrial output value (RMB mn)	Industrial sales value (RMB mn)	Export delivery value (RMB mn)	Employees (mn)	Legal entities
Inner Mongolia	91.363	108.603	12.652	112.50	109.088	3.192	0.162	685
Guangxi	74.177	91.224	4.301	101.295	93.053	5.541	0.239	1072
Chongqing	82.576	104.308	5.904	106.645	104.508	8.253	0.304	1156
Sichuan	237,904	345,616	20,292	360.58	350.694	9.737	0.783	2956
Guizhou	28.75	36.351	2.928	39.851	37.682	0.437	0.093	471
Yunnan	56.104	51.168	4.088	55.877	51.759	0.72	0.126	461
Tibet	0.245	0.067	−0.01	0.096	0.078	0.0	0.0	2
Shaanxi	64.164	69.626	4.71	77.542	72.166	1.877	0.189	823
Gansu	27.336	22.881	1.509	24.577	22.622	0.994	0.089	443
Qinghai	14.256	6.727	1.322	6.792	6.069	0.065	0.015	71
Ningxia	28.488	24.643	1.268	25.882	23.954	2.238	0.055	213
Xinjiang	42.549	29.772	2.824	28.276	26.991	1.153	0.063	334
Western average	**62.326**	**74.249**	**5.149**	**78.326**	**74.889**	**2.851**	**0.177**	**724**
National average	**213.476**	**322.427**	**20.465**	**333.25**	**324.756**	**38.903**	**0.652**	**3019**

Source: Enterprise database of China National Bureau of Statistics

and fast track of development, without a thought towards long-term planning or development. This has been severely affecting the long-term development of the non-governmental economy and is going against its structural optimization. Hence, NGEs themselves must design their own long-term development plans while the state should implement appropriate regulations of their development through policies. In accordance with the trend of China's economic development and the characteristics of non-governmental economy development, China's NGEs are likely to develop in the following ways.

2.3.1 NGEs' Development Models

2.3.1.1 Expansion of Scale

For over 30 years, the non-governmental economy has practically grown out of nothing and developed from small to large, and accounts for half the national economy at present. Similar to the general characteristics of China's economic growth, NGEs' development is a process of expansion.

In the future, China's economy will continue its process of acceleration, which will last until the year 2035, according to our calculations. An estimation of the Logistic Model of China's growth—arrived at by use of the Three-Sum Method (三和法, sān hé fǎ)[7]—shows that the inflection point will appear approximately at Period 49 or 50 (2034–2035) on the simulated Logistic growth curve (t) of China's GDP per capita (Fig. 2.9). Also according to our calculations, the peak value of China's working-age population will be 1.02 billion (first peak value) in 2015, and the total supply of the labor force is estimated to be 0.79 billion. The working-age population, however, will not immediately drop in succession thereafter. There will be a short period of rise (second peak value) or slow decline between 2022 and 2030. By around 2035, China's working-age population will begin continuously declining. It can be inferred that China's demographic dividend will not completely disappear until the year 2030. Under these circumstances, there is still a powerful internal driving force for China's economy in the following years.

Thus it is clear that the continuous expansion of NGEs is supported by the objective national conditions. Over the past 30 years, China has conducted the borderless expansion of its industrial products worldwide through the resource-allocation mechanism of low-priced industrialization, the result of which is that the secondary industry now accounts for nearly half its GDP. China's industrialization is highly resource-input driven, and such a development is typical of low cost and high input models. In the transition from the planned system to the market economy, the commercialization of production factors usually falls behind that of

[7]Estimation methods to be found in Li Zinai, & Ye Azhong. (2000). *Advanced Econometrics*. Beijing: Tsinghua University Press, pp. 40–42.

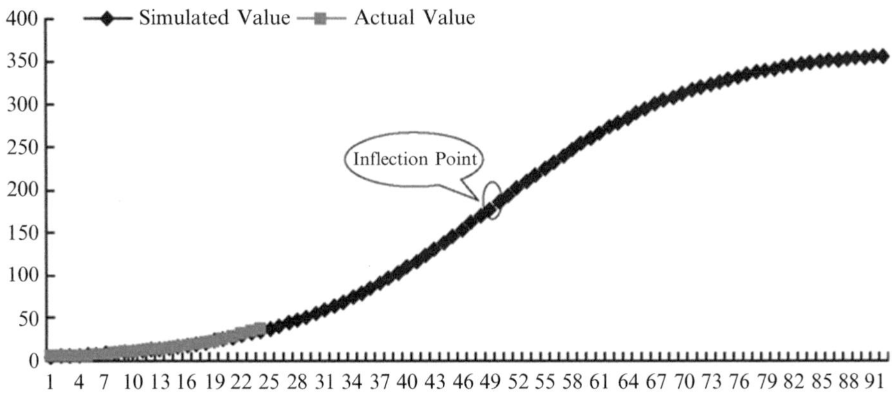

Fig. 2.9 Simulation of China's long-term economic growth (Provided by Chen Changbing)

commodities. In order to encourage enterprises to develop more rapidly and finish their primitive accumulation, the government has controlled the prices of the input production factors and maintained relatively low prices of land, the labor force, and investment products. For example, the prices of energy and water have long been lower than the international equilibrium prices; the cost constraint has been low in terms of environment, natural resources, and the social security of employees, and, in some cases, there is no such cost constraint at all. The government has also monopolized the country's financial resources and has used all available means to motivate and create a cheap supply of financing, as well as given priority to these enterprises in financing. By means of the global allocation achieved through the country's national opening up, the government has encouraged the introduction of international productive capital and the export of commodities, as well as integrated the "infinite domestic labor supply," international capital, and the broad overseas market, so as to solve the three major problems facing economic development, namely, capital, resources, and the market. In the context of opening up, the hand-in-hand procession of the country's marketing reforms and internationalization has both induced and activated the formation of domestic capital due to the "learning-by-doing" effect and the establishment of a competitive mechanism of innovation. But this model of expansion seems hard to sustain, because the period is basically over once there is a progressive increase in the returns to scale of the globalization-based industrialization, and China has entered the mid-late stage of industrialization. It is the theme of China's economic growth in the future to find a new resource allocation mechanism to facilitate the continuous structural transformation of China's economy. Therefore it should be noted that the old model of expansion would only result in higher costs and poorer returns. For NGEs, this is particularly true, because they are weaker than SOEs in terms of the ability to take risks. But, as we have seen clearly, NGEs have been changing their models of development, for the increase in the number of industrial NGEs has greatly slowed down since 2004.

In short, China's NGEs will continue the expansion of their scales in the future, but the scale-oriented model of development will change. The most likely way forward for NGEs is the integration of scale and benefits.

2.3.1.2 Consistence with China's Urbanization

Since the beginning of the new century, urbanization has become the dominating force acting upon China's economic growth and driving industrialization. With all kinds of developmental resources rapidly gathering in cities, the improvement of the level of urbanization has directly promoted the efficiency of the country's industries and the contribution of the tertiary industry to the economy, stimulated the rapid expansion of cities by means of economies of scale, and thus spurred the economic growth of the country as a whole. Urbanization is key to China's efforts to restore the domestic demands being made upon it and to transform its industrial structure, and will be the major power behind long-term economic growth in the years to come.

In 1975, Northam concluded that the regularity of worldwide urbanization displayed the S-shaped curve of urbanization, which is made up of apparent phases and can be divided into three stages. The first stage of urbanization is below 30%, when the city population grows slowly; only when the urban population accounts for over 10% of the total population will urbanization speed up a bit. The second stage of urbanization is between 30% and 70%. Urbanization accelerates when the city population accounts for more than 30% of the overall population, and will not stabilize until it reaches 70%. The third stage of urbanization is over 70%, when society and the economy have developed towards maturity and the city population remains steady.

In 2008, China's urbanization rate was at 45.68% and accelerating. By use of the Logistic function of urbanization and regarding the year 1800 as the base period, we can find in the simulation of China's urbanization from 1978 to 2007 that the growth rate of urbanization was 0.04357, far quicker than the world's average growth rate of 0.01729. China will end its urbanization acceleration stage around 2013 (between 2011 and 2016 as is predicted). In that stage, the growth rate of urbanization will be approximately 1.09%, and the urbanization rate will be between 47.93% and 53.37%. After that, China's urbanization growth will slow down gradually, but still maintain a high growth rate. According to the predictions made by use of the Logistic Model of Growth, China's urbanization rate will be 52.28% in 2015 and 57.67% in 2020, and will reach 67.81% in 2030. On the basis of the 45.68% found in 2008, to realize the urbanization rate of 67.81% in 2030 would mean to raise the rate nearly 1% annually across the following years, which means that over 14 million people must move into the cities each year. If the current trend of urbanization remains unchanged, it is possible to realize the urbanization rate of about 68% in 2030. Nevertheless, if we take into consideration the influences of the large proportion of the rural population on China's overall population and the advent of the aging society, 68% is very likely to be the roof of China's possible urbanization in the following 20 years. For a long time after that, the urbanization rate will keep stable at around 68%. Therefore, urbanization will continue to be the dominating force in China's economic growth in the following 20–30 years.

It can be inferred from the above analysis that urbanization will become a new growth point for NGEs, because urbanization means many more people will change their original ways of life and also their modes of production. In the era of urbanization, more people will gather in cities, but factories will no longer be the principal focus, since they are small in terms of space. More people will choose to enter the service industry, providing featured products and services for each other and for people living outside the cities. The high population density will bring about intense population concentration as people take part in economic activities through different service networks. In this way, the service industry in urban areas will become the mainstay of the economy. NGEs' services in China are far from developed, however, even though they have some competitive advantages in the traditional service industries such as catering, circulation, traffic, and transportation. Many of the modern service industries in cities are beyond the reach of NGEs, as they are still dominated by SOEs. Moreover, according to the existing policies, NGEs are forbidden from accessing many sectors. Although the state has issued two successive regulations concerning NGEs this year, it still remains to be seen what the practical effect will be.

The practice in those countries with developed market economies proves that urbanization will be the major driving force behind economic growth in the future and that the service industry will play an increasingly important role when a country has reached a certain level of industrialization. Statistics show that the service industry has accounted for over 70% of the overall GDP of some countries, while the proportion is still below 50% in China. Therefore, there is an enormous space for the growth of China's service industry. Undoubtedly, once policy permits, NGEs will play a greater part in the service industry, and with the furtherance of urbanization, the service industry must be the main direction of NGEs' development in China in the future.

2.3.1.3 Motivation by Technological Innovation

Experience shows that economic development is the constant capitalization of economic resources. On the basis of clarified ownership or the usufruct of existing visible or invisible assets, such capitalization is the determination of asset values by means of a cash inflow that discounts their anticipated values in the future and the circulation of such rights in the market in order to realize benefits through a competitive pricing mechanism. For developing countries, it is impossible to capitalize their economy in one step. What they can do is to obtain a greater economic surplus through the rapid accumulation of capital in certain fields (usually industry) with high expected benefits when there is an economic surplus (For developing countries, the primitive economic surplus can be obtained from agriculture or foreign countries) and promote their economic growth through the constant process of capitalization.

For material investment, material operation rents come from two aspects: the production rents(the excess marginal benefits realized by production with acquired machinery and equipment) and the material capitalization rents (or capital returns, the premium brought by the property right transactions of physical assets). Comparatively, material operation rents are under better control, because physical assets like machinery and equipment are tangible and the production capacity is predictable. Furthermore, material operation rents are more certain and controllable, as the physical assets are less exclusive than intangible properties like human capital and technology and are thus easily priced in the capital market. Investment in research and development, organizational innovation, and technological innovation will bring about technological innovation rents, which consist of technological monopoly rents and technological capitalization rents. The former refers to the excessive part of the marginal material output with the marginal costs deducted, brought about by the application of new technologies; the latter refers to the variation of property prices in the capital market or the transfer of technology. On the other hand, however, since there are considerable risks in investment in innovation, technological monopoly rents are extremely uncertain; what's more, as the technological exchange markets are immature and lacking an effective venture investment market in developing countries, technological capitalization rents are difficult to realize. Therefore, investment in technological innovation is generally characterized as rather uncertain and unpredictable. As the available capital of an enterprise is generally fixed at a certain point in time, the possible benefits must be weighed in order to decide to make technological innovation investments or material capitalization investments. If the anticipated material operation rents exceed the technological innovation rents, enterprises usually tend to discount invisible assets and invest more in ready-made machinery, equipment, and supplementary technology. This results in the accumulation of physical capital and reflects technological progress, and, meanwhile (to a certain degree), improves the country's total-factor productivity with the increase of resource allocation efficiency. On the contrary, if the technological innovation rents exceed the anticipated material operation rents, enterprises are inclined to invest in independent research and development and conduct purely technological innovation, which inhibits the accumulation of material capital but promotes an increase in total-factor productivity.

The above analysis indicates that:

(1) Under the condition of resource constraint, all enterprises have to face the choice between material investment and innovative investment. The former is relatively definite and controllable, while the latter is more uncertain and unknowable. The enterprises' investment decisions are based on their judgment concerning the two types of rents.
(2) In the economic context of rapidly-developing capitalization, the rational choice of economic actors is material investment or the overt trade of invisible assets instead of technological innovation, as there are always assets premiums.

Such a microscopic choice will precipitate, at the macro level, the capital formation of a country and the promotion of total-factor productivity as a result of the improved allocative efficiency.

(3) The accelerative effect of "learning-by-doing" makes enterprises inclined to buy or import ready-made machinery, equipment, and technology, rather than to implement independent technological innovation. This will further help in terms of capital formation and capital-reflected technological advancement, but technological advancement in the broad sense will be repressed, which is brought about by technological innovation.

(4) In the pure sense of economics, an economy can only transform a growth model based on the domination by material capital accumulation into the innovative model characterized by the explicitation and capitalization of the broad-sense resources—such as knowledge and technology—when all the following three conditions are met: the common explicitation of fixed assets stock, the return of assets premiums to their basic values, and the exhaustion of the "learning-by-doing" effect in capital accumulation and expansion (the approximation of internationally advanced technology).

Accordingly, the choice of industrial technology must be based on the enterprises' meditation on the natural endowment of production factors in order to adapt themselves to extant conditions. For the technological progress of developing countries, the first stage is imitation, when merchants and engineers play the leading role; the second stage is quantity expansion, characterized by simple and low-quality products, market expansion, the joining of new enterprises, the rapid development of industries, a slow increase of TFP (total factor productivity), and lowered profitability; the third stage is quality improvement when the branding strategies and product quality certifications are adopted, characterized by constant innovation, concurrent imitation, quality improvement, the withdrawal of low-efficiency enterprises, the slow development of industries, and the rapid increase of TFP.

In light of China's reality, technological advancement is currently in the second stage. Most enterprises' technological progress comes from learning and absorbing foreign technologies, which may sustain them for some time but cannot last forever. New theories on technological innovation prove that most large-sized enterprises, especially those of a monopolistic nature, are not the main actors of technological innovation. It is the medium- and small-sized enterprises that are the major force behind innovation. Such is the general situation in present-day China. NGEs' innovation has not yet been raised to the height of a national policy, however, and the environment for innovation has not been significantly improved. To encourage more enterprises to adopt the path of technological innovation, it is a necessity that the policies and the market play a joint role so as to enable them to gain benefits from innovation. From the perspective of the market, it is necessary to arouse the consumers' interest in innovative products and concurrently create an atmosphere of social innovation. From the perspective of policies, it is compulsory to lower the costs of innovation and to make innovation the major channel for enterprises' opportunities for development. To sum up, innovation is the only way to further NGEs' development.

As can be concluded from the above analysis, China's NGEs must accelerate their rate of technological innovation and exploit the important field of urban services while maintaining their expansion of scale, so as to develop both in quality and quantity.

2.3.2 *The Role of NGEs' Development in the Sustained Rapid Growth of the National Economy*

As is widely acknowledged, China's success in national economic transformation has benefited from the rise of NGEs, which have not only made up for the economic burden caused by the country's declining SOEs, but have also revitalized China's economy and created more points of growth. With the arrival of the new century, SOEs are receiving a new lease on life, while NGEs' development is facing fresh uncertainty; there is even the phenomenon of the "advance of SOEs and retreat of NGEs." It is the general trend that China's economic scale will keep expanding in the future and there will be enormous space for the development of both SOEs and NGEs. Based on the flexible operation mechanisms and their rapid adaptation to market variation, NGEs in particular will probably become the main types of enterprises in China in the future. Therefore, NGEs will play an increasingly important role in China's economic growth. Specifically, their role will be reflected in the following aspects:

First of all, NGEs' proportion of the overall economic aggregate will further increase. Although there have been no formal statistics released by the state so far, it is estimated by many that NGEs' total output accounts for more than 60% of China's GDP, and we believe this proportion will continue to rise. Since the future development of urban services will primarily be realized by NGEs and, furthermore, the share of the services industry in relation to overall GDP will keep increasing, the proportion of NGEs in China's GDP will also increase accordingly.

Secondly, NGEs will continue to shoulder the responsibility of expanding employment. With their large numbers and bright future, NGEs' function in employment will become increasingly evident.

Thirdly, NGEs will be the pioneers in China's future technological innovation. In order to gain larger space and more opportunities for their own development, NGEs have been acting as the major force behind China's innovation. This will not change in the future, because innovation is the core of NGEs' development and is fundamental to the survival of NGEs. For NGEs' development, innovation is the motivating power that will facilitate the formation of an innovative mechanism of society as a whole and raise China's overall innovation to a new level.

Fourthly, NGEs will continue to integrate with SOEs. The ownership of enterprises is never completely fixed. With the ongoing improvement of the business environment and the ceaseless development of China's economy, the integration of ownership is a significant trend of global economic development, and the policy environment where SOEs and NGEs were pitted in opposition to each other will also change. In the future, NGEs and SOEs may no longer be so clearly distinguished in China, but will tend to integrate more and more with each other, and both will act as major promoters of the country's economic development.

Lastly, NGEs will achieve a more balanced development in China. Their scale will keep expanding, the structure of large-, medium-, and small-sized enterprises will continuously change, and the unbalanced distribution between the eastern, central, and western regions of the country will also change. NGEs will develop prevalently throughout the country, and more and more medium- and small-sized enterprises will have the opportunity to grow into giants.

2.4 Conclusions

First, China's NGEs are developing under the special background of reform and are playing an increasingly great part in the national economy as a whole. Characterized by its quick start and rapid expansion, NGEs' development is of objective inevitability and follows its own law of development. At present, China's NGEs are still in a period of rapid expansion, but mere expansion may not be enough to support and sustain their development. They will need more power to spur their development in the future.

Second, China's NGEs are closely tied to the reform of SOEs. The current policy environment is not exactly favorable to their further development. It is definitely necessary for the government to create more favorable external conditions and guide NGEs onto the normal path of development as soon as possible.

Third, China's NGEs should combine their expansion of scale with technological innovation and urbanization in the future and, in doing so, constantly transform their structure and promote their industrial culture in the development.

Bibliography

Atkeson A, Kehoe P (1997) Industry evolution and transition: a neoclassical benchmark, NBER working paper, 6005. NBER, Cambridge, MA

Chen R, Zhang Q, Zhou M. Report on export of Zhejiang's NGEs. http://www.zj.xinhuanet.com/. Accessed 29 Sept 2007

Jiang L (2006) Eight contributions of China's NGEs. J Cent Inst Soc (8)

Jovanovic B (1995) Learning and growth, NBER working paper, 5383. NBER, Cambridge, MA

Liu G (1988) Models of China's economic system reform. China Social Sciences Press, Beijing

Liu X (2003) Long-term growth of China's economy. Econ Res J (5)

Research Group of Non-Governmental Investment Mechanism and Development of Shaanxi's NGEs (2006) Evaluation of NGEs' contributions to economic developemnt of Shaanxi. West Econ Dev Res (3)
Shao G, Zhang R (2004) Evaluation of NGEs' contributions to development of Guangdong. Stat Decis (12)
Sheng H (1994) Transitional economics of China. Shanghai People's Press, Shanghai, China
Song Y, Yang Y, Dong M (2004) Development and growth of NGEs. Rev Econ Res (22)
Wu J (2004) Economists, economics and China's reform. Econ Res J (2)
Xue M (1990) On China's reform of the economic system. Tianjin People's Press, Tianjin, China
Yang Q (2004) Has China's economic reform improved enterprise performance? A DEA evaluation of China's large and medium enterprises, Working paper, no. 287. ESRC Centre for Business Research, University of Cambridge
Zhao Z (2007) Contributions of China's NGEs to industrial structure adjustment. Mark Mod (6)
Zheng X (2005) Contributions of Shanghai's NGEs to GDP of Shanghai and relevancy analysis. Shanghai Bus (2)

Chapter 3
Industrial Transformation and Upgrading: The Inevitable Choice for NGEs' New Growth and Development

Mengjuan Li and Muzi Li

Industrial transformation and upgrading is rich in implications. There are three levels of a complete industrial transformation and upgrade. The first is structural adjustment—or transformation and upgrading within an industry—which is a process of promoting the value chain of enterprises' products and the accompanying escalation and extension of enterprises' value chain from manufacturing to development and design, branding, and the marketing of products. The second is cross-industrial upgrading, which entails structural change among different industries and the transformation from traditionally labor-intensive, low processing, low value-added manufacturing to that of emerging industries. The third level is the adjustment of the structures and positions of the primary, secondary, and tertiary industries in the national economy. Essentially, industrial transformation and upgrading includes both the rationalization and advancement of the industrial structures overall. It is an ongoing process that starts with the product escalation within an enterprise, proceeds to the flow of resource stocks between industries that impels the changes of industrial scales, to the transformation of industrial structures from the lowest level to the highest level, and finally ends with the adjustment and transition of the industrial organizations and structures.

M. Li (✉)
Electronic Information Institute of MIIT, Beijing, China

M. Li

Y. Liu (ed.), *New Interpretations on the Development of China's Non-Governmental Enterprises*, Research Series on the Chinese Dream and China's Development Path, DOI 10.1007/978-981-10-3872-3_3

3.1 The Environment and Mechanisms of NGEs' Industrial Transformation and Upgrading

3.1.1 Disadvantages in NGEs' Industrial Transformation and Upgrading

China's NGEs are now facing pressure to survive in the process of their industrial transformation and upgrading, such as shrinking demands in both the domestic and overseas markets, deteriorating trade conditions, the adjustment of industrial structures, and more, all of which have become disadvantages in their industrial transformation and upgrading as well as disadvantages to the very survival and development of NGEs.

3.1.1.1 Unsteady Demands in Domestic and Overseas Markets

Under the influence of the U.S.-instigated financial crisis, a marked decrease in demand has swept across the international market in general and Europe and the U.S. in particular, which are China's major export destinations. In the first three quarters of 2008, China's exports to the U.S. dropped by 4.6% over the same period as compared to the previous year, and the growth rate of China's exports to Europe was down by nearly 8% compared with that of 7 months before. Due to the unstable economic performance, there is no clear recovery of consumer confidence in the U.S. and Europe. According to statistics provided by the European Commission, the consumer confidence index was −14.3 in December, 2009 and −13.3 in January, 2010, marking a clear lack of confidence among consumers in Europe and the U.S. This has directly affected the export of China's labor-intensive products. An analysis of NGEs' products in January, 2010 shows that the export of footwear, cases and bags, and plastic products was declining, down 5%, 8.5%, and 40.6%, respectively, over the same period of the previous year. There is still no fundamental improvement in the market environment of NGEs.

3.1.1.2 The Deterioration of the Foreign Trade Environment

While the demands in domestic and overseas markets are shrinking, the foreign trade conditions of Chinese enterprises are also degrading, which manifests in the following two aspects.

One is that trade protectionism is on the rise in developed countries. With declining consumer demands worldwide, many countries have adopted a series of trade protection measures to protect the market for local product sales and to strictly restrict the sales of foreign products. As World Bank international trade expert Chad Bown pointed out, in the first three quarters of 2009, newly-made requests for protectionism were up 30.3% throughout the world over the same period the previous year.[1] There has been a marked increase of trade restrictions on China by foreign countries. According to statistics released by the Chinese Ministry of Commerce, 19 countries/regions had initiated 101 trade relief investigations targeting Chinese products by early November of 2009, an increase of 639% over the same period the previous year, with trade disputes being particularly bitter between China and the U.S.[2] In 2009, the U.S. had launched 23 trade relief cases, a rise of 53%, and the value involved accounted for 65% of China's total amount involved in trade relief investigations throughout the world. This rise in trade restrictions has increased the export costs of Chinese enterprises and narrowed their profit margin. The rise of international trade protectionism reflects not only limitations on import/export products by various countries, but, more importantly, new changes in their developmental strategies. As more countries are paying closer attention to their domestic markets, the trade conditions of China's NGEs promise to take a turn for the worse.

The other way in which the foreign trade conditions of Chinese enterprises are degrading is the depreciation pressure being applied to the major settlement currencies used in China's foreign trade. In the major export destinations of China's NGEs, the US dollar has been devaluating since the financial crisis, and the same is true of the euro under the influence of the sovereign debt crisis in European countries. The exchange rates of the euro and the dollar have declined to historically low levels. Under the increasing pressure of competition in the international market, China's NGEs usually export on credit to promote product sales, which, in turn, prolongs the billing cycle. The depreciation of the euro and the dollar has directly impaired the price advantage of China's exported products in competition and caused China's NGEs to lose the price advantages of their products. On the other hand, the devaluation of the settlement currencies has also raised the foreign exchange risk for China's NGEs.

3.1.1.3 The Increasing Pressure of Industrial Structural Adjustment

Great changes have also taken place in the developmental environment of China's NGEs. In the process of marketization, China has ensured its position as the "world's factory" with its cheap labor and resource advantages. But this rapid industrialization has greatly increased the country's resource consumption, which

[1] Liu Qian, & Tang Chunlin. (Feb. 9, 2010). Frequent Trade Frictions Predicted by Experts in Second Half of This Year, Guangdong Trade Association Unable to Play Leading Role in Coping Trade Wars. *South Daily*.

[2] (Jan. 28, 2010). NY Fed Economic Indicators on Sharp Rise in January. *China Industry Security Guide*.

has made China a resource-importing country due to the shortage of its own resources.[3] The rise of resource prices has greatly reduced the return of low-end product exports and thus made it impossible to sustain an export-oriented, extensive model of development, which has also caused serious environmental pollution. Of the 20 worst polluted cities in the world, 13 are in China, and 3/5 of its rivers are severely polluted. It involves an enormous amount of effort to make any headway against serious pollution, a process which is seriously damaging to the capacity for development.

In order to realize the sustainable development of its economy, the Chinese government has stipulated strict binding indexes of energy saving and emissions reduction in *The National Economic and Social Development Plan for the 11th Five Year Plan* and proposed the establishment of "an industrial system and consumption mode characterized by low carbon emissions." In pursuing the goal of energy saving and emissions reduction, the central government has also targeted the tasks necessary for eliminating outdated industrial capacity in 18 trades, and set up corresponding assessment mechanisms for different levels of governments, which have quickened the structural adjustment of local industries.

While China is in urgent need of adjusting its industrial structures under the pressure of energy saving and emissions reduction, the developed economies—represented by the U.S.—reflect the reasons for the financial crisis and have formulated a "strategy of green economic growth"—the "re-industrialization" and the "export doubling" plan. As these developed countries accelerate their industrial structural adjustment, great changes are bound to take place in the industrial pattern of the world's economy in the future. Under these circumstances, the Chinese government should actively adjust its industrial structures not only from the perspective of saving energy and the reduction of emissions, but also from the perspective of promoting the international competitiveness of the overall national economy.

Limited by their technology and financial resources, a significant proportion of NGEs are engaged in high pollution, high energy-consuming industries, and quite a number of them will be subjected to the new round of industrial structural adjustments. Such enterprises will be faced with a severe struggle for survival if they cannot carry out timely and successful adjustments and upgrade their industrial structures.

3.1.1.4 Highly Competitive Domestic Markets

NGEs are mainly concentrated in labor-intensive and low value-added fields or industries, whose relatively low thresholds for capital and technology make it easy for new enterprises to enter. There are always large numbers of enterprises in such

[3]Jin Leqin, & Liu Rui. (2010). Low Carbon Economy and Transformation of Development Models of China's Economy. *Explorations on Economic Issues*, (1), 84–87.

industries that fiercely compete with each other. The producers usually adopt a low-price strategy to promote their product sales, which, in turn, has greatly compressed their space for profits. Many enterprises resort to improper means of competition to survive, such as misappropriation of trademarks, the replacement of quality products with shoddy ones, false advertising, and framing their rivals. Worse, some enterprises even evade their duty of paying taxes for their own short-term benefit. Take Guangdong Province for example. Of the 1002 medium- and small-sized enterprises surveyed, 22.8% believe that there are serious problems of tax evasions and the production and sale of counterfeit goods, while 23.4% believe that there are serious cases of trademark misappropriation, replacement of quality products with shoddy ones, false advertising, and framing of rivals among such businesses. In addition, regional protectionism has, to a certain degree, aggravated disorderly competition among NGEs. Local protectionism may benefit the development of NGEs inside the region, but prevents the free flow of products and production factors and is thus to the disadvantage of NGEs' expansion and large-scale operations.[4]

3.1.2 Advantages in NGEs' Industrial Transformation and Upgrading

While China's NGEs face certain disadvantages in their industrial transformation and upgrading, there are also many factors that favor their further development.

3.1.2.1 Lower Thresholds for NGEs' Entry Access

China's economic reform is a process of loosening economic controls by the government, which will give the country's economic entities more freedom of economic activities and activate their vitality and creativity.

Through years of economic reform, the non-governmental sectors of the economy have become an important part of the market economy. However, NGEs have not yet been given equal competitive chances in certain areas as SOEs have. There are still capital access restrictions on NGEs' participation in such monopolistic fields as transportation, energy, and so forth. To eliminate the institutional barriers to NGEs' development, the State Council issued *Opinions on Encouraging, Supporting, and Guiding the Development of Individual, Private, and Other Non-Public Sectors of the Economy* (State Issuance No. 3, 2005) in 2005. But as specific rules were not set to be implemented, there was no substantial expansion of

[4]Liu Erli, & Cui Yi. (2007). Market Environment for Development of Medium and Small NGEs of Guangdong. *Modern Enterprises*, (1), 35–38.

NGEs' investment fields, and a "glass door" still existed for those NGEs entering certain monopolized fields.

As the overseas market environment of China's NGEs has been deteriorating since the breakout of the financial crisis in the U.S., the State Council issued *Several Opinions of the State Council on Encouraging and Guiding the Sound Development of Non-Governmental Investment* (State Issuance No. 13, 2010) in May, 2010. The document clearly states that its purpose is to "encourage and guide non-governmental capital to enter all industries and fields unless clearly prohibited by laws or regulations" and requires there to be no additional conditions on non-governmental capital. In accordance with the stipulations of the document, the government allows and encourages non-governmental capital to enter the key fields of fundamental industries, infrastructure, municipal public utilities, medical care, finance, defense-related science and technology, and so forth., which used to be monopolized by state-owned capital. This shows that the government is further relinquishing its investment controls on non-governmental capital, providing new investment channels for it to retreat from high energy-consuming and high pollution fields, and guiding it to actively invest in those high-return fields. All this will help motivate non-governmental capital to withdraw from the high energy-consuming and high pollution industries and promote NGEs' industrial transformation and upgrading.

3.1.2.2 Clearer Policy Guidance on Industrial Transformation and Upgrading

Industrial upgrading should be driven by profit motivations and realized through enterprises' choices regarding their own economic behavior. It is a long and difficult process to upgrade industries, as is dependent upon the choice of market mechanism. To finish the industrial upgrading more rapidly, it is also necessary to draw support from the guidance and intervention of governmental industrial policies. As a matter of fact, China is now actively guiding its industrial structural adjustment with industrial policies in order to achieve the goal of energy saving and emissions reduction.

China has formulated and revised its *Catalogue of Industrial Structural Adjustments* to guide the elimination of outdated industrial capacity in steel and iron, nonferrous metals, light industry, the textile industry, and so forth., and has adopted and is currently implementing an industry revitalization plan. To speed up the adjustment of industrial structures, China's Ministry of Industry and Information Technology has established annual objectives and implementation schemes by industry for the elimination of outdated industrial capacities and assigned objectives and tasks level by level to ground-level governments and enterprises. To promote further structural adjustment, it has also established both strict industrial access conditions and the definitive criteria for outdated industrial capacities, raised the admittance thresholds with indicators of security, environmental protection, energy consumption, material consumption, quality, land, and so forth., and encouraged the development of advanced industrial capacity of low energy-consumption and low pollution. Through the revision of the *List of Investment Projects Approved by the Government*, it has strengthened the examination and administration of its investment projects, inhibited low-level, redundant construction, and prevented any increase in outdated industrial capacity.

In pursuing its goals of industrial adjustment, the Chinese government has established a set of economy-based, differential motivation and restraint mechanisms to enhance enterprises' enthusiasm for industrial transformation and upgrading, e.g., increasing the electricity price of outdated industrial capacity with a differential electricity pricing policy; reforming the country's resource taxation and increasing the prices of certain resources; canceling the export tax rebates of 406 resource products or high energy-consuming and high pollution products of six categories, including steel products, medical products, chemical products, nonferrous metal processing materials, and so forth.; supporting and guiding enterprises to exercise industrial transformation and upgrading by using the available technological transformation funds; providing more tax preferences and financial support for the emerging industries; and so on.

The clear orientation of the country's industrial structural adjustment provides specific guidance for NGEs' capital investment and industrial withdrawal. The execution of administrative and differential economic policies has made a big difference in the existing business environment and profit margins between enterprises of outdated industrial capacity and those in emerging industries and fields, as well as provided the driving force behind enterprises' industrial transformation and upgrading.

3.1.2.3 Further Improvement Among the Financing Environments

At present, the major financing channel of small- and medium-sized NGEs is still bank loans. It is generally difficult for NGEs to obtain loan financing due to the small scale and low risk resistance capabilities of most NGEs, however, and because their product innovation and development are at the lower end in the industrial chain. Accordingly, the government has adopted a series of measures to solve the difficulty small- and medium-sized NGEs face in obtaining loans.

First of all, the China Banking Regulatory Commission has taken into consideration risk reductions and the exemption from responsibility of bank employees issuing loans for SMEs. It will reduce the employment risks of bank personnel and make them willing to offer loans to SMEs.

Secondly, the state-owned shareholding commercial banks have established financial service institutions for SMEs, improved the qualification examinations and the approval and guarantee institutions, and increased the efficiency of both examinations and approval. For example, the Agricultural Bank of China (ABC) has reduced the radius of banking management by expanding authorization to the second-level branches, where loans for SMEs can be approved. It has also worked out special customer standards for SMEs, innovated its guarantee system, shortened the process for examinations and approval, and increased the efficiency of examinations and approval. All these measures will ensure that SMEs are entitled to bank services and are able to obtain loans forthwith. The Industrial and Commercial Bank of China (ICBC) formulated the *Business Procedures for Small- and Medium-sized Enterprises* in 2009, which has simplified the examination and approval of SMEs for loans, opened a green channel for the financing of SMEs, and ultimately given priority to their loan applications. It has also shortened the examination and approval period by adopting the rule of "responsibility for first inquiry" and the electronic processes for examination and approval. Moreover, according to state industrial policies, the ICBC has formulated differential supporting policies for different industries and exercises loan controls over industries with high pollution, high energy consumption, or redundant construction, but implements favorable supporting loan policies for the emerging sci-tech industries, new energy sources, new technologies, and cultural industries.

Thirdly, SMEs are actively encouraged to seek financing by listing on the stock market and experimenting with issuing collective bonds.

Fourthly, the guarantee institutions behind SMEs' credit loans are receiving increased financial support and enjoying the preferential tax policy of a reduction or exemption of 3 years' business tax. The number of provinces/municipalities/regions where this is available is being increased, where such institutions are established and have already provided guarantee services for SMEs.

The improvement of SMEs' financing environment will help solve the shortage of funds during the industrial upgrading of NGEs.

3.1.3 Motivation for NGEs' Industrial Transformation and Upgrading

Since the beginning of the financial crisis, China's NGEs have gone through various changes in external market environment, business conditions, and policy environment for their survival and development. At the same time, severe restrictions on the domestic resource environment and the pressure of industrial structural adjustment continue to challenge the survival and development of backward NGEs. With the rising costs of labor, land, and other resources in China, the profit margin is becoming smaller and smaller for NGEs pursuing low-end paths of survival and development. With a view towards greater development in the long run, NGEs must follow the general direction of the state's industrial structural adjustment and pursue the path of industrial transformation and upgrading, as their increased admittance into monopolized industries and the financing environment are being further enabled in China. In the short run, however, NGEs will have to pay huge costs for their industrial transformation and upgrading. Withdrawing from the old industries is bound to result in sunken costs, while their entry into new industries not only involves enormous investment but also demands higher levels of technological strength and management capabilities. In addition, during their industrial transformation and upgrading, they will have to face the risk of market demands, which are affected by both income levels and consumptive habits. If the market demand risk is great and the profit chance in future is rather uncertain, it would be difficult for NGEs to commit to industrial transformation and upgrading.

As independent market entities, most enterprises will consider the situation from both their current and long-term interests to decide whether or not to carry out industrial upgrading, though the government may adopt some obligatory measures and force them to withdraw from high energy-consuming and high pollution industries.

3.2 The Status Quo of NGEs' Industrial Transformation and Upgrading

The process of industrial transformation and upgrading is an important form of NGEs' development under new economic conditions. To better understand the industrial transformation and upgrading of NGEs, it is necessary to analyze the current situation of their industrial development. By use of the basic data of China's National Bureau of Statistics on NGEs' development, this section analyzes the industrial distribution, regional distribution, and industrial innovation capacities of NGEs and provides realistic grounding for the further exploration of NGEs' industrial transformation and upgrading.

3.2.1 NGEs' Industrial Distribution

Without enough resources like capital, land, and so forth. and due to the lack of a complete system of financial support, China's NGEs had very limited opportunities for survival and development at the beginning of the period of economic reform, since they had no technological and market advantages. At the beginning of the country's market reforms, NGEs were mainly distributed in traditional trades and fields, such as manufacturing, construction, commerce, catering and services, real estate, and so forth.[5] Since the mid-1990s, NGEs have developed considerably in the tertiary industries, mainly in commerce, catering, and services, whereas NGEs in the secondary industries have remained in the traditional fields and at the low end of the industrial chain. We select 61,684 sample NGEs in 2006 and 63,776 in 2008 from the data of China National Bureau of Statistics for further investigation. The

[5]Wang Jinsong, Shi Jinchuan, & Li Yingchun. (2005). On Industrial Structure Evolution of China's NGEs and Concurrently on Competitive Relationships Between NGEs, SOEs and FFEs. *Management World*, (10), 82–91.

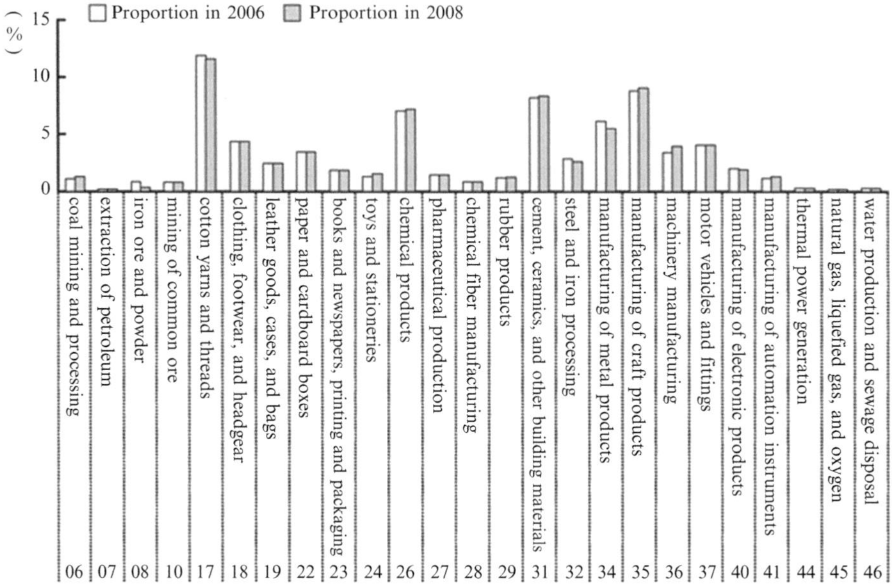

Fig. 3.1 The industrial distribution of China's NGEs (Source: Enterprise database of China National Bureau of Statistics (sorted and calculated))

analysis shows that NGEs in the secondary industry are still engaged in the traditional fields of production.

The comparison of these data points that NGEs are mainly engaged in the fields of cotton spinning, craft products, cement and other building materials, fertilizer production, metal products, clothing, footwear and headgear, motor vehicle fittings, paper production, and machinery manufacturing, among others. Very few of them are engaged in the manufacturing of automation instruments or resource products such as coal, petroleum, natural gas, or thermal power. Compared with the same data in 2006, the proportion of NGEs involved in the manufacture of cotton yarn and metal products declined in 2008, while the number of those involved in fertilizer production and the manufacturing of craft products and rubber products increased. This roughly reflects the fact that China's NGEs are mainly involved in low-end manufacturing and processing, and seldom engaged in resource-based or capital-intensive industries. See Fig. 3.1 for NGEs' industrial distribution.

3.2.2 NGEs' Regional Distribution

China's NGEs are unevenly distributed not only in industries, but also among regions. Data from the National Bureau of Statistics shows that China's NGEs are mainly in the developed eastern regions. In 2008, of all the enterprises above the designated size, 64.5% were in the eastern region, 16.9% in the central region, and

10.7% in the western region. In light of the administrative divisions, China's NGEs are mainly concentrated in the coastal provinces of Zhejiang, Jiangsu, Shandong, and Guangdong. NGEs in these four provinces account for 51.6% of all statistical samples. In the central part of China, NGEs are concentrated mainly among the four provinces of Henan, Hunan, Hubei, and Anhui. In the eastern region of China, NGEs are primarily engaged in textile processing and building materials. Here, we choose garment production and processing (Industry code 1810) and cement and other building materials (Industry code 31) as representative samples, and use them to analyze the uneven regional distribution of NGEs' industries overall.

3.2.2.1 The Regional Distribution of Garment Processing NGEs

From the perspectives of enterprise numbers and regional distribution, Chinese garment processing enterprises are mainly distributed along the coastal and developed regions in the east, such as Zhejiang, Jiangsu, Guangdong, Shanghai, and Shandong. Garment processing makes up the largest proportion of all NGEs' industries in Shanghai, Tianjin, and Beijing, where the numbers of such enterprises are small, however. The proportion of garment processing declined in Beijing and Shanghai in 2008, compared with that in 2006. With greater and increasing numbers of such enterprises, Zhejiang, Jiangsu, and Guangdong Provinces were behind Shanghai and Beijing in the proportion of garment processing enterprises. Compared with 2006, the proportions of the garment processing industry had also declined in these three provinces in 2008. In the central and western regions, the number and proportion of garment processing enterprises were smaller. All these facts reflect the uneven regional distribution of the garment processing industry in China. See Figs. 3.2, 3.3, and 3.4 for the statistical results.

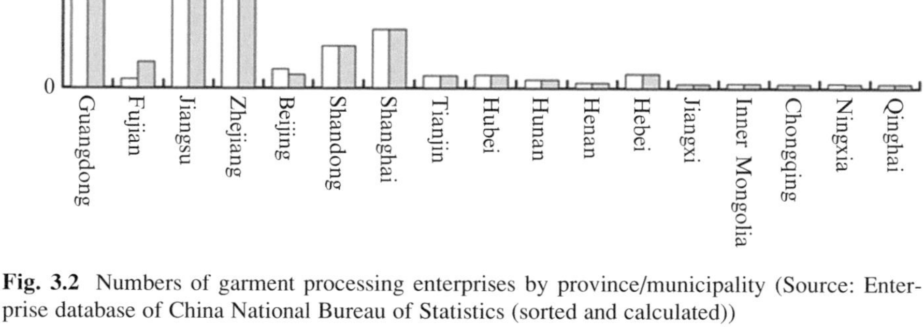

Fig. 3.2 Numbers of garment processing enterprises by province/municipality (Source: Enterprise database of China National Bureau of Statistics (sorted and calculated))

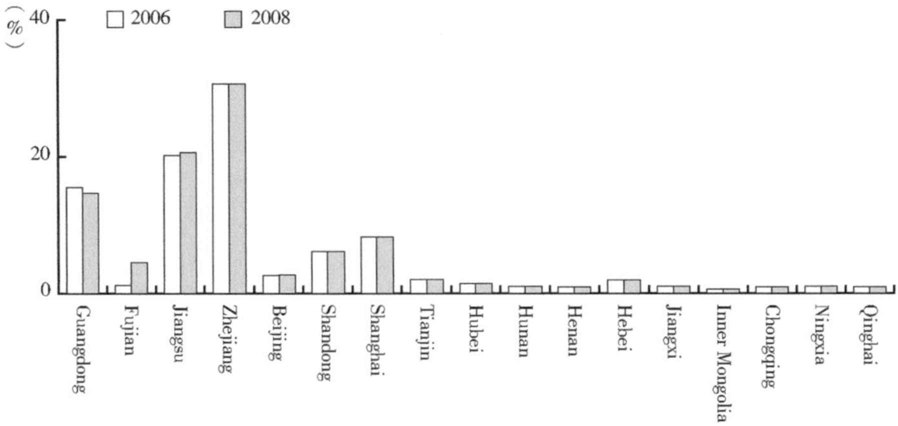

Fig. 3.3 Proportions of garment processing among all industries by province/municipality (Source: Enterprise database of China National Bureau of Statistics (sorted and calculated))

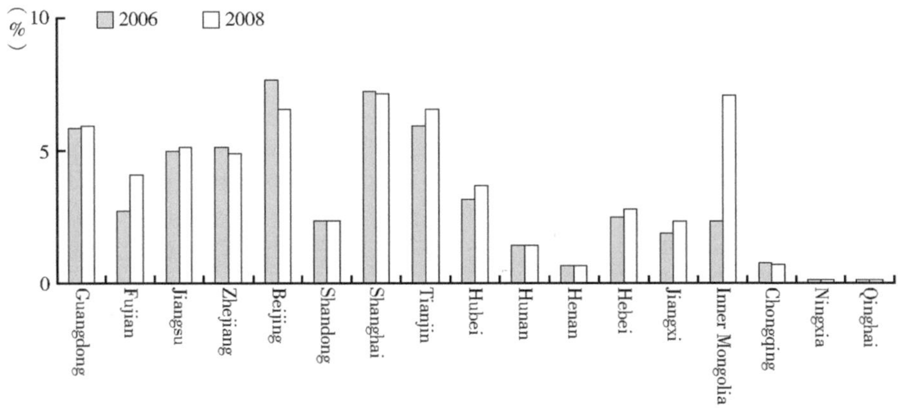

Fig. 3.4 Proportions of garment processing enterprises among all NGEs by province/municipality (Source: Enterprise database of China National Bureau of Statistics (sorted and calculated))

3.2.2.2 The Regional Distribution of Cement and Other Building Materials NGEs

According to our analysis, the industry of cement and other building materials is mainly distributed in the eastern and central regions, with the largest number of enterprises located in Shandong Province. The proportion ofbuilding material enterprises has declined in Jiangsu, Fujian, Shandong, Hunan, and Jiangxi Provinces and increased in Guangdong, Zhejiang, and Henan Provinces. This industry is less distributed in Beijing, Shanghai, and Tianjin Municipalities. Compared with garment processing, the building materials industry develops more evenly. See Figs. 3.5 and 3.6 for the statistics.

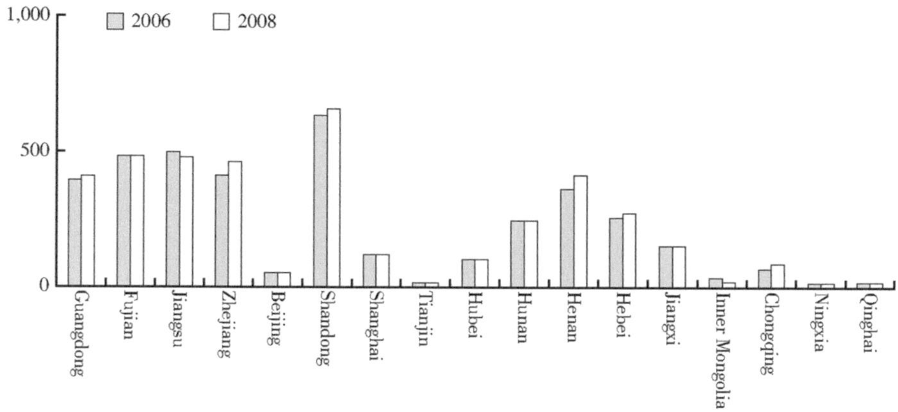

Fig. 3.5 Numbers of building materials NGEs by province/municipality (Source: Enterprise database of China National Bureau of Statistics (sorted and calculated))

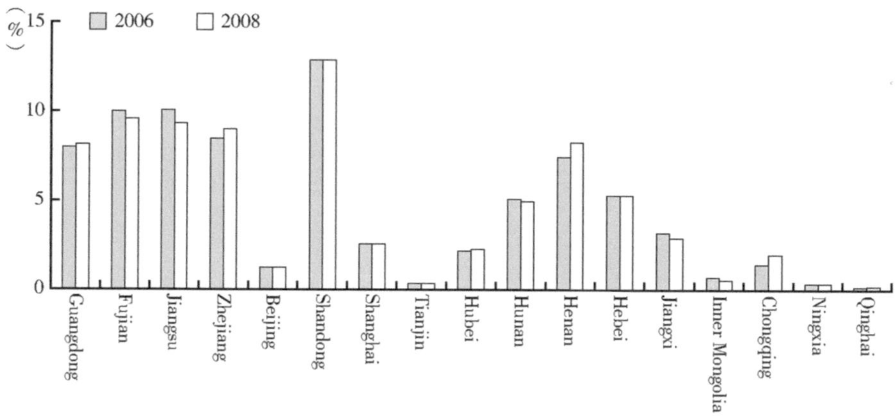

Fig. 3.6 Proportions of building materials of all industries by province/municipality (Source: Enterprise database of China National Bureau of Statistics (sorted and calculated))

It is thus clear that not only are China's NGEs unevenly distributed across regions, but the distributive features of different industries vary from each other as well. The garment processing enterprises of China are basically export-oriented and the industry is mainly concentrated in the eastern coastal regions. In contrast, the building materials industry is geared to meet the local market and therefore mainly distributed in the central regions and those parts of the eastern region exhibiting concentrated demands. Compared with the export-oriented industry of garment processing, the building materials industry reflects fewer regional differences.

3.2.3 The Development of NGEs' Industrial Chains

To analyze the industrial chains of NGEs, we chose to investigate the chemical industry and the metal processing industry (steel and iron), where the industrial chains are relatively long, since shorter chains—for example in textile processing or building materials—cannot reflect the higher levels of NGEs' industrial development.

3.2.3.1 The Development of Industrial Chains in the Chemical Industry

The chemical industry ranks fourth among all industries in the number of China's NGEs, and chemical NGEs correspondingly make up a large proportion of all NGEs—6.93% in 2006 and 7.11% in 2008. Some branches of the chemical industry are longer in industrial chains and thus have higher demands on capital, and higher-end products enjoy higher value rates. To some degree, the development of the chemical industry represents the capital strength and development level of all NGEs. In light of the distribution of the chemical industry, China's chemical NGEs are mainly engaged in the production of general auxiliaries or basic chemical materials, while only a small part of enterprises are engaged in the macromolecule resins or plastics industries, though they feature a relatively high proportion of technical assets. This indicates that China's NGEs are still at the lower end of the value chain of the chemical industry and need to be further upgraded. See Figs. 3.7 and 3.8 for the statistics.

3.2.3.2 The Development of Industrial Chains of the Metal Processing Industry

In this section, we analyze NGEs' distribution in resource-based industries with the example of the metal industry, including pig iron processing, steel processing, and alloy steel. In light of the regional distribution of the pig iron industry, the numbers of NGEs are relatively large in the central provinces of Hebei, Jiangsu, Hubei, Hunan, and Henan, but make up a very small part of the total numbers of NGEs in these provinces. In contrast, the numbers of NGEs are small in the western regions of Inner Mongolia and Ningxia, but make up a larger proportion of the total numbers of NGEs in these regions. This indicates that the pig iron industry of China is mainly concentrated in the central regions, and is a small proportion of the industries in economically developed regions like Beijing, Zhejiang, Tianjin, Shanghai, Guangdong, and so forth. In light of the regional distribution of the steel processing industry, there are relatively large numbers of NGEs in the provinces of Zhejiang, Jiangsu, Hebei, Guangdong, Shandong, Hubei, and Henan. According to the changes in this industry in 2006 and 2008, the enterprise numbers dropped in Zhejiang, Henan, Hebei, Hunan, and Jiangxi but increased in Shandong,

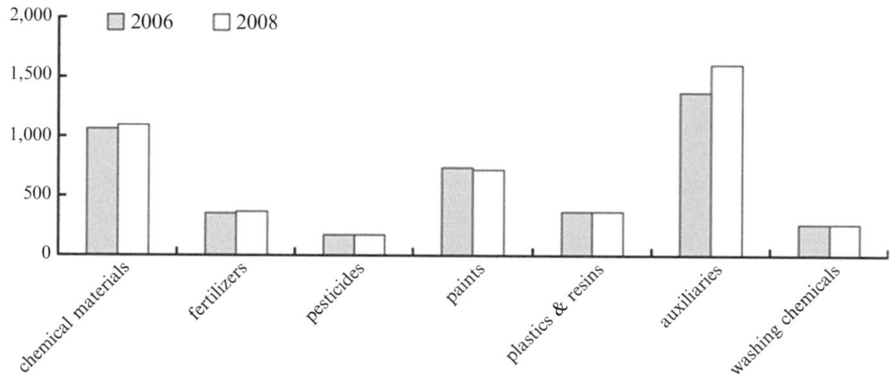

Fig. 3.7 Enterprise numbers in branches of China's Chemical Industry (Source: Enterprise database of China National Bureau of Statistics (sorted and calculated))

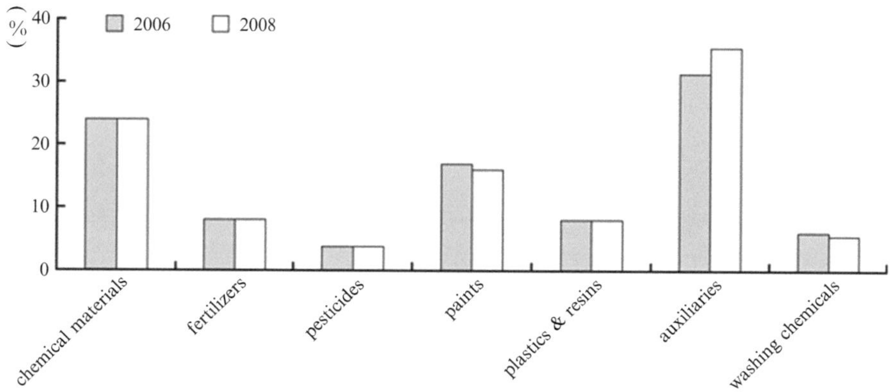

Fig. 3.8 Proportions of branches in China's Chemical Industry (Source: Enterprise database of China National Bureau of Statistics (sorted and calculated))

Hubei, Tianjin, and Chongqing in 2008. NGEs of alloy steel production are concentrated in Hunan, Henan, Inner Mongolia, Ningxia, and Jiangsu, and less distributed in other regions.

As we can see in the distribution of the steel and iron industry, China's NGEs are different in the degree of concentration at different product stages. In provinces supporting larger productions of pig iron such as Jiangsu, Hebei, and Shandong, there are fewer enterprises of steel or alloy steel production; whereas in Hunan, Henan, Inner Mongolia, and Ningxia, there are more enterprises of steel alloy production. To some degree, this proves that China's NGEs in the steel and iron industry have not yet formed a relatively complete industrial chain on the basis of resource advantages. See the statistics in Figs. 3.9, 3.10, 3.11, 3.12, 3.13, and 3.14.

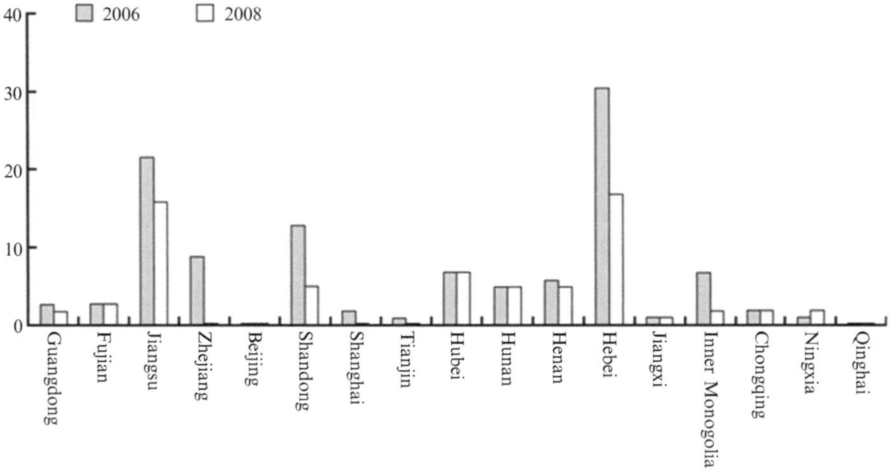

Fig. 3.9 Enterprise numbers in the Pig Iron Industry by province/municipality/region (Source: Enterprise database of China National Bureau of Statistics (sorted and calculated))

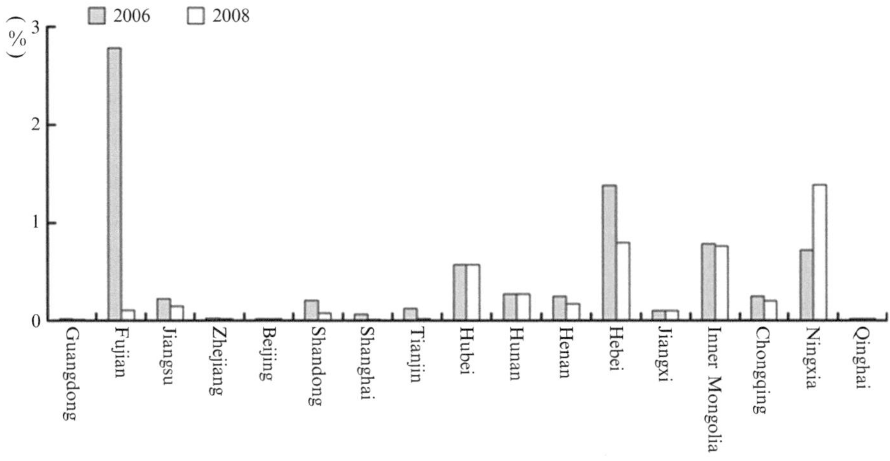

Fig. 3.10 Proportions of Pig Iron Enterprises by province/municipality/region (Source: Enterprise database of China National Bureau of Statistics (sorted and calculated))

3.2.4 NGEs' Capacities for Innovation and Industrial Shift

We chose the value rate of new products and the cross-industrial production of enterprises to describe NGEs' levels of industrial upgrading. As the value rate of new products was not included in the statistics for 2008, we selected the statistics of 2006 and 2007 as the sample years for analysis. We chose and analyzed the garment processing industry (Industry code 1810) and the electrical tools industry (Industry code 3912) as representative figures of industrial shift and innovation, respectively,

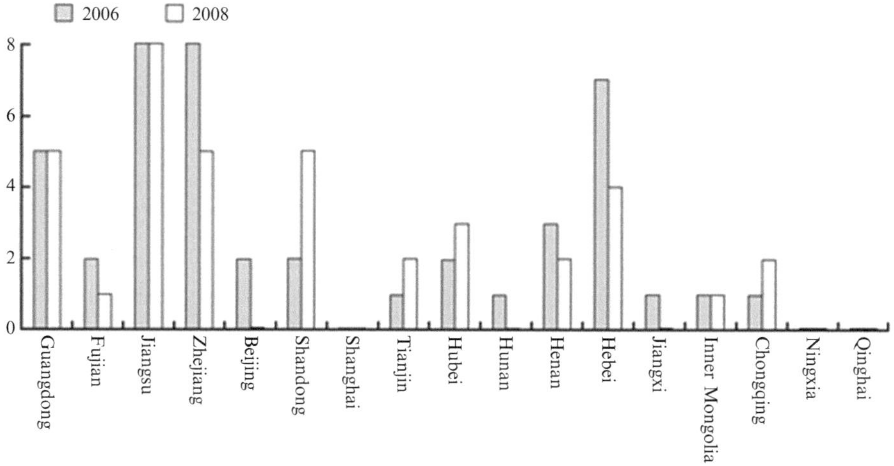

Fig. 3.11 Enterprises in the Steel Pipe Industry by province/municipality/region (Source: Enterprise database of China National Bureau of Statistics (sorted and calculated))

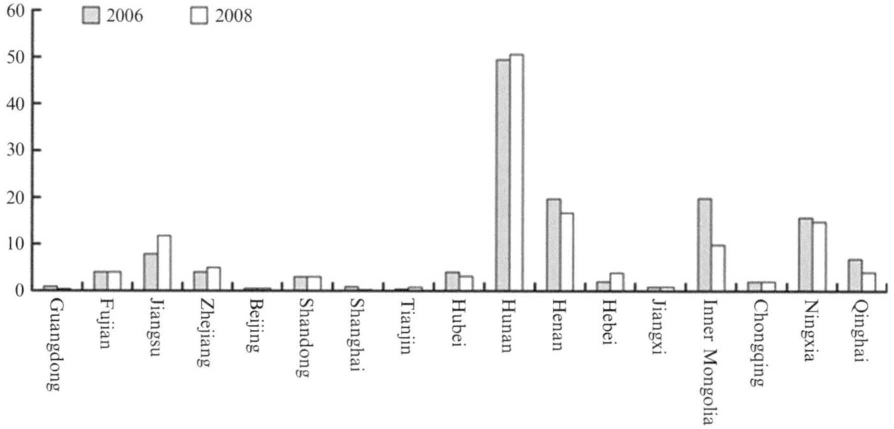

Fig. 3.12 Enterprises of the Steel Alloy Industry by province/municipality/region (Source: Enterprise database of China National Bureau of Statistics (sorted and calculated))

for the garment processing industry is now facing the greatest pressure of industrial shift with its uneven regional distribution, decreased profitability, and the shortage of migrant labor force in the coastal regions in the southeast, while the electrical tools industry is of a higher technological level, and its development is closely related to the available levels of technological innovation.

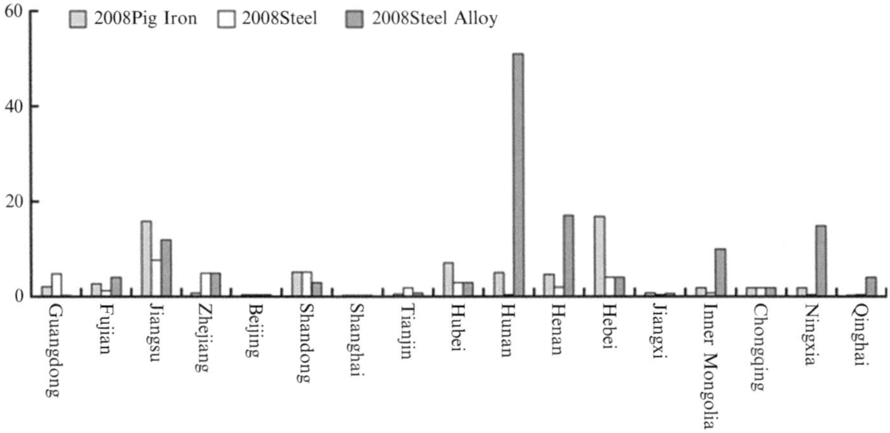

Fig. 3.13 Distribution of steel and iron industrial chains, 2006 (Source: Enterprise database of China National Bureau of Statistics (sorted and calculated))

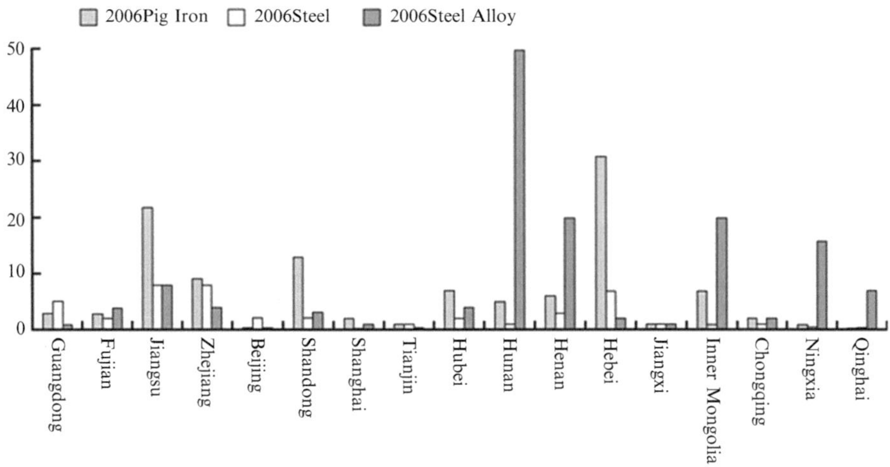

Fig. 3.14 Distribution of steel and iron industrial chains, 2008 (Source: Enterprise database of China National Bureau of Statistics (sorted and calculated))

3.2.4.1 The Garment Processing Industry

As there are many enterprises in the garment processing industry (Industry code 1810), we only selected the non-governmental holding enterprises above a certain designated size in this industry and analyzed their product innovation capacities and cross-industrial operations.

In 2006, of all the 2428 enterprises above the designated size in this industry nationwide, 173 had new products and their average value rate of new products was 43.8%, with the average of all the 2428 sample enterprises being 3.7%. In 2007, of all the 2599 sample enterprises, 299 had new products and their average value rate of new products was 43.35%, with the average of all the sample enterprises being 5.12%. According to the statistics, the value rate of new products was generally low among China's garment processing enterprises.

We chose to analyze the cross-industrial operations of garment processing enterprises in Zhejiang Province, where there is a relatively concentrated distribution and the largest number of such enterprises. Of the 68 sample enterprises in 2006, 15 were producing two or more products. Five of them were producing upstream and downstream products—namely garment producers were simultaneously producing either fabrics or yarns. Two enterprises were conducting cross-industrial production: in addition to garment products, Wenzhou Zhongyi Group was producing central- and low-pressure valves and sanitaryware, and Wenzhou Fapai Group was engaged in the production of hardware and computer equipment and the export of garment processing technology. Of the 38 samples in 2007, 8 were producing two or more products, and 1 was engaged in cross-industrial operation. Of the 78 samples in 2008, 16 were producing two or more products, and 1 was engaged in cross-industrial production. Clearly, the diversified operation of the garment processing of Chinese enterprises is basically within the textile industry, and very few enterprises are really capable of operations across the textile industry and other industries. This indicates a low capacity for industrial shift among China's garment processing NGEs.

3.2.4.2 The Electrical Tools Industry

We chose the electrical tools industry (Industry code 3912) in Zhejiang Province as another sample for analysis. In 2006, there were 42 enterprises in the electrical tools industry in Zhejiang Province, of which six were medium- or large-sized and the rest small-sized enterprises. Fourteen enterprises were producing two or more products and ten were turning out new products. For these ten enterprises, the average value rate of new products was 16.46%, but of all the 42 sample enterprises, that made up only 4.31%. Only one of the 42 enterprises was manufacturing permanent magnet motors. Of the 53 sample enterprises in 2007, 9 were medium- or large-sized and the rest were small-sized enterprises. Twenty three enterprises were producing two or more products and nine of them had extended to other fields. For example, motor manufacturers were producing fans, motorcycle accessories, heat radiators, mahjong machines, waxing machines, barbeque articles, and so forth. Of the 53 enterprises, 20 were turning out new products and their average value rate of new products was 22.2%, but the average value rate of new products was 8.3% for all the 53 enterprises taken together. Of the 73 sample enterprises we analyzed in 2008, 21 were producing two or more products. The major cross-industrial products were textile machines, plastic wrappings for hardware, stainless-steel kitchen and bathroom equipment, fans, precision castings, and so forth. by motor manufacturers. Compared with those in the garment processing industry, the enterprises in the electrical tools industry are more capable of diversified and cross-industrial production.

To further analyze the correlation between diversified products in the electrical tools industry, we studied 29 non-governmental holding manufacturers of electric motors and/or electrical tools in Zhejiang Province in 2006. Ten enterprises had secondary products, which were more or less correlated with their major products. For example, the Superman Group was producing electric shavers and electric hair driers besides micro-motors, and had further extended to the manufacture of electric components. The Zhengda Industry Co., Ltd. in Yongkang City was producing aluminum castings in addition to electrical tools.

Therefore, the enterprises in the electrical tools industry are generally better off than those in garment processing in so far as the value rate of new products and cross-industrial production. Nevertheless, they can hardly enter new industries either, as their cross-industrial products are also highly correlated. The value rate of new products is closely related to the research and development input of enterprises—the more input, the higher the value rate. Among the sample enterprises, 27.23% made up the average percentage of research and development funds in overall profit. Zhejiang Yida Electrical Appliance Co., Ltd. had injected 1.47 times its total profit in research and development; Huzhou Yueqiu Motor Co., Ltd., 1.26 times; and Hongda Group, the major product of which is electric motors, had spent 1.15 times its total profit on research and development.

From the statistics and analysis of the industrial development of China's NGEs, we can see that China's NGEs are mainly medium- and small-sized, and concentrated in the labor-intensive light industry and the traditional manufacturing and processing fields of heavy industry. Though the industries of China's NGEs are rather different, most of these industries are characterized by their concentration in certain provinces (mainly the eastern coastal provinces of Zhejiang, Jiangsu, and Guangdong), which reflects their relatively mature development in these regions and the industrially-clustered feature of China's NGEs, in particular the labor intensive enterprises. Most enterprises are hardly capable of innovation and produce only one single product, however, and only a few of them are able to carry out cross-industrial production. Even though a number of enterprises are engaged in cross-industrial production, their products are usually limited within the same range; only a very few enterprises manufacture products of an industrially-chained relationship. The investment of China's NGEs in research and development is obviously insufficient, which indicates that they are generally weak in technological and capital strength. In general, China's NGEs are still in the lower stages of development.

3.3 NGEs' Choices in Industrial Transformation and Upgrading

The strategies and models outlining industrial upgrading provide directional and theoretical guidance for the industrial innovation of NGEs. Limited by their technological capability and economic strength, however, China's NGEs have to first improve the capability of value creation in the traditional industries before they are encouraged to engage in the emerging industries.

3.3.1 NGEs' Choices in the Transformation and Upgrading of Traditional Industries

NGEs are mainly engaged in traditional industries, the development of which has created many job opportunities. Under the huge pressure of employment, it is against China's basic national conditions to discard the traditional industries. To upgrade their industries, China's NGEs must strengthen the research, development, and innovation capabilities of the country's traditional products, improve the added worth of their products, and enhance the division and collaboration between industries while promoting the collective competitiveness of industries through the development of industrially-clustered areas.

3.3.1.1 The Integrated Innovation of Traditional Industries

Industrial agglomeration is a basic form of industrial development. It may not only be capable of bringing about certain economies of scale and reducing enterprises' cost of operations, but also form an external economy and lower the cost of transactions between enterprises while realizing the flow and share of labor markets, specialized inputs and services, information, and knowledge. The collaboration and competition between enterprises within a specific area can help realize resource complementation and overcome the problem of insufficient innovative resources of a single enterprise. Therefore, industrial agglomeration is a very important geographical structure for industries in the pursuit of resource allocation efficiency and industrial competitive advantages.

China's traditional industries mainly earn their competitive advantages by means of their low costs, so the value added potential of products is also low. Due to increasingly intense market competition, the country's traditional industries have gradually and spontaneously formed certain industrial clusters for survival and growth, most of which are still in the initial stage and therefore limited in the promotion of their own competitiveness, and are thus far from being considered modern industrial clusters. For the traditional industries, the major method of promoting industrial competitiveness is to strengthen their independent innovation abilities. While a single enterprise is limited in innovative capacity, the establishment of an ecosystem for the innovation of a whole industry can realize the complementation of technological innovative capacities of the enterprises within an industrial cluster and overcome the innovation risks and high costs of single enterprises, and therefore benefit the continuous promotion of the cluster's competitiveness. In this regard, the integrated innovation of industrial clusters is the basic method by which to upgrade traditional industries.

The integrated innovation of industries not only increases enterprises' income through an increase in product amounts and scales, but also enhances the added worth of products and the overall competitiveness of industries from the perspectives of product development, information network construction, modern logistics, and so forth. It is the basic direction of industrial clusters' development. It retains the existing costs and market advantages of the traditional industries while promoting the core competitiveness of such industries. It is one of the basic ways in which to upgrade traditional industries as well as being the basic direction of their development.

Take the textile industry for example. For a long time, China's textile industry has won an advantage in competition mainly by its low labor costs, but the enterprises are small in size and redundant their product structure. The industry has developed essentially through expansion of scale and is weak in its overall international competitiveness. The low-cost competition has caused frequent trade frictions among textile products. Since the financial crisis broke out in the U.S., the textile industry has been facing many disadvantages, such as the slow-down of overseas demand, the appreciation of the RMB, rising labor costs, and so forth., and faced unprecedented severe challenges in its production, profit-making, and exports. Quite a few enterprises are already faced with a crisis of survival. With a good variety of difficulties like the excess production capacity, the rising production cost of raw materials and human resources, shortages of funds, an increased responsibility on the part of the enterprise for energy saving and environmental protections, and intensifying market competition, it has become an inevitable choice for the textile industry to fully realize its transformation and upgrading. The transformation and upgrading of China's textile industry must rely on already-formed industrial clusters and accomplish the integrated innovation of the whole industry.

China's textile industry clusters started to take shape spontaneously in 2002 and are characterized by their homogeneity. Operating extensively on the basis of their low labor costs as an advantage, most of these industrial clusters are limited to counties or towns and with small areas, and are still some way from being considered modern industrial clusters. It is rational to realize their integrated innovation through the following channels:

(1) The quantity-to-quality transformation of the development model. With intensifying competition in the global market, it is impossible to sustain the current extensive development of China's textile industry that is featured by the low-level expansion of production capacity and severe waste of resources. This transformation is a must for gaining competitive advantages by means of branding, research and development, management, and quality improvement, and to increase the value added worth of the product. It is obligatory to change the development model of low-cost and low-price competition and to transform from quantity expansion to quality promotion.
(2) The transformation of the operations model from foundry to independent brands. Foundry production is based on low costs, but with the rise of labor

costs and the state's strict restriction on energy saving and emission reductions, it is impossible to sustain the foundry model of operation that relies on low costs and meager profits through mass production. The enterprises must establish their own brands according to local tastes and culture, and, in doing so, develop towards the higher end of the industrial chain.

(3) The transformation of the resource utilization model from material-based to knowledge-based. The Smiling Curve theory summarizes that more value added worth is obtained at both ends of the industrial chain. That is to say, the front end of research and development and the back end of sales and logistics, both relying on the advantage of knowledgeable resources, are the more profitable links on the industrial chain; while the production or manufacturing links gain the lowest value added and lower profits, relying mostly on cheap raw materials and the labor force. China's enterprises will have to face the severe pressure of increasingly lower profits if they continue to limit themselves in the production or manufacturing of products. Therefore, for the long-term development of the industry, it is both a critical strategy for and measure to motivate enterprises to upgrade their operation from the lower end of the manufacturing spectrum to the higher end of development, design, and sales on the industrial chain, and to encourage them to promote their competitiveness through independent innovation, branding, and marketing, to raise their position and discursive power on the industrial chain, and to increase the value added of their products and services.

3.3.1.2 Cross-Regional Industrial Shift

Industrial transformation and upgrading is in itself a process of industrial structural adjustment and upgrading. The adjustment of industrial structure is bound to go together with industrial shift, which is the large scale movement of production capital from one place to another. Industrial shift may take place between countries or between regions in the same country. It is a basic form of industrial structural evolution, which is rooted in the unbalanced economic development between regions. This unbalanced economic development and the difference in labor resource quality between regions requires different economic structures that adapt to local economic development. Different levels of economic development have provided space for the industrial shift taking place in China. The industrial shift from developed regions to less developed regions will help the former eliminate its outdated industrial capacity and develop the industries of high value added, while benefitting the latter by providing new opportunities for development.

The traditional industries of China are unevenly distributed in space: many labor-intensive industries are concentrated in the eastern, developed regions (such as textile and garment processing and the manufacturing of toys, cases and bags, and stationeries); such enterprises are sparsely distributed in the western regions, where some resource-based primary products are made. To create space for the development of emerging industries, it is necessary for the eastern regions of China to move the production of labor-intensive products to the central regions. Some of China's provinces and regions have already initiated the regional shift of industries.

Guangdong Province has implemented the policy of "vacating the cage to change the bird" (腾笼换鸟, téng lóng huàn niǎo) and have actively pushed ahead the industrial transformation and upgrading between regions within the province. The levels of economic development also vary considerably between the regions in Guangdong. For the industrial transformation and upgrading of the Pearl River Delta, for example, Guangdong Province has implemented the industrial shift strategy of "vacating the cage to change the bird" along with restrictions leading to the gradual elimination of the labor-intensive industries of high energy-consumption, high pollution, and low value added in the Pearl River Delta. In this way, it has made space (land) for the development of those advanced manufacturing and modern services industries featuring high technology and higher value added. Under this policy, some projects saddled with high energy consumption and high levels of pollution have been closed or moved out of the Pearl River Delta, and related investment has been guided to the less developed regions of Guangdong. The Pearl River Delta is now focusing on the development of the advanced manufacturing and services industries and has optimized the internal structure of the manufacturing and services industries found therein. On the other hand, after accepting the industrial shift from the Pearl River Delta, the less developed regions of Guangdong have accelerated their process of industrialization and urbanization, increased job opportunities, and attracted part of the surplus labor force to flow from the rural areas to the secondary and tertiary industries, which has, in turn, promoted the adjustment and upgrading of industrial structures in these regions.

Some of the enterprises in China have volunteered to adopt the strategy of cross-regional industrial shift under the pressure of increasing costs. For example, the Foxconn Group in Shenzhen has chosen a northward shift under the increasing pressure of costs. It has additionally adopted this strategy because Shenzhen has lost its geographic advantages due to internal and external customs integration and the implementation of a minimum-wage policy. The construction of new factories in Henan, Hebei, Shanxi, and Chongqing has enabled it to obtain cheap labor and land resources therein. In order to solve the problem of employment and raise their tax revenues, the governments of these newly-located regions have all welcomed Foxconn to build new factories in their jurisdictions, provided it with land and preferential policies, and enthusiastically conducted the technical trainings of laborers.

3.3.1.3 The Integration of Innovative Design into Traditional Industries

The main approach to the upgrading of the country's traditional industries is to increase the value added of products, and product innovation is one of the most important ways to increase the value added. Product innovation involves not only product functions, but also the exterior appearance and cultural values associated with products. By integrating new ideas and concepts into product design, innovation enables the products to meet the diversified, individualized, and fashionable demands of the market, to greatly raise the cultural and intellectual content of traditional manufacturing products, and, in doing so, to increase their value added. The integration of innovation into traditional manufacturing is an important direction in the upgrading of traditional industries, which will help push forward the upgrading of traditional manufacturing to the advanced manufacturing industry of high value added and expand the development space available for manufacturing. Hence, the development of innovative industries to propel the upgrading of the preexisting traditional industries is an important method by which to transform the model of economic growth and realize the sustainable development of the country's traditional industries.

For traditional methods of manufacturing, the integration of innovative industries with traditional industries may start with industrial design. There is large space for the development of innovative industries in the industries of textiles, garments, toys, and household electrical appliances, all of which are industries in which China's NGEs are primarily concentrated. With their large proportions of the export of Chinese products, these industries are the representatives of China's manufacturing, but are more frequently subjected to export restrictions and the anti-dumping practices of the Western countries perpetuated upon China. The development of innovative industries in these fields and the combination of innovation and traditional industries can increase the value added of the products and help maintain the competition advantages of these industries.

In Zhejiang and Guangdong Provinces, great importance has been attached to the significant role of innovative industrial design in facilitating the economic transformation and upgrading of China's enterprises, and the active development of innovative industries is well underway for the transformation and upgrading of the country's traditional industries. According to the industrial advantages and the characteristics of industrial clusters in different regions, Zhejiang Province has projected a specific focus of its innovative industry development on each region. For example, the key field of innovative industrial development is industrial design in Hangzhou, while Wenzhou will focus on the innovative design of garments, shoes, and leather products, and Shaoxing will mainly develop the innovative design of textile products.

In 2005, Guangdong Province proposed the evolution from "Made in Guangdong" to "Designed and Made in Guangdong," and has since been actively developing industrial design while cultivating large numbers of industrial design talents. At present, there are over 60,000 employees and more than 600 companies engaged in industrial design in Guangdong. A good example of this is Shenzhen, which was awarded "City of Design" by UNESCO in 2008. The industrial design industry of Shenzhen has seamlessly integrated Chinese culture with the market and, in doing so, formed an unreplicable core of competitiveness. Design centers of considerable scale have been established in the leading commercial enterprises of Huawei, ZTE, TCL, Skyworth, Midea, and so forth., whose product competitiveness in the international market is closely tied to their innovative industrial design. With industrial design as the theme, Comix Stationery in Shenzhen has sought financing by listing on the stock market, which has pushed forward its development. In Foshan City, Weishang Furniture Manufacturing CO., Ltd. has improved its daily production capacity and material utilization rate by relying on its innovative design, and was fittingly honored as a model of "industrial-design to promote the transformation and upgrading of traditional industries" (工业设计推动传统产业转型升级, gōngyè shèjì tuīdòng chuántǒng chǎnyè zhuǎnxíng shēngjí) as a result.

In summary, if NGEs consisting of traditional industries attach enough importance to the positive role of innovation in their industrial development and make certain investments in it, they will be able to increase the value added and strengthen the market competitiveness of their products. Moreover, it will also help establish unique enterprise brands and benefit the survival and development of NGEs as a whole.

3.3.2 NGEs' Transformation, Upgrading, and Entry into Strategic Emerging Industries

According to their present industrial and value-chain distribution, China's NGEs are still at the lower end of industrial development and cannot fully advance their industries in the short run. Under the triple pressures of resources, environment, and existing market demands, China must transform its model of economic development for the sustainable development of the economy. As many countries have successively adjusted their development strategies and have been developing a "green economy" following the financial crisis (which also presents an international pressure for China), it must also "boost its technological innovation and develop the green economy," adjust and optimize the country's industrial structure, and realize the transformation and upgrading of China's industry during its 12th Five-Year Plan. The transformation and upgrading of the industry is a means by which to eliminate outdated industrial capacity and develop its emerging industries, which is in itself the replacement of a country's industrial structures. In the context of industrial upgrading, there must be good investment outlets for non-governmental capital to be able to withdraw from outdated industrial capacity while some NGEs continue to realize the upgrading of their traditional industries.

To promote industrial restructuring, China has proposed to vigorously develop the country's strategic emerging industries from the perspective of sustaining its economic growth, while speeding up the elimination of outdated industrial capacity. Moreover, it has determined the key industries for support, i.e., its new energy sources, new materials, new medicines, electric cars, information and communication, and the energy-saving and emission-reducing industries, and has planned to invest a total of RMB five trillion between 2011 and 2020 to support their development. After the financial crisis, to increase non-governmental investment, the State Council released *Several Opinions of the State Council on Encouraging and Guiding the Sound Development of Non-Governmental Investment* in May, 2010, and has encouraged non-governmental investment in energies, environmental protection, public utilities, and more. For further implementation of the policies and measures documented, the State Council released a *Notice on the Division of Key Work in Encouraging and Guiding the Sound Development of Non-governmental Investment* on July 26, 2010, and further defined the task division among the departments and local governments concerned in encouraging and guiding the investment of non-governmental capital and has determined the specific measures necessary to encourage non-governmental investment. Under these circumstances, the "glass door" that impedes China's non-governmental investment may hopefully disappear, indeed. In that case, non-governmental capital and state-owned capital will be more equal in terms of investment policies, environment, and opportunities to participate in strategic emerging industries. The non-governmental capital from eliminated industries may then try to enter some of China's strategic emerging industries.

3.3.2.1 Entry into New Energy Industries: Solar Energy and Wind Power

According to the prediction of the International Energy Agency (IEA), global coal resources will be exhausted in 220 years, with extraction peaking in 2012, while petroleum and natural gas will run out in 30–60 years. China is a country with relatively poor levels of natural resources, whose remaining proven reserves of the primary energy sources are without exception smaller than the world's average. For example, its remaining proven reserve of coal can only last about another 81 years; petroleum, about 15 years; and natural gas, about 30 years. Therefore, it is necessary to adjust the country's energy structure for the sustainable development of human beings, and in doing so, the proportion between renewable energy, e.g. solar energy, and conventional energy will change drastically. It is predicted that the proportion of renewable energy, including solar energy, will be about 28% in 2020, about 37% in 2030, about 46% in 2040, and about 55% in 2050.[6]

To ensure the country's energy security, China is vigorously developing its renewable energy resources, including solar energy, wind power, hydraulic power, and geothermal energy. As ideal renewable and environmental-friendly sources of energy, solar energy and wind power are the most sustainable approaches to relieving the energy crisis and the energy products being developed globally. China's *Plans for the Medium- and Long-Term Development of Renewable Energy Sources* stipulated that, by 2020, the proportion of renewable energy will be 15%, with solar energy and wind power as the major sources of China's renewable energy. It is rational for NGEs to engage themselves in solar energy application and wind power generation.

[6]Cui Rongqiang, & Wang Jianqiang. (2008). The Future of Solar Photovoltaic Power Generation. *Renewable Energy Resources*, (3), 26.

3.3.2.1.1 Entry into Solar Energy Application

Solar energy application includes photothermal application, optoelectronic application, and more. With increasing investment in its research and development, rapid progress is being made in solar energy technology. Thanks to a dramatic decline in the cost of the silicon material necessary for solar photovoltaic power generation, the payback period of investment in any given photovoltaic power generation system with amorphous silicon films/silicon crystal cells has been shortened to less than 1 year. While the material cost is declining, the efficiency of photovoltaic cells is rapidly improving. Currently, the cost of photovoltaic power generation has been reduced to the point where commercialized development is possible for the industry. In China's first-round franchise bidding for photovoltaic plants in March 2009, the accepted feed-in tariff was RMB 1.09 per kilowatt hour, while the lowest accepted price had declined to RMB 0.7288 in the second-round of bidding on August 16, 2010.[7] With the feed-in tariff lowered, the enterprises running the photovoltaic plants will strive to expand the scale of photovoltaic power generation so as to achieve the scale effect, which in turn will push forward the commercialization of photovoltaic power generation. As the government is to facilitate the grid-connected operation of photovoltaic power generation, China is vigorously developing off-grid power generation in remote areas with power shortages and popularizing the solar energy lighting system in cities. The scale of China's photovoltaic industry will grow increasingly larger in the future.

The overall industrial chain of photovoltaic application is very long, and includes several sub-chains such as the raw material chain, the auxiliary material chain, the equipment chain, the industrial service chain, and even the manufacturing of specialized machinery and equipment. Limited by their capital scale, China's NGEs hardly have any advantage over SOEs in the current competition of photovoltaic plant operation. But as it is such a long industrial chain, NGEs have enough chances to enter the fields of silicon raw materials, auxiliary materials, solar cells, photovoltaic product components, the manufacturing of specialized machinery and equipment, and related supporting industries. There are already a number of successful enterprises in these fields in China, e.g., Suntech in Wuxi City, Trina Solar in Changzhou City, Tianwei Group in Baoding City, LDK Solar in Jiangxi Province, and so forth. In addition, China's NGEs may also be engaged in the production of solar building materials, furniture, and lighting equipment as a way to transform and upgrade more traditional industries. Moreover, at present, Chinas' NGEs are vigorously exploring the international market, as many other countries are actively developing photovoltaic power generation and consequently their demands for photovoltaic components are on the rise, which provides a good opportunity for NGEs to develop in the photovoltaic industry.

[7]Wang Xiaoming. (Aug. 23, 2010). Photovoltaic Bidding: Exclusive Feast of "National Team"? At http://www.cqn.com.cn/news/xfpd/szcj/qyfc/gscy/338807.html.

3.3.2.1.2 Entry into the Wind Power Industry

China is rich in its wind energy resources, with an estimated 1.6 billion kilowatts. Affected mainly by topography, wind energy resources are abundant on China's Shandong Peninsula and Liaodong Peninsula, the Yellow Sea shores, the South China Sea coast and islands, Hainan Island, and in Inner Mongolia, Xinjiang, and Gansu, as well as Northeast China; the potential of wind power utilization is enormous in these areas. Nowadays, the wind power industry is developing rapidly in China, and its installed wind-power capacity ranks second in the world. However, an incomplete industrial chain is limiting the further development of the country's wind power industry.

The industrial chain of wind power can be broadly split into two parts, the upper industrial echelon of wind-power equipment manufacturing and the downstream industry of wind-power construction and operations, and the former may be further divided into machine manufacturing and component manufacturing. In China's wind power industry, the productivity of the upper industry can hardly meet the development speed of wind-power construction in the downstream. China is still at the initial stage of megawatt-class machine manufacturing and weak in the production of the most important components, which makes it impossible to manufacture wind-power machines domestically. Such a weak industrial chain has provided NGEs with new opportunities for industrial transformation, however. NGEs have already started their entry into the sub-chains of the wind power industry. In 2007, there were 36 enterprises nationwide manufacturing wind turbines, of which 17 were state-owned holding companies and 12 were NGEs. In 2009, 87 enterprises were engaged in the manufacturing of wind-power generators, of which 39 were SOEs and 24 were NGEs. A considerable proportion of NGEs are capable of the mass production of wind turbines. Some NGEs have entered the field of key components and parts necessary for the production of wind power machines. For example, in Tongxiang of Zhejiang Province, Huazhang Electric Co., Ltd. has been producing wind power rheostats since the second half of 2009; meanwhile, Hengshi Corporation of Zhenshi Group has started producing wind-power generator blades and the material necessary for combo mats. A complete industrial chain is being formed in Tongxiang, from the upper industries of generator blades, fiberglass weaving, and controllers to the downstream industry of wind-power machine manufacturing. In the general context of economic stagnancy, Tongxiang's sales within the wind power industry increased by 70% in the first quarter of 2009.[8] As China examines and begins to give approval to wind-power farm operations that require a capital ratio of 20%, most NGEs are unable to participate in and benefit from such franchise-based projects due to their insufficient funds. Some of China's NGEs, however, have begun entering the construction of wind farms. For example, China's first NGE 30,000-kW wind-farm project was approved in Jinzhou in

[8]NGEs of Zhejiang: Rise and Market Exploration of Wind Power Industry. At http://tvshow.smgbb.cn/dianshi/zixun/changsanjiaozhoubao/2009-03-17/9196.html

December 2009, which is a key planning program for wind power development in Liaoning Province. What's more, China's NGEs have turned towards joint development of the wind power industry. In August 2010, the offshore wind project in the salt regions of Laizhou was officially launched, which is a cooperation between two NGEs, China Creative Wind Energy Company Limited and Laizhou Chengyuan Salt Chemical Co., Ltd. When the first period of the project is finished, they will be able to produce 600 doubly-fed and direct-driven wind turbines of three megawatts each year, and a high-standard technical service center will provide for the repair and maintenance of wind power equipment. In the second period, a production line of 3–5 MW wind turbines and offshore wind turbines will be constructed. The annual output value is estimated to be over seven billion RMB when the overall project is completed and put into operation. The entry into the wind power industry will definitely create a new growth point for NGEs.

3.3.2.2 Entry into the Electric Vehicle Industry

China has already entered the era of popularized automobile consumption and its auto consumption market is expanding rapidly. With the rapid increase of its automobiles, environmental pollution and petroleum resource consumption are also on the rise. To realize energy savings and emissions reduction in auto consumption, China has determined to pursue a particular structural adjustment of the automobile industry, that is, the development of new energy vehicles, e.g., electrical vehicles. It is projected in the *Program for the Development of the New Energy Vehicle Industry,* formulated by the government, that China should rank first globally in the scale of the industrialization and marketization of new energy vehicles by 2020, and that electric hybrid vehicles and pure electric vehicles are to be the focus in the development of new energy vehicles.

To industrialize new energy vehicles, China must first realize the industrialization and automation of the industry's key components and parts, such as power batteries, electric motors, electric controllers, and so forthand so forth. Specifically, the level of the mass production of power batteries determines the degree of the industrialization of new energy vehicles. Accordingly, China will establish a system of standards for electric vehicles, construct research and experimental bases of the components and parts, formulate industrial gathering areas of lithiumion power batteries, and cultivate two or three leading power-battery enterprises, which are of a production-sales scale of over 20 billion watt-hours and capable of developing and producing the key materials necessary for new energy batteries.

China's NGEs can actively participate in the production activities on the overall industrial chain of electric vehicles. For example, they may engage in the production and recycling of electric vehicle batteries, as China's NGEs are currently capable of the mass production of cell phone and electric bicycle batteries, and the production technology of an electric vehicle battery is quite similar to that of the above two types of battery. It is possible to realize the industrialization and mass production of electric vehicles in a short time if appropriate policies and technological support is given to non-governmental capital. On the other hand, the development of new energy vehicles on a large scale will give birth to the power-battery maintenance and recycling industry, which will provide another opportunity for NGEs' transformation and upgrading. On August 18, 2010, SASAC (the State-Owned Assets Supervision and Administration Commission) organized and established the State-Owned Enterprise Electric Vehicle Industry Alliance to promote the industrialization of new energy vehicles. For China's non-governmental capital, it is a good opportunity for equity participation with SOEs and entry into the industry of new energy vehicles. There are already precedent NGEs that are successful in the production of electric vehicles.[9] BYD Auto and New Meijing Auto Group are good examples. For more than 10 years, New Meijing Auto Group has invested RMB 200 million into the research and development of electric vehicles. It has finally achieved key breakthroughs in the development of pure electric buses and has currently mastered the four core technologies of electric vehicles. As the result of its weight reduction in vehicle body design, the electric buses it manufactures are the country's lightest at present. The power batteries it produces can be fully charged within 3 h for a ride of over 300 km, and is of lower cost and more stable performance than comparable products and, further, is guaranteed for 8 years' use. China's NGEs are technologically competent enough to manufacture new energy vehicles of technological leadership. An academician of the China Engineering Academy and president of the World Electric Vehicle Association, Chen Qingquan, believes that, compared with traditional automobile enterprises, NGEs newly engaged in new energy vehicles are more enthusiastic in technological research and development and are more likely to achieve technological breakthroughs as they are free from any historical baggage.

3.3.2.3 Entry into the Environmental Protection Industry

With environmental deterioration caused by rapid industrialization, greater and greater demands are being placed on the environment. For the coordinated development of the economy, society, and environment, China implemented an energy saving and emissions reduction plan as part of the country's 11th Five Year Plan. Investments in environmental improvements have been on the rise ever since, and the development of the environmental protection industry is accelerating at an unprecedented speed. Preliminary calculation of the State Environmental Protection Administration shows that China's environmental protection industry has maintained an average annual growth rate of 15–17% from 2006 to 2010. It is predicted in the *Study on Macro Strategies of China's Environment* that the output value of China's environmental protection industry will exceed RMB 1 trillion in

[9] An NGE's Electric Vehicle Dream. At http://finance.ifeng.com/leadership/ppgl/20100626/2346987.shtml.

2010, more than 3% of the GDP. It is also predicted in the industry planning for energy saving and emission reduction, formulated by the National Development and Reform Commission, that China's investment in environmental protection will reach RMB 3.1 trillion in the 12th Five Year Plan, a growth of 121% compared to the RMB 1.54 trillion in the 11th Five Year Plan, and that the total output value of China's energy saving and environmental protection industry will reach 7–8% of the GDP by 2015. Far into the future, the environmental protection industry will be a real sunrise industry and a pillar of the green development of the economy. As China will further reinforce those binding indicators of energy saving and environmental protection in the country's 12th Five Year Plan, investment in environmental protection will increase and the environmental protection industry will have a broader margin for development.

Due to its long industrial chain and strong correlation with other industries, the environmental protection industry has a very strong capacity for dynamic employment compared with other industries, an extensive permeability in the national economic system, and an omnidirectional and multilevel correlation with other industries. The development of the environmental protection industry can drive in an all-round way the technological upgrading of the economic system and industrial structural transformation. No one should underestimate the greatly stimulating effect of the environmental protection industry on the overall economy. The development of the environmental protection industry will help realize and bring about the green growth of China's economy. China's environmental protection industry is now actively pushing forward the disposal of sewage, industrial pollution, and waste, as well as the treatment of municipal refuse. To encourage the development of the environmental protection industry, China will reform its environment-related fees and taxes, promote the marketization of sewage and waste disposal services and operations, and increase governmental investment in these areas. The environment for the development of the environmental protection industry will be improved. It is now feasible for NGEs to enter the environmental protection field, and there are successful cases of NGEs' entry into the environmental protection industry.

As a listed company of Tianjin Municipality, Teda Corporation became involved in waste-incineration power generation in 2001, and chose to construct its first incineration plant in Shuanggang, Tianjin—a project which was completed in 2004. By the end of 2008, the garbage power plant in Shuanggang had finished the innocuous treatment of 400 thousand tons of domestic waste, generated 129 million kilowatt-hours of energy, and delivered 108 million kilowatt-hours onto the power grid. Thanks to the excellent operation of this project, Teda won the bid for the Dalian urban area domestic-waste incineration project with an investment of RMB 657 million in June 2009.[10]

Everbright International has also successfully entered the industry of municipal refuse disposal and formed a replicable business model. On September 17, 2009,

[10]Teda Corp. Fighting for 80-Billion Market of Garbage Power Generation. At http://www.topcj.com/html/0/GSXW/20100330/1092252.shtml

Everbright International reached a framework agreement of mutual cooperation with Jiangyin Municipal Government of Jiangsu Province. According to the agreement, Everbright International will conduct wastewater recycle and reuse, the development of new materials and the utilization of new energy including solar energy, wind power, and bio-energy, the development and construction of town-level sewage disposal projects, and the integration of the sewage disposal facilities in Jiangyin City. On October 19, 2009, Everbright Environmental Energy (Zhenjiang) Limited, a wholly-owned subsidiary of China Everbright International Limited, signed a franchise agreement and a refuse-disposal service agreement regarding the waste incineration power generation project of Zhenjiang City with the Urban Administration Bureau of Zhenjiang, Jiangsu Province. It was entitled to 30 years of franchised operation and was to invest in the construction—operation—transference model. Up to this point, Everbright International has organized and carried out 26 garbage power projects in the Pearl River Delta, the Yangtze River Delta, and the Bohai Rim areas; its garbage power plants have been constructed, put into operation, and are developing well in Suzhou, Yixing, Jiangyin, Changzhou, Jinan, Qingdao and Zibo.

Garbage power generation is a considerable prospect for development in China. At present, China is the largest producer of urban solid waste in the world. As waste landfills not only consume much land but may also cause secondary contamination, incineration has become the first choice for urban waste disposal. As predicted in the *Analysis Report on Investment in the Domestic Waste Industry of China 2010*, the proportion of incineration to overall waste disposal will rise from 2–3% to 10–20% in 10 years. The former State Construction Department had also previously planned to raise the proportion of garbage power generation from 2% in 2002 to 30% in 2030. Solid-waste incineration and power generation can not only greatly reduce the volume of solid waste, but also avoid the air pollution caused by methane emissions caused by other methods of waste disposal. The power and heat produced in the incineration process can effectively replace fossil energies, which results in the recycling of resources and conforms to the basic orientation of China's sustainable development. Currently, the state implements supportive policies for garbage power generation. As a franchise program of municipal public utilities, garbage power generation receives a waste disposal fee from the government; what's more, the generated electricity can be fully delivered onto the state grid and is given governmental financial subsidies. As the innocuous treatment of solid waste is still of a low proportion in China, NGEs should take advantage of the state policy to encourage non-governmental investment in public utilities, and actively engage themselves in the disposal of urban waste.

3.4 Conclusion

Currently, NGEs are a new economic and industrial force that pushes ahead China's economic development and hold a significant position in the national economy. Following the global financial crisis, NGEs are now faced with various pressures, such as shrinking domestic and overseas markets, the deterioration of trade conditions, the acceleration of industrial structure adjustment, and more. They must implement a process of industrial transformation and upgrading to progress, which is consistent with the transformation of the development model of China's national economy.

NGEs must first make clear the direction of their industrial transformation and upgrading. China's NGEs are mainly engaged in labor-intensive processing industries and are relatively weak in technological strength, capacity for innovation, and in the value added of their products. What's more, the regional development of NGEs is extremely uneven. Though the development and policy environment of NGEs has been improved considerably and the scope of non-governmental investment has already been extended in China, NGEs cannot be said to have equal opportunities for competition with SOEs and are faced with factual access restrictions in their entry into the highly profitable or monopolized industries and fields, due to the monopoly of SOEs and the high capital threshold of the strategic emerging industries.

For their survival and development, China's NGEs must carry out industrial transformation and upgrading, but it is impractical for them to completely abandon their previous labor-intensive industries and enter capital-intensive industries during the industrial upgrading. At present, it is more feasible for NGEs to implement industrial transformation and upgrading on the basis of traditional industries, and to gradually increase the value added and competitiveness of their products through product innovation and the improvement and integration of product value chains.

Considering that many countries are accelerating their industrial structural adjustment, China must also strive to transform and upgrade its domestic industry so as to realize an optimal degree of sustainable development and promote the overall competitiveness of its economy. Under this circumstance, the existing high energy-consuming and high pollution industries of NGEs are inevitably faced with the pressure of being eliminated. The capital withdrawn from the adjusted industries will have to find new investment channels. For such capital, it is worthwhile to try entering those industries and fields encouraged by the government, such as new energies, electric vehicles, environmental protection, and so forth. While encouraging NGEs to enter these strategic emerging industries, the government must further lower the threshold of these industries, give NGEs stronger financial support, and provide an environment for competition equal to that of SOEs.

Bibliography

Cui R, Wang J (2008) The future of solar photovoltaic power generation. Renewable Energy Resour (3):26

Deng G (2006) Industrial transformation—experience, problems and strategies. Economic Management Press, Beijing

Du P (2009) Basic drivers of industrial development, transformation and upgrading. Zhejiang Econ (4)

Gan C (2006) Industrial economics: courses and cases. China Machine Press, Beijing
Jin L, Liu R (2010) Low-carbon economy and transformation of China's economic development model. Inq Econ Issues (1):84–87
Liu E, Cui Y (2007) Market environment for development of Guangdong's SMEs. Mod Enterp (1):35–38
Liu Q, Tang C (2010). Frequent trade frictions predicted by experts in second half of this year, Guangdong Trade Association unable to play leading role in coping trade wars. South Daily, 9 Feb
Wang J, Shi J, Li Y (2005) On industrial structure evolution of China's NGEs and concurrently on competitive relationships between NGEs, SOEs, and FFEs. Manage World (10):82–91
Wang X, Huang R, Guo L (2010) Direction choice in development model transformation of Guangdong's SMEs in post-crisis era. Rev Econ Res (40)
Zhang Y (2002) Industrial innovation: models of industrial upgrading under new economic conditions. J Quant Tech Econ (1)

Chapter 4
Barriers to Entry in Monopolistic Industries: NGEs' Difficulties and Solutions

Jinwen Ju

4.1 Barriers to NGEs' Entry in Monopolistic Industries: Introduction

The monopolistic industries hold the dominant position in China's national economy. Sustained high relative prices directly lead to high profits for China's monopolized industries, such as telecommunications, petroleum, tobacco, finance, electricity, water, and gas. On August 20, 2010, SASAC (the State-Owned Assets Supervision and Administration Commission) released the *Table of Central Enterprises' Respective Operations of State-Owned Assets 2009*, which includes 108 of the 129 central enterprises. According to the table printed here, the total net profit attributable to the parent companies of these 108 central enterprises came out to RMB 398.96 billion, and China Mobile, CNPC (China National Petroleum Corporation), and Sinopec Group ranked as the top three companies, with net profits of RMB 79.63 billion, 70.17 billion, and 39.32 billion, respectively. As reported by *The Beijing News* on August 30, 2010, the four major state-owned banks were far ahead of the industry in terms of net profit; their net profits added up to RMB 255.9 billion, 74.5% of the total net profit of the 16 listed banks; with its net profit of RMB 84.603 billion, ICBC (Industrial & Commercial Bank of China) was the most profitable of all. Many studies show that the fat profits of monopolized industries come from their privileges, rather than any kind of improvement of economic efficiency in the technological sense (Bai Ming and Lei Jingqing 2006; Yu Chunliang and Zhang Wei 2010). According to data put forward in the *Report on the Development of China's Information Society 2010*,[1] the average broadband expenditure was 7.4% of China's per capita GDP in 2008, ranking 71st of all

[1]Quoted from a report on *Beijing Morning Post*, Aug. 23, 2010.

J. Ju (✉)
Chinese Academy of Social Sciences, Beijing, China

Y. Liu (ed.), *New Interpretations on the Development of China's Non-Governmental Enterprises*, Research Series on the Chinese Dream and China's Development Path, DOI 10.1007/978-981-10-3872-3_4

99 countries compared in the study. The figure was 1.15% in South Korea, which ranked 9th, but the per capita national income of South Korea was 6.9 times that of China, which means the broadband expense of a Chinese individual was 124 times that of a South Korean. The high profit of these monopolized industries ensures much higher incomes for their employees than for those employed in other industries. Through a comparison of the employee wages between the post and communications industry and other industries, Xie Di (2007) discovered that, each year, the average wages of the post and communications industry are 70% higher than those of other industries, and over 160% higher than that of agriculture, forestry, animal husbandry, and fishery, and that the gap is widening yearly (Table 4.1). Wang Junhao et al. (2010) also pointed out that the average employee income within the monopolistic industries is much higher than the national average, and the income gap is growing. In 2005, the average wage in telecommunications and other information transmissions was RMB 36,941, 101% higher than the national average. In 2003, the average income in the production and distribution of electricity, gas, and water was 34% higher than the national average, while in 2005 the gap had widened to 37%. Similarly, the income gap between the transportation, storage, and postal services industries and other industries had grown from 14% to 16%. Now that monopolies are not conducive to efficiency but, rather, cause huge losses of efficiency (Yu Chunliang and Zhang Wei 2010), it is of great significance to a country's Pareto Optimality in terms of the economy and social welfare to break existing monopolies.

The most important way to break a monopoly is to introduce competition. In recent years, we have indeed done much work in introducing competition into the monopolistic industries, the main method of which being the demerger of the state-owned monopolistic enterprises. The effect, however, has been far from what might have been expected. Many scholars do not accept this choice of reform but deem NGEs' entry in large numbers necessary to break a monopoly (Wang Junhao 2006; Zhang Xinzhu 2007; Ju Jinwen 2009).To strengthen competition, the central government has repeatedly introduced policies that encourage

Table 4.1 Comparison of employee wages between select industries 1995–2002 (RMB)

Years	Average annual wages of all industries studied	Post and communications	Agriculture, forestry, animal husbandry, and fishery
1995	5500	9201	3522
1996	6210	10,569	4050
1997	6470	12,056	4311
1998	7479	13,017	4528
1999	8346	14,424	4832
2000	9371	16,359	5184
2001	10,870	19,991	5741
2002	12,422	23,582	6398

Notes: (1) The statistics are the average annual wages of the whole industry/industries studied; (2) Post & Communications is regarded as a sub-sector
Source: Xie Di (2007)

NGEs' entry into the country's monopolized industries. As has been pointed out, however, there are, practically, several "glass doors" facing NGEs' entry. These invisible but extant obstacles are essentially the barriers to such industries. It is possible to break, or at least greatly reduce, an existing monopoly once NGEs are able to overcome these barriers.

What are the barriers of China's monopoly industries at present? How high or strong are they? What leads to these barriers? What policies or measures should we take to reduce them? These questions are exactly what are addressed in this chapter.

4.2 The Chinese Experience: The Universality of Institutional and Administrative Barriers

In this section, we will reveal new changes in the barriers to entry and several feasible approaches to breakthroughs on the basis of the latest state of NGEs' entry into different monopolistic industries. For difficulties in access to certain statistics, related events or sample cases are used to expound the authors' viewpoints.

4.2.1 Electric Industry

In order relieve the long-term shortage of the country's electricity supply, as early as 1985, the administrative department of China's electric power started to implement the policy of "raising funds to build power plants" based on the principle of "power plants run by the people, power grids managed by the state," and in doing so attracted huge social investment in the construction of power plants. In particular, the power generation projects of Chinese-foreign joint venture or cooperatives, as well as those that were foreign funded, developed rapidly. From the mid 1990s on, NGEs that have grown up in some eastern developed regions (such as Zhejiang) began to advance towards becoming involved in the electricity industry. Huiming Corp., an NGE of Zhejiang, launched a 230 million RMB investment in the construction of the Baihe Hydroelectric Station in Jingning. The installed capacity was 33,000 kWh and the annual generating capacity was 100 million kilowatt-hours, which meant an annual income of about RMB 50 million through power generation. What's more, NGEs of Zhejiang also purchased some small- and medium-sized hydroelectric stations that were combined with the grid and in operation. Moreover, they also participated in the management of several rivers in small- and medium-sized cities in the west of China. For example, Huiyang Corp. was engaged in development projects in Hubei, Guangxi, Sichuan, and Guizhou. The total investment was RMB 1.1 billion and the installed capacity added up to 160,000 kWh. Up to the present, the total installed capacity of all its projects has exceeded 2 million kilowatt-hours. Other NGEs soon followed suit, such as

Zhejiang Guangsha Group, Songcheng Group, Hangzhou Kailida Group, and so forth. Zhejiang Hongyang Hydroelectric Development Corporation invested RMB 100 million and constructed hydroelectric stations in Yuexi County, Liangshan Prefecture, of Sichuan Province. Zheng Jie, a private entrepreneur of Jingning, Zhejiang Province, invested RMB 70 million in the development of the hydroelectric resources along Xiapu River. Private entrepreneurs of Linhai invested RMB 30 million and constructed two hydroelectric stations in Tangjiashan of Sichuan Province. Sinowisdom Group invested and built Changzhou Water Control Project in Guangxi, the cascade hydropower stations in the central reaches of the Jinsha River, Nina Hydroelectric Station in Qinghai, Helanshan Win Farms Project in Ningxia, and the Wind Power Project on the Kangxi Grassland, among others. The electric industry has been subjected to the earliest and most profound of China's monopolized industrial reform. In January 2004, Chint Group and Huafon Group invested and participated in the construction of Zheneng Yueqing Electric Power Station, the total investment of which was about RMB 11.8 billion. It was the first large-sized project of a power facility construction in which Wenzhou's NGEs were involved. In the twenty-first century, following the government's encouragement of new energy development, many NGEs have started entering the fields of garbage power generation, solar power generation, and wind power generation. Wenzhou Weiming Environmental Protection Co., Ltd. entered the field of garbage power generation in the late 1990s, and invested and constructed Dongzhuang Garbage Power Plant in BOT (Build-Operate-Transfer) mode, which functions as Wenzhou's first garbage power plant. The corporation is the first of China's NGEs to operate garbage power projects and possesses four garbage power plants at present. In March 2002, HEAG Group of Wenzhou invested RMB 10.8 million and founded Huayi Wind Energy Co., Ltd., and started the operation of wind power projects. The total installed capacity of the wind farms invested in and constructed by HEAG has reached 1 million kilowatt-hours. The installed capacity of the first-phase project completed at the end of 2004—an investment of over RMB 70 million—is 46.5 thousand kilowatt-hours. As the first NGE of Foshan to enter the wind power industry, Dongxing Fengying Wind Power Equipment Manufacturing Co., Ltd. of Guangdong Province started its engagement in the industry in 2007 and initially engaged in technological cooperation with a German wind power corporation. Later, Dongxing Fengying cooperated with DWD (Danish Wind Design Co., Ltd.) in the development of a 2 MW wind turbine. By 2009, Dongxing Fengying had produced seven wind turbines of a combined 800 kWh, the first two sold to Haiwanshi Wind Farm of Yudean Group and the other five carried to its own wind farm under construction in Guizhou. In January 2010, Shandong RealForce Group held the launching ceremony of its 1 MW solar power station in Weishan, which is the first NGE-invested solar photovoltaic energy station in China. With its internationally advanced technology, this MW-level solar power station has overcome the technical difficulty of the islanding effect in photovoltaic power generation. In the near future, Shandong RealForce Group will complete the establishment of a solar-energy base that integrates research, development, and production.

Through an analysis of NGEs' entry into the electric industry and the barriers they face therein, we have come to the following conclusions:

First of all, the electric industry is one of the monopolistic industries/fields with the earliest and largest-scale entry of NGEs. In particular, some small- and medium-sized hydroelectric plants/stations have been mostly invested in and operated by NGEs. This indicates a weaker monopolistic intensity and lower barriers to entry in the generating segment of the power industry. On the other hand, new energy projects like garbage power generation, typical of huge investment, low risks, and slow returns, always require enterprises to advance enormous funds, which is an insurmountable barrier to smaller NGEs' entry into these fields.

Secondly, the monopolistic pricing of the power generation enterprises by the administrative department has already become a strong barrier to entry into this industry. Take, for example, the small hydroelectric stations in Xishui County of Guizhou Province. There are currently 88 small- and medium-sized hydroelectric stations operated by NGEs in the county, about 80 of which have been completed and put into operation; the total installed capacity of over 150 turbines in the county is 15,000 kWh. According to related documents provided by the China National Development and Reform Commission, the price of hydroelectricity should be 0.215 RMB per kilowatt-hour in Xishui. The one who sets the online electrovalency in Xishui, however, is the local government and pricing department, who have decided the online electrovalency without holding a price hearing. Consequently, the electrovalency remained 0.1914 RMB per kilowatt-hour until July 2007, at which point it was raised to 0.1974 RMB per kilowatt-hour starting in August 2007. The full cost of private hydropower enterprises is 0.3956 RMB per kilowatt-hour. This means a loss of 0.1982 RMB per kilowatt-hour for these enterprises—the more they generate, the larger their loss. It has led to a survival crisis for the private hydroelectric enterprises in Xishui.

Finally, from another perspective, NGEs' entry into the electric industry is hampered by certain high thresholds made by the country's administrative and regulatory departments. In 2009, the Equipment Industry Division of China's Ministry of Industry and Information Technology compiled their *Industry Access Standards* of wind power equipment manufacturing, which brought up three key demands being made on wind power equipment manufacturers. First, enterprises concerned with wind power turbine manufacturing should be equipped with the appropriate production conditions and all the supporting facilities for a single-turbine capacity of 2.5 MW or above and for an annual output of 1 million kilowatts or more. Second, enterprises involved with wind power turbine manufacturing should achieve a total capacity installation of no less than 500,000 kW before they are allowed to engage in further reconstruction and/or expansion. Third, new enterprises of wind power turbine manufacturing should have at least 5 years of experience in the manufacturing of large-sized electrical machines. For the overwhelming majority of NGEs, it is difficult to meet these three demands. Even some NGEs already in this industry will have to withdraw from it or seek joint operation with those large-sized SOEs that are able to match these conditions, at the cost of the control of their own management.

4.2.2 Urban Public Utilities

After the country's reform and opening up, China's general guidelines on urban public utilities were to distinguish public and private sectors, governmental and market mechanisms, and both the macroscopic administration of government and the microscopic operation of enterprises, to incrementally break the monopoly of urban public utilities by the government and public sectors, and, finally, to open the industry to non-governmental organizations and FFEs. In recent years, the marketization of urban public utilities has continued to increase. In December 2012, the Ministry of Construction introduced *Opinions on Accelerating the Marketization of the Municipal Utility Industry*, which clearly intended to quicken the marketization process and introduce competition mechanisms, as well as to allow non-governmental capital to participate in the investment, construction, reconstruction, and operation of municipal gas, heat, water, and electricity networks and public transportation.

In the field of municipal water utilities, Suez Lyonnaise des Eaux of France had invested in Tanzhou Water Company of Zhongshan City, Guangdong Province, as early as 1992, which marks the beginning of foreign investment in China's water services market. In January 2003, Santong Mechanical Maintenance Company, an NGE of Guangdong, bought out the permanent operation of the water company of Xinzhou District, Wuhan City at the price of RMB 8.8 million. In the field of gas, ENN Energy Corporation, an NGE, has been supplying gas for the Langfang Development Zone of Hebei Province since 1993 and begun extending to other cities since 1998. So far it has obtained the exclusive operation of gas networks in over 30 cities, including those in Beijing, Hebei, Shandong, Anhui, Jiangsu, Zhejiang, Henan, and so forth. Its service covers an urban population of approximately 10 million. In early 2002, Qionglai City of Sichuan Province signed an agreement with the non-governmental Ruiyun Group on the development and construction of its new urban area and handed over to the latter the overall construction of the 5 km^2 new urban area and the operating rights to its public utilities. In this way, Ruiyun Group obtained the right to the construction and management of this new area and a franchise monopoly on the municipal public utilities, including water, electricity, gas, public transportation, and so forth., for 50 years.[2] Since 2000, Beijing has loosened the restriction on NGEs' entry into the public utilities fields, such as the production and distribution of electricity, gas, and water. For example, in the first quarter of 2005, Beijing had absorbed social capital of about RMB 11 billion in this industry and had introduced non-governmental capital into 11 projects concerning 10 types of urban public infrastructure, such as water, heat, gas, waste disposal, toll highways, rail transit, and so forth. In Jiangsu Province, 849 NGEs had entered the public infrastructure or monopolistic industries in the production and distribution of electricity, gas, and water by the end of

[2]Lu Hongyou. (2007). *Studies on Operational and Administrative Mechanisms of China's Urban Public Utilities*. Beijing: Economic Management Press, p. 60.

2005.[3] In Zhejiang Province, NGEs in the industry of social security and welfare totaled 620, while those involved in the production and distribution of electricity, gas, and water totaled 717 by the end of 2006, an increase of 42% and 53%, respectively, on an annual basis.[4] In the field of public transportation, Shiyan City of Hubei Province introduced Fivehorse Auto Hire Company, an NGE based out of Wenzhou, which bought out the operation of 22 bus lines already opened in Shiyan for 18 years at the price of RMB 8 million each year. Though the public utilities enterprises were nationalized again by the municipal government in May 2008, the reform of Shiyan has had a profound influence on other cities in China. As a matter of fact, many cities have introduced NGEs in their ongoing reformation of public utilities enterprises. In the field of urban infrastructure construction, the best known example is Hangzhou Bay Cross-Sea Bridge in Zhejiang Province, which represents an investment of RMB 11.8 billion. In the non-governmental investment of 35%, Songcheng Group has a share of 17.3%; Cixi Jianqiao Investment Corp., 12.83%; Youngor Group, 4.5%; and Cixi Tianyi Investment Co., Ltd. and Cixi Xingqiao Co., Ltd. both have limited shares. In the sewage disposal field, Shanghai Union—85% of which is made up of non-governmental investment—has won the franchise rights of Zhuyuan Sewage Treatment Plant, the largest sewage disposal project in Shanghai.

Through this analysis of NGEs' entry into the urban public utilities industries, we find that it is different from other monopolized industries—it represents a divided rather than chained monopoly, it involves quite a number of disparate fields, and the country's urban infrastructure construction requires enormous funds in the context of rapidly-increasing urbanization. Limited by the financial strength of the local government, almost all the cities involved have taken the measure of lowering investment barriers and introducing non-governmental capital, which has made this industry one of the monopolistic fields with the largest-scale entry of NGEs. The key problem in the process of NGEs' entry, however, is that policy continuity cannot be guaranteed. The present municipal policy encouraging NGEs' entry cannot guarantee the same attitude will be present in future policies. It is not rare that new policies deny the practice of the old and NGEs suffer for the change.

4.2.3 The Air Transport Industry

As early as January 1987, the State Council approved the *Report on the Reform Program and Implementation Procedures of the Civil Aviation Management*

[3] Huang Mengfu. (2006). *Report on the Development of China's NGEs (No. 4) 2005–2006*. Beijing: Social Sciences Academic Press, p. 460.

[4] Huang Mengfu. (2007). *Report on the Development of China's NGEs (No. 4) 2006–2007*. Beijing: Social Sciences Academic Press, p. 375.

System and subsequently implemented the management system reform of the industry with a focus on the separation of administration, airline companies, and airports. In 1990, the SOE monopoly of China's air transportation industry was broken and an oligarchic competition within the domestic airline market started to take shape. By the end of 2000, there were 35 national and local airline companies in China, but their debt-to-equity ratio was generally above 80%. For some airports, the figure was between 30% and 40%. All the airline companies ran into a funding bottleneck in the course of their development. To alleviate capital pressure on the civil aviation industry, the State Council passed the *Notice of the State Council on the Issuance of the Civil Aviation System Reform Program* at the 121st premier office conference in January 2002, which marked the kick-off of the second round of reforms of China's civil aviation system. Against this background, China Eastern Airlines Wuhan Company was founded on August 18, 2002. At the same time, an NGE called the Juneyao Group (Shanghai) appeared in the shareholding structure of the company. Wenzhou Juneyao Group was the first NGE to enjoy equal participation in China's civil aviation industry. At the end of January 2003, Wang Junyao, a private entrepreneur, invested RMB 550 million and hosted Yichang Sanxia Airport in Hubei Province, which was the first officially approved purchase of an airport by an NGE in China. Sometime after that, Guangdong Huahao Industry Group acquired 10% of the stock shares of Baiyun International Airport Business Travel Service Co., Ltd., and Chengdu Gingko Restaurant Group obtained 1% of the stock shares of Sichuan Airlines. In March 2003, the largest freight airline company in China was founded. The total investment was RMB 2.5 billion with a registered capital of RMB 2.2 billion. Citic Pacific, a corporation with 16 years of investment experience in the aviation industry, became the first joint-venture enterprise in civil aviation through its equal participation in the industry.[5] In October 2004, China's civil aviation administration approved the operation of Funing Airport in Suifenhe City, Heilongjiang Province, which was the first privately invested and constructed new airport within China while also being a small-sized general aviation heliport covering 130,000 m^2. This marked the first step of China's opening of airport investment to NGEs.[6]

On January 15, 2005, the policy *Business License Stipulations on Public Air Transport Enterprises* was formally implemented in China. According to the stipulations contained therein, NGEs are entitled to the establishment of airlines companies. On August 15, 2005, *Stipulations on Domestic Investment in Civil Aviation Industry (Trial)* was implemented, which further encouraged non-governmental investment in the civil aviation industry. For the first time in

[5]Liu Pingqing. Situation, Problems, and Trends of NGEs' Participation in Public Utilities. In Zhan Houyi, Ming Lizhi, & Liang Chuanyun. (Eds.). (2004). *Report on Development of China's NGEs 2003*. Beijing: Social Sciences Academic Press, pp. 82–98.

[6]Wang Junhao, et al. (2005). *Structural Reorganization, Classified Administration and Coordination Policies of China's Monopoly Industries*. Beijing: The Commercial Press, p. 306.

history, the document has made clear—in the form of regulations—that non-governmental capital is permitted to function as the major shareholder(s) of civil aviation properties and has fully defined the scope of non-governmental investment in the civil aviation industry, including in the fields of public air transport, general aviation, civil airports, air traffic control systems, fuel sales, the storage, transport, and filling of aircrafts, aircraft maintenance, cargo storage, ground services, airline food production and sales, passenger and cargo sales agency, computer reservation system services, aviation settlement, and other related fields. Since 2005, the Civil Aviation Administration of China, following the spirit of these documents, has approved the establishment of 14 civil aviation companies and the operation of over 30 domestic air routes. These include Okay Airways, Spring Airlines, United Eagle Airlines, East Star Airlines, Dazhong Airlines, Kunming Airlines, Eastlink (predecessor of Juneyao Airlines), China Express Airlines, West Air, Datang Qili Aviation, Great Wall Airlines Cargo, YingAn Airlines, Donghai Airlines, and Delong Airlines. Furthermore, according to the *Report on NGEs' Development in Guangdong Province*, Powerfirst Industrial and Zhongfudi Industrial of Shenzhen City succeeded in the joint control of Shenzhen Airlines in 2006, and thus made it the largest non-governmental aviation corporation in China.[7]

In 2008, however, the sudden breakout of the international financial crisis had an enormous impact on China's civil aviation industry. Of the 14 non-governmental aviation companies operating in the country, only Spring Airlines, Juneyao Airlines, and Donghai Airlines were profitable, while all others suffered losses. In particular, Datang Qili Aviation and Dazhong Airlines were abortive before their maiden flights, even though they had previously received their air operator's certificates. The non-governmental aviation sector was faced with seemingly inevitable extermination (Table 4.2).

Founded in 2005, East Star Airlines had to file for bankruptcy in early 2009, because it was unable to repay its debts to China Aviation Oil and Hubei Airport Group (RMB 140 million and 60 million, respectively). As the first licensed non-governmental aviation company, United Eagle Airlines ended up as part of a merger by state-owned airlines. In November 2006, the state-owned Sichuan Airlines invested RMB 20 million and became a shareholder of United Eagle by increasing its capital and number of shares; in July 2007, Sichuan Airlines further invested RMB 20 million and obtained the management rights of United Eagle; in March 2009, Sichuan Airlines owned the controlling share of United Eagle with another investment of RMB 200 million. On October 15, 2009, the Commercial Aircraft Corporation of China (COMAC), Sichuan Airlines Group, and Chengdu Communications Investment Corporation Group (CCIC) signed a cooperation agreement in Chengdu. According to the agreement, the three parties were to restructure United Eagle Airlines and raise its equity capital from RMB 300 million

[7]Huang Mengfu. (2007). *Report on the Development of China's NGEs (No. 4) 2006–2007*. Beijing: Social Sciences Academic Press, p. 440.

Table 4.2 Operating status of select non-governmental aviation companies

Company	Age (year)	Aircraft fleet	Distribution of flights/ routes	Enterprise condition
Spring	5	12 aircrafts including 1 wholly purchased	Based in Shanghai; over 30 domestic air routes	Profited RMB 21.04 million in 2008
Juneyao	4	2 A319 & 6 A320 aircrafts, all rented	Based in Shanghai	Profited RMB 11.5 million in 2008
China Express	4	3 CRJ200ER aircrafts, all rented	Based in Guiyang	–
East Star	4	3 A319 &7 A320 aircrafts, all rented	Based in Wuhan	Bankrupted
Okay	5	11 aircrafts (8 B737-series passenger-cargo carriers, 1 Modern Ark 60, & 2 Y8 general purpose airplanes)	Based in Hangzhou; Tianjin Branch Company; 14 business departments; 20 air routes	Flights suspended in December 2008; all restored on February 16, 2009
United Eagle	5	1 A320–200 & 3 A319–100 aircrafts	Based in Chengdu	Purchased and nationalized by Sichuan Airlines for debts

Source: Wang Xin (June 2010)

to 680 million, with the shareholding ratio being 48% (COMAC), 40.97% (Sichuan Airlines), and 11.03% (CCIC). By then, United Eagle had been completely turned into an SOE. In December 2008, the suspended Okay Airways restored its flights, but it was unable to recover from the setback, as the United States' FedEx had already ended their cooperation. What's more, it was still being confronted with earlier lawsuits. Spring Airlines, whose performance now relies on its travel platform, is also having a hard time keeping its head above water.

Through this analysis of NGEs' entry into the civil aviation industry, we find the following barriers face NGEs looking to enter the field:

First of all, the barrier of economics of scale poses a problem. Aviation companies are complex in terms of construction and operational costs. Unable to make profit in the short run, they have to rely on the support of additional outside funding before they can develop into a certain size. Otherwise, their capital chain is likely to fracture. It has thus far proved to bean insurmountable barrier for NGEs.

Secondly, the administrative control of civil aviation administration is a barrier. Usually, the authorities tends to protect the interests of market developers according to the Grandfather Clause established by the IATA (International Air Transport Association). Naturally, some popular and major air routes are operated by state-owned aviation companies rather than NGEs in spite of their applications for management.

Thirdly, China has an environment that fosters unequal competition. Three of China's largest aviation companies posted losses in 2008, namely, China

Southern Airlines, China Eastern Airlines, and Air China. That being said, Eastern Airlines and Southern Airlines received a state injection of RMB 7 billion and 3 billion, respectively, and Air China Group received an injection of RMB 0.5 billion from the Tianjin Municipal Government. Whereas non-governmental aviation companies, since they cannot and do not enjoy such support, are put at a competitive disadvantage and even go bankrupt or are forced to merge.

Fourthly, NGEs run into the problem of non-market-based pricing mechanisms. The supply of China's aviation fuel is monopolized by China Aviation Oil, and the fuel price is decided by the National Development and Reform Commission and Civil Aviation Administration. As a result, fuel prices cannot accurately or topically reflect the fluctuation of supply and demand in the market. This makes it impossible for non-governmental aviation companies to make management decisions according to the latest market quotations.

4.2.4 Petroleum and Telecommunications

At present, the extraction and refining of China's oil represents a typical oligopoly. The vast majority of the country's oil resources are divided up among the large-sized SOEs, i.e., CNPC, Sinopec, and CNOOC (China National Offshore Oil Corporation). According to the data of Meng Xianduo et al. (2007), CNPC and Sinopec have obtained the exploration rights to about 90% of China's petroliferous sedimentary basins (over 4 million square kilometers); external cooperations concerning oil from neritic to offshore areas are monopolized by the three giants and predominated by CNOOC; the petroleum refineries are made up of CNPC, Sinopec, and some local refining enterprises; in the sales of petroleum, CNPC and Sinopec are in charge of wholesale distribution, while CNPC, Sinopec, some special users, and private gas stations are in charge of the retail of oil products. Thus, the large state-owned groups have completely taken on the petroleum refinery capacities and entirely control the supply channels of oil products in China.

In spite of all this, the reformation of the petroleum industry has been indeed attempted by introducing NGEs into the upper, middle, and lower segments. The first civil chamber of the petroleum industry, CCPI (China Chamber of Commerce for Petroleum Industry), has been founded; the first non-governmental joint venture in the field of petroleum, Great Wall Union Oil Co., was established; some petroleum-based NGEs have begun a project of joint investment and cooperation with the country's large-sized SOEs or FFEs (foreign-funded enterprises); non-governmental and other forms of capital has entered such fields as oil extraction, pipeline transportation, petroleum refining, the wholesale and retailing of oil products, and so forth. According to a 2007 study by Meng Xianduo, there are currently more than 80 NGEs engaged in oil extraction; about 100 NGEs are engaged in petroleum refining (with a total capacity of 80 million tons); in the wholesale oil products field, there are about 200 NGEs, or 8% of the total enterprise in this field (which sell 5% the total oil products in China); in the retail field, NGEs have a 13% market share of oil products and possess over 40,000 oil stations, 43% of the total amount in China.

For a long time, telecommunications has been an industry with high monopoly prices and profits in China. From 1998 to 2008, China's telecommunications industry had experienced several separation-oriented reforms. An oligopoly market has already taken shape in the basic telecommunications services field, which is currently dominated by China Telecom, China Mobile, China Nand so forthom, and China Unicom. With the increasing marketization within industries, the country's administration has introduced some policies that encourage NGEs' entry into the telecommunications industry, but the main field being opened in practice is that of value-added services.

In 1993, the State Council approved the opening of some value-added telecommunications services to future private investment and permitted NGEs' entry into these fields, including radio paging, telephone information services, electronic mail, and electronic data interchange.[8] *Regulation of the People's Republic of China on Telecommunications*, released by the State Council in 2000, has given explicit permission to investment by NGEs, as well as their operation of or participation in all telecommunications services.[9] According to the data in *Yearbook of China's Information Industry 2007 (Telecommunications Volume)*, by the end of 2006, there were 22,000 operators of value-added services in telecommunications nationwide, of which 20,800, or 95%, were NGEs or inclusive of non-governmental investment; in the basic telecommunications services field, nearly 500 enterprises were inclusive of non-governmental investment and operating basic telecommunications services, as opposed to value-added services.[10] Statistics from the former Ministry of Information Industry show that in the newly approved mobile terminal producers, 70% are NGEs, and in the manufacturers of telecommunication equipment, NGEs also make up a considerable proportion, the best known being Huawei and ZTE.

As opposed to the entry barriers of other industries, the barriers to NGEs' entry into the petroleum industry are mainly the strategic prevention of the dominant enterprises, that is, the dominating state-owned petroleum enterprises place obstacles to NGEs' entry by means of the administrative power of the government. Take, for example, the oil extraction in Yulin of Shaanxi Province. In April 1994, CNPC and Shaanxi Provincial Government signed the *Agreement on the Exploitation of*

[8]Editorial Board. (2007). *Yearbook of China's Information Industry 2007(Telecommunications Volume)*, p. 203.

[9]Huang Mengfu. (2006). *Report on the Development of China's NGEs (No. 4) 2005–2006*. Beijing: Social Sciences Academic Press, p. 186.

[10]Editorial Board. (2007). *Yearbook of China's Information Industry 2007(Telecommunications Volume)*, p. 203.

Petroleum Resources in Northern Shaanxi, which crossed out an area of 1080 km^2 from the Changqing and Yanchang Oilfields for the entrusted or joint development of related counties/districts (like Yanan and Yulin) and determined an area of 3500 km^2 south of Jingbian to be under the joint exploration and development of Changqing Oilfield and associated local enterprises. Due to the lack of funds and technology, some of the local drilling and extracting enterprises learned from the central oil enterprises the experience of "joint drilling, divided entrusting, and oil-well contracting." By the end of 2000, 1039 individual and private investors had been introduced, 4473 oil wells had been sunk, and the oil production capacity had reached 1 million tons, or 1/6 of the total capacity in the region. Later, however, Shaanxi Yanchang Petroleum (Group) Corp. Ltd. unincorporated all the NGEs of oil extraction therein and centralized their management, with the help of the administrative power of the provincial government and on the pretext of chaotic management caused by too many small joint operators with no technology. The NGEs involved in oil extraction at that point had to withdraw from the region once and for all.

The telecommunications industry shows a similar situation to that of the petroleum industry. With a high profit rate of 20% in China (it is no more than 10% in other countries and less than 1% in U.S., even with a developed telecommunications industry.), SOEs of telecommunications tend to strategically prevent non-state-owned enterprises' (NSOEs') entry by way, for example, of the government's promulgation of related regulations regarding administration, and, in doing so, ensure their own high monopoly profits.

4.2.5 Railway Transportation

The railway transportation industry is deemed to be the strongest fortress left over by the earlier state-run planning system of China. Huge social demand has created the urgent need for various types of investment, however, including non-governmental investment. In July 2005, the Ministry of Railways (dissolved as of 2013) released the *Executive Opinions on Encouraging, Supporting, and Guiding the Participation of Non-Governmental Sectors of the Economy in the Construction and Operation of Railways*, which clearly states the fields of the railway industry that are to be opened to non-governmental capital, namely, railway construction, passenger and cargo transport, manufacturing of railway transportation equipment, and the diversified operation of railways. Moreover, the marketing reform of the railway sectors have long been attempted. In the first half of 1998, the railway administration approved a schedule for those baggage trains contracted by Huang Wu-xue, owner of a private automobile transportation enterprise in Guangzhou, and for the container trains contracted by Huayu Container Trains Transport Co., Ltd. of Shaoxing, Zhejiang Province. This broke the existing monopoly on baggage and container trains by state-owned railway enterprises held up until that point. By the end of 2005, there were 26 joint-venture railway companies in operation, with the total assets of RMB 113.8 billion and an operating kilometrage of 8777 km.[11] A number of construction projects, e.g., Shijiazhuang-Taiyuan Passenger Line and Qianan-Caofeidian Railway, absorbed over RMB 40 billion of equity funds from non-governmental investors.[12] According to the *Report on NGEs' Development in Guangdong Province*, Shenzhen Sinotech Logistics Co., Ltd. had acquired 100% equity of Luoding Railway through the process of auctioning and bidding, which thus made it the first railway in China under the absolute equity control of an NGE.[13] Nanjing Weilong Corporation, an NGE, joined hands with the Nanjing Railway Economic Development Corporation and established Nanjing Yiyuan Logistic Company, which manages the state-owned railway asset, Andemen Freight Yard. Nanjing Weilong holds 60% the equity of the newly founded company and has pioneered NGEs' entry into the railway freight transport field.[14] In November 2005, Jianan Railway Project in Jingcheng was approved by the Ministry of Railways. It was a RMB 2.3 billion project invested in by the non-governmental Yufeng Jianan Railway Co., Ltd. Jianan Railway covers 64.92 km and links Jiafeng Station on the Houma-Yueshan Line in the west and Chenpu Station on the Taiyuan-Jiaozuo Line in the east, and is China's first railway completely invested in and constructed by non-governmental capital. According to a report by the Xinhua News Agency on August 20, 2009, the first-phase project of Bayanwula-Xinqiu Railway was started on November 10, 2007. Covering 487 km, Baxin Railway was controlled by the non-governmental Chuncheng Group of Liaoning Province, with equity participation by the Ministry of Railways, Tiefa Group, Fuxin Mining Group, Fuxin City Investment Corp., Datang Group, China Resources Group, and Beijing Energy Group. The first-phase project represented an investment of RMB 5.87 billion.

There are three prominent problems in NGEs' entry into the railway transportation industry at present.

The first is that the administrative system overseeing the railway industry is still a mixture of certain functions of the government and enterprises. The Ministry of Railways dominates enterprises' behavior by means of administrative regulations and allocates all the transport resources mainly by way of administrative orders. As the Ministry of Railways holds too much power to be contended with, railways invested in and constructed by local governments are usually taken over by the Ministry at low prices, to say nothing of those invested in and built by private

---

[11]Huang Mengfu. (2006). *Report on the Development of China's NGEs (No. 4) 2005–2006*. Beijing: Social Sciences Academic Press, p. 186.

[12]Huang Mengfu. (2007). *Report on the Development of China's NGEs (No. 4) 2006–2007*. Beijing: Social Sciences Academic Press, p. 163.

[13]Ibid., p. 440.

[14]Huang Mengfu. (2006). *Report on the Development of China's NGEs (No. 4) 2005–2006*. Beijing: Social Sciences Academic Press, p. 460.

investors. As a result, railway transportation has remained the industry with the least amount of entry by NGEs even up to now. For NGEs, the height and strength of entry barriers mainly lie in the overall system of a monopolized industry, rather than the policy preferences.

Secondly, NGEs are faced with the great risks brought by the unique pricing and settlement mechanisms of the country's monopolistic industries. In China, the Ministry of Railways decides the prices of both passenger and freight railway transport and centralizes the railway transport liquidation accordingly. According to *Measures for the Liquidation of Railway Transportation Revenue* released by the Ministry of Railways, the ministry collects the transportation income of all the railway bureaus and other railway transport enterprises and reallocates the money among the bureaus and enterprises on the basis of pricing policies and allocation rules also made by the Ministry. Then the bureaus and enterprises identify their respective business incomes and costs in accordance with the allocated sums of money. Railway transportation enterprises have practically no right to participate in setting prices, neither can they respond quickly to the market, and thus there is no guarantee of their profitability. All these elements are something that NGEs have to take into consideration before their entry into the market.

Thirdly, the strong barrier of economies of scale stands in the way. As is widely known, railway construction requires huge funds, and it takes a long time to recover any initially-invested capital and see profits. Nevertheless, as we have seen, it is possible to break through the even remarkable scale-economy barrier of such an industry as railway transportation with the growing power of NGEs.

4.3 Breakup of Monopolies: A Logical Deduction

Even with so many barriers and risks of entering the monopolistic industries, NGEs' entry is inexorable. Not only have the central and local governments released several policies and measures that encourage NGEs' entry into the monopolistic industries, NGEs have also made various explorations and attempts of their own in order to facilitate their entry into these industries. The following are our suggestions and countermeasures regarding NGEs' entry into the monopolistic industries.

4.3.1 Propel the Overall Reformation of Monopolistic Industries and Lower Their Admittance Threshold

As we have analyzed previously, the institutional and administrative monopoly is at the root of monopolized industries. Therefore, the fundamental measure necessary to lower the existing barriers to entry is to strengthen the reformation of these industries. The State Council released the 36 Provisions on Non-Public Sectors of Economy in 2005 and the new 36 Provisions on May 7, 2010, which shows the determination and policy orientation of the central government in this regard. Due to the overall institutional restriction of these industries, however, the reality of NGEs' entry is far from what has been expected. Hence, in order to break the monopoly, the primary task going forward must be to conduct an overall reformation of the monopolized industries, improve and elaborate the system for accessing them, and convert the country's short-term policies and principles into regular systems and executive mechanisms.

To accomplish this, the first thing that must be done is to formulate as soon as possible a general plan and implement rules outlining the marketing reform of the monopolistic industries. By learning from the experience of SOE reform, we must establish goals, steps, and paths to the relaxation of control and marketing reform of each monopolized industry according to their respective features and on the principle of pragmatic implementation and key-point breakthroughs, and only then work out the corresponding supportive measures.

Secondly, settle the legal status of NGEs in terms of their entry into the monopolistic industries as soon as possible. In coordination with the implementation of *The Anti-Monopoly Law of the People's Republic of China*, modify monopoly-related laws such as the *Telecommunications Act*, the *Railways Act*, the *Electric Power Law*, and the *Civil Aviation Law* on the principle of fairness, justice, and equality. Free NGEs entering the monopolistic industries from the discriminations and restrictions previously imposed by the monopolistic enterprises, and ensure their legal status and treatment as equal to those of SOEs and their own interests under the effective protection of the country's laws.

Finally, it's important to speed up the reformation of the administration system of monopolistic industries. The key is to make breakthroughs in the following areas:

First, speed up the reformation of investment examinations and the approving institution. For privately invested projects in those monopolistic industries involving no additional government-monopolized resources like land, cancel the administrative examination and approval procedure and introduce the project registration system; once they are registered and listed on the annual construction plan, investment and construction should be allowed to start immediately. For those requiring additional government-monopolized resources, construction may start directly if the resources are obtained by the enterprises in fairly-competitive ways, such as through auctions and bidding; if the resources are obtained through governmental examination and approval, the administrative department should make public the examination and approval procedures, simplify the associated steps, and exercise online or one-stop examination and approval so as to improve the efficiency of the process.

Secondly, make government affairs public and establish a system of information disclosure for the administrative department. Release to the public the major measures and polices associated with governmental development and reform adopted by the administration, information about industrial investment guidance, the bidding and tendering information related to key projects, and predictions on the general development of both the economy and society by means of semi-regular disclosures of information, media bulletins in magazines, on TV, and through the internet, news articles, interviews, and so forth., and guide non-governmental investors to make scientific decisions and their reduce risks of investment in order to avoid redundant construction and the waste of social resources.

Third, speed up the establishment of the agency service market. Develop normatively private agency service institutions related to investment consultation, assessment, accounting, legal services, auditing, designing, supervision, bidding and tendering, technological innovation, and more. Actively cultivate those investment agency institutions of strong economic and technical power and high authority. Optimize the service system of non-governmental investment by strengthening its management and establishing a self-disciplining mechanism for the agency industry, while promoting the market competition of agency services and improving the quality of agency services.

4.3.2 Re-examining China's Strategy for Large Enterprises

In the context of economic globalization, we do, in fact, need a number of large enterprises with that are strongly competitive, but it is rather risky to pin the hope of realizing this strategy merely on the country's SOEs, due to their institutional and administrative defects as well as the increasingly strong control of interest groups. On the other hand, the NGEs of China have gone through 30 years of fierce competition and market practice, and some excellent enterprises have subsequently come into prominence and are equipped with the preliminary competence and power necessary for international competition. Therefore, it is important to re-examine China's large-enterprise strategy and regard NGEs as an important part of that strategy. On this basis, allowing powerful NGEs to enter the basic monopoly industries and encouraging them to grow bigger and stronger will allow some symbiotic clusters of large governmental and non-governmental enterprises to form. Meanwhile, it is necessary to transcend the "capitalization" strategy of SOEs' growth and change it into "privatization"[15] when conditions permit, and restructure the SOEs in competitive fields into enterprises of diversified ownerships or even put them under the control of non-governmental capital, so as to promote the international competitiveness of China's large enterprises through the optimization of enterprise systems. What's more, it is necessary to inhibit the influence of interest

[15]Here "privatization" refers to the state of new NGEs' entry into the monopolized industries; while "capitalization" refers to the entry of private capital into the ownership structure of state-owned monopolized enterprises. Only when the equity of non-governmental investors exceeds the holding proportion of an SOE is the "capitalization" of significance to "privatization."

groups' behaviors on governmental policy-making while strengthening the independent administration and supervision of the government itself.

4.3.3 Exploring Mechanisms of Aid for NGEs' Entry into Monopolistic Industries

Though some large-sized NGEs are powerful enough to enter the monopolized industries themselves, most NGEs still lack the strength required. The most outstanding problems facing them are financing difficulties and the shortage of the key production elements, such as human capital. Accordingly, the establishment of an aiding mechanism will enable NGEs to obtain the necessary production elements at lower costs and, in doing so, grow larger and stronger, and ultimately spur more NGEs to enter the monopolistic industries.

First of all, it is necessary to speed up the development and innovation of all sorts of industrial investment funds, industrial bonds, and trust investment certificates, and to support qualified NGEs to seek financing by listing on the stock market. This can be accomplished by selecting some large monopolistic projects with excellent economic benefits and market prospects and initiating a pilot trial for both industrial investment funds and specialized trust investment funds. Furthermore, it would be beneficial to encourage some NGEs with sound performance to list and seek financing on the stock market or to issue enterprise bonds in the form of straight bonds, convertible bonds, and so forth.

Secondly, governmental funds and resources should be used to flexibly assist NGEs' entry into the monopolistic industries. For public-welfare or some quasi productive monopoly projects, the government should encourage NGEs' entry by means of capital injection, discount loans, financing guarantees, return compensation, tax reduction, the preferential supply of land for construction, and a combination of projects with different income rates. The capital injection by the government should be strictly limited to public-welfare projects and a few quasi productive projects existing under a strong natural monopoly. It is necessary to reasonably decide the proportion of governmental injection, appropriately lower the governmental proportion of involvement and correspondingly increase NGEs' investment in these projects according to their degree of public welfare or marketization and on the principle of promoting the enterprises' capacity for financing in the market and the virtuous circle of their operation. In terms of return compensation, compensation standards should be calculated and determined on the basis of a development plan for the country's monopolistic industries, the reasonable costs of enterprises, and the average profit margin of the society, and done in association with the existing resource supply and product purchases promised by the government. The government and enterprises should create contracts to legally restraint and regularize the behavior of all parties concerned, as well as to guarantee the fulfillment of the promises made by associated administrative departments and enterprises. For enterprises of relatively strong levels of investment, financing, and comprehensive operational strengths, project portfolios should be adopted when possible. By this method, when such enterprises undertake the construction and operation of public-welfare or quasi productive infrastructures, they will be entitled to the advertising operations of the infrastructures, priority in developing a certain amount of real estate, or the construction and operation of some profitable projects within related regions.

Thirdly, the investment of pioneering capital, venture capital, and private equity funds should be encouraged for those NGEs already in the monopolistic industries. With the opening of the Growth Enterprise Market, some NGEs preparing to enter or already in the monopolistic industries can consolidate their economic and technological strengths by taking advantage of these types of capital. The government should release related provisions on the investment of pioneering and venture capital in the monopolistic industries so as to provide an institutional guarantee for the entry and withdrawal of such types of capital.

4.3.4 Constructing Withdrawal Mechanisms for Monopolistic Industries

To encourage NGEs' entry into the monopolistic industries, it is very important to construct a mechanism for the withdrawal of non-governmental investment from these industries. If investors deem it hard to withdraw once they enter these industries, they tend to be extremely cautious about their entry in the first place. Therefore, it is necessary to construct an exchange market for the smooth transactions of property rights by way of bidding and auctioning according to the characteristics of monopolistic industries, such as petroleum, electricity, telecommunications, aviation, urban water, electricity, the gas supply, expressways, rail transit, and so forth., and to make it possible for the quick compensation of transfers or retransfers of the property and management rights of the enterprises involved, so as to establish an institutional system for the normalized entry and withdrawal of non-governmental capital. The governmental should study and, as soon as possible, formulate laws and regulations outlining the transfers of property and management rights in the monopolistic industries, including those aspects related to property rights definition, assets evaluation, approval procedures, transfer contracts, transferee qualifications, and so forth. At the same time, the government should establish an assistance mechanism for NGEs' withdrawal under special circumstances. For example, it is possible that the government used to encourage NGEs' entry into certain fields but now restricts their entry and development in these same fields. In this case, the government should compensate for the losses to NGEs caused by the withdrawal. For small enterprises with obsolete production equipment and outdated technology, which are unable to meet the environmental protection requirements of the state and incapable of independent withdrawal, the government can even take the assistive measure of acquisition and invalidation necessary for their withdrawal.

4.3.5 Encouraging Innovation of the Mode of Entry and Improving the Entry Success Rate

As they enter into the country's monopolized industries, Chinese NGEs have innovated several practical modes and adopted various strategies that have effectively improved the success rate of their entry. Thus, as NGEs enter the monopolistic industries, they must not follow the same pattern previously set by large SOEs, but should create different entry modes according to the specific conditions of their own management and following applicable regulations, technology, and spatial features of the monopolistic industries themselves. For example, in the field of infrastructure construction, the BOT, BT, and CBOT modes have proved feasible; in the fields of electricity, railway transportation, municipal public utilities, aviation, and so forth., it is highly recommended for NGEs to adopt a pattern relying on independent decision-making units with control rights. In addition, it is necessary to study the changes in governmental policies as they relate to the country's monopolistic industries and to avoid direct engagement in the naturally monopolized businesses, and so forth., which are empirical principles set up to improve the rate of entry success. Only in this way can NGEs improve their success rate of entry into monopolistic industries.

Bibliography

Bai M, Lei J (2006) Performance analysis of monopolistic SOEs. Res Dev (5)
Bain JS (1956) Barriers to new competition. Harvard University Press, Cambridge, MA
Baumol W, Panzar J, Willing R (1982) Contestable markets and the theory of market structure. Harcourt, Brace, Jovanovich, New York
Carlton DW, Perloff JM (1998) Modern industrial organization (Chinese version). The Joint Publishing Company & Shanghai People's Publishing House, Shanghai
Dai Z (2006) Logic in the evolution of China telecom industry: a framework of analysis. Econ Manag (24)
Demsetz H (1982) Barriers to entry. Am Econ Rev 72(1):47–57
Fan H, Wang W, Liu X (2007) Administration of Beijing's public utilities: status, problems and countermeasures. In: ZUFE, CIRD (eds) China: reform of governmental regulation system. Economic Press of China, Beijing
Ju J (2009) NGEs' entry into monopoly industries. Economy & Management Publishing House, Beijing
Ju J, Han X et al (2004) Non-governmental enterprises, non-governmental capital & economic policies. China Financial & Economic Publishing House, Beijing
Li T (2002) Market barriers to entry. Shanghai University of Finance & Economics Press, Shanghai
Meng X, Peng J, Yu Z (2007) Some doubts on breaking industry monopoly. China Pet Enterp (8)

Shepherd WG, Shepherd JM (2007) The economics of industrial organization (Chinese version). China Renmin University Press, Beijing
Wang J (2006) Introduction to governmental regulation economics: basic theories and application in governmental regulation practice. The Commercial Press, Beijing
Wang X (2010) Development trends of China's non-governmental aviation sector under the financial crisis. Internal Draft
Wang J et al (2010) Studies on deepening the reform of China's monopoly industries. China Social Sciences Press, Beijing
Xie D (2007) Interaction between SOEs adjustment and government rule formulation reform in natural monopoly industries. Economic Science Press, Beijing, p 328
Yang T (2003) Reform of administrative examination and entry of non-governmental enterprises. Res Financ Econ Issues (11)
Yu L, Zhang W (2003) A research on the pricing theory of strong natural monopolies and the regulatory system of electricity price in China. Econ Res J (9)
Yu L, Zhang W (2010) Intensity and efficiency loss of industry administrative monopoly in China. Econ Res J (3)
Zheng S (2007) On restructuring of natural monopoly industries and ways of accession of private enterprises. J Ningbo Univ 20(2)

Chapter 5
Corporate Governance and Its Modernization: The Fundamental Basis of NGEs' Growth and Development in the New Stage

Fengyong Lü

As many research findings have revealed, it is beneficial in terms of ongoing and future enterprise performance for NGEs to adopt a governance model that fits best with their development at different stages and under circumstances, and, furthermore, that there is no fixed, optimal model of governance. Hence, the governance model of enterprises must change in accordance with the corresponding changes in their development and environment. Otherwise, it will inevitably impede the promotion of enterprise performance and even hamper potential development and growth. Globally widespread, the governance model of family enterprises can promote NGEs' growth at particular stages of development. Even when an enterprise has succeeded in listing on the stock market and appears as a public enterprise, it can still achieve excellent performance under the family control if the details of its governance model are arranged appropriately.

In the new stage, the development of NGEs is characterized by greater diversity in the form of variations in shareholding structure, scale, industry, technology, market, and so forth. As China's NGEs share rather notable family characteristics, the in-depth exploration of the family governance model, especially the arrangement of the specific governance mechanism, will help China's NGEs, in particular those inclined to exercise family governance, select a more appropriate governance model in the future, and promote their smooth development.

F. Lü (✉)
Chinese Academy of Social Sciences, Beijing, China

Y. Liu (ed.), *New Interpretations on the Development of China's Non-Governmental Enterprises*, Research Series on the Chinese Dream and China's Development Path, DOI 10.1007/978-981-10-3872-3_5

5.1 The Governance Structure of NGEs: Status and Classifications

5.1.1 The Status of NGEs' Governance Structure

According to the large-sample enterprise statistics of 2008, 93,596 enterprises were defined as non-governmental, of which, 7858—or 8.4%—were collective holding NGEs, 81,967—or 87.6%—were private holding NGEs, and 3771—or 4.0%—were holding NGEs of other types. Of the private holding NGEs, 56.5% were registered as private limited companies, the largest in number; the next were limited companies of other types and wholly-owned private companies, making up 15.7% and 14.6%, respectively, of the total overall; only 2.4% were registered as companies limited by shares. Figure 5.1 shows the distribution of registered types of private holding NGEs.

In order to perform an in-depth analysis of the governance structure of NGEs and its influence on enterprise performance, we selected the data of 597 NGEs from the competition survey database of NGEs' competitiveness in 2007, collected by the CASS Center for Private Economic Studies, and used them as the basis for our analysis. Of the 597 enterprises distributed in 13 provinces/municipalities, 185 were in Zhejiang Province, 75 in Jiangsu Province, 62 in Beijing Municipality, 58 in Guangdong Province, 51 in Hebei Province, 46 in Liaoning Province, 35 in Fujian Province, 31 in Shanghai Municipality, 25 in Yunnan Province, 20 in Hubei Province, seven in Shandong Province, one in Jiangxi Province, and one in Sichuan Province.

We approached the status of NGEs' governance structure from the following perspectives: shareholding structure, organizational structure, board structure, the status of ownership and control and management rights, the structure of senior management sources, and incentive mechanisms, and then classified and analyzed NGEs' governance models according to their characteristics.

5.1.1.1 Shareholding Structure

Table 5.1 shows the shareholding structure of NGEs in 2006. Of the 597 NGEs, 92 (15.4%) are below 30% in the proportion of enterprise equity held by the owner/s and their immediate relatives, 60 (10.1%) are between 30% and 50%, and 445 (74.5%) are above 50%. As judged by the shareholding structure, the majority of NGEs are still under the absolute equity control of the owner/s and their immediate relatives, which indicates the highly concentrated ownership of NGEs in general.

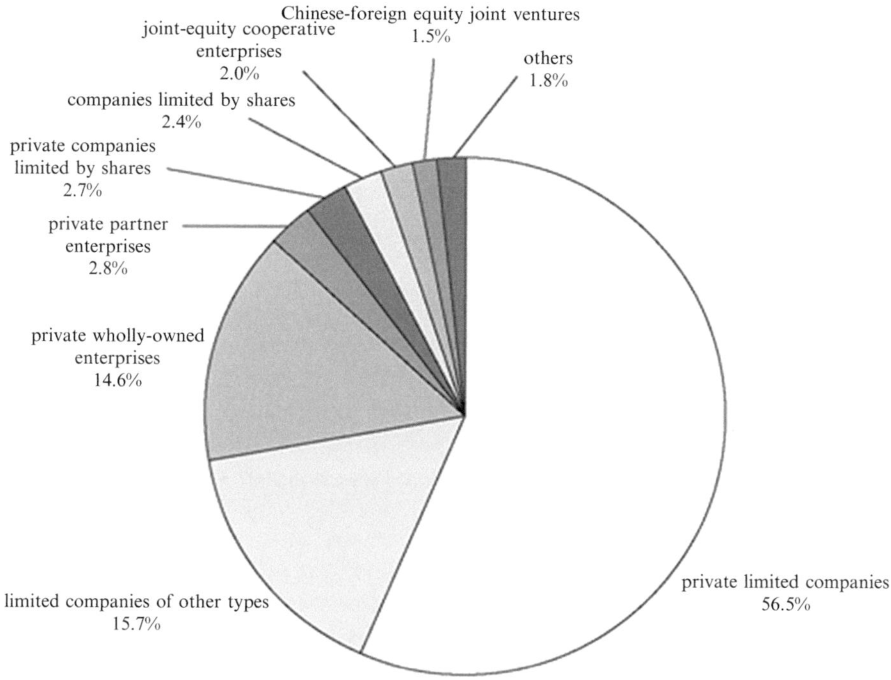

Fig. 5.1 Registered types of private holding NGEs 2008 (Source: Survey data of industrial enterprises in 2008, CASS Center for Private Economic Studies)

Table 5.1 Shareholding structure of NGEs 2006

	Proportion of equity held by owner/s and immediate relatives(%)		
	≤30	30 ~ 50	≥50
NGE numbers	92	60	445
Proportion (%)	15.4	10.1	74.5

Source: Competition survey database of NGEs' competitiveness in 2007, CASS Center for Private Economic Studies

5.1.1.2 Organizational Structure

Table 5.2 shows the organization structure of NGEs in 2006. Of the 597 NGEs, 524 (87.8%) have formed boards of directors, 346 (58.0%) have formed boards of supervisors, and 320 (53.6%) have both. As the majority of NGEs have boards of directors, quite a number have boards of supervisors, and more than half have both, we can conclude that the organization structure of NGEs is relatively complete at least in the form, which indicates they have made much progress in the exploration of organizational structural modernization.

Table 5.2 Organization structure of NGEs 2006

	Board of directors	Board of supervisors	Both
NGE numbers	524	346	320
Proportion (%)	87.8	58.0	53.6

Source: Competition survey database of NGEs' competitiveness in 2007, CASS Center for Private Economic Studies

Table 5.3 Board composition of NGEs 2006

	Owners' relatives	Independent directors	Major operators	Worker representatives
NGE numbers	135	67	264	67
Proportion (%)	25.8	12.8	50.4	12.8

Source: Competition survey database of NGEs' competitiveness in 2007, CASS Center for Private Economic Studies

5.1.1.3 Board Composition

Table 5.3 shows the board composition of NGEs in 2006. Of the 524 boards of directors formed in 597 NGEs, 135 (25.85%) included the relatives of the owners, 67 (12.8%) include independent directors, 264 (50.4%) include major operators, and 67 (12.8%) include worker representatives. According to the composition of the boards of directors, board participation by major operators is common; many boards have included owners' relatives; but the inclusion of worker representatives and/or independent directors is relatively rare. This indicates that NGEs are still relatively undeveloped in terms of board composition and have further room for improvement.

5.1.1.4 Structure of Ownership and Control and Operational Rights

Table 5.4 shows NGEs' ownership structure, control rights, and operation rights in 2006. Of the 597 NGEs investigated, 470 (78.7%) were represented by the owners or their immediate relatives as the legal representative, which indicates the strong control of the owners or their immediate relatives over the enterprises in general and the common unity of ownership and control rights; 379 (63.5%) hold the position of executive general manager (president)filled by the controlling shareholders, which indicates the common unity of ownership and operation rights; 55 (9.2%) have that position filled by close relatives of the controlling shareholders, suggesting that a growing number of NGE' may be transforming into family enterprises; 82 (13.7%) have that position filled by non-controlling shareholders, which indicates the pursuit of some balance between power and responsibility by the controlling and non-controlling shareholders in some NGEs; 81 (13.6%) have

Table 5.4 NGEs' ownership structure, control rights, and operational rights 2006

		Identities of executive general manager/ president			
	Owners/immediate relatives as legal representatives	Controlling shareholders	Immediate relatives of controlling shareholders	Non-controlling shareholders	Others
NGE numbers	470	379	55	82	81
Proportion (%)	78.7	63.5	9.2	13.7	13.6

Source: Competition survey database of NGEs' competitiveness in 2007, CASS Center for Private Economic Studies

Table 5.5 NGEs' structure of senior management sources 2006

	Proportion of family members(%)				Proportion of outsiders(%)			
	0	≤30	30 ~ 70	≥70	0	≤30	30 ~ 70	≥70
NGE numbers	223	153	188	33	144	137	256	60
Proportion (%)	37.4	25.6	31.5	5.5	24.1	22.9	42.9	10.1

Source: Competition survey database of NGEs' competitiveness in 2007, CASS Center for Private Economic Studies

that position filled by other personnel and still fewer by professional managers, which indicates NGEs' weak desire to employ professional managers as senior executives. From this data, we can infer that NGEs have maintained a high degree of unity between ownership and control and operation rights.

5.1.1.5 Senior Management Structure

Table 5.5 clearly shows NGEs' structure of senior executives sources in 2006. Of the 597 NGEs, 223 (37.4%) have not included family members (of the owners) in the senior management; conversely, 62.6% have family members in their senior management, which is a rather high ratio. In light of the proportion of family members in the senior management, 153 NGEs (25.6%) have management structures where the number of immediate family members was below or equal to 30%, 188 (31.5%) are between 30% and 70%, and 33 (5.5%) are above or equal to 70%. Of all the samples included, 144 (24.1%) have hired no outsiders as senior executives, while, conversely, 75.9% of the NGEs included here have hired outsiders as senior executives. In terms of the proportion of outsiders in senior management, 137 NGEs (22.9%) were below or equal to 30%, 256 (42.9%) were between 30% and 70%, and 60 (10.1%) were above or equal to 70%. If we compare the data in Tables 5.4 and 5.5, we can find that though outsiders seldom take the position of executive general manager (president), they generally make up a considerable proportion in the senior management, far larger than that of family members. This indicates that NGEs have made some efforts in the opening and professionalization of enterprise management.

Table 5.6 NGEs' incentive mechanisms by ESOP 2006

Enterprises with ESOP	
NGE number	Proportion (%)
108	18.1

Source: Competition survey database of NGEs' competitiveness in 2007, CASS Center for Private Economic Studies

5.1.1.6 Incentive Mechanisms

Table 5.6 is about NGEs' incentive mechanisms by means of employee stock ownership (ESOP) in 2006. Of the 597 NGEs, 108 (18.1%) have implemented ESOP, which indicates that many NGEs have tried to improve their incentive mechanisms by implementing ESOP.

5.1.2 Categorization and Comparison of NGEs' Governance Models

5.1.2.1 Categorization of NGEs' Governance Models

Classification of NGEs' governance models can be made according to the features of NGEs' governance as described above. In accordance with some theories of corporate governance and the features of NGEs' governance, family equity and the identity of executive general manager (president) have been used as the major criteria of our classification. That is, NGEs are classified into three categories on the basis of their ownership and control rights, namely, as Classical Family Enterprises, Modern Family Enterprises, or Non-Family Enterprises. Classical Family Enterprises are NGEs where the proportion of family representation is above or equal to 50% and the position of executive general manager (president) is filled by the controlling shareholder/s or their immediate relatives. Modern Family Enterprises may be further divided into two types. The first type, marked as Modern Family Enterprises (I), are NGEs where the proportion of family representation is above or equal to 50% but the position of executive general manager (president) is not filled by the controlling shareholder/s or their immediate relatives, while the second type, marked as Modern Family Enterprises (II), are those where the proportion of family representation is below 50% but the position of executive general manager (president) is filled by the controlling shareholder/s or their immediate relatives. Non-Family Enterprises are those where the proportion of family representation is below 50% and the position of executive general manager (president) is not filled by the controlling shareholder/s or their immediate relatives. Classical Family Enterprises, Modern Family Enterprises (I) and Modern Family Enterprises (II) are all governance models of family enterprises.

Table 5.7 shows the classification of NGEs' governance models according to the chosen criteria. Of the 597 samples, 354 (59.3%) are Classical Family Enterprises, 91 (15.2%) are Modern Family Enterprises (I), 77 (12.9%) are Modern Family

Table 5.7 Classification of NGEs by governance models, 2006

Category	Corporate governance: Proportion of family representation(%)	Corporate governance: Identity of executive general manager/president	Number	Proportion (%)
Classical family enterprises	≥50	Controlling shareholder/s or their immediate relatives	354	59.3
Modern family enterprises (I)	≥50	Not controlling shareholder/s or their immediate relatives	91	15.2
Modern family enterprises (II)	<50	Controlling shareholder/s or their immediate relatives	77	12.9
Non-family enterprises	<50	Not controlling shareholder/s or their immediate relatives	75	12.6

Source: Competition survey database of NGEs' competitiveness in 2007, CASS Center for Private Economic Studies

Enterprises (II), and 75 (12.6%) are Non-Family Enterprises. It is easy to see that the majority of NGEs are still family enterprises (87.4%), most of which (over 2/3) are Classical Family Enterprises. This shows that with respect to governance model many NGEs in China still strongly resemble family enterprises.

5.1.2.2 Characteristics of NGEs' Assets Under Different Models of Governance

Table 5.8 shows those assets characteristic of different categories of NGEs. In light of the average assets scale, Non-Family Enterprises rank largest (RMB 501.026 million), followed by Modern Family Enterprises (II) and Classical Family Enterprises, while the category of Modern Family Enterprises (I) is the smallest (RMB 185.771 million). In light of the average per capita assets, Non-Family Enterprises are the largest (RMB 0.651 million), followed by Classical Family Enterprises and Modern Family Enterprises (I), with Modern Family Enterprises (II) as the smallest (RMB 0.345 million). The difference in average per capita assets is relatively small between the three categories of family enterprises, however, but is rather large between Family Enterprises and Non-Family Enterprises. The differences in assets between different categories of NGEs, especially between Classical Family Enterprises and the other categories, are related to their scales and labor-intensiveness. As can be found in Table 5.8, there are 139 labor-intensive enterprises in Classical Family Enterprises, 39.3% of all the enterprises in this category. While in Modern Family Enterprises (I), Modern Family Enterprises (II), and Non-Family Enterprises, labor-intensive enterprises become smaller and smaller in number as well as in proportion, or 36.3%, 29.9%, and 28.0%, respectively. Judged by the data in the tables, Non-Family Enterprises are generally large in scale and obviously capital-intensive. Modern Family Enterprises (II) are of considerable scale and technology-intensive. Classical Family Enterprises and Modern Family Enterprises (I) are smaller in scale due to their single equity structure, but as they are typically

Table 5.8 Characteristics of NGEs' assets under different models of governance, 2006

Category	Average assets		Labor-intensive enterprises	
	Average assets scale (mn RMB)	Average per capita assets (mn RMB)	Number	Proportion (%)
Classical family enterprises	241.538	0.356	139	39.3
Modern family enterprises (I)	185.771	0.350	33	36.3
Modern family enterprises (II)	326.582	0.345	23	29.9
Non-family enterprises	501.026	0.651	21	28.0

Note: Labor-intensive enterprises here only include those in the industries of agriculture, forestry, animal husbandry and fishing, construction and real estate, food and beverages, textiles and clothing, hardware products, household supplies, paper making and printing, and home appliances, but do not include those in the fields of automobile, motorcycle and auto parts, telecommunications and software, and tourism and catering

Source: Competition survey database of NGEs' competitiveness in 2007, CASS Center for Private Economic Studies

labor-intensive, they are generally larger than Modern Family Enterprises (II) in average per capita assets. Modern Family Enterprises (I) are smaller than Classical Family Enterprises in average per capita assets, which may imply the Classical Family Model is better for enterprises of highly concentrated equity because it can promote the management's care for the enterprises, whereas the complex principal-agent relationship may limit the development such enterprises.

5.2 The Relationship Between NGEs' Governance Structure and Performance

A study of the relationship between NGEs' governance structure and performance may be able to serve a significant guidance for NGEs' choice and improvement of an appropriate governance model for its own needs. This section analyzes NGEs' performance under different models of governance and the influence of different variables in governance models on enterprise performance, and discusses how NGEs should choose a governance model that best fits their own development.

5.2.1 NGEs' Performance Under Different Governance Models

Our study mainly focuses on the profitability and operational effectiveness of NGEs under different governance models. It is easy to see in Table 5.9 that Non-Family

Table 5.9 NGEs' performance under different governance models, 2006

Category	Profitability		Operational effectiveness		
	Average profit-tax rate of capital (%)	Average profit-tax rate of sales (%)	Average asset turnover ratio	Average labor productivity (mn RMB)	Average profit-tax ratio of wages
Classical family enterprises	10.61	7.67	1.38	0.4928	2.52
Modern family enterprises (I)	10.41	7.46	1.40	0.4887	2.19
Modern family enterprises (II)	14.57	8.99	1.62	0.5597	2.81
Non-family enterprises	25.10	16.54	1.52	0.9876	9.11

Source: Competition survey database of NGEs' competitiveness in 2007, CASS Center for Private Economic Studies

Enterprises are better in terms of profitability and operational effectiveness. With the average profit-tax rate of capital 25.10%, the average profit-tax rate of sales 16.54%, an average labor productivity of RMB 0.9876 million, the average profit-tax ratio of 9.11, and the average asset turnover ratio of 1.52, they rate much higher than other categories of NGEs and rank first among all indicators except that they are a little lower than Modern Family Enterprises (II) in the average asset turnover ratio. Modern Family Enterprises (II) are second only to Non-Family Enterprises and better than the other two categories of NGEs among all indicators, with their average profit-tax rate of capital of 14.57%; their average profit-tax rate of sales of 8.99%; their average labor productivity of RMB 559,700 million, their average profit-tax ratio of wages of 2.81, and their average asset turnover ratio of 1.62. The other two categories are almost at the same level of performance. But Classical Family Enterprises are generally better than Modern Family Enterprises (I) in profitability and operational effectiveness, and their data are slightly better than those of the latter except for the average asset turnover ratio. For Classical Family Enterprises, the average profit-tax rate of capital is 10.61%, the average profit-tax rate of sales is 7.67%, the average labor productivity is RMB 0.4982 million, the average profit-tax ratio of wages is 2.52, and the average asset turnover ratio is 1.38. The data of Modern Family Enterprises (I) in these same regards are, respectively, 10.41%, 7.46%, RMB 0.4887, 2.19, and 1.40.

Although Non-Family Enterprises generally outperform Family Enterprises according to the data, that does not mean family enterprises must choose the non-family model of operation. This model is suitable for Non-Family Enterprises most likely because it fits in with their scale and stage of development, while most family enterprises are small and therefore may not work well with the non-family

Table 5.10 Performance of NGEs of similar assets scales under different governance models, 2006

Category	Profitability		Operational effectiveness		
	Average profit-tax rate of capital (%)	Average profit-tax rate of sales (%)	Average asset turnover ratio	Average labor productivity (million RMB)	Average profit-tax ratio of wages
Classical family enterprises	10.84	7.91	1.37	0.6836	3.25
Modern family enterprises (I)	11.24	7.00	1.61	0.6499	2.42
Modern family enterprises (II)	15.26	9.04	1.69	0.7124	3.39
Non-family enterprises	28.98	17.46	1.66	1.4824	10.89

Source: Competition survey database of NGEs' competitiveness in 2007, CASS Center for Private Economic Studies

model of operation. To discuss this, we have selected some enterprises of the same assets scale from among the four categories of NGEs, and compared their profitability and operational effectiveness. Table 5.10 is the comparison result of enterprises with an asset scale of over RMB 500 million. If we compare Tables 5.9 and 5.10, we can find that there is little change in the ranking of the indicators, except that Classical Family Enterprises are no longer higher but slightly lower than Modern Family Enterprises (I) in the average profit-tax rate of capital. In addition, the gap between the categories remains almost the same. Non-Family Enterprises once again rank highest in terms of profitability and operational effectiveness; Modern Family Enterprises (II) rank second; while Classical Family Enterprises are still generally better than Modern Family Enterprises (I). Our conclusions in Table 5.10 are consistent with what we find in Table 5.9, which indicates that the assets scale is not the key factor that determines the performance of NGEs under different models of governance.

5.2.2 *Performance of NGEs with Different Governance Characteristics: A Regression Analysis*

To explore the relationship between the governance characteristics and performance of NGEs, we have made regression analyses of their relationship by using regression models based on the ordinary least square method (OLS). The following are two analyses based on the regression models. One is to study the influence of variables in the overall governance characteristics on NGEs' performance, and the other is to study the influence of the governance characteristics of different categories of NGEs on enterprise performance.

5.2.2.1 Overall Analysis: General Characteristics of Performance and Governance

We take the logarithm of an enterprise's sales as the explained variable representing enterprise performance, the logarithm of an enterprise's total assets and employees as the explanatory variable, and using these, express the ownership, organization structure, board composition, ESOP, the identity of executive general manager, and status of family members in senior management as different governance characteristics, and set them as dummy variables. According to these settings, the regression model takes the following form.

$$\text{LOGGS} = \text{C} + \beta_1\text{LOGGA} + \beta_1\text{LOGGE} + \text{D}_1 + \text{D}_2 + \text{D}_3 + \text{D}_4 + \text{D}_5 + \text{D}_6 + \varepsilon \quad (5.1)$$

In the equation, LOGGS represents the logarithm of sales, LOGGA represents the logarithm of total assets, and LOGGE represents the logarithm of total employees. D_1, D_2, D_3, D_4, D_5 and D_6 are dummy variables representing the governance characteristics of the enterprises. Representing shareholding structure, D_1 is 1 when the equity proportion of the owner/s and their immediate relatives is above 50%, and 0 otherwise. Representing organization structure, D_2 is 1 when there are both a board of directors and a board of supervisors, and 0 otherwise. Representing the composition of the directors' board, D_3 is 1 when there are independent directors and representatives of major operators or workers, and 0 otherwise. Representing the status of ESOP, D_4 is 1 when ESOP is implemented, and 0 otherwise. Representing the identity of the executive general manager, D_5 is 1 when the position is filled by the owner or her/his immediate relative, and 0 otherwise. Representing the status of family members in senior management, D_6 is 1 when the proportion of family members is above 30%, and 0 otherwise.

Based on the above models, we conducted the regression of Eq. (5.1) by using the ordinary least square method (OLS). Table 5.11 shows the results.

As we can see in the regression results, the absolute values of t-statistics of the coefficient estimates of Constant term C and Variables LOGGA and LOGGE are relatively large and can pass the critical value test of 1% significance. For the dummy variables, the absolute values of the t-statistics of coefficient estimates of D_3, D_4, and D_6 are large enough to pass the test of 5% significance, while those of D_1, D_2, and D_5 are small and the test results are not significant. The related statistical information is listed in the lower part of the table. The F stats reflect a significant linear regression of the equation. But the goodness of fit of the equation is not satisfactory, which is shown by the low sample determination coefficient (0.374) and modified sample determination coefficient (0.366). Nevertheless, from

Table 5.11 OLS analysis results of NGEs' performance with different governance characteristics (all samples)

Variable	Coefficient	Standard error	t-statistics	Probability
C	1.220	0.169	7.223	0.000
LOGGA	0.443	0.056	7.859	0.000
LOGGE	0.306	0.066	4.631	0.000
D_1	0.062	0.072	0.862	0.389
D_2	0.023	0.062	0.369	0.712
D_3	0.117	0.062	1.974	0.056
D_4	0.166	0.076	2.172	0.030
D_5	0.049	0.069	0.713	0.476
D_6	−0.139	0.063	−2.193	0.029
Sample determination coefficient R2	0.374	Akaike information (AIC)		2.167
Modified sample determination coefficient	0.366	Schmitz information		2.234
D.W statistics	1.748	F stats		43.776

the perspective of our research purposes, the regression results have been able to adequately reflect the influence of the governance characteristics on enterprise performance. The coefficients of D_3, representing board composition, and D_4, representing ESOP, are both positive, so their test results are statistically significant. This indicates better performance is achieved by those enterprises where there are independent directors, major operators, and workers' representatives serving on the board and where ESOP is implemented. The coefficient of D_6, representing the status of family members in senior management, is negative and the test result is statistically significant. This indicates a poorer performance of enterprises where the proportion of family members is above 30% in senior management positions. The coefficient estimates of the other dummy variables have no statistical significance, which indicates the insignificant influence of the shareholding structure, the identity of the executive general manager (president), and whether or not both a board of directors and supervisors exists on enterprise performance.

Enterprises with independent directors, major operators, and workers' representatives serving on the directors' board are more rational in terms of the composition of the board and are less driven by the sheer interests of the shareholders when making decisions regarding the enterprise's development, which therefore helps promote their performance. ESOP is a good incentive mechanism for enterprises, which successfully coordinates the long-term development of enterprises and the career objectives of its employees, in particular management personnel and skilled workers, and therefore helps promote enterprise performance. A high proportion of family members in senior management positions indicates a large number of informal administrative relationships in enterprise operations, which goes against standardized operations and the promotion of an enterprise's performance. Shareholding structure is no more than the allocation of ownership, and has a relatively insignificant influence on a given enterprise's performance unless a rational analysis of the organization's operational and administrative power is made accordingly. As for the board of supervisors, it is not particularly necessary for the development of enterprises; while the establishment and composition of the board of directors is somewhat more significant. This explains why the relatively complete governance structure of both boards have no significant effect on the promotion of enterprise performance. The identity of the executive general manager (president) also has an insignificant effect on the promotion of enterprise performance. This is because many enterprises of different shareholding structures may or may not separate their ownership and operational rights. If we leave aside the shareholding structure and observe the identity of the executive general manager (president) alone, we find a statistically insignificant influence of the identity on the promotion of enterprise performance. But some combination of the ownership and the identity of the executive general manager (president) may have a significant influence on future enterprise performance, which will be further analyzed in the following section.

5.2.2.2 Categorized Analysis: Performance and Governance Characteristics Under Different Models of Governance

We again take the logarithm of an enterprise's sales as the explained variable (representing enterprise performance), the logarithm of an enterprise's total assets and employees as the explanatory variable, and set NGEs' governance models as dummy variables. According to these settings, the regression model takes the following form:

$$\mathrm{LOGGS} = \mathrm{C} + \beta_1 \mathrm{LOGGA} + \beta_1 \mathrm{LOGGE} + \mathrm{E}_1 + \mathrm{E}_2 + \mathrm{E}_3 + \varepsilon \tag{5.2}$$

In this equation, LOGGS, LOGGA, and LOGGE represent the same things as in Eq. (5.1). E_i are dummy variables representing corporate governance models. E_1 is 1 when the enterprise is a Classical Family Enterprise and 0 otherwise; E_2 is 1 when the enterprise is a Modern Family Enterprise (I)and 0 otherwise; E_3 is 1 when the enterprise is a Modern Family Enterprise (II) and 0 otherwise. Based on the above models, we can conduct the regression of Eq. (5.2) by using the ordinary least square method (OLS). Table 5.12 shows the regression results.

As we can see from the regression results, the absolute values of the coefficient estimates of the t-statistics of Constant term C and Variables LOGGA and LOGGE are relatively large and pass the critical value test of 1% significance. The absolute values of the coefficient estimates of t-statistics of dummy variables E_2 and E_3 are large enough to pass the test of 5% significance, while that of E_1 is small and can only pass the test of 10% significance. The related statistical information is listed in the lower part of the table. The F stats reflect a significant linear regression within the equation. The goodness of fit of the equation is not satisfactory, however, as the sample determination coefficient is only 0.374 and the modified sample

Table 5.12 OLS analysis results of NGEs' performance under different governance models

Variable	Coefficient	Standard error	t-statistics	Probability
C	1.401	0.168	8.347	0.000
LOGGA	0.466	0.055	8.411	0.000
LOGGE	0.328	0.066	4.980	0.000
E_1	−0.143	0.090	−1.588	0.113
E_2	−0.351	0.111	−3.163	0.002
E_3	−0.365	0.115	−3.166	0.002
Sample determination coefficient R2	0.373	Akaike information (AIC)		2.158
Modified sample determination coefficient	0.368	Schmitz information		2.203
D.W statistics	1.816	F stats		70.232

determination coefficient is only 0.366. But again, from the perspective of our research purposes, the regression results have been able to reflect the influence of the governance models on enterprise performance.

The coefficients of the dummy variables of Classical Family Enterprises, Modern Family Enterprises (I), and Modern Family Enterprises (II) are all negative. This indicates poorer performance on the part of family enterprises in contrast with non-family enterprises. The absolute value of the coefficient estimate of Modern Family Enterprises (II) is the largest of the three, indicating the poorest enterprise performance, and that of Modern Family Enterprises (I) is the second largest. The governance model of Classical Family Enterprises has a relatively small influence on enterprise performance and is less significant statistically, which indicates a smaller negative effect of this model on enterprise performance as compared to either categories of modern family enterprises.

It must be pointed out that the conclusions of the regression results here seem to be somewhat inconsistent with those drawn from Table 5.9. What remains unchanged is that Non-Family Enterprises have the best performance. In Table 5.9, Modern Family Enterprises (I) demonstrated the poorest average performance, followed by Classical Family Enterprises, while Modern Family Enterprises (II) perform better on average. But in our regression analysis here, the governance model of Classical Family Enterprises has a smaller negative influence on enterprise performance than the two models of Modern Family Enterprises being presented, and the model of Modern Family Enterprises (I) has a smaller negative influence on enterprise performance than do Modern Family Enterprises (II). The inconsistency between these conclusions is because of the following two reasons. One is a statistical reason. In Table 5.9, the performance data points represented are the average values of the enterprises in each category, easily affected by particularly large or small values of certain enterprises, while the regression analysis has overcome this problem and can better reflect the relationship between the governance models and enterprise performance. The other is that enterprise performance is mainly defined by the profit-tax rate of capital and profit-tax rate of sales in Table 5.9, while enterprise sales income is adopted for the same purpose in the regression analysis, as the regression result is statistically insignificant when the profit-tax rate of capital and profit-tax rate of sales are used as dependent variables to represent enterprise performance. Therefore, in spite of the low sales income of Modern Family Enterprises (II), it is possible for them to achieve a relatively high profit-tax rate of capital and profit-tax rate of sales because of their high degree of technology-intensiveness.

The regression results show that the performance of non-family enterprises are better than those of family enterprises. This accords with what may be practically expected. It is true that the preliminary governance models of family enterprises adapt well to enterprise development in the initial stage, but family enterprises are still faced with many problems in their governance. For example, the informal administrative relationship may play an important role in corporate governance, but its advantages in enhancing trust and reducing opportunity costs can be offset by arbitrariness and exclusiveness, which may result in a poorer enterprise performance compared with that of non-family enterprises.

5.2.2.3 Conclusions Drawn from the Regression Analysis

Through this analysis of the relationship between governance characteristics and enterprise performance, we have come to three conclusions: the shareholding structure, the identity of the executive general manager (president), and whether the NGE includes both boards, all have insignificant influence on enterprise performance; a high proportion of family members in senior management has a negative influence on enterprise performance; the inclusion of independent directors, major operators, and workers' representatives on the board of directors and the implementation of ESOP have greater positive influence on enterprise performance. Through our analysis of the relationship between governance models and enterprise performance, we draw a fourth conclusion that Non-Family Enterprises are the best in performance, Classical Family Enterprises are the second best, Modern Family Enterprises (I) are poor, and Modern Family Enterprises (II) are the poorest. It can be inferred from the above conclusions that although the shareholding structure and the identity of the executive general manager (president) have an insignificant effect on enterprise performance, some combination of the two may have a certain degree of influence, that is, the governance model of relatively decentralized ownership and moderately separated operation also has a positive influence on enterprise performance, whereas a high proportion of family members in the senior management has a negative influence on enterprise performance. Nevertheless, Classical Family Enterprises generally perform better than the other two categories of family enterprises. These conclusions, however, are not universal. For technology-intensive family enterprises, the governance model of Modern Family Enterprises (II) may be better, since this model makes it possible for them to achieve a relatively high profit-tax rate of capital and profit-tax rate of sales in spite of their low sales income. Also, we can further infer from these conclusions that Non-Family Enterprises are the best in terms of performance, followed by Classical Family Enterprises; the model of Modern Family Enterprises (II) fits better technology-intensive enterprises; while Modern Family Enterprises (I) is the poorest governance model.

5.2.3 NGEs' Performance and Governance Structure

According to the above analysis, the six governance variables we have studied are either directly or indirectly related to enterprise performance. NGEs—which includes independent directors, major operators, and workers' representatives serving on the board of directors and implementing ESOP—have better performances; those with a high proportion of family members in their senior management structure have poorer performance; the shareholding structure and the identity of the executive general manager (president) have no significant relationship with enterprise performance, but some combination of the two is significant, which is manifested by the better performance of Non-Family Enterprises and the poorer performance of Family Enterprises, and in particular the poorest performance of Modern Family Enterprises (I); whether the NGE makes use of both boards is not significantly related to enterprise performance, but as those NGEs including independent directors, major operators and workers' representatives on their board of directors and implementing ESOP have better performance, this proves the positive effect of the board of directors on enterprise performance and the necessity of its establishment, while the board of supervisors is not quite necessary for NGEs.

These conclusions have supplied us with some measure of enlightenment. Firstly, Non-Family Enterprises have relatively complete and modern governance structures and better operational effects. Thus, Family Enterprises must develop and transform their governance model into that of Non-Family Enterprises. Secondly, the governance model of Classical Family Enterprises is still effective. For enterprises under the absolute control of the first major shareholder, it is unnecessary to fill the position of the general manager with someone other than her/his family members, but there should not be a high proportion of family members in the senior management. Thirdly, the governance model of Modern Family Enterprises (II) has relative weak features of family enterprises. The ownership of an enterprise is decentralized to some degree, but the ownership and operation rights are not separated. This decentralized ownership leads to a rise in concerns of the other owners about the enterprise, which may cause a loss of managerial efficiency to some degree and can have a negative effect on the sales income of the enterprise in question. But such concern is beneficial to cost savings and ultimately results in a higher profit-tax rate of capital and profit-tax rate of sales.

5.3 NGEs' Choices of Governance Structure: Models and Paths

5.3.1 *Problems in NGEs' Governance Structures*

Through our analysis of the characteristics of NGEs' governance structure and their influence on enterprise performance, we can surmise some problems in NGEs' governance structures.

5.3.1.1 The Severe Problem of Family Members in Senior Management

Our study shows that a high proportion of family members in senior management positions have a negative influence on enterprise performance. As the data in Table 5.5 indicates, however, 62.6% of the sample enterprises had a proportion of above 30% in that respect in 2006. It has already become a severe problem. A high proportion of family members in senior management can affect corporate governance and performance in two ways. On the one hand, it will reduce the number of non-family members, in particular professional managers, participating in senior management, which is detrimental to the cultivation and introduction of senior talents and seriously affects the human resource reserve of enterprises. On the other hand, a high proportion of family members in senior management may cause a serious imbalance between the two governance mechanisms of family enterprises, namely, the formal contract governance based on social trust and the informal relationship governance based on private or family trust. Once the informal relationship governance dominates the daily management of an enterprise, it is likely to cause managerial confusion during the period of rapid development and expansion, which is detrimental to the effective operation of the enterprise.

5.3.1.2 Insufficient Implementation of ESOP

Our study also shows that the implementation of ESOP has a generally positive influence on enterprise performance. As the data in Table 5.6 indicates, however, only 18.1% of the sample NGEs had implemented the incentive mechanism of ESOP in 2006. The proportion is definitely too low. As an incentive mechanism, ESOP is good for motivating the enthusiasm of managers and key technicians and coordinating their career objectives and enterprise goals, which is beneficial to the long-term development of the enterprise as a whole. The fact that relatively few NGEs have implemented ESOP reflects to a certain degree the singularity and stagnation of NGEs' shareholding structure in China, which is impeding the improvement of NGEs' governance structure and operational effects.

5.3.1.3 Composition of the Board of Directors to Be Improved

Our study shows that the inclusion of independent directors, major operators, and workers' representatives on the board of directors has a positive influence on enterprise performance. The data in Table 5.3, however, indicates that the participation of major operators on the board of directors is relatively common, but that few NGEs have included independent directors and workers' representatives on the board. This is not good for the structural integrity of the board and may hinder the board from weighing the interest of all parties and making correct decisions as to the long-term development of the enterprise.

5.3.1.4 Large Proportion of Family Enterprises

Our study also shows that non-family enterprises are better than family enterprises in terms of performance. In spite of certain advantages held by family enterprises, their long-term developmental goal is to gradually realize the socialization of their ownership and the professionalization of their operation. As the data in Table 5.7 indicates, of the NGEs sampled in 2006, only 12.6% were non-family enterprises, while 87.4% were family enterprises. The large proportion of family enterprises is harmful to the promotion of the overall quality and operational effects of China's NGEs.

5.3.2 NGEs' Choices of Governance Models

Despite so many problems in their governance structure, NGEs must pay the closest attention to their governance models for their long-term and sound development. In this part, we will focus on the choices of NGEs target models of governance.

According to the previous analysis, modern stock corporations are better than family enterprises in terms of performance, and Classical Family Enterprises are better than the other categories of family enterprises being considered, but during their transition to modern stock corporations, some governance models of family enterprises are not adequately effective. On this basis, we can summarize the principles backing NGEs' choices of their governance models.

First, the most effective model is that of modern stock corporations. As the governance model of non-family enterprises, it is featured by ownership decentralization and ownership-operation separation. NGEs under the governance models of family enterprises must make it the ultimate goal of their transformation.

Second, family enterprises should give priority to and implement the Classical Family Enterprise model before they are able to adequately enact the model of modern stock corporations, and avoid ownership-operation separation only as a form that occurs under the condition of the absolute majority of shares.

Third, NGEs must pave the way for the separation of ownership and operations as soon as possible and transform themselves into normative modern corporations. Otherwise, they will have to bear some loss of their operational effect if they are unwilling to adequately separate ownership and operations under the pressure of the scale of expanded assets and capital shares.

So far we have concluded the principles for NGEs' choices of governance models, but there is one more type of family enterprises that we have not yet studied thoroughly and clearly, namely, those NGEs that are under either the absolute or relative control of extended family members with their total shares holding a majority in the shareholding structure and having appropriately exercised the separation of the ownership and operational rights. In our analysis, NGEs under the relative control of family members are categorized as non-family enterprises in the form of modern stock corporations, but internationally they are generally regarded as family enterprises when there are multiple family members involved in the enterprise with an obvious relative advantage vis-à-vis shareholding. Such NGEs have all the formal characteristics of modern stock corporations. As family members are closely related, they are easily united in the goal of restricting the behavior of the first major shareholder to bring up important issues. This helps protect the right of the statistically significant minority of shareholders and promote the operational effect of the enterprise. All this can even bring about a better performance than that of normative modern corporations. It is a more complex case, however, when an enterprise is under the absolute control of family members. In our analysis, when it is simultaneously under the absolute control of the first major shareholder and her/his immediate relatives, such an enterprise is categorized within the umbrella of the Modern Family Enterprises (I) model, which has a bad effect on the enterprise's performance. When it is under the relative control of the first major shareholder and her/his immediate relatives, such an enterprise is categorized as a non-family enterprise in the form of a modern stock corporation. This model would be effective if the other family members chose to stand by the minority shareholders and restrict the behavior of the first major shareholder and her/his immediate relatives. It would be ineffective, however, if the other family members chose to join hands with the first major shareholder and her/his immediate relatives. Thus, it is uncertain how this governance model of family enterprises will affect enterprise performance on a broad scale. For this reason, it should not be NGEs' ultimate goal insofar as governance models, but it may be regarded as a temporary goal in the evolution of their governance models.

Our analysis has shown that the model of modern stock corporations is the most effective form of governance, but this does not mean that all NGEs should adopt this model. In fact, the majority of NGEs will continue to be medium- and small-sized enterprises for some time. Given their scale and industrial characteristics, it is more likely for these enterprises to adopt the governance models of family enterprises, in particular the model of Classical Family Enterprises, so as to bring into full play its inherent advantages. Besides, even for some larger enterprises, it is still debatable whether they should fully implement the modern corporation model of governance based on complete ownership-management separation. For example, the fight for the control of Gome Electrical Appliances between the major shareholders and professional senior management has proven that, under specific conditions, the modern corporation model based on complete ownership-operation separation also has significant problems and can even lead to the splitting up and ineffective operation of a company. All these factors indicate that enterprises fitted with family management have a specific radius of effective management. Even when they have grown larger, it is the institutional structure and governance environment of the enterprises that determine whether they should modernize their governance structure and enterprise management. Particularly when the effective internal management of an enterprise has encountered a deterioration of its external environment, the enterprise will have to face new challenges in the improvement of its governance structure and adapt itself to the new environment. Therefore, the judgment of NGEs' governance structure must be based on business efficiency, rather than any kind of analysis as to whether it is modern or not.

Generally, however, the system of modern stock corporations is still the most effective model of governance. Thus, it is necessary to create fertile conditions for the establishment of a complete system of modern stock corporations when possible. As the governance structure of modern stock corporations with distinct familial traits, sometimes called family institutions, is likely to be highly efficient, it is favored by NGEs in the transformation of their governance structures. It may also be the choice of some NGEs as their target model of governance structures. Moreover, based on the appropriate selection of their governance models and structures, NGEs must pay adequate attention to other governance-related issues, such as the implementation of ESOP, the improvement of board composition, and the prevention of excessive family occupation in their senior management.

5.3.3 Paths Available for NGEs' Governance Model Transformation

Most NGEs begin their existence in the form of family enterprises. There are two important features of family enterprises. One is that a family possesses all or the major equity of an enterprise and ownership is basically in the hands of the family, and the other is that the operation of the enterprise is under the direct or indirect control of one family or several closely related families. Family ownership and control are the essential features of family enterprises. According to the three-dimensional model of family business development proposed by Kelin E. Gersick in *Generation to Generation: Life Cycles of the Family Business*, family enterprises usually go through three stages: creation, growth, and maturity. Accordingly, the ownership of an enterprise is first controlled by the founder alone or together with his or her spouse, then by the founder's siblings, and finally by the founder's cousins. Similarly, the operational rights also go through three stages. First, the enterprise is controlled by the creator. Then the creator's children enter the enterprise and work with their parents. Finally, leadership is passed down from one generation to the next. In this way, the enterprise grows from the original home business into a family enterprise of close relationships, then develops into a family enterprise of relatively distant relationships, and gradually evolves into a socialized enterprise. Such an evolutionary path of family enterprises is consistent with their inherent laws of development, and those able to complete this process of transformation usually turn out to be successful enterprises.

According to the three-stage theory of the natural evolution of family enterprises and the above relevant analysis, the ultimate goal of the governance transformation of family enterprises is the modern stock corporation model. Such a transformation is also a gradual process of socialization, which usually includes three perspectives: namely, the socialization of property rights, the socialization of management control, and the contracting of enterprise culture. In fact, these three aspects are widely reflected by the organization structure of an enterprise itself. Therefore, it is an important task for family enterprises to normalize their organizational structures during their transformation.

5.3.3.1 Socialization of Property Rights

Property rights structure is the principal factor in deciding the governance models of enterprises, and the step-by-step socialization of property rights is a prerequisite for the establishment of the governance model of modern stock corporations. For a family enterprise—with its expanding scale, increasingly complicated market environment, growing management procedures and difficulties, and the sharp rise in its financing demands—it is imperative to establish formal institutions as the major mechanisms of its daily management through property rights socialization, and to reduce or even eliminate the influences of kinship on the enterprise operations. There are several possible approaches to property rights socialization. The first approach is socialization through the self-evolution mechanism. It goes like this: a family enterprise is created and managed by the first generation, and the equity is centralized in their hands; the equity is decentralized and held by more family members in the second generation; in the third generation, the equity is further dispersed as the family members become more distant. In this way, the ownership of the family enterprise is gradually transformed into the common shareholding of more and more distant family members. Meanwhile, the proportion of public shareholders increases, which dilutes the equity of the family members bit by bit and finally takes away their absolute and even relative holding positions. The second approach is the deliberate introduction of strategic investors or cooperators. According to possible changes in its development environment and future development demands, a family enterprise may cooperate with upstream and downstream enterprises or horizontally-relevant enterprises, and in doing so dilute its over-centralized ownership by means of cross shareholding, absorption of equity investment, and so forth., so as to gradually transform the ownership structure away from the relative control of the family. The third approach is the dilution of family equity and increase of equity held by managerial and technical personnel by means of equity incentives and management stock ownership. This not only brings into play initiative on the part of key personnel in the managerial and technical sectors, but also guarantees the sustained vitality and aggressiveness of an enterprise, and results in the structural transformation of an enterprise from family ownership to management ownership. The fourth approach is to go public by listing on the stock market. If the equity of the family members has not been adequately dispersed after the initial public offering (IPO), it can be further diluted through refinancing or directional add-issuance. Of the four approaches to property rights socialization, most family enterprises prefer the first, the self-evolution method. Even if some family enterprises adopt the other approaches to dilute their equity, they are still inclined to maintain a position of absolute and familial control—very few families are willing to lose their controlling stake. With all these options available, however, family enterprises may choose either one or more of the above approaches to socialize their property rights.

5.3.3.2 The Professionalization of Operators

One of the most important ways for family enterprises to improve their governance model is to professionalize their operators, that is, to introduce or cultivate professional managers. Many family enterprises have attempted the introduction of professional managers from the outside, only for it to turn out to be a failure in most cases. The reason for this is that equity is over-centralized in these family enterprises and the informal governance mechanism plays a dominant role in the daily management of the enterprises. As a result, the professional managers are unlikely to get used to the working environment and the introduction ends fruitlessly. For family enterprises, a precondition of professionalizing their operators is stock ownership socialization. Even though the socialization may not have adequately diluted the family equity, it will have increased some external supervisory force, which can help eliminate or reduce the influence of informal governance mechanisms on the enterprises. The professionalization of the operators also requires evolution of power by the owners. Family enterprises must change the old dictatorial model of decision making and management and implement managerial stock ownership, so as to encourage the professional managers to make full use of their energy and wisdom for the enterprise's development. On the other hand, to avoid possible failures caused by ignorance of the enterprise conditions on the part of the newly-introduced professional managers, family enterprises may also exert greater effort to cultivate their own professional managers. They may recruit potential talents from the personnel market, arrange all sorts of tasks for them, give them the necessary training, and speed up their promotion. In this way, they can cultivate their own professional managers who are not only competent, but also familiar with the state of the business. Another significance of operator professionalization, it should be noted, is that it can prevent the relation-based appointment of management staff, create a smooth and healthy mechanism for personnel cultivation, growth, and employment, and bring into full play the initiative and creativity of the employees.

5.3.3.3 The Contracting of Enterprise Culture

The non-contractual culture of family enterprises, such as the casual decision-making and relation-based management resulting from relationships and emotional connections, has a very harmful effect once the enterprises in question have developed to a certain degree. Hence, for family enterprises, the contracting of enterprise culture is a very important part of their transformation towards a more advanced and efficient governance model. They may realize it by decentralizing ownership and the reduction of family members serving on the boards and in senior management. At the same time, they should strictly define the duties and responsibilities of each member of the corporation, the operational mechanisms of the enterprise, and the processes of daily management through the designing of regulations and rules. In addition, they should severely punish violators, in particular delinquent family members, so as to give warning to the other staff members and family members. Finally, they can realize the contracting of enterprise culture and adapt themselves to the increasingly complicated market environment and management processes.

5.3.3.4 Normalization of Organizational Structures

The normalization of an enterprise's organizational structures is an important requirement for the full play of professional managers' roles and the contracting of enterprise culture, as well as a necessary result of property rights socialization. The normalization of the organizational structure of family enterprises involves not only the board of shareholders, the board of directors, and the board of supervisors, but also the employees' congress. In the normalization process, the composition of the board of directors and the decision-making mechanism are particularly significant. When considering the board of directors, it is important to prevent the excessive participation of family members and properly limit their voting rights based on equity amounts while also increasing the decision-making voting rights based on the number of board members, so as to reduce the detrimental effect of family interest on the enterprise in question. In terms of the board of shareholders, it is especially important to increase the participation of minority shareholders, allow them to enjoy their voting rights by entrusting other shareholders, and increase and ensure their voting rights to the utmost extent. The employees' congress should be brought into full play. It should be entitled to some veto power in decisions concerning the employees' interests and the right to make suggestions on important decisions of the enterprise. To sum up, the principle of organizational structure normalization is to moderately restrain the rights of family members and properly increase those of other related stakeholders in various organizations, and to validate and guarantee it by means of regulations and institutions.

5.3.4 Major Constraints on the Transformation of NGEs' Governance Structures

It is true that NGEs' governance structures need further improvement and reformation, but NGEs are still faced with many constraints on what they are capable of doing. Some of these constraints are inherent, while others are caused by external environmental factors. The inherent problems in the improvement of NGEs' governance structure include the familial governance concepts of the enterprises, the informal interest groups, the non-contractual enterprise culture, and so forth.; while the external environmental problems include deficiencies within the social credit institution, the immaturity of the managerial labor market, difficulty in financing, industrial barriers, the imperfection of the legal system, the adverse effect of some traditional thoughts, and even the one-child family planning policy of China.

5.3.4.1 NGEs' Inherent Constraints on Governance Structure Improvements

First, the deep-rooted concepts of the familial governance of enterprises. NGEs are usually created and developed through the painstaking efforts of one or more members of a family. In most cases, they are regarded as the private property of the members who have attached much sentiment to them, which is different from what can be found in public enterprises. The result is that they lack the due social attributes of enterprises. In terms of corporate governance, this sentiment may be manifested in the form of a dictatorship, egotism, relation-based appointment, rejection of the introduced management personnel, and the absence of a wish to socialize the enterprises (unless forced to). These imperial or familial governance concepts are universal among a great deal of NGEs. They have become an impediment to NGEs' property rights socialization, operator professionalization, organization normalization, and management regularization, and they work against the further improvement of the corporate governance structure.

Second, the powerful invisible interest groups inside NGEs. Due to such informal governance factors such as relation-based appointments, sentiment, and so forth., it is easy for invisible interest groups to come into shape within NGEs. Such interest groups are powerful in enterprise management and operations. Violation of managerial regulations is common among members of these groups but they seldom receive real punishment. Meanwhile, they usually obey in public—but oppose in private—the instructions and orders of their leaders or superiors who are not members of the owner's family. With their perfunctory attitude and sluggish ways, they seriously interfere with the normal management and operation of the enterprises. Worst of all, when different interest groups are formed around different family members within an enterprise, they tend to fight for power and money and attack each other, which may even threaten the very survival of NGEs. In addition, the existence of interest groups also makes it difficult for professional managers to establish themselves and display their talents in NGEs. Consequently, it is very difficult to really promote the management level of enterprises.

Third, the severe problem of non-contractual enterprise culture. The culture of NGEs, especially SMEs, has integrated too much sentiment but little contractual spirit, and humanity is always above regulations in the governance. Such a culture has increased the arbitrariness inherent in enterprise decision-making and management and has made enterprise management and operations less normative and procedural, and thus caused confusions in enterprise operation. In such a non-contractual enterprise culture, the staff members no longer value their own efforts towards a promotion or pay raise, but are willing to resort to flattery for some benefits. Consequently, it is difficult for the enterprise to formulate a positive atmosphere of initiative, unity, and endeavors. On the contrary, a culture of overt contentiousness and covert fighting between gangs and cliques may come into shape. Once such a culture is formed, it is very difficult to eradicate it because some factors are already internalized as part of the daily actions and thoughts of the staff members, which will, in turn, make it even more difficult to contract the existing enterprise culture.

5.3.4.2 Environmental Constraints on the Improvement of NGEs' Governance Structure

The improvement and transformation of NGEs' governance structure requires certain social and environmental conditions. As NGEs develop to a certain stage, they would be in urgent need of the improvement of their governance structure. This much-needed improvement would be delayed and even impeded, however, if the social and institutional environment cannot meet the need of enterprises. The social and environmental constraints on NGEs' governance structure primarily include incomplete market mechanisms, the undeveloped capital market, deficient social credit institutions, the immature managerial labor market, the country's imperfect legal systems, and the one-child family planning policy.

First, the Incomplete Market Mechanism Currently in China, NGEs are still rejected by many monopoly industries; financing channels are insufficient; resources cannot be allocated and are restricted from flowing freely according to the principle of efficiency; and SOEs are entitled to more resources while NGEs are subjected to unfair competition. All these factors are implicitly limiting NGEs' development and expansion, but the expansion of scale and business-related fields is an important driving force for the improvement of NGEs' governance structures. In other words, the incomplete market mechanism of China is limiting the driving force behind the improvement of NGEs' governance structures.

Second, the Under-Developed Capital Market Relatively small in size, China's institutional investors rarely participate in the investment of NGEs except insofar as they are involved for the promotion of NGEs' listing on the stock market. The newly-opened Growth Enterprise Market has provided a possible channel for NGEs to seek financing by listing on the stock market and improving their shareholding structure, but it is far from sufficient for such a huge number of NGEs and can hardly be expected to fully perform its designed role. As the country's property rights trading market is still immature, NGEs are incapable of attracting institutional investors and are unable to find smooth approaches to participate in other types of corporations, in particular SOEs, through property right trades. These factors are all limiting the further improvement of NGEs' property rights structure and are to the disadvantage of NGEs' property rights socialization.

Third, the Deficient Social Credit Institution There are two forms of social credit, namely, the legal form and the cultural conception. With urbanization rate continue to increase in China, large numbers of rural residents have rushed into cities. But the organizational model of rural communities is nowhere to be found in cities. People do not know each other. The idea of relations-based social credit has lost its previous foundation of blood relationships or friendship. Social credit based on such a cultural conception has become fragile for lack of effective supervision by public opinion and can no longer perform its original function. At the same time, the legal form of social credit has also become deficient due to the country's incomplete legal system and poor execution, as well as the declining constraints of the law. Under these circumstances, private entrepreneurs have a strong impulse to count on their family members, relatives, and friends to govern their enterprises, which greatly constrains the further improvement of NGEs' governance structure.

Fourth, an Incomplete Professional Managers' Market With the growth and development of NGEs, the introduction of professional mangers and the utilization of external wisdom has become an important method by which to break the management bottleneck and realize the promotion of enterprises. The domestic professional managers' market is now suffering from a shortage of professional managers, however, in particular excellent mangers. Meanwhile, there is no evaluation of integrity or supervision of professional managers, the effective restraint mechanism has not yet been formulated, and the punishment mechanism for the discreditable behavior of professional mangers is weakening. All these problems may easily subject NGEs to unnecessary frustrations in their introduction of professional managers and cause a loss of confidence in and enthusiasm for the employment of professional managers from the outside.

Fifth, the Country's Flawed Legal Systems Currently in China, the private property rights protection system, the trade secret and patent protection system, and the professional ethics system are all incomplete. These imperfect legal systems have encouraged the moral hazards of private entrepreneurs and professional managers and blocked the principal-agent relationship, and thus have made it more difficult to separate the ownership and operation of enterprises.

Sixth, Challenges Posed by the Family Planning Policy Through efforts being made over several generations, NGEs can gradually evolve into public companies with less distinct family traits. But the premise is that there must be quite a number of related individuals in the later generations. Otherwise, the organization's equity cannot be adequately or gradually decentralized through increasingly distant blood relationships, and the basis for the natural evolution of NGEs into public companies would no longer exist. As China has implemented its rather strict one-child family planning policy, the creators of NGEs usually have only one child. Moreover, the basic national policy will remain unshakable in the short run. Therefore, it is almost impossible for NGEs to evolve naturally and gradually into modern stock corporations with indistinct family traits and dispersed ownership.

Due to the above constraints, it is more difficult for China's NGEs to improve their governance structure. NGEs should not seek overnight success in this process, however, but must steadily create and wait for appropriate conditions and improve their governance structure in due course. At the same time, they must also try to prevent failures in this process and avoid possible losses incurred by such failures.

5.3.5 Approaches to the Improvement of NGEs' Governance Structure

5.3.5.1 The Creation of Internal Conditions Propitious to NGEs' Governance Structure Transformation

With various constraints of the internal environment for improvements to NGEs' governance structure, it is necessary to make a conscious effort to create agreeable conditions, change the existing status quo, and break the constraints on enterprises, so as to better push forward the proposed improvements to the governance structure. In this way, it is possible to eliminate those factors impeding the transformation of enterprises' governance structure through education and publicity, the reinforcement of rules and regulatory management, the improvement of the supervisory mechanism, the determination of benefit compensation, and more.

First of All, Establishing a Baseline Awareness of Serving the Society at Large NGEs are indeed the fruit of private entrepreneurs through arduous pioneering efforts, but they are also the result of the common efforts of all the staff members working for them, and their earnings come, ultimately, from society. Therefore, private entrepreneurs should discard the idea of private ownership, avoid regarding the enterprises as their private property, and of conducting arbitrarily. They must establish an awareness that enterprise development is rooted in society and should serve society, respect the enterprise managers and their employees, and actively push forward property rights socialization.

Secondly, Reinforcing the Management of Rules and Regulations and the Supervision System With the strong familial makeup of NGEs, it is common that family members serve as senior managers. The result is that enterprises cannot be operated and managed according to their established regulations, rules, and institutions, which has a detrimental effect on enterprise development and makes it difficult for professional managers to fully play their roles. Accordingly, NGEs must reinforce the management of rules and regulations and of the supervision system, strengthen the behavioral restrictions placed on family members in the enterprises by means of institutional factors so as to make them comply with enterprise regulations, rules, and institutions, and act as role models to others, to create a good institutional environment and operational circumstances, and to remove all the artificially-imposed obstacles for professional managers.

Thirdly, Strengthening Education and Transparency The reinforcement of management and the improvement of the supervision system are definitely important measures to regulate the behavior of family members. To achieve a better effect and reduce conflict , however, NGEs must value the important role of education and transparency , teach family members the significance of institutionalized management to the operation and long-term development of the enterprise, and reduce the formation of cliques and gangs as well as arbitrary decisions based on personal inclinations.

Fourthly, Constructing a Compensation Mechanism In order to contend with the adverse effect of non-contractual management, NGEs must minimize the proportion of family members or co-founders in their senior management. This may give rise to a series of inevitable conflicts. In this case, it is necessary to construct a benefit compensation mechanism, through which family members or co-founders dismissed from senior management positions can be compensated with a certain amount of shares or a one-time subsidy. This is an important measure to lessen resistance to reform and to press ahead towards the socialization of their industries and the professionalization of their management.

5.3.5.2 The Construction of an External Environment Favorable to NGEs' Governance Structure Transformation

The improvement of NGEs' governance structure is also hampered by external constraints to varying degrees. This requires that governmental departments actively push forward various reforms and construct an external environment favorable to NGEs' governance structure transformation. On the other hand, NGEs must themselves make every effort towards and actively look for available solutions under existing circumstances and conditions, rather than merely wait until the best opportunity passes them by.

Firstly, Further Improving NGEs' Financing Environment Deepen the systemic reform of banks and non-bank financial institutions and improve the system coordinating NGEs' indirect financing, which includes accelerating reform of the state-held commercial banks to increase their loan support for NGEs and establishing local shareholding banks to support the indirect financing demands of NGEs. Construct a multi-level capital market system, encourage NGEs to seek financing by listing on the stock market, give priority to the development of the over-the-counter market, give full support to the development of venture capitals, improve the environment available for NGEs' direct financing, and further optimize the property rights structure of NGEs.

Secondly, Constructing an Institutional Environment Conducive to Honesty and Trustworthiness Strengthen education in professional ethics as well as people's credit awareness. Carry out wide awareness-raising and education about credibility by administrative means, newspapers, TV programs, networking, and so forth. Establish and develop a credit rating system for both enterprises and individuals. By way of legislation, clearly define the record of, transfer, management rating, disclosure, and use of credit files, as well as the responsibilities and rights of rating agencies and rated organizations. Strengthen the implementation of related laws and raise the default costs of enterprises and other credit subjects. Only in this way can we construct a truly law-based credit system in China.

Thirdly, Improve the Professional Managers' Market Complete the credit system, build up the credit records of managers, raise the behavioral costs for untrustworthy managers, and force them to restrain their behavior out of self-interest. Implement a disclosure mechanism outlining managers' information, so as to enable any party involved in a transaction to have access to the credit information of the other parties. Establish an evaluation system of managerial personnel, one with both Chinese characteristics and in accordance with international standards, and which has overcome the weaknesses of the old system as being too general and abstract in assessment indexes. At the same time, make clear NGEs' responsibilities as the employers of managerial personnel and create an excellent operational environment for professional managers to fully perform.

Fourthly, Adjust the Family Planning Policy in Due Course For over 30 years, the one-child family planning policy has played an important role in checking the over-rapid population growth and relieving resource and economy pressures in China. With the most changes in the environment, however, some drawbacks of this policy are becoming visible, e.g., the earlier ageing of society, the decreasing labor population, and the employment difficulties in some regions, which have somehow restricted the natural evolution of NGEs' property rights socialization. On the other hand, as some researchers hold, most of China's small- and medium-sized NGEs fit in with and have a preference for the family corporate governance model, and for those family enterprises with relatively concentrated equity, many would prefer natural evolution as the method by which to further socialize their stock ownership. Hence, even though it may not be the best time to adjust the family planning policy, it is necessary to make accessions for the future, undertake studies of and plan for the optimal family planning policy in the coming years, and make adjustment to the current policy in due course.

Bibliography

Anderson R, Mansi S, Reeb D (2003) Founding family ownership and the agency cost of debt. J Financ Econ 68(2):263–285

Bi Y (2007) The introduction of professional high-level managers and the evolution in the governance characteristics of family enterprises. Econ Surv (1)

Chen L, Lu L (2009) Family business, corporate governance and performance: an empirical study of manufacturing industry in Zhejiang Province. J Sun Yat-Sen Univ (3):203–212

Chrisman C (2004) Comparing the agency costs of family and non-family firms: conceptual issues and exploratory evidence. Entrep Theory Pract (28):335–354

Chrisman J, Chua J, Steier L (2003) An introduction to theories of family business. J Bus Ventur (4):441–448

Ding J, Chen C (2007) Trust, specialized division and the choice of the family corporate governance mechanisms. Financ Econ (12)

Gao Z, Wu H (2008) The evolution of governance structure in China's family-owned enterprises—from family operation to family ownership. J Wuhan Metall Manag Inst (1)

He J (2008) An analysis of the family management of China's private firms. Econ Manag (9)

He Y, He B (2009) Empirical studies of the influence of NGEs' governance structure on enterprise performance. China Manag Inf (6)

Hu Z (2009) Explorations on governance development of China's private enterprises and firms. North Econ (10)

Huang S, Wang Q, He J (2008) Institutional constraints, demand driven and adaptive choice: an analysis of governance evolution of China's private firms. China Ind Econ (6)

Liao K (2007) Factors analysis: governance structure changes of China's family enterprises. Contemp Econ (9)

Liu Y (2008) Coordination of formal and informal institutions in the governance of family enterprises. Enterp Vitality (10)

Liu M (2009) Path selection and obstacles in family business governance model transformation. Enterp Econ (7)

Liu J, Song L (2007) Stakeholder governance pattern and the importing obstacles of Chinese family business. Financ Econ (1)

Mao J (2007) Study on management model innovation of private corporations in our country. Mod Bus Trade Ind (9)

Mustakallio M, Autio E, Zahra SA (2002) Relational and contractual governance in family firms: effects on strategic decision making. Fam Bus Rev 15(3):205–222

Schulze WG, Lubatkin MH, Dino RN (2003) Exploring the agency consequences of ownership dispersion among the directors of private family firms. Acad Manag J 46(2):179–194

Song L (2007a) Modern governance pattern and the importing logic obstacles of Chinese family business. Lanzhou Acad J (4)

Song Y (2007b) The governance model of family enterprise—considering of an international comparative visual angle. North Forum (1)

Tang X (2008) Contractual and relational governance between owners and managers in family firms. J Beijing Jiaotong Univ (2)

Wang F, Zhang X, Mo M (2008) Approaches to improvement of governance structure of China's private enterprises and firms. Manag Obs (22)

Xu W (2008) Issues in stakeholder governance of NGEs. Financ Account Mon (27)

Yang L, Zhu S (2006) An empirical analysis of the relationship between family businesses governance structure and their performance. Bus Econ Adm (10)

Yu J, Shi B (2008) Research on corporate governance performance of listed family companies—based on factor analysis. J Shanxi Financ Econ Univ (10)

Yu X, Wang X, Wang C (2007) Comparison and analysis of governance structure of family enterprises before and after being listed. Shanghai Econ Rev (9)

Zhan D, Zhou L, Yu X (2008) Evolution of family corporate governance: from close to open model. Mod Manag Sci (10)
Zhang C (2006) Changes in governance structure of SMEs: based on an interpretation of capital structure theory. J Shandong Inst Bus Technol (3)
Zhang H (2009a) Trust restraint, transaction cost, and internal relation governance: behavior models of Chinese family enterprises. Mod Econ Res (3)
Zhang M (2009b) The governance structure of family enterprises and its evolution paths: analysis of a survey among 99 SMEs of Wenzhou (2009). North Econ (10)
Zhao H, Chen X, Xia H (2009) Process of NGEs' growth and dynamic evolution of their governance structure. Reform Econ Syst (3)
Zhou M (2008a) Shift between NGEs' shareholding structure and governance mechanisms. J Cap Univ Econ Bus (4)
Zhou S (2008b) Social capital, governance structure and agency problem of family business. Zhejiang Soc Sci (12)
Zhou X (2008c) Contracted governance, relation management and governance model selection of family enterprises. Seeker (6)
Zhu S, Mao Z (2009) On equity diversification and governance of family enterprises. Commercial Times (1)
Zhu W, Tang G (2008) A new governance viewpoint on private companies—key interest parties governance mode research based on life cycle theory. J Cent Univ Financ Econ (5)

Chapter 6
Scale and Efficiency: Basic Paths to NGEs' Growth and Development in the New Stage

Bai Xue

6.1 New Characteristics of NGEs' Expansion

As NGEs are one of the most active microscopic entities within the market economy, the rational expansion of their scale can enhance the vitality of the socialist market economy, meet diversified market demands, and contribute to the optimization of China's industrial structure and the promotion of its international competitiveness. In terms of input, NGEs' expansion of scale takes the form of an increase in the quantity of production factors under their direct ownership and indirect control; in terms of output, the expansion of scale manifests as the promotion of NGEs' output levels.

6.1.1 Changes to the Scale of NGEs in the New Stage

Enterprise sales can be used to roughly reflect the scale of enterprises, as it can respond to the short-term fluctuations of demands and is neutral in proportion to the input factors (Scherer 1965). According to the statistics of the China Enterprise Confederation, the number of NGEs is increasing yearly on the sales-based list of Top 500 Chinese Enterprises. In 2002, there were only 19 NGEs on the list, while in 2009, there were 104. In particular, Jiangsu Shagang Group Co., Ltd., with a sales revenue of RMB 145.232 billion, ranked 35th on the list and the 1st of all NGEs in 2009 (See Table 6.1). With their rapid expansion of scale, however, NGEs are still worlds apart from SOEs. For example, Jiangsu Shagang Group realized a sales revenue growth of 25.73% over the previous year, which indicates an evident

B. Xue (✉)
Graduate School, Chinese Academy of Social Sciences, Beijing, China

Y. Liu (ed.), *New Interpretations on the Development of China's Non-Governmental Enterprises*, Research Series on the Chinese Dream and China's Development Path, DOI 10.1007/978-981-10-3872-3_6

Table 6.1 Top Chinese SOEs and NGEs by sales revenue 2009

Ranking	Enterprise	Sales revenue (RMB bn)	Revenue growth (%)	Profit (RMB bn)	Profit growth (%)	Assets (RMB bn)	Owners' equity (RMB bn)	Employees (mn)
1	Sinopec	1462.439	19.10	13.630	−58.53	1044.849	378.265	0.6397
2	PetroChina	1273.003	27.21	71.382	−43.92	1804.447	1310.871	1.6184
3	State Grid	1140.737	12.86	4.618	−86.27	1643.458	577.197	0.9372
35	Jiangsu Shagang	145.232	25.74	8.521	−3.11	102.333	39.809	0.0282
50	Lenovo	115.211	−21.41	0.483	−75.67	64.422	7.718	0.0246
54	Suning Appliance	102.342	19.73	2.260	48.37	21.619	9.112	0.1104

Note: The first three enterprises are the largest SOEs and the other three are the largest NGEs by sales revenue on the list of Top 500 Chinese Enterprises, 2009
Source: Website of China Enterprise Confederation, http://www.cec-ceda.org.cn/

expansion of scale. But it is only 10%, 63%, and 10% of Sinopec's (which ranked 1st on the list) listed figures in terms of sales revenue, profit, and assets, respectively.

Other indicators—such as total profit, operating profit, asset size, owners' equity, and employee number—are also frequently used to judge the changes in enterprise scales. As Table 6.2 shows, the annual sales revenue of Shagang increased 11.85 times, from RMB 11.298 billion in 2002 to RMB 145.232 billion in 2009. Meanwhile, its profit, total assets, and number of employees had increased from RMB 3.556 billion, RMB 10.192 billion, and 7.9 thousand persons, respectively, to RMB 8.521 billion, RMB 102.333 billion, and 28.2 thousand persons, up 12.11 times, 9.04 times, and 2.57 times. Similarly, Lenovo Holdings has also shown a trend of rapid large-scale expansion. Its sales revenue, profit, and total assets increased by 3.45 times, 0.56 times, and 3.45 times, respectively, from 2002 to 2008. Under the influence of the financial crisis, Lenovo was hindered in its expansion in 2009 and the growth rate of its revenue and profit dropped −21.41% and −75.67%, respectively, as its business mainly covers IT, real estate, and finance, and the demand elasticity for its products is relatively high compared with that of Shagang. This indicates that NGEs' expansion is affected by their different levels of growth risk tolerance.

6.1.2 *The Expansion of NGEs' Financing Models*

The expansion of capital elements is at the core of the scale of a given enterprise's expansion. At present, bank loans and commercial credit are still the major channels of NGEs' debt financing. A rising proportion of enterprise liabilities in their assets structure can help relieve the problem of entrusted agency and therefore promote an enterprise's values (Myers 1984; Bharath et al. 2009). Some NGEs are relatively weak in terms of risk tolerance, however, due to their small scale and lack of core competence in the process of growth and development, and their demand for funds is relatively small and uncertain. All these factors have increased the difficulty of credit ratings and the supervision of commercial banks, and are likely to result in a lack of direct financing capacity and higher financing costs for NGEs (Research Group of Enterprise Survey Unit, NBS 2004). Since the beginning of the twenty-first century, thanks to the development and improvement of China's capital market and the relaxation of institutional restrictions and financial constraints, NGEs financing difficulties have been relieved to some degree and their financing modes are now characterized by new traits.

Through their analysis of Chinese NGEs' financing, Hu Jun and Chen Jian-lin concluded that, with NGEs' growth and development, their financing modes generally tend to evolve from internal financing to debt financing and then to equity financing, and that their external financing channel changes from the private market to the public market (Hu Jun and Chen Jianlin 2009). At present, NGEs' models of financing are going through a period of diversified development. Equity financing is

Table 6.2 Expansion of the scale of Jiangsu Shagang and Lenovo holdings 2002–2009

	Sales revenue (RMB bn)	Revenue growth (%)	Profit (RMB bn)	Profit growth (%)	Assets (RMB bn)	Owners' equity (RMB bn)	Employees (thsd)	Ranking
Jiangsu Shagang Group Co., Ltd.								
2002	11.298	35.56	0.650	26.11	10.192		7.9	95
2003	14.512	28.44	0.799	22.91	14.471		8.9	97
2004	20.402	40.58	0.784	23.64	21.402	9.260	9.9	86
2005	31.124	52.29	2.346	216.64	26.453	11.739	9.8	75
2006	40.548	30.48	1.045	−48.62	35.760	11.931	10.0	66
2007	58.772	44.95	2.906	178.22	52.547	19.572	13.1	63
2008	115.504	96.53	8.771	118.08	81.885	30.135	26.7	36
2009	145.232	25.74	8.521	−3.11	102.333	39.809	28.2	35
Lenovo Holdings Co., Ltd.								
2002	32.877	15.59	1.405	37.29	15.327		14.5	37
2003	35.542	8.10	1.416		15.888		16.4	37
2004	40.331	13.47	1.237	−12.63	17.908	7.619	18.5	39
2005	41.922	3.94	1.481	19.71	22.202	8.649	16.6	56
2006	108.189	158.07	0.809	−2.84	62.255	6.960	27.3	24
2007	138.947	29.31	0.103	−85.79	65.138	12.297	30.3	22
2008	146.201	5.73	2.197	2339.57	68.261	15.731	27.2	28
2009	115.211	−21.41	0.483	−75.67	64.422	7.718	24.6	50

Note: "Ranking" refers to their ranks on the list of Top 500 Chinese Enterprises over the years
Source: http://www.cec-ceda.org.cn/ (Website of China Enterprise Confederation)

developing rapidly among China's NGEs. Apart from the traditional modes of financing, there is also a considerable rise in the proportions of short-term and long-term overseas loans, institutional investment, and financing by listing on the stock market. Take financial listing, for example. Listed non-governmental companies are the product of the development of both China's NGEs and the stock market. But since 1992—when Shenzhen Huayuan Industry was listed as the first NGE on the China's A Share Market—due to control by the capital market, the participation of NGEs had been rare in China's stock market, a situation that lasted until the late 1990s. By the end of 2001, there were only 145 non-governmental companies listed, accounting for only 12.72% of all the companies listed on the A Share Market, while the majority were state-owned companies (Fig. 6.1). Since 2000, thanks to the reform of the economic system and the gradual opening up of the capital market, NGEs have been developing rapidly by listing on the stock market. By the end of 2009, there were 667 non-governmental companies listed on the A Share Market,[1] 39.70% of all total listings. Moreover, the target domain of NGEs' equity financing has been extended from China to foreign countries, and a number of NGEs are also listed on overseas markets, such as Country Garden, Wanxiang Group, Qiaoxing Universal, and so forth. The following are the general features characterizing China's non-governmental companies as they are listed in the new century: the innovative spirit and entrepreneurship of their leaders, family holdings across many companies, managerial ownership in most companies, flexible mechanisms and high efficiency, the high market concentration of some industries, and imperfect governance structures and managerial institutions within most companies.[2]

In addition, the institutional shift characterized by the implementation of the new *Company Law*, *Securities Law*, and *Property Law* has opened up new paths for NGEs' private placement and mortgage/pledge financing. As a mode of financing, financial leasing has been applied by some large- and medium-sized NGEs. These changes in NGEs' modes of financing have provided new, more feasible approaches to the funds necessary for their growth and development, reduced their financing constraints, and enabled enterprises to expand their scale based on the expansion of their capital use and control.

---

[1]In fact, some listed companies controlled by the collective, social groups, or ESOA (Employee Stock Ownership Association) are of a non-governmental nature. If they are taken into account, the figure can be bigger.

[2]Shenzhen Stock Exchange. (2009). Features of Non-Governmental Companies Listed at Present. http://www.szse.cn/main/nssqyfwzq/wtjd_news/fxssgy/39741016.shtml. Accessed Aug. 15, 2009.

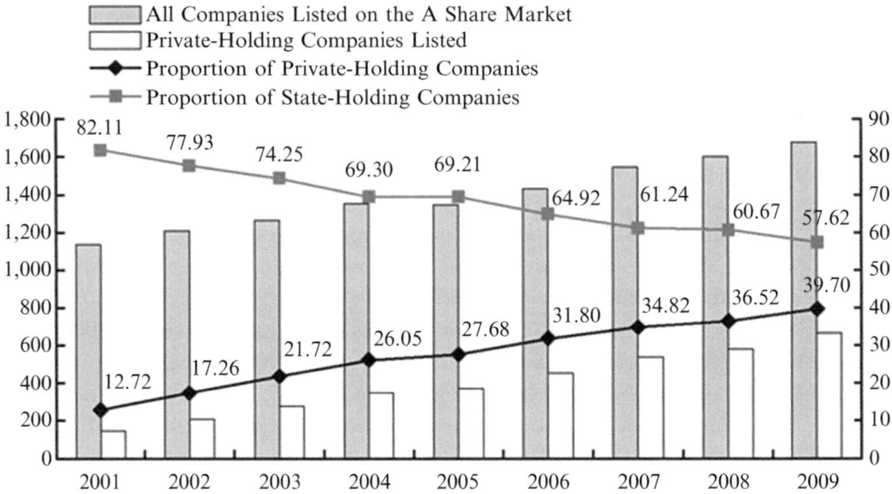

Fig. 6.1 Changes in proportion of China's NGEs listed on a share market
Note: 1. *Left axis*: Enterprise numbers; *right axis*: %
2. According to the data classification standard of CEIC, all the listed companies are classified by the ultimate controlling shareholder of the largest shareholder, i.e. the actual controller of the listed companies, into six types: state holdings, private holdings, foreign holdings, collective holdings, social-group holdings, and ESOA holdings
Source: CCER governance structure database and wind database (Sorted)

6.1.3 The Industrial Extension of Enterprise Boundaries

In terms of industrial boundary extension, NGEs' scale of expansion tends to take the form of a choice between diversification and specialization. There has been quite a bit of controversy over the relationship between diversification and an enterprise's performance in the process of growth (Hall 1994). By using the CASS Center for Private Economic Studies' 2005 NGE Database, Li Chunyu (2006) discovered that diversification is a rather common choice among NGEs, and this is because it contributes to their risk aversion and promotion of competitiveness at the early stages of development. Based on Wrigley's criteria of diversification[3] and the characteristics of listed companies as they exist in China, and according to the proportion held by the largest-income industry in the businesses discussed here, we divide the non-governmental listed companies into those categorized as Complete Specialization (corresponding to 100%, Column 2 in

[3]Enterprises may be classified according to the degrees of specialization or diversification: (1) -Single-product enterprises—one business consists of over 95% of the total revenue; (2) Dominant-product enterprises—one business consists of 70–95% of the total revenue; (3) Relevant-product enterprises—none of the businesses consist of over 70% of the total revenue, but there is an industrial correlation between them; and (4) Irrelevant-product enterprises—none of the businesses consist of over 70% of the total revenue, and there is no industrial correlation between them.

Table 6.3 Scale and diversification matrices of listed NGEs

	100 100%	95 ~ 99 95–99%	70 ~ 95 70–95%	50 ~ 70 50–70%	Less than 50 < 50%	
2004						
>10,000	1	0	2	0		**1.06**
5000–10,000	1	0	0	1		**0.71**
1000–5000	12	13	23	18	5	**25.09**
500–1000	11	6	12	14	7	**17.67**
100–500	37	16	42	22	14	**46.29**
<100	5	3	8	6	4	**9.19**
Total	67	38	87	61	30	283
	23.67	**13.43**	**30.74**	**21.55**	**10.60**	
2009						
>10,000	1	4	2	2	0	**1.91**
5000–10,000	0	3	10	4	0	**3.61**
1000–5000	8	66	52	26	12	**34.82**
500–1000	13	46	35	21	7	**25.90**
100–500	19	51	26	19	11	**26.75**
<100	7	3	10	11	2	**7.01**
Total	48	173	135	83	32	471
	10.19	**36.73**	**28.66**	**17.62**	**6.79**	

Notes: 1. According to the classification of listed NGEs in Fig. 6.1 and after the rejection of those with incomplete data, the samples include 283 and 471 NGEs in 2004 and 2009 respectively
2. The enterprise scale intervals in Column 1 are divided according to the major business income (RMB mn) of listed NGEs. The diversification intervals in Row 1 are divided according to the proportion of the largest-income industry in the main business
3. The values in bold refer to the proportions (%) in the corresponding intervals; the other values refer to the numbers of listed NGEs that fall into the interval crossings
4. Source of values: Wind database (Computed)

Table 6.3), Relative Specialization (95–99%), Relative Diversification (50–95%), and Decentralization/Diversification (<50%). A comparison of the data from 2004 to 2009 shows that the proportion of Complete Specialization Enterprises to the whole declined from 23.67% to 10.19%, that of Relative Specialization Enterprises increased from 13.43% to 36.73%, while the proportions of Diversification Enterprises also declined (to varying degrees). This indicates that, with such changes to their growth environment, China's NGEs have probably begun their transition from a diversified strategy to a specialized strategy of development. We come to similar conclusions when we take into consideration the scale of enterprises. In Table 6.3, the greatest value in the changes between intervals from 42 NGEs (corresponding to an enterprise size of RMB 0.1–0.5 billion and a major business income of 70–95%) in 2004 to 66 NGEs (corresponding to an enterprise size of RMB 1–5 billion and a major business income of 95–99%) in 2009. This means the expansion of NGEs' scale is in line with a corresponding increase in their degrees of specialization.

During NGEs' expansion, the integration of industrial and financial capital has become a new characteristic of the industrial boundary extension of China's NGEs in the new economic stage. At present, by means of equity participation, shareholding, holdings, and personnel participation, the industrial capital of China's NGEs has entered those emerging financial institutions such as commercial banks, securities, insurances, trust investments, and so forth. Haier Group[4] and Haima Automobile Group are representatives of such NGEs.

In addition to traditional input-output boundaries, NGEs' expansions of scale may also go beyond accounting boundaries, which is a new characteristic in this stage. For example, with the promotion of its capabilities in terms of the market allocation of resources, an enterprise may affect external economic allocation through its own decision-making. The main forms of NGEs' extension of accounting boundaries are collectivization and transnationalization. With their parent companies as the mainstay, China's NGEs have formed economic unions with many enterprises and institutions by means of investment, production, and operational cooperation, and so forth., and have therefore strengthened their capability for production factor allocation beyond the enterprises themselves. This has become a trend, as well as a main means by which large- and medium-sized NGEs, especially those that are export-oriented, to avoid market and policy risks in the context of globalization.

6.2 NGEs' Expansion of Scale and Dynamic Efficiency

There are two classes of economies arising from an increase in the scale of production—"firstly, those dependent on the general development of the industry; and, secondly, those dependent on the resources of the individual houses of business engaged in it, on their organization and the efficiency of their management. We may call the former external economies, and the latter internal economies".[5] At present, agglomeration is the major characteristic of external economies involved in NGEs' development, and a positive correlation can be observed between the degree of industrial concentration and variation among enterprises' technological efficiency (Lall and Rodrigo 2001; Onder et al. 2003; Xue Bai 2007), which contributes to the promotion of internal efficiency among enterprises. This section will discuss the evolutionary characteristics of NGEs' dynamic efficiency in the process of their expansion.

[4]Haier Group is the first NGE engaged in the financial industry. In 2002, Haier Group and New York Life Insurance Company founded a joint venture, Haier New York Life Insurance Co., Ltd., in Shanghai, each holding 50% of the shares.

[5]Marshall, A. (1958). *Principles of Economics*. (8th Ed). New York: McGrau-Hill, pp. 136.

6.2.1 The Malmquist-DEA Method and Data Processing

NGEs' scale is determined by the number of production factors they possess, and their efficiency is determined by the allocative mode of the input factors within enterprises. An improvement in dynamic efficiency as manifested in the input-output or cost-return relationship reflects the optimized resource allocation and strengthened competitiveness of enterprises. For NGEs, efficiency is of top priority in their objective function; while for SOEs, the scale of an enterprise is more important in their decision functions due to the existence of the principal-agent mechanism. It is true that some NGEs also have the principal-agent problem. Compared with SOEs, however, the change in agency or income may bring higher risks to NGEs, and therefore their primary operational goal is basically the maximization of profit.

To analyze the dynamic evolution of NGEs' efficiency in China's new economic stage, we adopt the Malmquist-DEA nonparametric estimation method to estimate changes in their technical advancement by comparing the production frontiers between the points in a time series. DEA can be used to describe the distance function of technical efficiency in the decision making units (DMU) regardless of the specific production function (Charnes et al. 1978). On the basis of Malmquist's work, Cave and Christensen (1980), and further developed DEA and enabled it to be widely applied in the calculation and decomposition of productivity. By using the Malmquist-DEA method, we can decompose the total-factor productivity change (tfpch) into efficiency change(effch), pure efficiency change (pech), and scale efficiency change(sech)with constant returns to scale.[6] The decomposition of this function is expressed as follows:

$$y_{ijt} = A_{ijt} f_{ijt}(\cdot) + \mu$$
$$A_{ijt} = \mathrm{tfpch}_{ijt} = \mathrm{effch}_{ijt} \times \mathrm{techch}_{ijt}$$
$$= \mathrm{pech}_{ijt} \times \mathrm{sech}_{ijt} \times \mathrm{techch}_{ijt}$$

In the equation, y represents the output; $f(\cdot)$ represents the allocation mode of the input production factors; A represents technical advancement; i, j, and t represent the enterprise, industry, and year, respectively. Further division of the technical advancement may make an analysis of NGEs' efficiency more accurate.

It is necessary to scientifically select the input-output variables in the data processing stage of Malmquist-DEA. For the input variables, we selected NGEs' major business income as the indicator of the scale of a given enterprise scale. It can not only measure the enterprise's scale, but also enable us to avoid, to a certain degree, any inaccuracy in the efficiency calculation, a result of the difference in production functions of different industries, as NGEs may engage in more than one

[6]For details of the derivation, refer to Cave, D., Christensen, L., Diewert, W. E. (1982). The Economic Theory of Index Numbers and the Measurement of Input, Output, and Productivity. *Econometrica*, 50(6), 1393–1414.

industry due to their diversification strategies. As for the output variables, the number of employees and total fixed assets are usually taken as the indicators of labor and capital input, respectively. Considering the increasingly prominent role of intangible factors, such as knowledge, in NGEs' growth in the new century, we have included intangible assets[7] as another major input indicator. Besides, in light of the difference between industries in terms of their institutional backgrounds, technical levels, and market demands, we have divided the input-output data by industry before processing them.

From the listed non-governmental companies included here in Fig. 6.1, we select only those in continuous operation from 2004 to 2009. A total of 169 listed non-governmental companies are analyzed after the rejection of those DMUs with incomplete data, of which 5 are engaged in agriculture, 121 in manufacturing, 1 in the production and supply of electricity, gas, and water, 5 in construction, 3 in transportation and storage, 11 in information technology, 8 in wholesale and retail trade, 10 in real estate, 3 in social services, and 1 in the communications and cultural industry, according to the industrial division of the China Securities Regulatory Commission(CSRC).[8] By processing their panel data with the software DEAP 2.1, we obtained the efficiency results of these companies in Tables 6.4 and 6.5.

6.2.2 Changes in NGEs' Dynamic Efficiency

A comparison of the averages of total-factor productivity change (tfpch) from 2004 to 2009 shows an obvious difference in technical advancement between different industries. The average tfpch is above 1 in manufacturing (C[9]), information technology (G), real estate (J), and associated services (F, H, K, L), indicating an actual technical advancement in these industries. In the areas of agriculture (A) and construction (E), the average tfpch is below 1 (0.880 and 0.801, respectively) from 2004 to 2009, but the average tfpch of these two industries generally increases yearly, indicating certain technical advancement in these industries.

[7]From the perspective of enterprise accounting, intangible assets include those without physical existence, such as long-term non-monetary assets, land use rights, franchises, patent rights, non-patent technologies, and so forth. Intangible assets can not only increase the profit of enterprises, but also promote their market competitiveness due to their exclusivity.

[8]According to the industry division of CSRC, "agriculture" includes not only agriculture, forestry, animal husbandry, and fishery, but also related services; "information technology" includes communications and related equipment manufacturing industries, computer and related equipment manufacturing industries, the communications service industry, and the computer application service industry. The classification and division of "manufacturing" are different between CSRC and NBS. The analysis in this section is based on CSRC classifications.

[9]CSRC industry code. The same hereinafter.

Table 6.4 Efficiency decomposition of listed NGEs by industry

Year	**A Agriculture ($N = 5$)**					**C Manufacturing ($N = 121$)**				
	Effch	**techch**	**pech**	**sech**	**tfpch**	**effch**	**techch**	**pech**	**sech**	**tfpch**
2004 ~ 2005	0.870	0.634	0.698	1.246	0.552	0.885	1.046	0.893	0.991	0.925
2005 ~ 2006	1.140	0.757	1.109	1.028	0.863	0.552	2.022	0.731	0.756	1.116
2006 ~ 2007	1.113	0.946	1.063	1.047	1.053	1.122	1.085	1.059	1.060	1.218
2007 ~ 2008	1.079	0.923	0.976	1.106	0.996	0.951	1.042	0.974	0.976	0.991
2008 ~ 2009	1.047	1.007	1.128	0.929	1.055	1.174	0.811	1.089	1.078	0.951
Average	1.045	0.842	0.980	1.066	0.880	0.906	1.142	0.940	0.964	1.035
Year	**E Construction ($N = 5$)**					**G Information technology ($N = 11$)**				
	Effch	**techch**	**pech**	**sech**	**tfpch**	**effch**	**techch**	**pech**	**sech**	**tfpch**
2004 ~ 2005	3.361	0.177	3.049	1.102	0.595	0.931	0.977	1.180	0.789	0.909
2005 ~ 2006	0.882	0.978	1.000	0.882	0.863	0.993	1.320	0.959	1.036	1.311
2006 ~ 2007	0.613	1.200	0.705	0.870	0.736	0.775	0.914	0.925	0.837	0.708
2007 ~ 2008	1.002	1.016	1.124	0.892	1.018	1.633	0.602	1.503	1.086	0.983
2008 ~ 2009	1.452	0.591	0.989	1.468	0.858	1.197	1.134	1.018	1.175	1.357
Average	1.215	0.659	1.191	1.021	0.801	1.070	0.957	1.099	0.973	1.024
Year	**J Real estate ($N = 10$)**					**F、H、K、L Other services[a] ($N = 15$)**				
	Effch	**techch**	**pech**	**sech**	**tfpch**	**effch**	**techch**	**pech**	**sech**	**tfpch**
2004 ~ 2005	1.209	0.935	1.261	0.959	1.131	1.765	0.526	1.301	1.356	0.929
2005 ~ 2006	0.933	1.341	0.798	1.170	1.252	0.897	1.032	0.971	0.924	0.926
2006 ~ 2007	1.091	0.816	1.575	0.692	0.890	0.770	1.728	0.846	0.910	1.330
2007 ~ 2008	1.917	0.778	1.247	1.537	1.492	1.094	0.743	1.181	0.927	0.813
2008 ~ 2009	0.556	1.856	0.812	0.684	1.032	0.996	1.186	0.932	1.069	1.181
Average	1.056	1.081	1.099	0.961	1.142	1.058	0.963	1.033	1.025	1.019

Note: Original data from wind database, processed with Malmquist-DEA on the basis of variable return to scale

[a]F, H, K, and L respectively represent transport and storage, wholesale and retail trade, social services, and communications and the cultural industry

In most industries, however, the tfpch in 2007 ~ 2008 or/and 2008 ~ 2009 declined to different degrees, especially as compared with what was seen before 2008, indicating the pronounced impact of the global financial crisis on NGEs' technical advancement. The non-governmental manufacturing industry is probably the most intimately affected by the financial crisis—its tfpch has declined from 1.218 in 2006 ~ 2007 to 0.991 and 0.951 by the following 2 years, and has not yet picked up as of the end of 2009. It should be noted that the non-governmental IT industry is least affected by the financial crisis, and its tfpch has maintained a rising trend, up from 0.708 in 2006 ~ 2007 to 0.983 and 1.357 in the following years. The development of information and communication technology (ICT) has blurred the line between manufacturing and services in the traditional sense, and led to an obvious trend of integration during the evolution of its industrial structure (Lundvall and Borras 1998; Kaufmann et al. 2003). This change has enabled the non-governmental IT industry, while advancing in its specialized technologies, to reduce the impact of external factors by adopting a diversified strategy towards development. This is probably why its tfpch has not showed a declining trend.

A comparison of the efficiency change (effch) and technical change (techch) further reveals that the effch of non-governmental manufacturing is below 1 from 2004 to 2009, which indicates no evident improvement in its production efficiency, for any increase in total-factor productivity is mainly caused by technical progress. In such industries as agriculture, construction, IT, and other related services, however, the average efficiency is above 1 while the technical change is below 1. This reflects that the rise of total-factor productivity in these industries is mainly caused by an improvement of enterprise efficiency rather than technical advancement. In real estate, both effch and techch are above 1, indicating some degree of promotion in both the enterprise efficiency and technical level from 2004 to 2009.

6.2.3 Enterprise Scale and Dynamic Efficiency

According to the theory of Cave et al. (1982), effch decomposition can be used to measure the roles of technology and scale in efficiency change. In Table 6.4, the pure efficiency change (pech) and scale efficiency change (sech) are 0.940 and 0.964, respectively, in manufacturing, which indicates the insignificant improvement of either the technical productivity or scale efficiency of enterprises. On the other hand, the average sech is above 1 in agriculture, construction, and other services, indicating relatively significant economies of scale. Whereas in the IT and real estate industries, efficiency improvement mainly results from the promotion of technical efficiency, and the role of scale efficiency is insignificant. Therefore, there may be diseconomies of scale among NGEs in both industries. Judging by the efficiency trend, the scale efficiency of real estate has declined from 1.537 in 2007 ~ 2008 to 0.684 in 2008 ~ 2009 due to external impacts as well as to the influence of policy adjustments, while that of other industries indicate a rising trend.

Table 6.5 Efficiency decomposition of listed manufacturing NGEs by size

	effch	techch	pech	sech	tfpch
C1 Large ($N = 61$)					
2004 ~ 2005	0.853	1.174	0.864	0.988	1.002
2005 ~ 2006	0.797	1.385	0.962	0.828	1.104
2006 ~ −2007	1.096	1.023	1.018	1.077	1.122
2007 ~ 2008	1.057	0.879	1.030	1.026	0.928
2008 ~ 2009	1.036	0.927	0.996	1.040	0.960
Average	0.960	1.062	0.972	0.988	1.020
C2 Medium ($N = 55$)					
2004 ~ 2005	1.036	0.823	1.024	1.012	0.852
2005 ~ 2006	0.428	2.658	0.525	0.817	1.139
2006 ~ 2007	1.231	1.019	1.172	1.050	1.254
2007 ~ 2008	0.978	1.097	1.032	0.948	1.073
2008 ~ 2009	1.150	0.826	1.122	1.025	0.950
Average	0.907	1.151	0.939	0.966	1.044
C3 Small ($N = 5$)					
2004 ~ 2005	0.985	1.231	0.948	1.039	1.213
2005 ~ 2006	0.890	1.414	0.872	1.020	1.258
2006 ~ 2007	0.881	1.334	1.071	0.822	1.175
2007 ~ 2008	0.707	1.245	0.802	0.882	0.880
2008 ~ 2009	1.263	0.732	1.264	0.999	0.924
Average	0.928	1.162	0.979	0.948	1.079

Notes: 1. Original data from wind database, processed with Malmquist-DEA on the basis of variable return to scale
2. Based on CSRC industry classifications, different from NBS classifications

To further judge the relationship between NGEs' scale and efficiency, we have divided the manufacturing NGEs according to the number of employees into large-sized (>2000 persons), medium-sized (300 to 2000 persons), and small-sized (<300 persons), as seen in Table 6.5.[10] We find in our analysis a steady increase of the average tfpch (total-factor productivity change) from large-sized NGEs (1.020) to medium-sized NGEs (1.044) to small-sized NGEs (1.079). This indicates a greater improvement of productivity among of small-sized manufacturing NGEs from 2004 to 2009. If we observe the data of 2008 ~ 2009 alone, however, it is the other way round—the tfpch is 0.960, 0.950, and 0.924, respectively, in large-, medium-, and small-sized NGEs, down by 0.162, 0.304, and 0.251 compared with the same data from 2006 to 2007. This indicates a stronger stress tolerance

[10]In the method of NBS (File No. 143 issued by State Economic and Trade Commission in 2003), industrial enterprises can be classified according to employee numbers, sales, and total assets. Considering the volatility of the indicators and their sensitivity to external impacts, we have selected the employee numbers in 2009 as the criterion of classification here, as it is relatively stable and easy to compare.

Table 6.6 Operational efficiency of listed NGEs by industry

	2004	2005	2006	2007	2008	2009
Agriculture	7.33	7.31	7.86	6.87	7.22	7.88
Manufacturing	9.37	10.42	7.55	7.35	7.94	8.69
Large and medium	9.47	10.58	7.59	7.34	7.79	9.47
Small	6.78	6.05	6.34	7.64	12.01	6.78
Construction	6.94	5.33	4.55	4.43	5.12	5.83
IT	14.23	15.62	13.21	13.51	15.12	15.60
Real estate	14.81	7.91	9.94	6.78	8.37	8.47
Services	11.49	15.24	12.34	9.12	13.82	12.84

Notes: 1. Operation efficiency (%) = administrative expenses/gross revenue
2. Sample numbers, industry classifications and original data source are the same as those of Table 6.5

among large-sized manufacturing NGEs in coping with external impacts, such as the international financial crisis.

In terms of technical change, the average techch of large-sized manufacturing NGEs is smaller than that of medium- and small-sized enterprises. This means that the scale-efficiency relationship has a certain influence on the total-factor productivity of all sizes of enterprises as well as to the ratio between them. If we compare the efficiency change among enterprises, we can find that the average scale efficiency (sech)of large-, medium-, and small-sized manufacturing NGEs is 0.988, 0.966, and 0.948, respectively. This indicates a probable positive correlation between enterprise scale and scale efficiency.

6.2.4 Changes in NGEs' Operational Efficiency

Besides production efficiency, the changes in NGEs' operational efficiency are also an important indicator of the improvement of enterprise efficiency. We have selected the administrative expenses[11] and the gross revenue from the financial data of the listed non-governmental companies and used the ratio between them to measure enterprise efficiency in operations and management. Table 6.6 shows the changes in the operational efficiency of the listed non-governmental companies of different sizes and across different industries. As we can see in the table, the operational efficiency of all industries surveyed has invariably gone through a decrease-to-increase process. For example, in the manufacturing industry, the average operational efficiency of the listed non-governmental companies fell from the maximal value of 10.42% in 2005 to 7.35% in 2007, indicating an

[11]In enterprise financial statements, administrative expenses refer to the costs incurred in the organization and management of the production and operation of an enterprise, which do not directly create economic output.

improvement of the operational and management efficiency of such companies in this period of time; but since 2008, the administrative expenses of the industry have been increasing due to changes in the international and domestic economic environment. The ratio to the gross revenue has also increased to 8.69% in 2009. This may indicate that, on the one hand, China's NGEs are limited in the control and management of risks in production and operations and weak in coping with external shocks, and, on the other hand, that external impacts cannot change the development trend of enterprise fundamentals—with the growth of the country's enterprises and the optimization of their external environment, NGEs' operational and management efficiency will return to its original trend of improvement.

Specifically, in the manufacturing industry, the ratio of administrative expenses to the gross revenue of large- and medium-sized NGEs was 9.47% and that of small-sized NGEs was 6.78% in 2004. That is, the operational and management efficiency of the former was lower than that of the latter in that year. Both generally declined over the following years. The administrative expenses of small-sized NGEs increased dramatically in 2008, however, due to changes in the external environment, while its ratio to the gross revenue (12.01%) was much higher than that of large- and medium-sized NGEs (7.79%). But in 2009, it returned to its original trend. In summary, the operational and management efficiency of larger manufacturing NGEs is lower than that of small ones, but over a short period of time, external impacts may cause a bigger rise in the administration expenses of small manufacturing NGEs.

6.3 Scale, Efficiency, and Paths to Growth for NGEs

When a dynamic equilibrium is reached between the expansion of scale and efficiency improvement of enterprises, rational paths to their growth are determined. Based on an analysis of NGEs' scale and efficiency, this section will study the relationship between them by using parametric and nonparametric regression models with Chinese data.

6.3.1 The Parametric Regression Analysis

In the process of NGEs' growth, their competitiveness is determined by their production and operational efficiency. As was analyzed previously, the improvement of both types of efficiency is probably correlated with the expansion of an enterprise's scale. We first construct the following parametric regression models:

$$\mathrm{tfpch} = \alpha \mathrm{I} \ln \mathrm{y} + \mathrm{C} + \varepsilon$$

Table 6.7 NGEs' scale and efficiency: parametric regression

	2005	2006	2007	2008	2009
tfpch					
lny	0.1814* (55.5117)	0.0945 (0.6785)	−0.0160* (−4.2383)	0.0302* (10.1125)	−0.0874 (−1.3092)
C	0.7060* (112.2465)	1.0419* (3.8466)	1.3597* (238.9880)	0.9879* (194.2796)	1.1926* (8.4811)
R^2	0.9628	0.0039	0.1312	0.4622	0.0142
DW	1.8755	2.0212	1.7083	1.6412	1.6402
lnma					
lny	−0.6055* (−4.3377)	−0.5727* (−5.0414)	−0.7632* (−6.7301)	−0.7226* (−6.9527)	−0.6902* (−7.1707)
C	3.1636* (12.0008)	2.9785* (13.2699)	3.3640* (14.1642)	3.3995* (15.3060)	3.4289* (16.6956)
R^2	0.1438	0.1863	0.2898	0.3015	0.3146
DW	1.6256	1.6631	1.7899	1.7606	1.8673

Notes: 1. The tfpch, ma and y values are the calculation results in Sects 6.2 and 6.3
2. The weighted linear regression is used for the empirical analysis of tfpch and lny in 2005, 2007 and 2008; the OLS regression is used otherwise
3. * indicates pass of test at confidence levels of 0.01 and 0.1 respectively

$$\text{lnma} = \beta \text{I} \ln y + \text{C} + \mu$$

In the models being examined, tfpch, lnma, and lny represent total-factor productivity change, operational efficiency, and enterprise scale, respectively; C is a constant term; $\varepsilon$and $\mu$are both disturbance terms. Then, using the Malmquist-DEA model, we can calculate the tfpch, the ratio of administrative expenses to gross revenue, and the main business revenue. Using the example of manufacturing NGEs,[12] Table 6.7 reveals the relationship between enterprise scale and efficiency from 2005 to 2009.

The regression reveals an unstable coefficient relationship between production efficiency and enterprise scale. In 2005, 2006, and 2008, we can see a positive relationship between the scale of expansion and the productivity expansion of the enterprises in question, but the coefficient αfluctuated remarkably—for example, there was a big difference between 0.1814 in 2005 and 0.0302 in 2008. In 2007 and 2009, however, the relationship between production efficiency and enterprise scale was negative. The regression also reveals a relatively stable relationship between operational efficiency and enterprise scale. The negative β reflects a declining trend of the ratio of administrative expenses to gross revenue with the expansion of enterprise scale, indicating that scale expansion is beneficial to the improvement of operational efficiency. It should also be noted, however, that the coefficient βfluctuated considerably in these years.

[12]As the data processing results of other industries are similar, typical manufacturing NGEs are chosen and analyzed here.

Although this linear result can directly reveal the relationship between the scale of expansion and the efficiency improvement of manufacturing NGEs, its defects should not be neglected. First of all, it is uncertain whether the coefficient $\alpha$is positive or negative, which may lead to contradictions in the interpretation of the relationship between production efficiency and enterprise scale. Secondly, under the assumption of a positive α,the infinite expansion of enterprise scale corresponds to the infinite optimization of production and operational efficiency. The result would be that only a very few enterprises survive to meet the market demands. But, in fact, due to resource constraints and transaction costs imposed on enterprises, the original functional relationship between enterprise scale and efficiency improvement will change after a certain degree of expansion. On this basis, we conclude that the relationship between enterprise scale and efficiency is likely to be non-linear.

6.3.2 *Nonparametric Regression Analysis*

Out of regard for the above-mentioned defects, we also use the nonparametric models to find out whether there is a non-linear relationship between enterprise scale and efficiency. We adjust the regression models as follows:

$$\text{tfpch} = m(\text{lny}) + \varepsilon$$
$$\text{lnma} = m(\text{lny}) + \mu$$

In the equation, $m(\cdot)$ is an unknown smooth function. Figure 6.2 shows the results of the nonparametric regression.

We first study the relationship between the production efficiency and expansion of scale of the enterprises in question. The regression results of 2005 show that, with the expansion, production efficiency experienced a period of rapid rise, but growth slowed down to between 1.5 and 2.0. The results from 2006 show a bimodal curve, indicating a trough of enterprise scale between 1.5 and 2.5, as well as an obvious decline of production efficiency when the enterprise scale reached 2.5. The 2007 data indicates that the production efficiency experienced a period of decline when the enterprise scale reached 1.6, but the trend would reverse and the production efficiency would continue to rise when the enterprise scale was around 2.5. The results from 2008 and 2009 were quite similar—both reflected an increase-to-decrease functional relationship, in an inverted U shape, between enterprise scale and production efficiency.

The nonparametric regression model resembles that of linear regression in that both reflect a significantly negative relationship between operational efficiency and the scale of expansion of the enterprises. The result of the nonparametric regression, however, has revealed a different evolutionary path. That is, the expansion is accompanied by a significant decline in the operational efficiency when the enterprise scale is between 0.0 and 2.0, but the decline slows when the enterprise scale

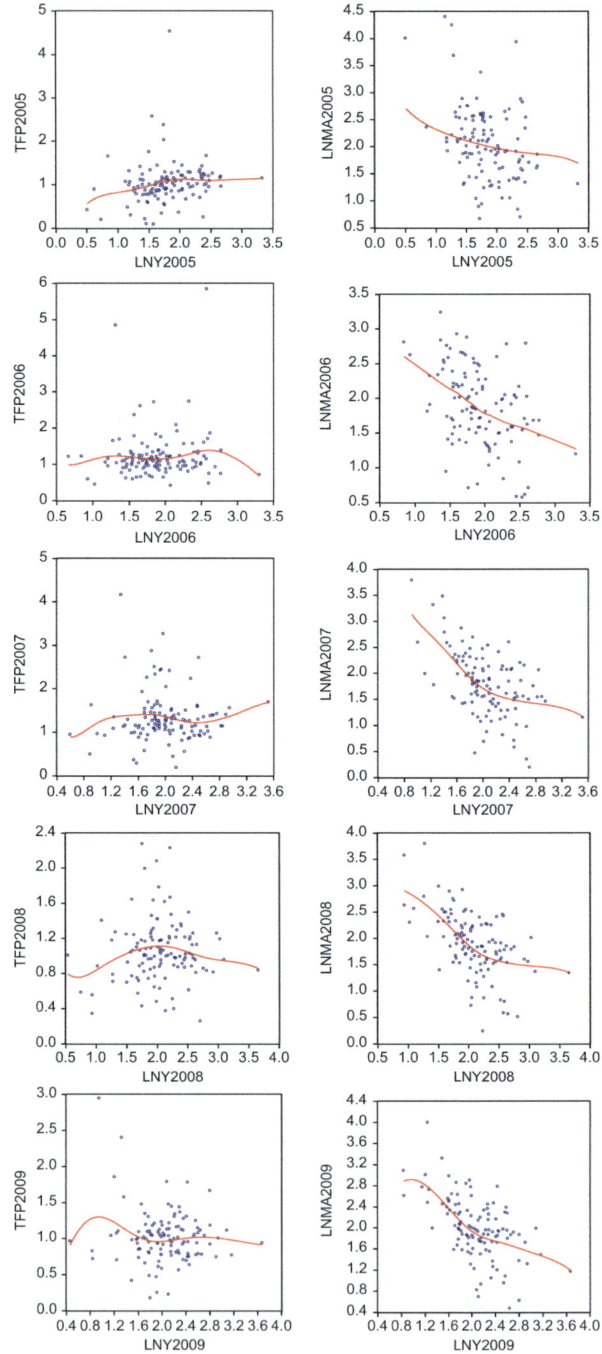

Fig. 6.2 NGEs' scale and efficiency: a nonparametric regression
Notes: 1. The same data information as that of Table 6.7
2. Nadaraya-Watson kernel estimation is used for the selection of the nonparametric regression models. The normal distribution function of "Normal" is chosen as the kernel form, and the bandwidth is chosen through the least squares cross validation

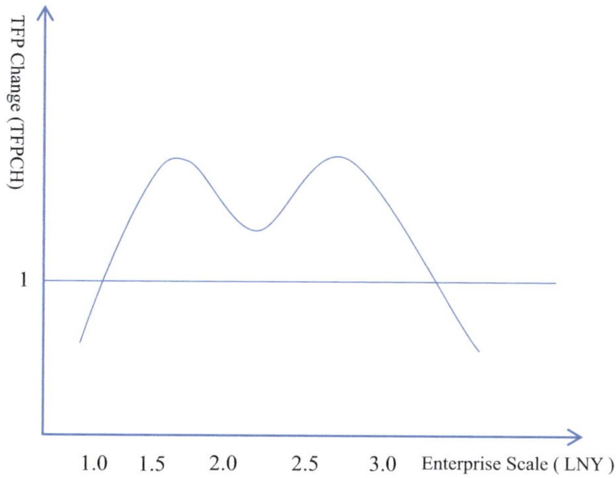

Fig. 6.3 NGEs' scale and TFP change (simulated)

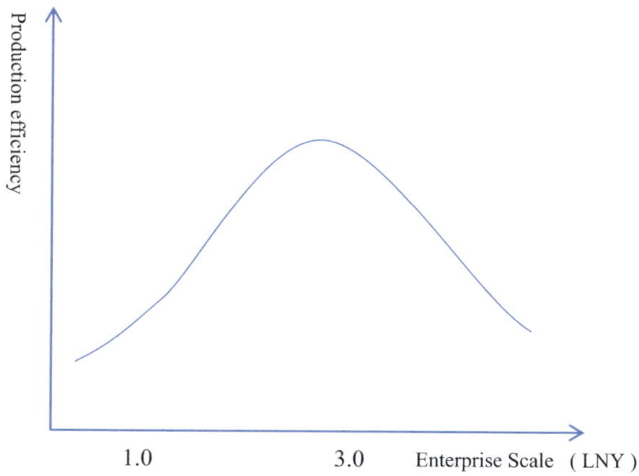

Fig. 6.4 NGEs' scale and production efficiency (simulated)

reaches 2.0. This indicates that, when the scale is expanded to a certain degree, some resistance within the enterprise will prevent the further decline of its operational efficiency. The functional relationship is well in line with observable reality.

6.3.3 Simulation of NGEs' Paths to Growth

Based on the empirical results reached here, we concluded and simulated the relationship between the scale and total-factor productivity in NGEs' growth as Fig. 6.3.[13] When TFPCH is above 1, it indicates actual technical advancement. According to the changes seen in TFPCH, we can divide an enterprise's growth into six stages. (1) When the scale is relatively small (LNY<1.0), TFPCH is below

[13]Either Fig. 6.3 or Fig. 6.4 is only the simulation of one possible form of the real economy.

1, indicating no significant production efficiency of the enterprise. But the rising trend of TFPCH indicates an on-going improvement of the enterprise efficiency. (2) When LNY is between 1.0 and 1.5, there is an obvious technical efficiency of the enterprise. (3) When LNY is between 1.5 and 2.0, the technical advancement slows. (4) When LNY is between 2.0 and 2.5, TFPCH is in the trough. In this stage, TFPCH can go below 1, or in other words, it is possible for there to be no efficiency of the enterprise whatsoever. (5) When LNY is between 2.5 and 3.0, TFPCH rises again, and finally, (6) When LNY is above 3.0, TFPCH enters a stage of absolute decline.

When we use total-factor productivity to illustrate NGEs' production efficiency based on Chinese data, we can conclude the relationship between NGEs' scale and production efficiency as the variation trends shown in Fig. 6.4. Specifically, in NGEs' scale of expansion, their production efficiency initially rises, indicating a positive relationship between scale and efficiency. After certain expansion of their scale, the increase of their production efficiency slows or even experiences an absolute decline, as their advantages are weakened and new constraints on their growth become more prominent. That is, the relationship between scale and efficiency may change into a negative one during this period. Afterwards, any further expansion of enterprise scale can bring about two results—the production efficiency may decline continuously or it may reverse and rise volatily.

6.4 Conclusions

In the new century, the production and operational environment of NGEs has been greatly changed by the infiltration of finance into every aspect of the real economy, the renovation of information and network technology, the weakening of economic boundaries, and the integration of industries. With the global financial crisis of 2008, China's NGEs have been and are currently faced with new tests of their development. They must actively adjust their growth and development paths, and adapt themselves to such changes as weak external demand and the loss of their original comparative advantages, as well as the rise of non-tariff barriers. Moreover, to cope with the financial crisis, the Chinese government has adjusted the macroscopic planning for NGEs' development in some industries. As a result, NGEs' development will have to face new ordeals brought about by frequent enterprise restructuring and institutional environment changes, e.g., the frequent adjustment of the export recovery rate. Under these circumstances, an empirical analysis on the dynamic evolution of NGEs' growth and development in the new stage can outline a feasible direction for NGEs' future development and guide governmental decision-making in the private sectors of the economy.

It is true that China's NGEs are limited by resource constraints, external demands, and the institutional environment during their growth, but their development and expansion is also a process of relaxation of these external constraints. To make it bigger or stronger? The two options contained within this question can be unified along the most basic path of NGEs' growth, namely, the dynamic expansion of their optimal scale. Through a study of the relationship between NGEs' expansion of scale and production efficiency improvements, we have discovered two transition points in NGEs' growth (i.e., the bimodal relationship seen in Fig. 6.3). In the process of expansion, enterprise efficiency first shows an increase-to-decrease curvilinear relationship in an inverted U shape, which is similar to the conclusions reached by He Yifeng et al. (2008) and Shi Qi and Lü Jiachun (2009). The turning point of efficiency in scale expansion is exactly the first transition point. What is different from other current conclusions is that further expansion of NGEs' scale will lead directly to the second transition point, where NGEs can reverse the evolutionary relationship of production efficiency and resume along a rising trend through their own efforts. This is a critical period for NGEs to narrow the gap with large-sized SOEs and FFEs, and a way to edge themselves into the list of Top 500 Chinese Enterprises and potentially even Global Top 500 Enterprises.

Accordingly, NGEs should not take the maxim of "making it bigger" as the constant goal of their growth. When they are small, "making it bigger" contributes to an increase in their market competitiveness and survivability. But once they have grown to a certain scale, "making it stronger" must be the core of NGEs' development; otherwise, they are likely to be trapped by an insufficient or even inefficient expansion of scale. On the other hand, in the process of NGEs' development, the government must guide them to attach greater importance to technological innovation in their expansion, encourage and foster NGEs' innovation by means of supportive financing and taxation policies, and establish a sound mechanism for market entry and exit. Moreover, it is necessary to enhance NGEs' market competitiveness, improve their awareness of "making it stronger," and guide them to avoid inefficient expansion of scale.

Bibliography

Bharath ST, Pasquariello P, Wu G (2009) Does asymmetric information drive capital structure decisions? Rev Financ Stud 22(8):3211–3243

Cave DW, Christensen LR (1980) The relative efficiency of public and private firms in a competitive environment: the case of Canadian railroads. J Polit Econ 88(5):958–976

Cave D, Christensen L, Diewert WE (1982) The economic theory of index numbers and the measurement of input, output, and productivity. Econometrica 50(6):1393–1414

Charnes A, Cooper W, Rhodes E (1978) Measuring the efficiency of decision making units. Eur J Oper Res 2(6):429–444

Cheng C (2004) Thought on Coase's theory about the boundary and scale of firms. Policy-Mak Ref (3)

Cheng H, Xing Y (2003) Capital structure, scale and growth of China's technology enterprises. World Econ (12)

Clarkson KW, Miller RL (1982) Industrial organization: theory, evidence, and public policy. McGraw-Hill Book Company, New York

Coase RH (1937) The nature of the firm. Econometrica 4(16):386–405

Dangl T (1999) Investment and capacity choice under uncertain demand. Eur J Oper Res 117 (3):415–428
Dewenter KL, Malatesta PH (2001) State-owned and privately owned firms: an empirical analysis of profitability, leverage, and labor intensity. Am Econ Rev 91(1):320–334
Dow GK (1987) The function of authority in transaction cost economics. J Econ Behav Organ 8 (1):13–38
Fan G (2000) On the dynamic process of institutional transition in China. Econ Res J (1)
Fang M, Nie H (2008) The empirical investigation of firm size determinants—evidence from Chinese enterprise panel. Nankai Econ Stud (6)
Ford J, Slocum J (1977) Size, technology, environment and the structure of organization. Acad Manag Rev 2(4):561–575
Gayle PG (2003) Market concentration and innovation: new empirical evidence on the Schumpeterian hypothesis. Department of Economics working paper, Kansas State University.
Gibrat R (1931) Les Inégalités Économiques. Librairie du Recueil Sirey, Paris
Hall B (1994) Enterprise restructuring and investment horizons in the United States, 1976–1987. Bus Hist Rev 68:110–143
Hargadon A, Sutton RI (1997) Technology brokering and innovation in a product development firm. Adm Sci Q 42:716–749
He Y, Su L (2008) Older is wiser?—evidence from a semi-parametric study of competitive power and experience in China's non-governmental enterprises. South China J Econ (5)
He Y, Su L, Shi W (2008) Experience effects and scale effects: an empirical study on labor productivity of China's NGEs. Paper at 8th China Economics Annual Conference. Available at http://down.cenet.org.cn/view.asp?id=83192
Honjo Y (2004) Growth of new start-up firms: evidence from the Japanese manufacturing industry. Appl Econ Lett 11(1):21–32
Hu J, Chen J (2009) Evolutionary characteristics of NGEs' financing modes: case study of typical enterprises. Guangdong Soc Sci (2)
Hu AGZ, Jefferson GH, Jingchang Q (2005) R&D and technology transfer: firm-lever evidence from Chinese industry. Rev Econ Stat 87(4):780–786
Jefferson GH, Rawski TG, Li W, Zheng Y (2000) Ownership, productivity change, and financial performance in Chinese industry. J Comp Econ 28(4):786–813
Kaufmann A, Lehner P, Todtling F (2003) Effects of the Internet on the spatial structure of innovation networks. Inf Econ Policy 15(3):402–424
Lall SV, Rodrigo GC (2001) Perspectives on the sources of heterogeneity in Indian industry. World Dev 29(12):2127–2143
Li C (2006) Brand competitiveness and diversification strategy for private enterprises. J Hebei Univ Econ Trade (2)
Li Y, Liu Z, Peng Z (2008) Decision-making on investment capacity under uncertainty. Oper Res Trans (2)
Liu X (2000) Impact of the structure of China's industrial enterprise's ownership on its efficiency. Econ Res J (2)
Liu B, Lin T, Liu Y (2010) On dynamic efficiency of steel and iron enterprises in China from scale and ownership perspectives—based on Malmquist TFP index. China Soft Sci (1)
Lundvall B, Borras S (1998) The globalizing learning economy: implication for innovation policy. Report to the DGXII, TSER, Bussels.
Malmquist S (1953) Index numbers and indifference surfaces. Trab Estad Investig Oper 4 (2):209–242
Myers S (1984) The capital structure puzzle. J Financ 39(3):575–592
Nie H, Tan S, Wang Y (2008) Innovation, enterprise size and market competition. World Econ (7)
Onder A, Deliktas E, Lenger A (2003) Efficiency in the manufacturing industry of selected provinces in Turkey: a stochastic frontier analysis. Emerg Mark Financ Trade 39(2):98–113
Pagan A, Ullah A (1999) Nonparametric econometric. Cambridge University Press, Cambridge

Qu Y (2009) Technological innovation performance of enterprises of various sizes and governmental policy orientation. Seeker (2)

Research Group of Enterprise Survey Unit, National Bureau of Statistics (2004) Studies on development and growth of NGEs. Rev Econ Res 22:2–12

Scherer FM (1965) Firm size, market structure, opportunity and the output of patented inventions. Am Econ Rev 55(5):1097–1125

Shi Q, Lu J (2009) Industrial chain positioning, firm scale, agglomeration and firm competence—an empirical research on listed manufacturing enterprises in the Yangtze River Delta. J Nanjing Univ Financ Econ (5)

Siddharthan NS (1992) Transaction costs, technology transfer, and In-House R&D: a study of the Indian private enterprise sector. J Econ Behav Organ 18(2):265–271

Wei L, Zhao J, Xiao H (2005) An empirical study on effects of company performance and equity ownership structure on listed firm size—exemplification of listed manufacturing companies in China. Soft Sci (3)

Worley JS (1961) Industrial research and the new competition. J Polit Econ 69(2):183–186

Wrigley L (1970) Divisional autonomy and diversification. Unpublished doctoral dissertation, Harvard Business School

Xu K, Ren F (1998) Economic models in East Asia and national industrial competitiveness. Soc Sci Abroad (3)

Xue B (2007) Analysis of industrial cluster life cycle from an angle of location decision. Ind Econ Res (3)

Zhou L, Luo K (2005) Firm size and innovation: evidence from China's province-level data. China Econ Q (3)

Chapter 7
The Labor-Capital Relationship: A Source of Strength for NGEs' Growth and Development in the New Economic Stage

Haoqing Xu and Lei Zhao

7.1 The Significance NGEs' Labor-Capital Relations

Since China's reform and opening up and with the development of China's economy under different types of ownership, domination of state ownership has been broken while the market-oriented "non-public sectors of economy" has grown significantly. By June 2009, there were 6.9 million NGEs nationwide, accounting for 70% of all enterprises in China; and they provide over 85% of urban jobs and more than 90% of rural employment , and NGEs had absorbed and accepted 75% of China's working population.[1] It can be said that the private sectors of the economy are already playing the dominant role in China's economy overall.[2] But during the rapid development of the private sectors of the economy, labor-capital conflicts and contradictions have been accumulated and have worsened, of which the "Foxconn Incident" is a typical example. As economic interest is the most basic unit of the labor-capital relations, it is crucial to determine a reasonable proportion of income distribution between labor and capital among NGEs. The report of the 17th National Congress of the CPC proposed to "gradually increase the proportion of residents' income in national income distribution and raise the proportion of labor remuneration in the primary distribution."[3] Chinese State Councilor Ma Kai pointed out that, currently, the proportion of resident income represents too small a share in the national income, and so is labor remuneration in the primary distribution. He proposed structure adjustment to of the

[1]Gu Jianfen. (2009). Perform Our Duty; Organize and Guide NGEs to Attract More Employment. http://www.zgjy.org/kwzl/kwzlshow.asp?messageID=259. Accessed 15 June 2010.

[2]Cheng Lu. (2006, Feb. 9). China's NGEs from 2001 to 2005. *China Business Times*.

[3]Report on the 17th CPC National Congress. http://www.xinhuanet.com/17da/index.htm. Accessed 23 July 2010.

H. Xu (✉) • L. Zhao
Graduate School, Chinese Academy of Social Sciences, Beijing, China

Y. Liu (ed.), *New Interpretations on the Development of China's Non-Governmental Enterprises*, Research Series on the Chinese Dream and China's Development Path, DOI 10.1007/978-981-10-3872-3_7

distribution of national income and, while retaining the continued growth of the enterprises and their normal income, that efforts be made to raise the proportion of labor remuneration and keep income inquality in check so as to ensure that the income growth of both urban and rural residents is no lower than the rate of economic growth, and that labor payment is not lower, but perhaps even slightly higher, than the growth rate of China's economy and corporate income.[4] Therefore, this chapter will study the construction of a reasonable income distribution system for the harmonious development of the labor-capital relations in NGEs—"an important part of the national economy"—in the new stage.

7.1.1 The Nature of the Labor-Capital Relations

Despite the superficial similarity between "labor-capital relations" and "labor relations," there are different ways of understanding of the two concepts among researchers and academics. As "the socialist transformation of the public ownership of the means of production" had been completed prior to the 8th National Congress of CPC, the non-public sectors of China's economy came to an end. Since then, the relationship of labor rights and those obligations between employees and employers has been referred to as the "labor-capital relations." Owing to historical reasons, some scholars have equated the two relationships indiscriminately in their studies. For example, Wang Daqing and Jiao Jianguo (2003) think that the "labor-capital relations is just a kind of labor relations, namely, the relationship of rights and obligations formed between individual laborers (or their organizations such as trade unions) and employers (or their groups and administrations) in the process of labor, including labor tasks, working conditions, working time and duration, labor remuneration, labor discipline, labor protection, social security, and welfare, as well as labor disputes and settlements."[5] Other scholars think that the two relationships indicate the broad and narrow senses of the same concept, without essential differences between them.

For example, Zhu Yan thinks that, from the perspective of law, the labor-capital relations has two meanings: one is that of the social labor-capital relations in the broad sense, namely, all those relations that occur in the process of social labor, including the use of the labor force, labor management, and labor services; the other is the relationship of labor rights and obligations in the process of labor between labor owners (laborers) and labor users (employers). This is the narrow sense of the labor-capital relationship, or the labor-capital relations as it is usually referred to.[6] In fact, the labor-capital relationship is one that occurs between people in the process of work. Therefore, as long as an enterprise is the subject of distribution

[4]Ma Kai. (2009). Quicken the Adjustment of Economic Structure When Coping with the International Financial Crisis. *Qiushi*, (20), 9–13.

[5]Zhu Weijun. (2001). *Labor Relations*. Beijing: China Labor and Social Security Publishing House, p. 5.

[6]Ibid.

for production elements and as long as it keeps operating, there will be some sort of labor-capital relationship between people in production and operations, and, consequently, there will be a labor-capital relation on the level of enterprise. At present in China, the labor-capital relations is an important part or a special form of labor relationship. The labor-capital relationship originates from the "employment relationship" of enterprises. The precondition of its existence is the separation of labor owners from the material conditions necessary to realize labor. The foundation of the labor-capital relationship is the public ownership of the means of production as well as the commercialization of the labor force. As Cheng Yanyuan has analyzed, the labor-capital relations is born out of the hiring behavior of an employment organization and basically refers to the relationship between management and an individual or group of laborers, caused by the interest of both parties, and manifested as cooperation, conflict, strength, and power[7] Feng Xiaotian argues that the labor-capital relations is, fundamentally, an interpersonal interaction based on employment, namely, the relationship between employers and employees.[8] Yet Chang Kai thinks that the so-called labor-capital relations usually refers to one between labor and capital in specifically non-public enterprises, which embodies the relationship between employees and employers (employer enterprises). It includes the relationship between an individual laborer and an employer, as well as that between the labor union, the employer, and the employees' group.[9] Therefore, a typical labor-capital relations predicated upon a system of wage labor, and the precondition is the separation of laborers from the means of production as well as the commercialization of the labor force. That is to say, a labor relationship based on joint labor and the public ownership of the means of production must never be equated directly with the traditional and ubiquitous labor-capital relations. Similarly, the labor-capital relations in the individual or private sectors of the economy is not a typical labor-capital relations, as the laborers are not completely separated from the means of production. In this sense, the labor-capital relations in China's NGEs is subordinate to the basic economic system of Chinese-style socialism and is therefore different from the labor-capital relations as it exists under a traditional capitalist system. In this light, it is justifiable to say that the two types of relationship are, in essence, labor relations.

7.1.2 The Labor-Capital Relations Within NGEs

Of the two subjects implicated within the labor-capital relations of China's NGEs, one is the entrepreneur who uses labor. As the owner of the means of

---

[7]Cheng Yanyuan. (2002). *Labor Relations*. Beijing: China Renmin University Press, p. 3.

[8]Feng Xiaotian. (2000). *Labor-Capital Relations in Private Enterprises*. Wuhan: Huazhong University of Science and Technology Press, p. 63.

[9]Chang Kai. (2004). *On Labor Rights*. Beijing: China Labor and Social Security Publishing House, p. 69.

production and the enterprise operator, he is entitled to the possession, control, and disposal of the means of production and is, at the same time, in possession of the surplus labor that workers create. The other is the workers, the labor owners employed by the entrepreneur for their physical or mental work in order to earn their wages, or a union that represents their interests. Under the conditions of incomplete labor contracts and asymmetric information, both labor and management have the urge to maximize their own benefits by means of information advantages.[10] Just as Mayo holds, both individuals and organizations desire to achieve a maximum output with the smallest amount of input.[11] Specifically, employees want to get more income or payment with as little labor input as possible, while employers want to pay their employees as little as possible to get as much labor. For employers, the objective is the maximization of profit, whereas for employees, the maximization of wages and welfare. The difference in their objectives determines the existence of their conflicts. For the two parties, neither are their interests completely in agreement nor completely in opposition. Despite their divided interests, both labor and management have one common interest—the production efficiency, the basis for realizing their individual power and interests. Therefore, both sides form a "community of interests" in the enterprise, and only when they value the rights and interests of each other and cooperate with each other can they improve the productivity, realize the Pareto improvement and increase their own interests.

7.1.3 The Labor-Capital Relations and Enterprise Performance

The influence of the labor-capital relationship on enterprise performance is an important concern for western scholars. For example, they are primarily concerned with such questions as whether the status of the labor-capital relations, e.g. its structure and quality, will affect enterprise performance, and the direction and degree of such an influence. An analysis of the possible modes for the division of the labor-capital relations mainly includes three views: labor-capital antagonism and conflict, labor-capital harmony or partnership, and labor-capital mutual benefit.

The major representative of labor-capital antagonism and conflict is behind the basic theory of Marxism. According to Marxism, the nature of the labor-capital relations of capitalism is the enforcement and exploitation of laborers by capital and

[10]Zhao Xiaoshi. (2009). Two-Way Moral Risks in Labor Relationship. *Financial Science*, (4), 65–72.

[11]Mayo, George Elton. (1964). *The Social Problems of an Industrial Civilization*. Beijing: The Commercial Press.

the possession of workers' surplus value by the capitalist without remuneration. "Capital is the opposite of workers, so the progress of civilization only increases the objective power of capital to dominate labor."[12] To improve their situation, the working class must resort to violent revolution and eliminate the system of wage labor and private ownership before they can solve their reconcilable labor-capital contradiction and conflict under capitalist conditions.

To the contrary, the advocates of labor-capital harmony hold that both the capitalist and the laborers (management and those under management) are part of the same enterprise, and there is no fundamental conflict of interest between them. The employer and employees hold basically common interests and are both committed to the pursuit of high efficiency, high profit, and high rewards within the enterprise. A good example of this is the labor relationship theory under the planned economy in China, whereby revolutionary comrades are only different in labor division, without a difference in position or status.

As the compromise between the above-mentioned two theories, the theory of the mutual benefit between labor and capital accepts the economic man hypothesis in mainstream economics. According to this view, both labor and management have the urge to maximize their own benefits by way of information advantages, under the conditions of incomplete labor contracts and asymmetric information.[13] For the two parties, their interests are neither completely in agreement nor completely in opposition. Despite their divided interests, both labor and management are united under certain common interests. Therefore, it is necessary for them to form a "community of interest" within the enterprise, share weal and woe, and cooperate with each other.

A comparison of the three views shows that either "antagonism/conflict" or "harmony" emphasizes only one aspect of the labor-capital relationship. On the one hand, the views held by those who espouse labor-capital harmony cannot explain disharmonious phenomena in the current labor-capital relations, such as labor disputes or even violent conflicts. On the other hand, according to the views of interested opposition, the opposite fundamental interests of both sides would make it impossible to implement the measures needed to improve the labor-capital relations, and any effort towards the improvement of enterprise performance would turn out to be in vain.[14] We are in favor of the theory of labor-capital mutual benefit. It is true that there are contradictions between them, as both labor and management pursue their own rights, but meanwhile they also have common interests. Only when they respect each other's rights

---

[12]Marx, Karl., & Engels, Frederick.(1975). *The Complete Works of Marx and Engels*. Beijing: People's Press, Vol. 23.

[13]Zhao Xiaoshi. (2009). Two-Way Moral Risks in Labor Relationship. *Financial Science*, (4), 65–72.

[14]Cappelli, P. & Neumark, D. (2001). Do High Performance Work Practices Improve Establishment-Level Outcomes? *Industrial and Labor Relations Review*, 54(4), 737–775.

and interests can they cooperate to improve productivity, realize the Pareto improvement, and pursue their own interests. In simple terms, this stable relationship for "cooperation and mutual benefit" is harmonious labor-capital relations; it emphasizes the cultivation and development of personnel abilities, values objective and fair performance appraisal, maintains the fair and rational level of and differentiation of payment, and, in particular, strengthens the awareness of mutual benefit and cooperation between the enterprise and employees, as well as the participatory awareness of common employees. In such harmonious labor-capital relations, the enterprise can establish a long-term and stable employment relationship with its employees by providing stable positions, fair remuneration, a friendly and cooperative work environment, and the chance for the long-term development of the employees' career. On the other hand, the employees contribute their working enthusiasm, talents, and loyalty to the enterprise. As Barnard pointed out, whether an organization can adequately function depends on whether or not it can organize the unanimous behavior of its members and ensure their cooperation.[15]

Many studies show that the proportion of labor in national income fluctuates with the stages of economic development. Although the proportion of labor income is on the decline in developed countries, it remains at a fairly high level compared with capital income. The proportion of labor income has also decreased in China's national income distribution. This has been proven by many scholars, who believe that SOEs' reform and NGEs' rapid development are the most important cause behind this phenomenon.[16,17] But it should also be noticed that few studies have been done on the labor-capital relations of China's NGEs, which are mainly qualitative analyses, and that the previous studies have not gone far in the systematic review of the history of NGEs' labor-capital distribution relationship and lack an empirical analysis of the relative contributions of NGEs' labor and capital, as well as the interaction between the labor-capital relations and enterprise development.

7.2 The Evolution of the Labor-Capital Distribution Relations Among NGEs

From the start of China's reform and opening to the early 1990s, the total wages of Chinese laborers accounted for 15–16% of China's GDP, and this proportion was stable. Since 1992, however, the proportion of labor income has been decreasing

[15]Barnard, C. I. (2007). *The Functions of the Executive* (Tr. Wang Yonggui). Beijing: China Machine Press.

[16]Bai Chong'en & Qian Zhenjie. (2009). Factor Allocation in National Income: a Story Beyond Statistics. *Economic Research*, (3), 27–41.

[17]Zhuo Yongliang. (2007). On Decrease of Labor-Income Proportion and Increase of Capital-Income Proportion. *Zhejiang Social Sciences*, (3), 26–33.

yearly. Many domestic scholars have analyzed and interpreted this trend from various perspectives. One important reason for the decline is SOEs' reform and NGEs' development, according to their analysis.

In the accounting system outlining China's national income, national income is divided into four types according to several factors—laborers' payment, net production tax, the depreciation of fixed assets, and operating surplus. Limited by the data of NGEs, the following analysis will cover only NGEs' wage income, profits, and taxes, so as to examine the evolution of NGES' income distribution between the labor and capital factors.

7.2.1 Wage Income in NGEs

The income of employees working for NGEs is mainly made up of two parts—wages and bonuses/dividends. According to data drawn from ACFIC's eight sampling surveys, in the early 1990s, if we add up the average annual wages, bonuses, and dividends of NGE employees, the sum was higher than the average income level nationwide, and it was also higher than that of state-owned and collective enterprises, nearly twice the national average at the time. In 1996, however, the average annual income of NGE employees was RMB 6115.56, less than RMB 6280 of on-post SOE employees, as well as lower than the annual average income of RMB 6210 throughout China. In 2003, the average annual income of NGE employees was only RMB 9043, but the average wages of SOE employees were over 1.6 times that of NGE employees. The latest survey data show that the average annual income of NGE employees was RMB 18,412 in 2007, which was RMB 8208 lower than that of SOE employees; the ratio was 1:1.45, a wider gap than the 1:1.19 seen in 2005. If we compare the annual growth of the average income across different types of enterprises, we can find the annual growth rate of wage income in NGEs is only 9.13%, which is significantly slower than the 15.99% found in SOEs and 14.27% in collective enterprises (Table 7.1).

7.2.2 NGEs' Profits

NGEs' profits, here, refers to what is left after the deduction of the costs and the payment of taxes and fees, including newly-added investment, investors' dividends, the payment of apportions and donations, social engagements, and more. It can be seen in Table 7.2 that most of Chinese NGEs' profits were put into reproduction. Especially in 2001, 94.98% of NGEs' profit was reinvested in production. After that, the proportion of reinvestment dropped significantly—in 2007 it was only

Table 7.1 Average annual income of employees in China's NGEs and other enterprises

Survey year	Average income in NGEs (RMB)	Average income in SOEs (RMB)	Ratio of SOEs' to NGEs' per capita income	Average income in collective enterprises (RMB)	National per capita income (RMB)
1993	4966	2878	0.58	2109	2711
1995	6027.66	4797	0.80	3931	4538
1997	6115.56	6280	1.03	4302	6210
2000	8000.04	8543	1.07	5774	8364
2002	10,250	11,178	1.09	6867	10,870
2004	9043	14,577	1.61	8678	14,040
2006	16,188	19,313	1.19	11,283	18,364
2008	18,412	26,620	1.45	15,595	24,932
Average annual growth	9.13%	15.99%	–	14.27%	15.94%

Note: The data in each line are based on the statistics of the previous year of the survey and calculated according to the prices of that year

Sources: ACFIC (2007); NBS. (2010); *China's Private Sectors of Economy Yearbook (June, 2006–June, 2008)*, Beijing: China Industrial & Commercial United Press

Table 7.2 Profit distribution across China's NGEs

Year	Average net profit after taxes (mn RMB)	Average net profit reinvestment (mn RMB)	Proportion of reinvestment (%)
1992	1	0.632	63.20
1994	1.82	1.247	68.50
1996	0.45	0.297	66.00
1999	1.279	1.015	79.36
2001	1.176	1.117	94.98
2003	1.965	1.623	82.60
2005	2.28	1.252	54.91
2007	3.122	1.608	51.51

Source: *China's Private Sectors of Economy Yearbook (June, 2006–June, 2008)*, China Industrial & Commercial United Press

51.51%, but still making up more than half of NGEs' profit. This can more or less explain the high investment rate seen in present-day China. As Xiao Zhuoji mentioned, because of the high returns on capital in China, non-public investment has been growing by 30% annually in recent years.[18]

[18]Xiao Zhuoji. Change the Exceedingly Unbalanced Situation and Coordinate Economic and Social Development. Address on the 10th Meeting of the 10th Session of the Standing Committee of CPPCC National Committee. http://cppcc.people.com.cn/GB/34961/50294/50298/3528737.html. Accessed August 11, 2010.

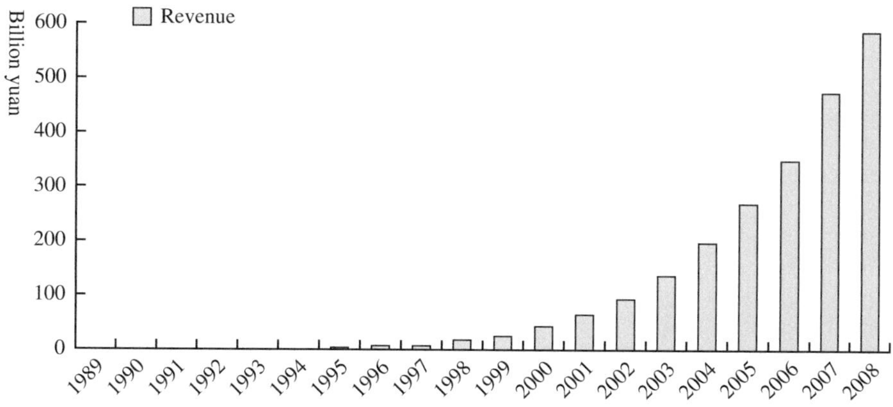

Fig. 7.1 NGEs' total revenue 1989–2008 (Sources: *Chinese Tax Yearbook (1990–2009)*)

7.2.3 NGEs' Revenue

The total revenue of China's NGEs has been increasing rapidly over the past 20 years. It has soared from RMB 0.34 billion in 1991 to RMB 589.97 billion in 2008. The average annual growth rate of NGEs' tax is 55.08%, far higher than their profit growth rate and also greater than the average growth rate of China's enterprise revenue (which was RMB 288.345 billion in 1991 and RMB 5.78618 trillion in 2008, with an average annual growth rate of 19.29%), and the proportion of NGEs' contribution to national revenue has increased from 0.12% to 10.2% of national taxes. Therefore, in the analysis of labor-capital allocation in NGEs, it is undesirable to simply discuss whether "the wages have encroached on the profit" or vice versus. Instead, it is necessary to include government taxation in the analysis, and study the proportional allocative framework of government, capital, and labor.

7.2.4 The Structure of NGEs' Income Distribution

Using the data from ACFIC's eight sampling surveys, Table 7.3 has listed the median of sales/output values, taxes, and profits, as well as their proportions among the sales of those NGEs surveyed since 1992.

As can be seen in Table 7.3, in the structural evolution of NGEs' labor-capital distribution in China, the proportion of profits is between 3% and 4% in recent years but declining. Taken together with NGEs' taxes, the proportion of taxes in sales was below 4.0% and basically stable, except for 1992. According to the 8th national sampling data, however, the average proportion of NGEs' five-item burdens (taxes, dues, apportions, donations, and public relations entertainment) in sales was around 12% in 2007, with the first three items accounting for 9.4% of sales. In general, the

Table 7.3 NGEs' taxes and dues, profits, and proportions in sales (mn RMB)

Year	Sales/ Output values	Taxes	Dues	Profits	Wages	Proportion of taxes (%)	Proportion of dues (%)	Proportion of profits
1992	1.00	0.05	0.008	0.127	0.154	5.00	0.80	12.70%
1994	1.82	0.07	0.012		0.229	3.80	0.60	
1996	3.35	0.128	0.039	0.282	0.306	3.80	1.20	8.40%
1999	4.00	0.14	0.02	0.20	0.440	3.50	0.50	5.00%
2001	5.80	0.22	0.03	0.21	0.615	3.79	0.52	3.62%
2003	4.40	0.16	0.02	0.15	0.407	3.64	0.45	3.41%
2005	6.54	0.25	0.03	0.21	0.858	3.82	0.46	3.21%
2007	7.84	0.26	0.02	0.25	0.773	3.32	0.26	3.19%

Note: There is no data of NGEs' profit in 1994. The data are output values in 1993 and 1995 and sales in the rest years. Generally, in the survey of NGEs, the median is smaller than the average, so the data in this table may be different from the actual data. But they are comparable since they are all median values

Sources: *Large-Scale Investigation of China's NGEs 1993–2006,* China Industrial & Commercial United Press. *China's Private Sectors of Economy Yearbook (June 2006–June 2008),* China Industrial & Commercial United Press

proportions of taxes and dues in NGEs' sales rose from 2001 to 2007, according to the report.[19]

Consequently, income distribution is not only a matter between labor and management, but the tax burden should also not be neglected. As China's NGEs are mostly engaged in competitive industries, to increase their labor-income proportion, the government, as an "external force," must reduce NGEs' burden. Only by doing so can NGEs raise the proportion of wealth to be allocated between labor and capital.

7.2.5 A Comparison with the Income Distribution of Industrial SOEs

To better study NGEs' labor-capital distribution structure in China, we have analyzed the ratio of wages and profits of industrial NGEs since 1999 and compared them with the same data of SOEs.

As Table 7.4 shows, without considering the price factor, the total profits of industrial NGEs and SOEs were RMB 12.152 billion and 99.786 billion, respectively, in 1999. In 2008, the data were RMB 830.206 billion and 906.359 billion, up by an annual rate of 59.90% and 27.78%, respectively. While over the same period, the annual growth rates of total wages were only 44.08% and 7.51%, respectively. The annual growth rate of NGEs' total profits was 15% higher than that of their total wages; for SOEs, the figure was 20%. Table 7.4 also shows the trends in variation in

[19](Mar. 26, 2009). Comprehensive Report on Data Analysis of the 8th Sampling Survey of China's NGEs. (summary). *China Business Times*.

Table 7.4 Profits and wages of industrial NGEs and SOEs (bn RMB)

Enterprise types	NGEs	SOEs	NGEs	SOEs	NGEs	SOEs
Year	Total profits		Total wages		Profits/wages	
1999	12.152	99.786	18.325	289.999	150.80%	290.62%
2001	31.256	238.856	55.506	299.0238	177.58%	125.19%
2003	85.964	383.620	92.927	315.2816	108.10%	82.19%
2005	212.065	651.975	273.924	362.0898	129.17%	55.54%
2007	505.374	1079.519	414.806	463.9839	82.08%	42.98%
2008	830.206	906.359	490.260	556.2607	59.05%	61.37%
Average annual growth rate	59.90%	27.78%	44.08%	7.51%	–	–

Note: The wages are based on ACFIC's survey of the average annual wages, multiplied by the total numbers of employees in *China Statistical Yearbook 2009*

Sources: (1) *China Statistical Yearbook 2009*; (2) *Large-Scale Investigation of China's NGEs 1993–2006*, published by China Industrial & Commercial United Press

the proportions of their total wages and profits from 1999 to 2008. The proportion of industrial NGEs' total wages to their total profits was 177.58% in 2001, but had dropped down to 59.05% in 2008. Meanwhile, the ratio of industrial SOEs' total wages to their total profits also decreased from 290.62% in 1999 to 42.98% in 2007, but rose slightly in 2008. Table 7.4 reveals two features in the overall profit distribution of China's industrial NGEs and SOEs. On the one hand, despite a certain amount of growth for both their profits and wages from 1999 to 2008, the growth rate of the latter was far less than that of the former. On the other hand, the proportion of laborers' wages had declined while the capital factor had become more significant in both NGEs and SOEs. Yet, it must be noted that, although the proportion of wages declined in both NGEs and SOEs, the number of SOE employees decreased and, consequently, the growth of average income among SOEs was much higher than that of NGEs (See Table 7.4). Meanwhile, what Table 7.4 shows is the proportions of wages to profits, but compared with the income of NGE employees, a greater part of SOE laborers' income was in the form of compensations and benefits. On the other hand, according to the *Report on China's NGE Studies (2006),* NGEs' medical care coverage, endowment, unemployment, and employment injury insurances were only 26.3%, 29.2%, 18.2%, and 10.7%, respectively, in 2005. Hence, the proportion of laborers' payment in SOEs is higher than that in NGEs.

From the features seen here in terms of income distribution, it can be inferred that a large part of industrial added value has been obtained in the form of capitalistic profits by China's industrial NGEs. In other words, the portion of laborers' income in industrial economic growth as a whole has been declining yearly, while the distribution of industrial NGEs has tilted their benefits away towards capital.

By observing the historical evolution of the labor-capital allocation among China's NGEs, we have come to these basic conclusions. In NGEs' development, laborers' average income grows slowly and their wages account for a small proportion of the profit in the overall economic distribution. With their high returns on capital, NGEs have a strong desire to reinvest, and their reinvestment rate to the after-tax profit has exceeded 50%, but they are also saddled with heavy tax burden. The distributive system as divided among the government, enterprises, and laborers is not rational.

7.3 Labor-Capital Income Distribution and the Performance of NGEs

7.3.1 Proportion of and Justifications for NGEs' Labor-Capital Distribution

We have made an empirical analysis of the ratio of distribution between labor and capital in China's NGEs in recent years by using the related data from the NBS enterprise sampling survey database. According to the ratio of labor income analyzed above, the proportion of labor income can be taken as a constant, unrelated to factor prices or the factor endowment structure, in a formula to be used in the following. The wide use of the Cobb-Douglas (C-D) Function has, to some extent, led to the belief that "the proportion of labor income is stable." As the early representatives of this view, Cobb and Douglas thought that changes in factor prices would not affect the proportion of labor income in the United States. Gollin (2002), after considering income from self-employment, was convinced of the existence of "Kaldor facts" and the validity of the C-D Function.[20] Since people have become aware of the existence of the intertemporal and transnational differences in the proportion of labor income, however, the Constant Elasticity of Substitution Function (CES) $Y_i = A\left[\alpha K_i^{(\sigma-1)/\sigma} + (1-\alpha)L_i^{(\sigma-1)/\sigma}\right]^{\sigma/(\sigma-1)}$ has been more widely used in research. Then, the proportion of labor income is determined by the following formula:

$$s_{Li} = 1 - \alpha \cdot k_i^{(\sigma-1)/\sigma} \tag{7.1}$$

In Formula (7.1), the proportion of labor income is decided by the capital-output ratio and unrelated to any other element, such as factor prices. The relationship between labor and capital (alternative or complementary, $\sigma > 1$ or $\sigma < 1$) determines the direction of the change in the labor-income ratio when the capital-output ratio is up.

So we first establish a C-D production function $Y = AK^{\alpha}L^{\beta}$ and then a CES production function for estimation purposes.

[20]Gollin, D. (2002). Getting Income Shares Right. *Journal of Political Economy*, 110(2), 458–475.

7.3.1.1 Overall Empirical Analysis

Data processing: a company's output Y is expressed as its industrial added value, and the producer price index (PPI) of industrial products is adjusted to the actual value; the capital stock$K$ is expressed as the net value of the company's fixed assets, and the price index of investment in fixed assets is adjusted to the actual value; the labor force L is expressed as the average number of employees of a company. A_0 is a technical coefficient. To eliminate the interference of heteroscedasticity, we take the logarithm of the above variables, as the logarithm can indicate the elasticity or the contribution of a factor's increase to output growth. As there is no available data of the industrial added value of 2004 and 2008 in the database, we have conducted a general regression of the data in 2005, 2006, and 2007.

C-D Production Function estimates:

3-year Overall Result (Balanced panel model).

The results of the Hausman Test are as follows:

Correlated random Effects—Hausman test			
Test cross-section random effects			
Test summary	Chi-sq. statistic	Chi-sq. d. f.	Prob.
Cross-section random	4064.534706	2	0.0000

Through the Hausman Test, we find the fixed-effect model should be adopted. Then we estimate the model with Eviews 6.0 and get the following results:

$$\begin{aligned} \log(Y) &= 5.974 + 0.196\log(K) + 0.287\log(L) \\ &\quad (220.81)(77.84) \qquad (67.59) \end{aligned} \tag{7.2}$$

$$R^2 = 0.8849, F = 15.37, DW = 2.51, N = 91{,}088$$

(Y is the output of a company, K is the capital stock, L is the number of laborers, and N is the sample number.)

Clearly, the equation shows a good degree of fit, as the t-statistics are all significant on the significance level of 1%. In the C-D Function, as the technical level is constant, the output growth comes from the contribution of capital and labor. According to the distributive principle of the market economy, all the production factors shall be participants in the distribution. The proportion of distribution depends on the contribution of each factor, and income should be fully distributed among all the factors. This is the famous Euler's Distribution Theorem.

Normalization of the equation estimation results shows that capital and labor contribute 40.57% and 59.43%, respectively, to the final output. Therefore, in terms of the distribution, laborers' remuneration should account for nearly 60% of the added value, which agrees with the ratio of distribution in countries with a mature market economy. If we compare the estimated and actual distribution, however, the proportion of laborer' payment was less than half the estimation. Hence, it is undeniable that laborers' remuneration is quite low in the primary distribution.

7.3.1.2 Empirical Analysis by Year

1. Estimation results of the cross-section data in 2005:

$$\begin{aligned} \log(Y) &= 4.103 + 0.302\log(K) + 0.493\log(L) \\ &\quad (232.53)(125.37) \qquad (135.86) \end{aligned} \tag{7.3}$$

$$R^2 = 0.4714, F = 40{,}618, DW = 1.690, N = 91{,}088$$

2. Estimation results of the cross-section data in 2006:

$$\begin{aligned} \log(Y) &= 4.115 + 0.300\log(K) + 0.464\log(L) \\ &\quad (238.80)(127.93) \qquad (131.37) \end{aligned} \tag{7.4}$$

$$R^2 = 0.4595, F = 38{,}725, DW = 1.746, N = 91{,}088$$

3. Estimation results of the cross-section data in 2007:

$$\begin{aligned} \log(Y) &= 4.097 + 0.330\log(K) + 0.475\log(L) \\ &\quad (221.42)(132.30) \qquad (125.60) \end{aligned} \tag{7.5}$$

$$R^2 = 0.4648, F = 39{,}553, DW = 1.647, N = 91{,}088$$

Based on the yearly cross-sectional data results and the normalization of the equation estimation results, we can find that the contribution of capital to output was 38%, 39.3%, and 41% in 2005, 2006, and 2007, respectively, while that of labor was 62%, 60.7%, and 59%, respectively. These proportions were close to the overall Panel Model results, so laborers' wages should account for nearly 60% of the added value. But again, if we compare the estimated and actual distribution, the proportion of laborer' payment was less than half the estimation.

7.3.1.3 CES Production Function

By use of Kementa's linear estimation and through the nonlinear transformation of the CES Function, we get a linear formula approximately as follows:

$$\begin{aligned} \log(Y) &= \log(A) + m\delta\log(K) + m(1-\delta)\log(L) \\ &\quad - \frac{1}{2}m\rho(1-\delta)\left[\log\left(\frac{K}{L}\right)\right]^2 \end{aligned} \tag{7.6}$$

Estimated Results of the CES Production Function:
3-year Overall Result (Balanced panel model)

Hausman Test

Test cross-section random effects			
Test summary	Chi-sq. statistic	Chi-sq. d. f.	Prob.
Cross-section random	3600.763820	3	0.0000

Through the Hausman Test, we find that the fixed-effect model should be adopted. Then we estimate the model with Eviews 6.0 and get the following results:

$$\log(Y) = 6.817 - 0.127\log(K) + 0.467\log(L) - 0.020\left[\log\left(\frac{K}{L}\right)\right]^2 \tag{7.7}$$

$$(164.83) \quad (-10.37) \quad (58.87) \quad (26.91)$$

$$R^2 = 0.8853, F = 5.44, DW = 2.52$$

Y is the output of a company, K is the capital stock, and L is the number of laborers.

As can be inferred from the above, the coefficient estimates of the CES Production Function are: $A = 342.364$; $\delta = -0.373$; $\rho = 0.229$; $m = 0.340$.

The resultant negative δ indicates something wrong in the data or elsewhere, as it goes against both our expectations and classical hypotheses. (The substitution elasticity $\sigma = 1/(1 + 0.229) = 0.813$ is close to 1, the substitution elasticity found in the C-D Production Function. This proves that the C-D Production Function is a more appropriate formula.)

7.3.2 *Collaborative Labor-Capital Relations and Enterprise Performance*

7.3.2.1 Enterprise Performance Promotion Through Collaborative Labor-Capital Relations: A Theoretical Basis

With the development of technology, more and more new technologies are being applied to the production process, which has gone from being characterized as labor-intensive to capital-intensive and then to technology- and knowledge-intensive. Inevitably, this requires that laborers bring into play their creative subjectivity in taking the initiative within enterprises. The establishment of collaborative labor-capital relations within an enterprise can better motivate enthusiasm for work, improve productivity, and increase output.

Firstly, in collaborative labor-capital relations, workers' efforts can not only be increased, but also better organized and coordinated into "effective effort." Under the condition of team production, enterprise labor consists of two closely related steps. One is the conversion of workers' labor capacity into actual labor effort; the other is the conversion of workers' labor efforts into effective labor efforts through reasonable organization and coordination. The labor effort as measured in unit time has a significant influence on the enterprise's productivity. Thus, without the second step, workers' labor efforts cannot turn into an effective joint force, products, or values, as part of it is wasted. This step is of the greatest importance and plays a more prominent role in China's technology- and knowledge-intensive modern labor. If NGEs intend to gain an edge in competition, they must rely more on the strengthened effectiveness of labor. Obviously, compared with non-collaborative labor-capital relations, collaborative labor-capital relations are more beneficial to the organization and coordination of the labor process, and are therefore more conducive to the formation of effective labor effort and creation of beneficial values.

Secondly, collaborative labor-capital relations contribute to strengthen enterprise cohesion and competitiveness. In their study of the relationship between labor-capital relations and productivity, Buchele and Christiansen raised the following questions: which type of unemployment are workers more afraid of? Dismissal as the punishment for violating labor regulations, or layoffs and bankruptcy as a result of an enterprise's failure to adequately compete? Knowledge of these questions can familiarize us with the main pressure acting on employees' behavior and better help us control their behavior accordingly. Reality shows that both types of pressure have an influence on workers, but the latter affects them more. There are two reasons. Firstly, in the daily management of an enterprise, it is rare that a worker is dismissed for disciplinary violations—this is especially true for those in key positions. Secondly, compared with key workers, those individuals in ordinary positions are under a greater threat of dismissal, but with their lower wages, any cost incurred from their unemployment is also lower. Hence, according to the positive correlation seen between unemployment cost, labor intensity, and labor productivity, the influence of such a threat on workers' attitudes towards labor is limited. Therefore, Buchele and Christiansen concluded that workers, especially the backbones, are more afraid of job cutting due to some threat to the whole enterprise, such as failure in operation, downsizing, production suspension due to obtainment of external resources, or close-down. This has laid a foundation for the establishment of collaborative labor-capital relations oriented to the overall benefit of the enterprise. The formation of a collaborative labor-capital relationship is highly significant to the enhancement of enterprise cohesion and further improvement of production and operation.

Thirdly, collaborative labor-capital relations positively involve workers and their interests in technological innovation, which can help facilitate further scientific progress and development. There are two types of technological innovation in production. One is product innovation, related to the results of labor itself, and the other is process innovation, or the innovation of labor conditions. In NGEs, both types of technological innovation are initiated by investment and dominated by capital, and their emergence and progressive transition is directly related to the lifecycle of industrial sectors, which rely on capital accumulation and competition. Both types are also subject to the labor-capital relationship, however, as technological innovation is not only completed solely through workers' efforts but also directly concerns their own interests—the former is beneficial to maintaining and enlarging the market share of an enterprise and increasing its sales, which makes it possible to expand employment and increase employee income, and has a positive (or at least not negative) influence on their interests; the latter is beneficial to improving the enterprise's output in unit time, and reducing the cost of each product by reducing labor consumption, which makes layoffs possible or even inevitable for some workers and thus is generally negative in regards to their interests. Therefore, only when workers are more directly and positively involved with technological innovation and productivity changes will they actively take part in this innovation. For example, in collaborative labor-capital relations, employees can share the fruits of product innovation by means of salary increases and bonus, profit sharing, and ESOP; the employer can increase job security through certain forms of insurance and long-term employment, and, in doing so, reduce the negative effect of technological innovation on the workers. On the contrary, if the workers feel a lack of security or do not have a positive relationship with their enterprise's technological innovation, they will realize that the increase of unit-time output may increase their chance of unemployment, or that any further innovation will bring nothing good to them. In this case, they will not volunteer to be party to technological innovation.

If we focus on those technicians within an enterprise directly engaged in innovation, we can see that collaborative labor-capital relations are more important for increasing their labor efforts. These technicians are the core workers of the enterprise and crucial to the promotion of its competitiveness. Due to their special roles and the enterprise's reliance on them, their management represents a dilemma—the enterprise has to instigate their initiative for technological innovation and, at the same time, make them respect the enterprise's authority. If key workers give their initiative in technological innovation full reign and display their innovative capacity, they may weaken the authority of an enterprise; if they respect the enterprise's authority too much, their own initiative and innovative capacity may be limited or weakened. It is our belief that the only way out of this dilemma is to provide them with further remuneration, job security, and opportunities for promotion; that is, to establish collaborative labor-capital relations.

7.3.2.2 Enterprise Performance Promotion Through Collaborative Labor-Capital Relations: A Factor Analysis

Based on the operation of China's NGEs, we believe the following factors are highly significant to the harmony and collaboration of labor-capital relations.

First, wages and bonuses. They are workers' main source of income, the amount of which influences their behavior. According to Akerlof, high wages will encourage workers to behave in accordance with the Gift Exchange Rules, raise their sense of mutual benefit and common responsibility, and reduce their opportunism. We believe, the higher the wages and bonuses, the more harmonious the labor-capital relations, and the easier it will be to motivate workers' enthusiasm and thereby improve enterprise performance.

Second, ESOP. Its implementation entitles workers to a share of an enterprise's profit, as well as the benefits brought about by enterprise growth. It can also improve the employees' sense of belonging, as they are shareholders of the enterprise, highlight the "common interests" between them and the employer, and strengthen the sense of unity and cooperation between labor and management. Moreover, this model of co-governance with employee stakeholders can realize a degree of self-restraint and mutual supervision on both sides and, to a certain degree, reduce their hidden actions. Obviously, ESOP can reduce bilateral moral hazards or ethical violations, improve labor-capital relations, and promote enterprise performance.

Third, worker supervision by management. The degree of supervision reflects the degree of management's trust in workers, as well as the degree of workers' autonomy. Through his experiments, Nagin found that, under an obviously loosened supervision, opportunistic behaviors increase among a large part of employees; however, at the same time, a significant number of employees respond little to the relaxation. Therefore, supervisory and incentivizing measures are necessary to the systematic management of these opportunistic employees. We believe, however, that too much supervision indicates a non-collaborative labor-capital relationship, which has a negative effect on enterprise performance.

Fourth, average worker tenure. Longer average indicate more stable labor-capital relations in an enterprise and a certain tacit agreement between management and employees that has been reached through a long-term interest bargain. For example, under the permanent employment system in Japan, many employees regard enterprises as their home, a situation that corresponds with a strong sense of belonging and has enabled Japanese enterprises to develop rapidly after WWII. On the other hand, the shorter the average number of working years, the stronger the personal mobility, the more unstable the enterprise, and the more difficult it is to form a stable work force. To reiterate, a longer average number of working years represents a more collaborative labor-capital relationship, which can effectively promote enterprise performance.

Fifth, the proportion of expenses used on employee benefits. Welfare is becoming an increasingly important factor in the competition for talents. A developed corporate concept of human welfare can raise employees' sense of belonging and loyalty and play a long-term incentivizing role among them. Therefore, the higher proportion of expenses spent on employee benefits, the more satisfied the employees will be with the enterprise, the more harmonious the labor-capital relationship, and the better the enterprise performance.

Sixth, the proportion of expenses on employee training. For an enterprise, employee training is an important human capital investment as well as an effective method for incentives, as it can improve employee skills and thus promote their job performance. For the employees, they can have better development after the training. Hence, the higher the proportion of expenses on employee training, the stronger the human capital of an enterprise, the more harmonious the labor-capital relationship, and the better the enterprise performance, as such training can improve the employees' individual human capital and cultivate their loyalty to the enterprise.

Apart from the above factors, labor-capital relations are also under the influence of labor unions, questions of scale, and the nature of the business engaged in by an enterprise.

7.3.3 *Labor-Capital Relations and Enterprise Performance: Empirical Tests*

According to related empirical research, besides the above-mentioned factors, the scale, liability ratio, and age of an enterprise also have important influences on its performance, so we have included them in the empirical models as control factors. In the following, we will test how collaborative labor-capital relations affect enterprise performance through multivariate linear regression modeling.

7.3.3.1 Multivariate Linear Regression Model

We will conduct an empirical test on their effects on enterprise performance. The equation used for estimation is:

$$\begin{aligned} roa = \beta_0 + \beta_1 \log(wage) + \beta_2 stock + \beta_3 supervise + \beta_4 moliblity + \beta_5 rwelfare \\ + \beta_6 rtrain + \beta_6 \log(scale) + \beta_7 rdebt + \beta_8 age + \mu \end{aligned} \tag{7.8}$$

In the equation, μ is a random factor and the content of the other variables can be seen in the table below (Table 7.5).

We estimate Eq. (7.8) with the survey data of 2004 and get the estimation results of Model 1. After eliminating the insignificant variables in Model 1, we re-estimate Eq. (7.8) and get the estimation results seen in Model 2 (See Table 7.6).

According to the Estimation Results of modeling, wages and bonuses have a significant positive influence on enterprise performance—the higher they are, the more likely to motivate employees' labor enthusiasm; the more harmonious the labor-capital relations, the better for overall enterprise performance. Employees' mobility has a significantly negative effect on enterprise performance—the higher the mobility, the worse enterprise performance. The other factors have relatively little influence on enterprise performance.

Table 7.5 Variable meanings and calculation methods

	Symbol	Variable meaning	Calculation method
Explained variable	*roa*	Enterprise performance	Return on assets = (Profit + Tax)/Total assets
Explanatory variables	*wage*	Wages and bonuses	Wages + Dividends + Equity incentive spending
	stock	ESOP	Virtual variable 1 = Yes, 0 = No
	supervise	Worker supervision by management	Number of operational and managerial staff members/number of all employees
	mobility	Employee mobility	(New employees+employees terminated)/ total number of employees
	rwelfare	Proportion of expenses on employee benefits	Employee benefits expenses/total wages
	rtrain	Proportion of employee training expenses	Employee training expenses/total wages
Control variables	*scale*	Enterprise scale	Total assets
	rdebt	Liability ratio	Total debt/total assets
	age	Enterprise age	Length of time from founding to sampling

Table 7.6 Estimation results of enterprise performance determinants 2004

		Model 1		Model 2	
	Variables	Coefficients	T-values	Coefficients	T-values
Explanatory variables	C	0.1149	4.5115	0.1166[a]	4.6484
	Log(Wage)	0.0238[a]	5.4634	0.0238[a]	5.6557
	stock	−0.0022	−0.1790		
	supervise	−0.0026	−0.0943		
	mobility	−0.0211[c]	−1.7140	−0.0210[c]	−1.7687
	rwelfare	−0.0025	−0.7148		
	rtrain	0.0074	0.6240		
Control variables	*Log(scale)*	−0.0131[a]	−3.1684	−0.0134[a]	−3.2795
	rdebt	−0.0758[a]	−3.8217	−0.0764[a]	−3.8667
	age	0.0015[a]	2.4553	0.0015[b]	2.4632
Test statistics	R^2	0.1106	–	0.1088	–
	F	7.1295	–	12.6906	–
	DW	1.9574	–	1.9475	–
Sample numbers	–	526	–	526	–

Note: [a]Indicates a significant estimated coefficient under 1% level
[b]Indicates a significant estimated coefficient under 5% level and
[c]Indicates a significant estimated coefficient under 10% level

7.3.3.2 Panel Data Model

The Panel Data Model can provide more information and effectively solve the multi collinearity that exists among the variables. With freer model estimation and more effective coefficient estimation, this method can appropriately handle the problem of individual heterogeneity and estimate the variable coefficients more accurately. Therefore, we also test how the factors affect enterprise performance by way of the Panel Data Model. Based on the general results, we recommend the Panel Data Model be employed as follows:

$$\begin{aligned} roa_{it} = \; & \beta_0 + \beta_1 \log(wage_{it}) + \beta_2 stock_{it} + \beta_3 supervise_{it} \\ & + \beta_4 moliblity_{it} + \beta_5 rwelfare_{it} + \beta_6 rtrain_{it} + \beta_6 \log(scale_{it}) \\ & + \beta_7 rdebt_{it} + \beta_8 age_{it} + \mu_{it} \end{aligned} \tag{7.9}$$

In the equation, i stands for the ith enterprise, t for the time, μ_{it} for the combination of random errors, and the meanings of the other variables are the same as those in Table 7.5.

In consideration of the unique heterogeneous elements of individual enterprises (enterprise culture, organizational structure, and so forth.) that may affect enterprise performance but will remain unchanged in the short term, we use the fixed-effect Panel Data Model in the test. Table 7.7 lists the estimation results of the Panel Data Model (Model 1). As the estimated coefficients of some explanatory variables are insignificant, we eliminate such variables and re-estimate the equation, and get the estimation results of Model 2.

The estimation results of the Panel Data Model are basically similar to those of the general multivariate linear regression model. Wages and bonuses have a significant positive influence on enterprise performance, while employees' mobility has a negative effect on enterprise performance. This accords with our expectations. An obvious difference is that employee training expenses have a significant influence on enterprise performance in the Panel Data Model results—the higher the expenses on employee training, the better the enterprise performance overall. We also notice the large co-efficient of this variable, which indicates a far greater influence than that of the other variables.

7.4 Conclusions

In the development of China's NGEs, the average income of laborers tends to grow rather slowly, and this growth obviously lags behind that of state-owned and collective enterprises. Compared with profits, wages account for only a small proportion of the distribution. Due to their high return on capital, NGEs are strongly inclined to reinvest, and their reinvestment rate to after-tax profit generally exceeds 50%. They are, however, saddled with a heavy tax burden. The distribution system among the government, enterprises, and laborers is irrational.

Empirical tests show that the contribution of capital to output must be around 40%, while that of labor must be approximately 60%. A comparison between the estimated results and the actual distribution results shows that the latter is less than

Table 7.7 Estimation results of enterprise performance determinants by the Panel Data Model 2004–2006

		Model 1		Model 2	
	Variables	Coefficients	T-values	Coefficients	T-values
Explanatory variables	C	0.1381[a]	3.6718	0.1458[a]	3.9829
	Log(Wage)	0.0344[a]	5.0294	0.0340[a]	5.2353
	stock	−0.0053	−0.2968	–	–
	supervise	0.0368	0.6488	–	–
	mobility	−0.0284[c]	−1.5942	−0.0275[c]	−1.5770
	rwelfare	−0.0058	−0.3082	–	–
	rtrain	0.1837[b]	2.2547	0.1752[b]	2.2062
Control variables	*Log(scale)*	−0.0310[a]	−5.0084	−0.0301[a]	−4.9240
	rdebt	0.0540[a]	3.3968	0.0541[a]	0.0007
	age	0.0012	1.3854		
Test statistics	R^2	0.0317	–	0.0301	–
	F	4.4907	–	4.4907	–
	DW	2.0152	–	2.0152	–
Sample numbers	–	507	–	507	–

Note: [a]Indicates a significant estimated coefficient under 1% level
[b]Indicates a significant estimated coefficient under 5% level and
[c]Indicates a significant estimated coefficient under 10% level

half the former, indicating a low level of laborer payment in the primary distribution.

In collaborative labor-capital relations, wages and bonuses have a significant positive effect on enterprise performance, while employee mobility is a negative factor. The factor of employee training expenses has a significant influence on enterprise performance—the higher the expenses, the better the enterprise performance.

In handling the labor-capital relationship and especially the labor-capital distribution of NGEs, the government should clearly define its roles as the "maker of the rules and procedures for expressions of interest, supervisor and facilitator of the expression and game of interest, and mediator of labor disputes." In coordinating labor-capital relations, the government should adhere to the maxim of the "equal importance of efficiency and fairness" and avoids such incorrect tendencies and short-sighted behavior as valuing investment above labor protection.

Bibliography

Acemoglu D (2000) Labor- and capital-augmenting technical change, NBER working paper no. 7544. Cambridge, MA, National Bureau of Economic Research

ACFIC (2007) Large-scale investigation of China's NGEs 1993–2006. China Industrial & Commercial United Press, Beijing

Alfred M (2005) Principles of economics (trans: Lian Y). Huaxia Publishing House, Beijing

Bai J, Fu T (2008) Explorations on NGEs' distribution models—building a contribution-based new model of distribution within NGEs. East China Econ Manag (8)
Bai C, Qian Z (2009) Factor allocation in national income: a story beyond statistics. Econ Res 3:27–41
Barnard CI (2007) The functions of the executive (trans: Wang Y). China Machine Press, Beijing
Bentolila S, Saint-Paul G (2003) Explaining movements in the labor share. Contrib Macroecon (Berkeley Electronic Press) 3(1):1103–1103
Bernanke B, Grkaynak RS (2001) Is growth exogenous? Taking Mankiw, Romer and Weil seriously, NBER working paper no. 8365. National Bureau of Economic Research, Cambridge, MA
Blanchard O (1997) The medium run. Brook Pap Econ Act 2:89–158
Buchele J, Jens C (1992) Industrial relations and productivity growth: a comparative perspective, international contributions to labor studies. University of Notre Dame, Notre Dame, IN, USA: Academic Press.
Cappelli P, Neumark D (1999) Do high performance work practices improve establishment-level outcomes? Ind Labor-Cap Relat Rev 54(4):737–775
Chang K (2004) On labor rights. China Labor and Social Security Publishing House, Beijing
Cheng Y (2002) Labor relationship. China Renmin University Press, Beijing
Cheng L (2006) China's NGEs from 2001 to 2005. China Business Times, 9 Feb
Clark JB (1997) The distribution of wealth (trans: Chen F, Chen Z). The Commercial Press, Beijing.
Ding W (2004) Labor relationship of enterprises and changes in economic performance. Fujian Tribune (Social Sciences Edition) (7)
Feldstein MS (2008) Did wages reflect growth in productivity? NBER working paper no. 13953. National Bureau of Economic Research, Cambridge, MA
Feng X (2000) Labor-capital relationship in private enterprises. Huazhong University of Science and Technology Press, Wuhan
Gershenfeld JC (1991) The impact on economic performance of a transformation in workplace relation. Ind Labor-Cap Relat Rev 44(2):241–260
Gollin D (2002) Getting income shares right. J Polit Econ 110(2):458–475
Gomme P, Rupert P (2004) Measuring labor's share of income, Policy discussion papers no.7. Federal Reserve Bank of Cleveland, Cleveland
Harrison AE (2002) Has globalization eroded labor's share? Some cross-country evidence. NBER working paper. University of California-Berkeley and NBER, Berkeley
Jayadev A (2007) Capital account openness and the labor share of income. Camb J Econ 31:423–443
Kaldor N (1961) Capital accumulation and economic growth. In: Lutz FA, Hague DC (eds) The theory of capital. St. Martin's Press, New York
Katz HC, Kochan TA, Gobeille KR (1983) Industrial relations performance, economic performance and QWL programs—an interplant analysis. Ind and Labor-Cap Relat Rev 37(1):3–17
Kessing SG (2003) A note on the determinant of labor share movements. Econ Lett 81(1):9–12
Kuijs L (2005) Investment and saving in China, World Bank policy research paper. World Bank, Washington, DC
Kyyr T, Maliranta M (2006) The micro-level dynamics of declining labor share: lessons from Finnish great leap, Discussion paper no. 1049. The Research Institute of the Finnish Economy, Helsinki
Lewis WA (1990) The theory of economic growth (trans: Liang X). Shanghai Joint Publishing Company, Shanghai, China
Li Y (1992) Adjustment of income distribution function: reflections on individual inclination of national income. Econ Res J (7)
Li J, Liu Z (2006) Demonstration research on private enterprise' assignment pattern. J China Univ Geosci (Social Sciences Edition) (2)
Li Y, Yin J (2007) Anatomy of high saving rate of China: analysis based upon flow of funds account of China from 1992 to 2003. Econ Res J (6)

Li X, Tian Z, Li J (2008) On the relationship between labor and capital distributions in NSOEs. Prices Mon (11)
Li D, Liu L, Wang H (2009) The U curve of labor share in GDP during economic development. Econ Res J (1)
Liang D (2008) Basic laws of formation and changes of primary distribution pattern. Economists (6)
Lu L, Wang Z (2003) On the relationship between capital, labor and distribution in private enterprises—based on a questionnaire survey and analysis. Comp Econ Soc Syst (1)
Lübker M (2007) Labor shares, Technical brief no. 01. International Labor Office, Geneva
Ma K (2009) Quicken the adjustment of economic structure when coping with the international financial crisis. Qiushi (20)
Marx K, Engels F (1975) The complete works of Marx and Engels, vol 23. People's Press, Beijing
Mayo GE (1964) The social problems of an industrial civilization. The Commercial Press, Beijing
NBS (2010) China statistical yearbook 2009. China Statistical Publishing House, Beijing
Norsworthy JR, Zabala CA (1985) Worker attitudes, worker behavior, and productivity in the U.S. automobile industry, 1959~1976. Ind Labor-Cap Relat Rev 38(4):544–557
Prados de la Escosura L, Rosés JR (2003) Wages and labor income in history: a survey. Economic History and Institutions Series 06, Working paper 03–10, Feb., Universidad Carlos III de Madrid
Tytell I, Jaumotte F (2007) How has the globalization of labor affected the labor income share in advanced countries? International Monetary Fund working paper no. 298. International Monetary Fund, Washington DC
Wang G (2006) Investigation of the present situation of income distribution in NGEs. China Labor Secur (10)
Wang D, Jiao J (2003) The theory of labor-capital relationship and its practice in western developed countries. Rev Econ Res (51)
Wooden M, Loundes J, Tseng Y (2002) Industrial relations reform and business performance: an introduction, Melbourne Institute working paper series. The University of Melbourne, Melbourne
Xiao H, Hao F (2009) Comparative research on the structure of primary distribution of income among China and foreign countries. Financ Trade Econ (2)
Xu X, Wang H (2008) Polarization in factor income distribution: evidence from China. Econ Res J (2)
Zhao J (2006) Analysis of distribution between labor and capital in China. Stat Res (12)
Zhao X (2009) Two-way moral risks in labor relationship. Financ Sci (4)
Zheng Z (2008) Study on annexation of wages by profit in China's enterprises. China Ind Econ (1)
Zhou M, Xiao W, Yao X (2010) China's unbalanced economic growth and national income distribution. China Ind Econ (6)
Zhu W (2001) Labor relationship. China Labor and Social Security Publishing House, Beijing
Zhuo Y (2007) On the decrease of labor-income proportion and increase of capital-income proportion. Zhejiang Soc Sci (3)

Chapter 8
Human Capital Investment: The Fundamental Means to Promote Enterprise Competitiveness

Jianxiong Liu and Xiongbing Zhu

China's NGEs have developed and grown under a dual track system in the process of reform. Judging by their initial conditions, NGEs did not have any particular developmental advantages in technologies, funds, or institutions. Experience shows that it has been the country's cheap labor that has most contributed to the large-scale development and expansion of China's NGEs. On the processing and OEM chains of the labor-intensive industries, China's NGEs have completed their period of capital accumulation and leapfrogged development by use of the cheap labor available at this particular stage of China's development. Even in the capital- and technology-intensive industries, China's NGEs are still inclined to use labor in place of capital and technology. In 2004, the major economic areas—such as the Pearl River and Yangtze River Deltas—were faced with a looming labor shortage, and cases of labor disputes repeatedly appeared in some areas. In the long run, China's NGEs will unavoidably face a new challenge of labor costs arising concurrently with the ongoing trend of China's demographic transition, which will undoubtedly hinder their competitiveness.

In understanding the source of Chinese NGEs' competitiveness, we have paid scant attention to the theory of human capital. Under the condition of an unlimited supply of labor, the objective pressure for more investment in human capital has not been felt by either SOEs or NGEs. For a long time, the dual economy of China has featured an unlimited labor supply, and the more-than-sufficient labor force has indeed been feeding the country's rapid economic growth with a demographic dividend. At present, there is still no sign of diminishing capital

J. Liu (✉)
Chinese Academy of Social Sciences, Beijing, China

X. Zhu
Tsinghua University, China

Y. Liu (ed.), *New Interpretations on the Development of China's Non-Governmental Enterprises*, Research Series on the Chinese Dream and China's Development Path, DOI 10.1007/978-981-10-3872-3_8

returns (Bai Chong'en et al. 2007), a fact which has broken the "Young-Krugman's Curse."[1] What China has formed and maintained, however, is an input-driven model of economic growth, which relies merely on capital and labor inputs to function. In such a model of growth, the contribution of technical progress, industrial structural upgrading, and improvements to productivity are relatively insignificant to economic growth (Cai 2008). In terms of demand-pull factors, this manifests as an over dependence on exports and investment, while the driving force of consumptive demand is relatively weak and limited. In the distribution of the national economy, the government and its enterprises possess the lion's share, leaving a small part for the people. With China's entry into the new stage of economic development, as the source of China's economic vitality and reservoir of its employment, NGEs are expected to sustain and promote their competitiveness with the new engine of human capital investment.

8.1 The Lewis Turning Point and NGEs' Comparative Advantages

8.1.1 NGEs' New Challenges Arising from Demographic Transition

According to the above-stated theory on human capital and our analysis of total-factor productivity, the overall economy of China must enter a new stage of development, that is, the transition from factor input to the improvement of total-factor productivity, which is the macro-background of the development of China's NGEs. The grass-root developmental history of China's NGEs shows that they are not only those institutions that have been capable of making breakthroughs during China's transition from a planned economy to market economy, but also the most typically marketized. They are the drivers behind market price liberalization in China and the most representative of market rules. They are the most sensitive to China's resource endowments, so their formation of factor prices is the most authentic. For example, in some areas of Zhejiang Province, private-sector credit rates usually reflect the supply and demand in China's capital market more truthfully than those of the Central Bank. In general, NGEs are now adjusting to the factor shortage in China; they will also be the first to feel the pressure to reform as the overall Chinese economy enters a new period of transformation.

The World Bank report, *The Quality of Growth* (Thomas et al. 2001), published at the end of 2000, clearly put forward a new framework of economic theory, which stresses the concept of three distinct types of capital: physical capital (which is of

[1]Young (1992) and Krugman (1994) cast doubts on the sustainability of the "East Asia Miracle," as they noted that these economies relied too much capital and labor inputs at that time with little contribution of total factor productivity.

much concern), human capital, and natural capital. In the future, China's resources and the physical environment can no longer afford to invest in the high-carbon model of economic growth. In terms of capital growth, China's domestic saving rate is about 40%, unlikely to go higher; the government has to bear increasingly expenses for public services; the marginal accumulation of enterprises will gradually slow; Chinese citizens have to use their own savings to prevent risks in education, medical care, housing, pension, and so forth., which should have already been settled by the country's social security system. Consequently, it can be predicted that the high savings and investment rates that currently exist in China will be unsustainable in the future. What's more, it is impossible for there to be a massive growth in the number of the labor force. For NGEs, the transition of the demographic structure brings new challenges to their development. Too much discussion of the country's physical and natural capital has left us with an optimistic impression of the abundant labor force, which has, in truth, lasted for many years. For the rise to prominence and growth of China's NGEs, in addition to the benefit they receive from the ideological, institutional, and environmental relaxation on the part of the government, the more important it becomes that they have made full use of the advantages of China's "demographic dividends" in terms of factor costs. Therefore, the fluctuations in China's population, as well as the supply-demand structure of the labor market, are of considerable importance to NGEs' in terms of sustaining of their competitiveness.

Like many other industrialized countries and regions, China has experienced a drastic demographic shift along with its rapid economic growth since the country's reform and opening up, namely, the accelerated transition from "high birth/growth rates and low rates of death" to a system better described as "low birth, low mortality, and low growth rates" of population reproduction 5.05‰. Since the 1990s, the total fertility rate has dropped to below replacement level, and by 2009, the natural population growth rate has decreased to 5.05%. This demographic transition usually manifests as changing trend in the increase of the working-age population, from a rapid growth to a decline in growth, and finally to a zero growth population (Fig. 8.1). In other words, according to the law of a demographic shift, this long-term low fertility level will inevitably result in the slowdown of labor supply growth and even, ultimately, negative growth. As is predicted, the turning point for China is 2015, when the working-age population between 15 and 64 will stop growing and enter a period of negative growth (United Nations 2009).

8.1.2 The Lewis Turning Point and NGEs' Comparative Advantages

According to Lewis's classical theory on economic development, developing countries featuring an indefinite labor supply must undergo a long process of a dual economy, that is, a process of capital accumulation accelerated by modern

Fig. 8.1 The working-age population and its growth in China 1950–2050 (Source: Population Division of the Department of Economic and Social Affairs of the United Nations Secretariat, World Population Prospects: The 2004 Revision and World Urbanization Prospects: The 2003 Revision. At http://esa.un.org/unpp, November 10, 2006 (Medium variant))

sectors' obtainment of the transferred agricultural labor with fixed wage rates (Lewis 1954). With abundant surplus labor, the wages of the transferred agricultural laborers are likely to remain at the subsistence level indefinitely. Industrial expansion can go without raising wage costs and thus bring very high industrial capital accumulation. This process of low wages and high accumulation will last till the surplus rural workforce is completely absorbed. In such a stage of the dual economy, an important turning point—the Lewis Turning Point—has come, when modern sectors' demand for labor exceeds the labor supply capable of being transferred from agricultural sectors, according to the current wage rates (Lewis 1972).[2]

[2]Although this theory has had a great influence on developing countries, many scholars have used it in the observation of such phenomena as "migrant laborers tide," "rural labor shortage," and supply and demand of labor in China. China's own economic development is not only made up of the industrialization from agriculture to industry, however, but is also a process of urbanization from the countryside to the cities, as well as the marketization from a planned economy to a market economy. The concurrence of industrialization, urbanization, and marketization has made it a complex matter to analyze China's economy. Lewis has established his theory of a dual economy from observing the European experience of urbanization, but in Europe there has been no transition from a planned economy to a market economy. Japan experienced the Lewis Turning Point at a time when his theory of dual economy was in vogue, and there appeared a series of related literature in the country (e.g. Minami 1968). But by the time the Four Asian Tigers started to rise, related discussions had obviously become less pronounced. What was prevailing then was the more neoclassical explanation of the "East Asian Miracle" by the World Bank. Both Japan and the Asian Tigers have government-led industrial policies, somewhat similar to the case in mainland China (Oi 1999; Walder 1995; Herrmann-Pillath and Xingyuan 2004). Neither Japan nor the Asian Tigers, however, have had the problem of transitioning from a planned economy to a market economy.

The history of and current changes to China's labor transfer consistently agree with Lewis's description of dual economic development and its turning point. As a result of its population policies and social and economic development, China has experienced the rapid growth of the working-age population during its period of reform and opening-up. The abundant labor supply and high savings rate have provided China's economic growth with a demographic dividend. The net increase of the working-age population in China's cities and towns is without exception transferred from the rural areas, however, which is on the decline every year. Accordingly, the dependency population has begun rising sharply, while the traditional demographic dividend is disappearing. The rise in wages for ordinary laborers and frequent shortage of migrant workers at present suitably reflect the conflict between the demographic changes and the huge labor demand for a rapid economic growth. Faced with structural changes to the labor force—such as the shortage of migrant workers—the Chinese Government has issued the *Law of the People's Republic of China on Employment Contracts* and the *Law of the People's Republic of China on the Mediation and Arbitration of Labor Disputes* to deal with labor disputes and protect the rights and interests of migrant workers; it is institutionally concerned with the means by which to increase their salaries. According to a study by Cai Fang (2010), many cities in China raised their minimum wages between 1996 and 2008. Of the 129 cities sampled in 1996, 32 adjusted the minimum wage; the sampled cities' average annual wage growth rate was 3.6%, while the average adjusted minimum wage growth rate was 14.4%. Of the 286 samples in 2008, 200 cities adjusted the minimum wage with an average annual wage growth rate for the cities as a whole of 13.6%, while the average adjusted minimum wage growth rate for these 200 cities was 19.4%.[3]

In interpreting China's economy using Lewis's theory of the dual economy, it should be noted that China's economic reform is both the disintegration of the dual economy and the integration of the planned economy into a market economy, as well as the transition of ownership in the process of a labor transfer. During China's reformation, the surplus rural labor force has been constantly transferring from agricultural to industrial sectors and from the rural areas to the cities, giving rise to a "rural labor rush" since The rise of China's private economic sectors is rooted in two basic problems that are insoluble under the planning system: the serious shortage of daily necessities and increasingly severe employment pressure (Shi Jinchuan 2006). To solve the two problems, the Central Government had to shrink the planning system, and that is why the private sectors of the economy took root and have grown on the edge of the planning system. From the very beginning, NGEs have been more dependent than SOEs on surplus rural labor in China's dual economic structure.

From 1970 to about 1978, the rise of the commune and brigade enterprises outside the planning system marked the sprouting of China's private economic

[3]Refer to Fig. 2 in Cai Fang. (2010). China's Farmers-Turned Workers in Global Spotlight: On Deepening of Urbanization with Chinese Characteristics. *International Economic Review*, (2), 50.

sectors. As the "complementary track" to China's double-track reform, NGEs began to play an increasingly significant role and grew stronger in the period from 1978 to 1988. In the early 1990s, as the private sectors of the economy operating within the "Sunan (Southern Jiangsu Province) Model" began restructuring, the commune, brigade, and township enterprises were transformed into private enterprises in line with the "Wenzhou Model," and their private property rights were further established. After 1992, to dissolve potential financial risks, the Central Government implemented a strategy of the "advance of NGEs and retreat of SOEs" and privatized a large number of loss-incurring SOEs, which constitutes the third path for the development of NGEs (Shi Jinchuan 2006). Either as the complement to SOEs in terms of the supply of products, raw materials, or early products, or in their later participation in the international division of labor by ways of processing and OEM at large scales, either as pure rural enterprises (as in earlier times) or as NGEs merging into cities, China's NGEs have made full use of the surplus labor force in the rural areas and are therefore obviously enjoyed the resultant demographic dividend. On the basis of the comparative advantage of an abundant labor force, China's NGEs have been able to display a stronger viability.

At an early period, NGEs were founded in villages and townships, which made it possible for peasants to leave their fields but remain in their hometown, and they thus became the second "reservoir" (after agriculture) of the country's surplus rural labor. Later, many NGEs started their geographical shift and moved into cities and towns, giving rise to the "rural labor rush"—the transfer of the surplus labor force into cities. As NGEs are part of the non-agricultural sector of the economy, the transfer of rural labor to cities lags behind the labor shift from agricultural to industrial sectors, which is determined by NGEs' urbanization. With the adjustment of national economic distribution, SOEs have begun transferring to the basic industries (such as the railway, highway, and associated resources) that involve the national interest and people's livelihood. These are generally heavy or chemical industries and require large funds, so their capital-labor input ratio is much higher than that of NGEs. On the other hand, following their local comparative advantages, NGEs are themselves vigorously developing within labor-intensive industries, and it is natural that, in the capital- and technology-intensive industries, they have also chosen to replace capital and technical costs with labor.

For NGEs, the difference in labor supply and demand before and after the arrival of the Lewis Turning Point means different things. Before its arrival, with abundant surplus labor, NGEs were able to absorb a continuous labor force with a fixed wage rate, and their marginal accumulation of industrial capital was very rapid, as their industrial expansion could be realized without a corresponding rise of the wage costs. With the arrival of the Lewis Turning Point, however, NGEs can no longer make up for their defects in capital, technology, and institutional support by using cheap labor. Instead, NGEs will have to shift from a reliance on cheap labor to a dependence on the improvement of efficiency and investment in human capital, so as to maintain and promote their marginal competitiveness (Fig. 8.2).

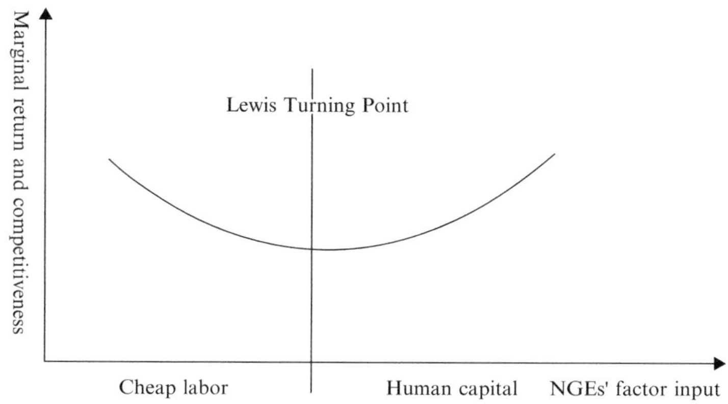

Fig. 8.2 NGEs required to promote human capital by the Lewis Turning Point

8.1.3 Human Capital Investment and the Dynamic Upgrading of NGEs' Comparative Advantages

For many NGEs, rural migrant workers have long made up the majority of their employees. Since the international financial crisis broke out in 2007, many of China's NGEs in the Pearl River and Yangtze River Deltas have suffered difficulties with exports and some are even on the verge of bankruptcy. On the one hand, this is a side effect of counter-cyclical macroeconomic policies; on the other hand, if we take a deeper look, it is caused by NGEs' loss of their traditional comparative advantages in globalization. After its founding in 1949, China implemented a "Catching-Up Strategy" (赶超战略, gǎn chāo zhànlüè) giving priority to the development of heavy industries and established a number of SOEs for the purpose of the development of capital- and technology-intensive big industries. Unlike the UK or US, however, without the long-term accumulation of material and human capital, China had no comparative advantage in its implementation of the "Catching-Up Strategy," and, for a long time, its SOEs involved in heavy and/or chemical industries operated without viability and had to count on a series of economic rules established by the government for continued survival, such as low interest rates, exchange rates, wages, and input prices. Since the implementation of the country's reform and opening-up, China raised the enthusiasm of peasants and workers and released the productive forces of the country through power decentralization and interest concession; second, by opening market access, it allowed NGEs and FFEs to enter those industries with comparative advantages but inhibited in traditional strategies, so as to improve its resource allocation, and, in doing so, avoided the collapse of its economy by providing those unviable SOEs with necessary protection and subsidies; and, finally, as market-track production and resource allocation became dominant, China abandoned the planned track and merged the dual track into a market system. Such a wide-scale reformation has indeed forsaken the traditional "Catching-Up Strategy" and follows the comparative advantages inherent in the structure of China's resource endowment, and has thus led to the "China Miracle" (Lin Yifu et al. 1999). NGEs are atypical representative of China's success in implementing a "strategy of comparative advantages" (比较优势战略, bǐjiào yōushì zhànlüè). By taking advantage of the demographic dividend in China's dual economy, they have first created a position equal to that of SOEs without government subsidies, and then won global prestige by participating in the international division of labor.

In the past, China's NGEs made their industrial and technical selections following the comparative advantages determined by China's resource endowment structure, and have therefore established their viability on a competitive market. This viability is more clearly manifested in Chinese NGEs' participation in the international division of labor. Since the end of the Asian financial crisis and China's entry into the WTO, NGEs have developed by leaps and bounds, a result of making use of their competitive advantages insofar as the "globalization dividend." The impact of the international financial crisis on China was first felt by NGEs, however, which exposed their vulnerability to the process of globalization.

On the surface, the financial crisis impacted NGEs' export orders and speed of development, but it had a more substantial impact on their development model. According to the classical theory of international trade, the enterprises of a country will first manufacture products in line with the domestic resource endowments and comparative cost advantages and act as the net exporter of such products, but will gradually change their role to ultimately become a net importer. During this role conversion, domestic enterprises need to dynamically upgrade their technology according to changes in the structure of resource endowment. From the ongoing trend in economic development, the comparative advantages of China's NGEs—based on traditional resource endowment and comparative costs—will gradually fade away. On the one hand, China's per capita resources are by no means rich, but its resource consumption has been soaring amidst rapid economic growth, resulting in the domestic prices of resource factors close to or even higher than those found in international markets; on the other hand, with the arrival of the Lewis Turning Point, changes in the country's population structure, and the gradual disintegration of the dual economy,[4] significant changes are taking place in the trend of migrant workers' employment: surplus rural labor that used to be attracted to cities is gradually disappearing; rural laborers' demands for wage adjustment are gradually intensifying; the new generation of migrant workers are more independent; and their wages will have to be raised with NGEs' development. As the international financial crisis has caused a decline in external demand, competition in the international market is increasingly intense, which requires NGEs to transform the

---

[4]The disintegration of the agriculture-industry dual structure is much faster than that of the rural-urban dual structure in China. Despite the acceleration of urbanization in recent years, a sufficient citification has not yet come into shape, which is marked by the conversion of farmers from migrant workers into city residents. This requires the reform of the household registration system and the equalization of public services, both of which will inevitably touch on the existing city welfare.

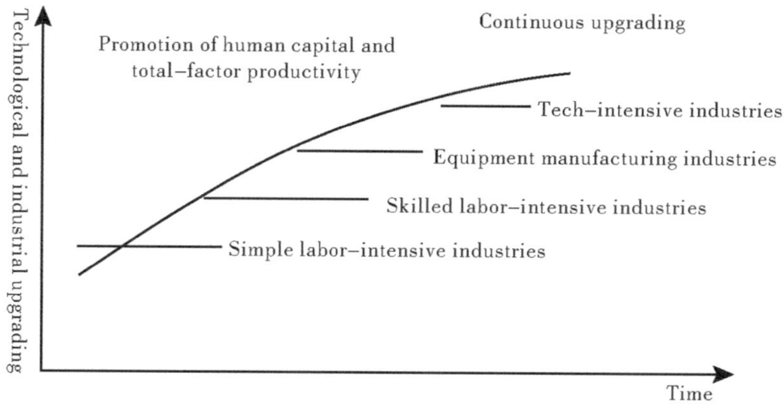

Fig. 8.3 NGEs' human capital enhancement and technological upgrading models

structure of their export commodities and dynamically upgrade their technology. For these objectives, it is extremely significant that NGEs strengthen their human capital accumulation and raise their total-factor productivity by promoting their human capital (Fig. 8.3).

8.2 NGEs' Human Capital Investment: Status and Problems

8.2.1 Characteristics of NGEs' Human Capital Investment

For lack of comprehensive follow-up surveys or statistics, there is no available data on the human capital investment of China's NGEs. Based on the data of a survey by the CASS Center for Private Economic Studies in 2007, we have made a basic analysis of the characteristics of NGEs' human capital at present. According to the enterprise data collected in 2007, NGEs are still at a low level of human capital, with a good variety of distribution across different regions, industries, and enterprises of different sizes.

First of all, NGEs are generally at a low level of human capital and vary as to their internal structure. In a relatively complete questionnaire survey from 2006, of the 234,085 employees in 327 NGEs surveyed, 1210 held a master's degree or above, accounting for only 0.5%; 12,848 held a university diploma, accounting for 5%; 27,422 were college graduates, accounting for 12%; 98,212 were graduates of senior high schools or secondary technical schools, accounting for 42%; and 94,393 had only received junior high school education or even below, accounting for 40%. All this shows that NGEs' human capital is still far from optimistic, though there has been a significant improvement since 2004.

Despite the overall low level of NGEs' human capital, entrepreneurs have received a rather high level of education. We have analyzed the questionnaires outlining 327 valid sample enterprises and calculated the education of the current general managers or presidents, whether or not they are demobilized soldiers, and whether or not they had ever been leaders of villages or other organizations. According to our analysis, 74.8% of them have received a college education or above; 25.1% have received a senior high school or technical school education; and only 1.2% received a junior high school education or below. In the questionnaires given to the 327 valid sample enterprises, 299 general managers/presidents presented themselves as demobilized soldiers, accounting for 91.7% of the total, and 138 used to be village leaders, 42.5% of the total (Liu Yingqiu and Xu Zhixiang 2007, 11–12). This data shows that NGEs, especially SMEs, are generally at a low level of human capital, but vary in their internal structure: as the top leaders, the entrepreneurs have high levels of human capital, while the middle and lower management personnel and ordinary employees tend to have low levels of human capital, a fact which has received insufficient attention.

The eastern coastal regions enjoy more and better educational resources along with more rapid economic and social development. They have overshadowed the central and western regions in such important conditions for human capital growth as cultural atmosphere, a convenient environment of education, easily-accessible and cheap access to information. According to the survey data, the eastern regions are the best in terms of NGEs' human capital, but the central regions are better than the western regions (See Table 8.1).

Thirdly, NGEs' human capital levels vary across industries. As Table 8.2 shows, the human capital level is high in industries with a high capital-labor ratio, e.g., communications and software, pharmaceuticals; but it is low in those industries with a low capital-labor ratio, e.g., construction and real estate or textiles and clothing. At the beginning of its reform and opening up, China was meeting the worldwide need for the transfer of labor-intensive industries to countries with abundant and cheap labor. NGEs followed China's structure of resource endowment at that time and thereby succeeded in accepting this transfer by taking advantage of the comparative advantages of the labor force. Labor-intensive industries, however, have fewer demands on human capital promotion than do capital- and technology-intensive industries. With the ongoing structural changes in the Chinese market (such as scarce factors and the disappearance of the demographic dividend), NGEs will have to drastically upgrade their technologies. The industrial features revealed in Table 8.2 have proven the critical role of human capital enhancement in the dynamic upgrading of technology.

Fourthly, human capital levels vary among NGEs of different sizes. Studies have found that the proportion of highly-educated personnel is high in large NGEs, while in smaller ones, the proportion of ill-educated personnel is high (See Table 8.3). A larger size of enterprises generally represents more advanced technologies, and the advanced technologies and equipment have higher demands on the laborers' skills. In addition, highly-educated people are more willing to work in large enterprises,

Table 8.1 The contrast among NGEs' human resource structure by province/municipality, 2006 (%)

Region	Percentage	Master's degree and above	Bachelor's degree	College graduates	Senior high school and technical school	Lower education
Beijing Municipality	100	1	9	15	44	31
Jiangsu Province	100	2	10	17	36	35
Yunnan Province	100	0.05	1.2	6	47	45.75

Source: Database on Human Capital and Competitiveness of China's NGEs 2007, CASS Center for Private Economic Studies

Table 8.2 Contrast among NGEs' human capital structure by industry, 2006 (%)

Industry	Master's degree and above	Bachelor's degree	College graduates	Senior high school and technical school	Lower education
Agriculture, forestry, animal husbandry, and fishery	0.5	9.4	22.1	35.8	32.2
Construction and real estate	0.6	5.5	11.5	22.5	59.9
Food and beverages	0.3	6.9	12.3	59.6	20.9
Biological medicine	0.8	7.8	24.9	45.5	21.0
Textiles and clothing	0.2	3.7	7.3	46.2	42.6
Electromechanical manufacturing	0.6	4.7	12.1	62.4	20.2
Automobile and motorcycle manufacturing	0.7	8.3	17.4	56.4	17.2
Household appliances manufacturing	0.3	3.0	6.4	36.9	53.4
Culture and media	2.1	12.9	26.4	37.3	21.3
Communications and software	7.8	33.2	28.9	30.1	0

Source: Database on Human Capital and Competitiveness of China's NGEs 2007, CASS Center for Private Economic Studies

not only out of a sense of honorability, but also because of the higher growth possible therein.

And finally, NGEs' human capital level also varies by their life cycle. NGEs' life cycles are very short in China, usually between 5 and 7 years from birth to death, which is indeed the result of their fragile and unsustainable competitiveness. Studies have found, the shorter NGEs' life cycle, the poorer their human capital, and the more fragile and unsustainable their competitiveness. There is a significant

Table 8.3 NGEs' average size and human capital structure by sales, 2006 (%)

Sales	Master's degree and above	Bachelor's degree	College graduates	Senior high school and technical school	Lower education
<50 mn RMB	0.44	6.78	12.23	34.12	46.33
50.01–100 mn RMB	0.22	3.52	8.05	43.14	45.07
100.01–300 mn RMB	0.33	4.29	9.87	30.29	55.22
300.01–1000 mn RMB	0.56	4.12	9.33	50.37	35.62
1000.01–3000 mn RMB	0.35	4.73	11.22	42.67	41.03
>3000.01 mn RMB	0.97	8.72	17.14	43.51	29.66

Source: Database on Human Capital and Competitiveness of China's NGEs 2007, CASS Center for Private Economic Studies

Table 8.4 The average human capital structure of NGEs by founding year (%)

Founding year	Master's degree and above	Bachelor's degree	College graduates	Senior high school and technical school	Lower education
Before 1985	0.61	5.71	15.79	47.78	30.11
1986–1990	0.51	4.41	12.11	50.71	32.26
1991–1995	0.47	6.21	11.88	42.71	38.73
1996–2000	0.65	5.45	11.11	31.62	51.17
2001–2006	0.34	5.25	10.53	37.13	46.75

Source: Database on Human Capital and Competitiveness of China's NGEs 2007, CASS Center for Private Economic Studies

correlation between their competitiveness, life cycle, and human capital structure (See Table 8.4).

8.2.2 *The Major Problems with NGEs' Human Capital Investment*

The above characteristics outlining NGEs' human capital development are consistent with the structure of China's resource endowment under the conditions of a dual economy. With the disintegration of that economic structure and the dynamic adjustment of the country's factor scarcity structure, these characteristics have turned into problems that constrain NGEs' development from multiple aspects.

First of all, NGEs' levels of human capital are generally low and vary sharply across different industries and by their life cycle, which derives from the "unlimited supply of surplus labor force" in the dual economy. There are many problems to be found with NGEs' management of human capital, which are caused by their long-term overdependence on the expansion model based on low labor costs. For example, they have often taken advantage of the "golden years" of migrant workers, e.g., those workers between 18 and 25 years old, who contribute a demographic dividend to enterprise development. Besides, as migrant workers will eventually return to their hometowns, NGEs would rather win their competitive advantage of labor costs through a constant rotation of workers than to cultivate human capital or accumulate social security for their employees. Under the conditions of a traditional demographic dividend, NGEs have paid scant attention to their human capital, resulting in outdated management ideas and unsound mechanisms for human capital cultivation. As migrant workers are hardly integrated into city life, lowly-paid, and lack social security, they tend to save as a precautionary measure. Consequently, the consumptive capacity cannot really be formed among migrant workers and their families as a huge group of consumers, which in turn constrains the demands being made on the entire market, its industries and enterprise products, and inhibits enterprises' marginal profitability.

Second, NGEs' human capital levels vary from region to region, with the levels of the eastern regions being the best and those of the central regions being better than the western regions, with this trend gradually strengthening. This characteristic of the human capital distribution of NGEs has posed a new question as to the geographical distribution of Chinese NGEs' human capital: can we change the unidirectional west-east migration of the country's huge labor force into the east-west migration of many NGEs, so as to reverse the unbalanced spatial distribution of human capital? China's NGEs first grew out of the "Wenzhou Model" and "Sunan Model," and later, with the privatization of SOEs and the collective enterprises of cities and towns, there sprung forth many more NGEs in other coastal regions. Despite public opinion and policies that encourage the development of NGEs' in the central and western regions, they have clearly fallen behind and failed to form a three-pillar system with the eastern and central regions in the development of non-governmental sectors of the economy. The implementation of the "Strategy of Western Development," the "Plan of Rejuvenating the Old Industrial Base in Northeast China," and the later "Rise of Central China Strategy" has effectively promoted the rapid development of NGEs in these areas, but limited by various subjective and objective conditions, they are still far behind the eastern regions in NGE development. Moreover, influenced by government-dominated investment strategies, the central and western regions are prematurely concentrated on capital-intensive industries, which has even led to a higher capital-labor ratio than that found in the eastern regions (Cai Fang et al. 2009). This has brought about a conflict: on the one hand, plenty of low-cost labor keeps moving to the east from the central and west, while on the other hand, these two regions are prematurely involved in the industrial development of low labor absorption. The result is the frustration of the east-central-west "flying geese"-type industrial shift and its ultimate failure. For NGEs, it is beneficial insofar as effectively extending their use of the "demographic dividend" if they can realize the industrial shift from the eastern to central and western regions, so as to replace or complement the government-dominated heavy and chemical industries in these regions. And it is equally significant to be able to push forward their human capital shift from the east to the central and western regions, compared with their increase of human capital investment in the east.

Third, China's NGEs also express distinct traits of family enterprises. A 2007 survey by the CASS Center for Private Economic Studies found that NGEs were not only low in their overall level of human capital, but also seriously unbalanced in their human capital structure, wherein entrepreneurs were higher in human capital level than middle and lower management personnel and ordinary employees. The human capital of entrepreneurs plays a more concentrated and prominent role in small enterprises than in larger ones, which indicates the critical and decisive role of SMEs' leaders, especially in maintaining enterprise competitiveness. It is the very nature of family enterprises that limits the will of NGEs to invest in general human capital or introduce professional managers from outside so as to standardize and specialize their operations and management (Dai Yuanchen 2005). Although many NGEs have modernized their governance structure in order to seek financing by listing on the stock market, the family traits are still reserved in their actual operations. For NGEs, only by integrating their family system with the modern system of human capital management can they possibly promote the marginal productivity of all their production factors (Li Xin chun and Zhang 2005).

Fourth, the motivation behind NGEs' investment in human capital is still weak. The structural changes in China's resource endowment have reminded many NGEs of the necessity of dynamically upgrading their "comparative advantages" and increasing their investment in human capital cultivation. But many excellent employees have chosen to leave or been "scooped up" by other enterprises once they have received human capital cultivation, which is a concern for many NGEs investing in human capital. Such worries have, in turn, restricted their technological upgrading and resulted in the early elimination and very short life cycle of many NGEs in market competition It is commonly believed that general human capital investment can bring individuals opportunities for economic mobility, and the greater the investment in general human capital, the more likely that mobility will be. On the other hand, an increase in specific human capital investment means the increase of capital-specific degrees, as well as a corresponding decline in the active mobility of human capital. Therefore, based on the "spillover effect" of human capital and the basic relationship between mobility and the allocative efficiency of human capital, there is, theoretically, a moderate scale of human capital investment (Zhou Lixin and Zeng Qingjun 2003). NGEs should distinguish the general and specific investments in human capital and maintain a moderate proportion and scale for both that is in line with specific enterprising characteristics.

8.3 Human Capital Investment by NGEs and the Government

It is true that the demographic dividend has manifested itself an advantage in the size of the labor force, but as the source of profit, it will eventually disappear. Whereas the improvement of human capital stock means the formation of a more sustainable profit source that can bring further increasing returns. In other words, it is a totally necessary measure against the transformative pressure to invest in laborers and increase human capital accumulation, as well as to replace quantity with quality. In fact, the "shortage of migrant workers," as a signal of labor force shortage overall, is more accurately recognized as the "skilled workers shortage." That is, as the demand for product quality rises in both domestic and international markets, enterprises have to adopt more advanced techniques and technologies, which require higher skills of workers. Unless the current and future laborers are able to meet the increasing demand for higher quality and a greater proportion of skilled labor, the problem of an imminent labor shortage will be all the more prominent. As the most dynamic part of China's economy, it is now imperative that NGEs recognize the abundant meanings the Lewis Turning Point has revealed. On the other hand, in the face of China's demographic changes, the government should grasp the situation accurately, adjust their policies rapidly, respond accordingly, and create conditions for NGEs' further development.

8.3.1 The Orientation of NGEs' Investment in Human Capital

For China's NGEs, in order to release the huge potential of qualitative human capital and turn it into a real productive force, the most critical necessity is to adjust their strategy of human capital development.

To do so, first, NGEs must integrate the training and development of their human capital and transform it into comprehensive and sustainable development. The formation of human capital depends not only on formal academic education, but also on the reinvestment of enterprises by providing the existing enterprise managers and workers within-service education and training, as well as chances for "learning while working," or experiential education. For some NGEs, their workers are mainly surplus rural laborers with a large degree of mobility who will eventually return to those rural areas, as the urban household registration system is not fully open to them and the cost of settling in cities is exorbitant. Generally, NGEs only invest in such manpower as senior technicians and middle and senior management personnel, including giving them generous incentives. As for migrant workers, the enterprises only organize some short pre-service training, with the result that investment in their continuous training usually ends up with nothing. NGEs' neglect of the career development of their ground-level employees reduces their loyalty, making it a short-sighted attitude to be held by the enterprises. As the older migrant workers born in the 1950s and 1960s have withdrawn, the labor market is also experiencing a replacement between laborers of different ages and generations. The younger migrant workers born in the 1970s, 1980s, and even 1990s are more independent and more conscious of their rights. Thus, NGEs are now faced with the challenge of modernizing their traditional management methods of human capital. After all, innovation among enterprises is the result of integrated collaboration. In the new stage, only when NGEs have established a concept of comprehensive and sustainable development regarding human capital are they able to sustain their competitiveness.

Second, in human capital distribution, NGEs must transfer their human capital from the east to the central and western regions. For a long time, there has been a geographical imbalance of China's economy, made apparent by an obvious cascade distribution from the east to the central and western regions. The eastern regions have long been the area where China's NGEs are persistently active, while the central and western regions have long been exporting their enormous labor forces to the east, which have been absorbed by various private sectors of the economy. This phenomenon has caused a series of problems, however. The laborers from the central and western regions always return home in large numbers on the Spring Festival or other holidays, and, taken together with the arrival of macroeconomic fluctuations, this cyclical backflow has delayed the otherwise rapid adjustment of the labor market. Upon the arrival of the Lewis Turning Point, NGEs in the eastern regions must now face the growing need to increase their human capital accumulation so as to cope with the looming migrant workers shortage and the appeal for pay raises that accompanies it. As a result, many foreign direct investments have transferred from eastern China to Vietnam and other countries since the promulgation of the new *Labor Contract Law* and the end of the international financial crisis. For NGEs, a possible choice is to move from the east to the central or western regions and to utilize the local labor force, so as to extend temporally their traditional comparative advantages through geographical transfer. But there are two problems with this solution. One is the premature development model of a high capital-labor ratio caused by the government-oriented Midwestern Development Strategy; and the other is the poorer investment environment created by the government in the central and western regions than that of the east, which restricts NGEs' investment expectations. Therefore, one feasible option is for the government to guide NGEs and industries of traditional comparative advantages to move to the central and western regions, rather than replacing them or "crowding them out," and at the same time, improve the institutional environment for property right protection in these western regions so as to induce the transfer of market and private forces.

Third, family NGEs must transform their exclusive governance structure into a structure based on modern recruitment and performance management. Following the traditional path of development, many of China's NGEs have established a closed family-type governance structure. With pressure from the standardization of market rules and the demand for financing by listing on the open market, such a governance structure has gradually developed into that of a standardized company, but it is still highly selective in the placement of high-level human resources within the company. There are many cases of private family enterprises throughout the world, which have received a mixed response (Chu Xiaoping 2004; Li Xinchun 2005; Lü Fuxin 2003). One positive aspect of this structure is that the family-type management has to dock with the governance structure of modern companies both in form and spirit; otherwise it is impossible to meet the demands of the sustainable operation required of modern companies. Family NGEs must introduce outside professional managers through the governance framework of modern companies, so as to avoid the negative problems inherent in familized management.

Fourth, NGEs must effectively arrange the structure of their human capital investment and efficiently solve the problem of human capital loss. As China's human capital and property market is still quite, the loss of human capital among NGEs is extremely serious. Generally, it is correct to increase investment inhuman capital as a method of promoting NGEs' competitiveness, but this has given rise to questions regarding the structure of NGEs' human capital investment—that is, whether the added input may turn out to be a case of "watering the crops for others." According to Gary Becker, there is a clear line between specific and general human capital investments and, in a human capital market of perfect competition, it is the individuals who receive all the returns on human capital investment, so enterprises will not invest in general human capital. General human capital investment initiated and enacted by enterprises usually exists only in human capital markets of imperfect competitions. In reality, however, even in a market of perfect competition, enterprises will usually make some investment in general human capital to remedy the investment that is "held-up" in specific human capital. Therefore, NGEs are supposed to find a proper ratio between their investments in general and specific human capital and give their employees both general training, as an important part of their career planning, and specialized education, which will cultivate them into a professional force that is able to contribute to the companies. Only by keeping and promoting the best ratio of human capital investment, rather than short-sighted employment strategies, are NGEs able to effectively solve the problem of staff turnover and maximize their profits.

Fifth, NGEs must internationalized their human capital management. The current state of economic globalization is favorable to their utilization of both domestic and international markets and resources, for their integration into the international market, and for their international competition and cooperation. At present, with the deepening of China's economic opening up, a new pattern of competition has taken shape—namely "the internationalization of the domestic market and the domestication of international competition". It has already become an inevitable demand of economic globalization, as well as an inevitable choice for NGEs' growth, to carry out international operations and participate actively in international competition.

There are two important aspects to consider for NGEs to go global: one is to maintain their competitiveness of export trades and the other is to participate in foreign investment. Since the international financial crisis in 2007, a phenomenon of "global acquisitions" by Chinese enterprises has existed. Local Chinese enterprises have accumulated considerable economic strength over the years; they have also gained certain experience in mergers and acquisitions by participating in the capital market. Some Chinese SOEs and NGEs have boldly gone abroad for overseas layout, as many foreign companies are trapped in their own financial crises—a result of the global crisis. Following the traditional "comparative advantages" available to them, China's NGEs already have the initial capability for foreign investment, since they have obtained a certain level of viability and achieved considerable capital accumulation by participating in the global trade. With the dynamic changes that have taken place in China's resource endowment structure, however, NGEs must dynamically upgrade their technology and human capital investment on their own soil if they are to maintain their strong viability and sustain their capital accumulation capacity. Without the dynamic upgrading of their comparative advantages, there would be no sustainable objective ground for NGEs' overseas investments and acquisitions.

To sustain their viability or obtain outstanding global talents, NGEs must upgrade and arrange their human capital for the objective of overseas expansion. For their going global, China's NGEs must invest in high-quality foreign talents, embrace mergers and acquisitions, and accelerate the internationalization of their talents, so as to avoid or reduce the risk associated with foreign investment. Faced with fierce competition on the international market, in order to adapt themselves to local laws and culture and to quickly gain a foothold in the local market, NGEs must, on the one hand, absorb local suitable high-quality personnel, and on the other hand, increase their own human capital investment in the cultivation of their own personnel and those managers with an international vision. Only by gradually cultivating an internationalized management team and talents skilled at overseas operation can NGEs meet the requirements of going global demanded by the allocation of factors and resources.

8.3.2 The Government's Roles in NGEs' Human Capital Investment

The most important roles the government plays in regards to the human capital investment of China's NGEs are those of changing the "government-dominated" model of development, deepening the reform of existing market orientations, and reducing and finally eliminating discrimination against NGEs. The government must promote the "entrepreneurship" of Schumpeter and facilitate the formation of NGEs' human capital. It is supposed to guide—rather than replace—NGEs' investment with regional policies and create a better investment environment as an important guarantee for the shift of NGEs' human capital from the eastern to the central and western regions.

Secondly, it must break the urban-rural dual economy and the urban-rural isolation system and construct a unified human capital market. It is necessary to further strengthen the protection of property rights in the labor market, promote integrity and civilization, and effectively restrict the disorderly flow of human capital between NGEs. In terms of social security, the government must play a timely back-up role and effectively lessen the social burden NGEs' carry concerning employment. In handling labor-capital disputes under new circumstances, the government should actively encourage solutions through voluntary negotiations between the two parties involved.

Thirdly and finally, the government must optimize the structure underlying governmental investment in education. As basic or high-school education with strong externalities is currently favored, whereas higher education is highly professional, it is important that the government optimize the proportion of their development. In the developmental mechanism of higher education, the government must communicate more with different parties and effectively coordinate the relationship between graduates and enterprises, as well as that between research institutions and enterprises. In addition, the government should invest more in vocational education and the cultivation and development of the professional manager market, which is also of a positive macroscopic significance to the promotion of NGEs' human capital.

8.4 Conclusions

As China's market-oriented reform is not yet finished, NGEs are more prone to counter-cyclical macroeconomic policies. With the extant changes to China's demographic structure, NGEs must face the challenges brought about by China's Lewis Turning Point and can therefore no longer enjoy the advantage of abundant cheap labor under the dual economy. This requires that NGEs change along with trends in the economic structure, dynamically upgrade their comparative advantages, and enhance their competitiveness on the market.

This new stage of China's economic transformation is oriented towards the improvement of the total-factor productivity. According to the economic theory of human capital, the promotion of human capital is of great significance to the improvement of the total-factor productivity. Therefore, NGEs must increase their human capital investment in order to drive the improvement of their total-factor productivity if they hope to lead SOEs in this aspect. Meanwhile, to expand their export trade and foreign investment in the new round of globalization, NGEs must dynamically upgrade their comparative advantages by taking note of changes to the country's resource endowment structure, in which the key to the upgrading lies in their human capital investment.

It is true that there are still various problems in the human capital investment of China's NGEs, such as outdated concepts and a generally low level of human capital investment, which are inherited from the traditional models of economic development. On the other hand, the characteristics of NGEs' human capital investment as reflected by such relevant variables as industry, size, and life cycle have repeatedly proven the importance of human capital investment. In terms of space, NGEs must fully realize their industrial shift from the eastern to the central and western regions and complement the government-dominated industrial development already found therein. In summary, it requires the joint effort of both enterprises and the government to promote NGEs' human capital and thus improve their competitiveness.

Bibliography

Bai C, Xie C, Qian Y (2007) China's capital returns. Comp Stud (28)

Becker GS (1987) Human capital, Chinese edn. Peking University Press, Beijing.

Becker GS (2002) The economic approach to human behavior (trans: Wang Y, Chen G). Shanghai People's Press, Shanghai

Cai F (2008) Approaching a triumphal span: how far is China towards its Lewis Turning Point? UNU-WIDER research paper no. 9

Cai F (2010) China's peasants-turned workers in the global spotlight: on deepening of urbanization with Chinese characteristics. Int Econ Rev (2)

Cai F, Yifu L (2003) Chinese economy. China Financial & Economic Publishing House, Beijing

Cai F, Wang D, Yue Q (2009) Flying geese within borders: how China sustains its labor-intensive industries? Econ Res J (9)

Chu X (2004) The growth of family enterprises and their integration with social capital. Economic Science Press, Beijing

Dai Y (2005) Miracles of Chinese economy: the rise of non-governmental enterprises. People's Press, Beijing

Dougherty S, Herd R (2005) Fast-falling barriers and growing concentration: the emergence of a private sectors of economy in China, Economics Department working paper no. 471. OECD

Herrmann-Pillath C, Xingyuan F (2004) Competitive governments, fiscal arrangements, and the provision of local public infrastructure in China: a theory-driven study of Gujiao municipality. China Inf 18(3):373–428

Krugman P (1994) The myth of Asia's miracle. Foreign Aff 73(6):62–78

Lewis WA (1954) Economic development with unlimited supplies of labor. Manchester Sch Econ Soc Stud (22):139–191. Reprinted in Agarwala AN, Singh SP (eds) (1958) The economics of underdevelopment. Oxford University Press, Bombay

Lewis A (1972) Reflections on unlimited labor. In: Di Marco L (ed) International economics and development. Academic Press, New York, pp 75–96

Li X (2005) Trust, loyalty and predicament of clannishness. New Econ (5)

Li X, Zhang S (2005) Family enterprises: organization, behavior and Chinese economy. The Joint Publishing Company& Shanghai People's Press, Shanghai

Lin Y (2008) Economic development and transition: thought, strategy and viability. Peking University Press, Beijing

Lin Y, Cai F, Li Z (1999) Miracles of China: development strategy and economic reform, Rev edn. The Joint Publishing Company, Shanghai

Liu Y, Xu Z (2004) Reports on Chinese non-governmental enterprise competitiveness, no. 1, 2, 3. Social Sciences Academic Press, Beijing

Liu Y, Xu Z (2005) Reports on Chinese non-governmental enterprise competitiveness, no. 1, 2, 3. Social Sciences Academic Press, Beijing

Liu Y, Xu Z (2006) Reports on Chinese non-governmental enterprise competitiveness, no. 1, 2, 3. Social Sciences Academic Press, Beijing

Liu Y, Xu Z (2007) Report on Chinese non-governmental enterprise competitiveness, no. 4. Social Sciences Academic Press, Beijing

Lü F (2003) Resource shortage of family enterprises and their philosophy continuation and extension. Manage World (12)

Minami R (1968) The turning point in the Japanese economy. Q J Econ 82(3):380–402

Oi JC (1999) Local state corporatism. In: Oi JC (ed) Rural China takes off: institutional foundations of economic reform. University of California Press, Berkeley

Schultz TW (1990) Investment in human capital (trans: Wu Z). Economic Institute Press, Beijing

Schumpeter J (1990) Theories on economic development (trans: He W, et al). The Commercial Press, Beijing

Shi J (2006) Report on the development of China's NGEs. Economic Science Press, Beijing

Smith A (1972) An inquiry into the nature and causes of the wealth on nations (trans: Guo D, Wang Y). The Commercial Press, Beijing

Solow R (1957) Technical change and the aggregate production function. Rev Econ Stat (The MIT Press) 39(3):312–320

The World Bank (1993) The East Asian miracle: economic growth and public policy. Oxford University Press, Oxford

Thomas V et al (2001) The quality of growth. China Financial & Economic Publishing House, Beijing

United Nations (2009) The world populations prospects: the 2008 Revision. http://esa.un.org/unpp/. Accessed 19 June 2010

Walder A (1995) Local governments as industrial firms. Am J Sociol 101(2):263–301

Young A (1992) A tale of two cities: factor accumulation and technical change in Hong Kong and Singapore. In: Blanchard O, Fischer S (eds) NBER macroeconomics annual. MIT Press, Cambridge, MA

Zhou L, Zeng Q (2003) Human capital investment and flow of enterprises. Quant Tech Econ (10)

Chapter 9
Efficient Technological Innovation: The Foundation of NGEs' Survival and Development in the New Stage

Yanbing Wu

Technological innovation is the inevitable choice for transforming models of economic growth and optimizing the economic structure; additionally, the promotion of NGEs' capacity for technological innovation is a measure of China's ability to meet the demands of economic development in the new period. *The 11th Five-Year Plan of China for National Economic and Social Development* proposed to "accelerate the establishment of a technological innovation system based around the centrality of enterprises, with the market as the orientation, and the integration of production, education, and research, and formulate a basic institutional framework of independent innovation." The *Decision on the Implementation of Science and Technology Development Plan and Enhancement of Independent Innovation Capabilities* released by the State Council clearly states its intention to "practically make enterprises the principal part of research, development, and investment, the subject of technological innovation, and the main implementer of innovation," and "to value and fully utilize the role of technological NGEs as the driving forces behind independent innovation and the development of high-tech industries, to create a fair competitive environment, and encourage NGEs to grow both larger and stronger and to participate in international competition." During the 12th Five Year Plan, the Chinese Government will give full support to the cultivation of the independent innovation capacities of the country's enterprises, and China's NGEs are likely to welcome the golden opportunity for technological innovation. During this period, in the face of fierce competition with SOEs and FFEs, only by relying on efficient technological innovation can China's NGEs gain competitive advantages in the future.

The most important factor in accelerating the transformation of the economic development model is to change the model of economic growth that mainly

Y. Wu (✉)
Chinese Academy of Social Sciences, Beijing, China

Y. Liu (ed.), *New Interpretations on the Development of China's Non-Governmental Enterprises*, Research Series on the Chinese Dream and China's Development Path, DOI 10.1007/978-981-10-3872-3_9

depends on factor input into one mainly depending on efficiency improvements, and the key to this is technological innovation. Although extensive research has been done on the economic effects of Chinese enterprises' technological innovations, empirical analysis on the efficiency of technological innovation of China's NGEs is almost nonexistent. As they make up a large proportion of Chinese enterprises, NGEs' technological innovation is critical to the construction of an innovation-oriented country. Therefore, the improvement of NGEs' capacity and technological innovation efficiency, as well as the extensive-to-intensive transformation of China's economic growth model, is an important approach to the new path of industrialization and the structural adjustment of China's national economy. This chapter analyzes the technological innovation of China's NGEs from the perspectives of its status quo and efficiency, which can not only fill in certain gaps in the existing literature but also contribute to the promotion of NGEs' technological innovation capacity and China's transformation of its economic growth model.

9.1 NGEs' Technological Innovation: Status and Problems

9.1.1 The Status Quo of NGEs' Technological Innovation

With their clearly defined property rights, China's NGEs are flexible in innovative mechanisms, clear about the target market of their technological innovation, and highly adaptive and diversified. Caught in the middle of severe market competition, NGEs have come to realize that cost-based expansion is no longer adaptive to market development. More and more NGEs have begun to emphasize the development of technology and new products alongside patent application. The following are the prominent characteristics of the technological innovation of China's NGEs.[1]

9.1.1.1 The Significant Enhancement of NGEs' Overall Capacity for Technological Innovation

In 2009, ACFIC released the result of an investigation into NGEs above the designated scale in 2008. Of the 500 NGEs investigated, 160 were registered as "China Famous Trademarks," an annual growth of 14.28%; the products of 150 were rated as NGEs "Chinese Top Brand Products," up by 8.70%; 245 were

[1]With reference to: Liu Yingqiu and Xu Zhixiang. (2006). *Report on Chinese Non-Governmental Enterprise Competitiveness, No. 3*. Beijing: Social Sciences Academic Press. Huang Mengfu. (2009). *Report on the Development of China's NGEs (No. 6), 2008–2009*. Beijing: Social Sciences Academic Press. Economics Division of ACFIC (2010). *Report on the Study of 500 Chinese NGEs in 2010*.

recognized as high and new technology enterprises, up by 3.38%; the key technologies of 320 were in independent development, up by 3.23%;and the 500 NGEs possessed a total of 28,562 patents of which 4420 were invention patents, up by 5.18% and 66.79%, respectively.

According to ACFIC's report of its survey of 500 Chinese NGEs in 2010, there was a significant increase in their brand building and technological innovation capacity, and they expanded to both ends of the industrial chain with higher added values. Of the 500 NGEs in 2009, 172 had "China Famous Trademarks," 12 more than that same figure in 2008, a momentously rapid growth for five consecutive years. What's more, the vast majority of the 500 NGEs had their own trademarks, which brought in income. In terms of technological innovation, 232 (or 46.6%) of the 500 NGEs were identified as high-tech enterprises by scientific administrative departments at or above the provincial level. The survey on the sources of enterprises' key technologies shows that 344 NGEs possessed key technologies from their independent research and development, 68.8% of the 500 NGEs and up by 4.8% over 2008.

9.1.1.2 Distinct Regional Gaps Within NGEs' Capacity for Technological Innovation

In 2006, the CASS Center for Private Economic Studies built a database of NGEs' independent innovative capacity following an investigation into 822 NGEs in 10 provinces and municipalities, including Beijing, Chongqing, Liaoning, Zhejiang, Guangdong, Yunnan, Hebei, Jilin, Jiangsu, and Hubei, and spanning over 20 industries such as communications, medicine, paper-making, metal products, equipment manufacturing, and chemicals. As the survey reveals, NGEs' technological innovation is characterized by distinct regional gaps, strong in the eastern region and weak in the western region of China. For example, by the end of 2004, 15,415 patents were applied for by those limited liability companies of NGEs above the designated scale, of which 11,397 (or 74%)were by enterprises located in the eastern region, while only 2380 (15.4%) and 1638 (10.6%) were applied for by those in the central and western regions, respectively. Obviously, compared with the central and western regions, technological innovation by industrial NGEs was far more active in the eastern region, which accounted for 70% of China's patent innovation and has become the major geographical area for technological innovation among NGEs.

Specifically, NGEs' capacity for innovation differs sharply between the provinces/municipalities either within the same region or in different regions. For example, in the eastern region, the top five provinces/municipality with patent applications were Guangdong (3721 applications), Zhejiang (1909), Shandong (1855), Jiangsu (1317), and Shanghai (933),with the number of Guangdong (ranking 1st) being four times that of Shanghai (ranking 5th). In the central regions, the top four provinces with patent applications were Anhui (574), Henan (451), Hebei (338), and Hubei (286), with the number in Anhui being twice that of Hubei.

Nationally, the gap was even wider between provinces/municipalities. For example, the province with the largest number of patent applications, Guangdong (3721), was 413 times higher than that of with the fewest applications (Hainan, 9).

In addition to the great difference evident in the quantities of patent application, there is a significant variety in the structures of patent application among the provinces, municipalities, and autonomous regions. Of the 15,415 applications, 5700 were for invention patents, accounting for only 37% of the total. The eastern region made 4583 applications for invention patents, which accounted for 80% of total patent applications overall and 40% of its own patent applications; the central region made 671 applications for invention patents, accounting for 11% of total patent applications overall and 28% of its own total patent applications; and the western region made 446 applications for invention patents, accounting for 9% of total patent inventions overall and 27% of its own total patent applications. Obviously, the eastern regions had a great advantage in the quantity of both patent applications and invention patent applications. What's more, in terms of the structure of patent applications, the eastern region, where 40% of all patent applications were for invention patents, fared far better than the central (28%) and western (27%) regions.

9.1.1.3 Obvious Difference in the Technological Innovation Models Between Industries

Of the 822 NGEs surveyed by the CASS Center for Private Economic Studies in 2006, 767 sample enterprises were listed as "Selection of Innovation Models." In answering what "major model of technological innovation" they used, 378 (49%) of the 767 sample enterprises wrote "original innovation;" 299 (39%) wrote "introduction, emulation, and re-innovation;" 65 (8%) wrote "integrated innovation;" and 25 (3%) wrote "other innovation models." According to the survey, in terms of the organization of technological innovation, 383 (50%) of the 767 sample enterprises selected "independent innovation;" 275 (36%) selected "joint innovation;" and 109 (14%) selected "other forms of innovation." Clearly, independent development was NGEs' first choice among all forms of technological innovation. The other forms of technological innovation were, successively, "cooperative development with domestic universities or research institutes," "cooperative development with other domestic enterprises," and "domestic introduction," in terms of the order of NGEs' adoption. In contrast, the proportion of international cooperation or introductions from abroad was small. This indicates that NGEs' current models of technological innovation rely mainly on the new technical resources available in China.

NGEs' technological innovation models vary greatly across different industries due to varying degrees of competition and speeds of technological development. As the survey results show, original innovation most obviously dominated those NGEs involved in communications equipment manufacturing, computer electronics equipment manufacturing, and professional equipment manufacturing. In these industries, the sample NGEs using "original innovation" methods were more than double those using "introduction, emulation, and re-innovation". This shows that innovation within China's electronics and communications industries has already transcended the lower stages of introduction, digestion, and renovation, and entered a new stage of technological development based on independent innovation. Meanwhile, the dominant innovation model in such industries as electrical machinery and equipment manufacturing, pharmaceutical manufacturing, metal smelting and pressing, automobile manufacturing, and chemical raw materials and chemical products manufacturing is still digestion and renovation based on introduction and emulation. The organizational models of technological innovation also vary distinctly from industry to industry. The proportion of high-tech enterprises that have chosen "independent development" and "cooperative development with higher education or research institutes" was much larger than that of other types of enterprises. Similarly, the proportion of listed companies, large-sized enterprises, high-tech enterprises, and eastern enterprises that have chosen to "introduce foreign technologies" was far larger than that among other types of enterprises.

9.1.1.4 Low Returns and the Poor Input-Output Correlation of Innovation

The purpose of innovation is to promote the competitiveness of enterprises and bring them greater economic returns. The economic returns on an enterprise's innovation are generally low and the correlation between innovation input and output is poor, a discovery made by the CASS Center for Private Economic Studies in its 2006 research on the input-output correlation of the technological innovation of 105 enterprises included in the index of NGEs' capacity for independent innovation. The technological innovation input of the 105 sample enterprises included here was measured by the proportion of research and development (R&D) input to their sales in 2005, and their economic returns on technological innovation were measured by NGEs' return on total assets in the same year. The researchers calculated the coefficients of correlation between the proportion of R&D input in sales income (R&D-salesproportion) and thereturn on assetsunder the four models of innovation by two standards of classification. The results show a generally low correlation between the innovative input and economic returns of the sample enterprises, or between their R&D-sales proportion and any return on assets. In the four models of innovation, the highest correlation coefficient was 0.248, which was not at all significant. This reflects, from one aspect, the generally low innovative benefit to China's NGEs. If we compare the correlations between the proportion of R&D sales and the return on assetsunder the four models of innovation, we can find the correlation tied to the "introduction, emulation, and re-innovation" model is higher than that attributed to "original innovation," "joint innovation," or "independent innovation."

9.1.2 NGEs' Difficulties in Technological Innovation

Despite their increasingly important position and role in the process of economic development, due to several intractable historical and institutional reasons, China's NGEs are still faced with difficulties during their process of innovation that require immediate solutions, such as shortages of funds, technologies, equipment, talents, and the information necessary for their future technological innovation; an incomplete environment and service system for their technological innovation; their weak capacity for independent innovation; their poor ability for production-education-research cooperation; and the fact that introduction and emulation are the dominant models of their technological innovation. Most of China' NGEs have neither developed the in-depth cooperation with higher education or research institutes at home and abroad necessary for their future innovation, nor made full use of the external resources available with such institutions, which has resulted, to some degree, in their low level of innovation. Most NGEs are still weak in any sort of original innovation capacity marked by the mastery of core or key technologies and independent intellectual property rights, as well as the capacity for re-innovation through integration and absorption. Specifically, China's NGEs are faced with the following difficulties in their technological innovation in the new era.

9.1.2.1 Unsound Mechanisms for Technological Innovation

Existing theories on technological innovation reveal that entrepreneurs are the primary movers of an enterprise's technological innovation. An outstanding entrepreneur is not only the decision-maker, but also the organizer and director behind an enterprise's technological innovation, whose innovative consciousness and ideas determine the overall implementation of the technological innovation of the enterprise. The great majority of China's NGEs lack either a complete mechanism or long-term strategies for independent innovation, and their leaders are additionally short of innovative consciousness and technical expertise. With their strong awareness of risk aversion, they are eager for quick success and instant benefits in enterprise operation and full of worries and hesitations about technological innovation. In enterprise management, they prefer stability to potential risk; they only focus on how to survive rather than how to grow strong and look more at short-term benefits rather than long-term development. Consequently, some NGEs are content to remain where they are and are further willing to accept the OEM pattern for profits, but are indifferent to independent innovation and reluctant to make any creative breakthroughs. NGEs usually rely greatly on their particular products or technologies. Once an innovative product or technology has made them a success, they tend to always expect to find their way by exclusively relying on this "knockout product." As a result, they are unable and unwilling to utilize the external resources or cooperate with other enterprises. The passive attitude of entrepreneurs to technological innovation has already become the Achilles heel of many manufacturing NGEs within China. Even though a few private entrepreneurs are indeed adventurous, they are prone to making mistakes in the strategies with which they choose to pursue technological innovation. Most commonly, they only "value original innovation but neglect simulated or improved innovation." This very model of "original innovation" is not at all a good choice for China's SMEs, however, as they are very limited in resources. While focusing on the economic benefits of technological innovation, they have indeed ignored the potential risks. In addition, the innovation of China's NGEs usually goes along with the separation between enterprises and innovation activities. The major model of their innovation is still the direct introduction and commercialization of technologies—technological achievements that are purchased from universities or research institutes. But in this process, the technological innovators themselves are not transferred, without whom the enterprises can hardly digest or absorb the technologies purchased. As a result, such enterprises are unable to sustain their innovation.

9.1.2.2 Imperfect Legal Environment

A fair and orderly market legal system is an important factor for enterprises' implementation of innovative processes. Enterprises engaged in technological innovation are subject to risks and costs inherent in the process, and their interests are bound to be damaged by all kinds of infringement (such as counterfeiting and copying) if the legal system is imperfect and market competition is in confusion. In fact, under the circumstance of disorderly competition, some enterprises can seize or encroach on the market by unfair means of competition and are likely to gain greater returns without taking any risk or paying any cost of technological innovation themselves. Therefore, such illegitimate behaviors in market competition are definitely a barrier to NGEs' own technological innovation.

9.1.2.3 Insufficient Financing Facilitation

For the majority of China's NGEs, due to their short history and small size, one of the bottlenecks to their technological innovation is financing difficulties, especially in obtaining long-term funds to sustain their development. Without enough funding, they are unable to commercialize their otherwise excellent technical achievements. Some NGEs involved in science and technology have to develop by incrementally improving upon their prior innovations, and therefore cannot realize the rapid formation of a large enough financial scale to seize any kind of market share. What's worse, some innovative programs have even withered on the vine for lack of funds. What's more, as the majority of China's NGEs are relatively small at present, the banks know little about the credit status of those private SMEs applying for credit facilities. On the other hand, the will and capability to repay the loan/s lies with the person in charge of the enterprise, or more exactly, in his/her personal capability and quality. Therefore, loans to NGEs are rather risky and hard to supervise. Moreover, the financial system is usually opaque in these enterprises, which can hardly meet the existing review standards or find a feasible guarantee system. Thus, small-and medium-sized NGEs have little chance of obtaining a loan from the bank, and their technological innovation is restricted by the shortage of funds.

9.1.2.4 A Shortage of Professional Technical Personnel

The accumulation of human resources requires a good mechanism for the introduction, utilization, and development of talent. Macroscopically, NGEs' severe shortage of technological innovation talents is caused by China's long-term planned economic system. Under this system, the distribution of talents is irrational, scientific personnel are over-concentrated in research institutes and large enterprises, and the flow of talents has been stagnated by the country's backward personnel system. Innovative talents have been impeded from flowing to NGEs by various man-made factors, but are now being robbed in large numbers by transnational corporations. All these have made China's NGEs the more frail in terms of technological innovation talents. Microscopically, one of the important reasons why NGEs, especially SMEs, can barely attract or retain technical personnel is that such talents are dissatisfied with their labor income. Many technical personnel have come to NGEs with the hope for a higher income; once this hope fails, it is very difficult to arouse their enthusiasm and creativity for further work. What's more, they are likely to leave if another enterprise happens to poach them with a fat salary at that moment. For technical personnel, the other important reason for their leaving is their dissatisfaction with the working environment. When they feel their talent or skills are not valued or being brought into full play in an enterprise, they tend to be disappointed and subsequently decide to leave.

9.2 The Efficiency of NGEs' Technological Innovation

In China, enterprises can be categorized into three types of ownership: SOEs, NGEs, and FFEs. The three types of enterprises differ not only in their behavioral characteristics, but also in their influences and roles in the growth of productivity and economy. To clearly interpret the efficiency of NGEs' technological innovation, we have made a comparative study of the three types of enterprises in China, discovered and revealed both the efficiencies of and problems with NGEs' technological innovation, and put forward some feasible policy suggestions.

9.2.1 Data Description

All the data used here is from the *China Statistical Yearbook on Science and Technology* and the *China Statistical Yearbook.* The *China Statistical Yearbook on Science and Technology 1999–2004* provides the basic information and statistics regarding the science and technology of SOEs and FFEs as well as the total data for each region from 1998 to 2003. We get the NGE data by subtracting those of SOEs and FFEs from the total data. Of the 31 provinces/ municipalities/regions in China, we have only included 30 in our samples for each year, since Tibet was rejected for having too much missing data. In each of the three types of enterprises, i.e., SOEs, NGEs, and FFEs, there are $6 \times 30 = 180$ observation samples. Therefore, there are a total of 540 observation samples of the three types taken together. Before establishing a set model, it is necessary to make clear the input and output variables of innovation. In various literatures, the number of patents is the most frequently used indicator of innovative output, but many scholars have pointed out its defects. For example, not all innovations are registered as patents; what's more, different patents can vary greatly in their economic value. To remedy such deficiencies, we chose to use the quantity of new products as proxy variables for innovation output. By the definition listed in the *China Statistical Yearbook on Science and Technology,* new products refers not only to brand-new products developed by use of new processes and/or new methods, but also to established products with improved design and quality; not only patented new products, but also those not yet patented. Obviously, compared with the number of patents overall, this definition of new products covers a wider scope of innovations than and thus can partially compensate for estimation bias in the use of patent numbers. Meanwhile, it must be noted that, in measuring innovative behaviors through patents and new product numbers, the implied assumption is that all patents or new products are of the same quality. This defect can somehow be overcome by the use of sales revenue generated by new products, for the higher the sales revenue of a new product, the greater its market value and the higher its quality of innovation. In order to verify the influence of different types of ownership on innovation efficiency from different angles, we take the number of patents applied, the number of new products, and their sales revenue as the innovation output variables. Compared with innovation output, innovation input is easier to measure. Here, we use technology development expenditure (R&D expenditure) and technology developers (R&D personnel) to represent innovation input. The data of all the above variables are from the *China Statistical Yearbook on Science and Technology* from the corresponding years. As for those variables affected by price fluctuations, the nominal values are translated into real values in accordance with the provincial price indexes in the corresponding years, which have been obtained from the *China Statistical Yearbook.* Technological innovation efficiency can be calculated in different ways. According to the general definition of efficiency, there are two types of innovation efficiency—single-factor innovation efficiency and total-factor innovation efficiency. The former refers to the innovation output from an innovation input, specifically expressed as R&D personnel efficiency (innovation output/ R&D personnel) and R&D expenditure efficiency (innovation output/R&D expenditures). This method is clear and easy to operate, but it can only be used to measure the contribution of a single factor to innovation and is likely to result insignificant estimation errors. The latter refers to the innovation output from factors other than the innovation factors of R&D expenditures and R&D personnel. Though this method is more complicated, its result is more reliable, as it takes into account the influence of different input factors on the output. In the calculation of total-factor innovation efficiency, the production function method is the one most commonly used in literatures, which is based on a solid foundation of economic theories and can strip away the potential effects of random errors. But this method requires the assumption of particular forms of the production function. Another method used to calculate total-factor innovation efficiency is data envelopment analysis (DEA), which is a pure mathematical planning method that requires no assumption of particular forms of the production function or of the efficiency distribution. It does, however, tend to neglect the effects of random errors on the output. With full consideration of the advantages and disadvantages of the above methods and to ensure the reliability of our tests, we have decided to simultaneously used the single-factor efficiency model, the production-function model, and the two-step DEA method in our empirical tests of NGEs' technological innovation efficiency.

9.2.2 *The Single-Factor Model of Innovation Efficiency and Estimation Results*

9.2.2.1 Model Specification

Single-factor innovation efficiency can be expressed by R&D personnel efficiency and R&D expenditure efficiency. According to its different definitions, we have established the following models for measuring single-factor efficiency:

$$Ln(Y/R)_{ijt} = a + \gamma_1 PRI_{ij} + \gamma_2 FOR_{ij} + \eta X_{it} + \varepsilon_{ijt} \quad (1)$$

$$Ln(Y/L)_{ijt} = b + \gamma_1 PRI_{ij} + \gamma_2 FOR_{ij} + \eta X_{it} + \varepsilon_{ijt} \quad (2)$$

In the models, i (i = 1,. . .,30) stands for the region, j (j = 1, 2, 3) for the type of enterprises, and t (t = 1998, . . .,2003) for the year. Y stands for innovation output, which can be measured using three indicators: the number of patents (P), the number of new products (N), and the sales revenue of new products (S). R and L, respectively, stand for R&D expenditures and the number of R&D personnel. By the definition of what constitutes innovation efficiency, Model (1) is an innovation efficiency model of R&D expenditures, where $(Y/R)_{ijt}$ is the R&D expenditure efficiency of Enterprise Type j in Region i in Year t. Model (2) is an innovation efficiency model of R&D personnel, where $(Y/R)_{ijt}$ is the R&D personnel efficiency of Enterprise Type j in Region i in Year t. Of the three types of ownership used in our sample enterprises, we take SOEs as the reference variable and the other two as dummy variables: PRI representing NGEs (private enterprises) and FOR representing FFEs (foreign-funded enterprises). As our focus is on NGEs' innovation efficiency, we shall pay special attention to the coefficient estimate γ_1. When γ_1 and γ_2 are significantly greater than zero, NGEs and FFEs are of higher innovation efficiency than SOEs, and their advantage in innovation efficiency is determined by the significance levels and values of the coefficient estimates γ_1 and γ_2.

To accurately evaluate the influence of different types of ownership on innovation efficiency, it is necessary to separate ownership from other factors likely to affect innovation efficiency, so we seta control variable (vector X in the models). As the two most important economic policies released during China's economic transition, the country's domestic reform and economic opening up both have a significant influence on enterprise goals and behavior. We therefore set them as important control variables, expressed as the degree of denationalization and the value of import and export, respectively. (1) Degree of denationalization. During China's transition from a planned economy to a market economy, SOEs continue to withdraw while the number of NSOEs are rapidly rising. The degree of denationalization, as a result of the country's ownership reform, reflects not only the clarity of the property rights being defined, but also the degrees of market economy activity and competition. A high degree of denationalization in a region can not only create a positive external environment for an enterprise's technological innovation, but also promote enterprise behavior and encourage enterprises to improve their level of innovation efficiency. Therefore, denationalization is expected to have a positive influence on innovation efficiency. Based on what data is available, we have measured the degree of denationalization by the proportion of employees in non-SOEs to the total quantity of employment, and subsequently marked it as NSOE. (2) Degree of openness. China's policy of opening up not only enables domestic enterprises to emulate and absorb advanced technology and management experience from abroad through "learning by doing," but also exposes them to intense competition in the international market, which can stimulate their technological innovation and improve their level of efficiency. We measure the degree of openness by the proportion of the total volume of import and export trade to GDP at the average exchange rate of the RMB against the USD (the central parity rate) for each year examined, and mark it as OPEN. (3) Time variables. Time variables reflect the variation in technological efficiency and also cover any variations in innovative efficiency caused by changes in the macro economy and related policies. We take 1996 as the reference variable of time and set five dummy variables representing the period from 1997 to 2003. (4) Region variables. Regional variables reflect the huge differences between the regions in terms of geographical conditions, resource endowment, and economic foundations. To compare the levels of innovative efficiency in different parts of China, we have divided the 30 chosen provinces/municipalities/regions into the eastern, central, and western regions.[2] We take the central region as the reference variable, and set the eastern and western regions as two dummy variables marked, respectively, as EAST and WEST. Meanwhile, to ensure the reliability of the estimation results, we have also adopted another set of region variables in which Shandong is taken as the reference variable, with 29 dummy variables representing the other provinces/municipalities/regions marked as PRO.

9.2.2.2 Estimation Results

Table 9.1 shows the regression results by use of the single-factor model of innovation efficiency. In the table, Columns (1) and (2) are the estimation results with the number of patents as the variable used for innovation output; Columns (3) and (4) are the estimation results with the number of new products as the variables outlining innovation output; and Columns (5) and (6) are the estimation results with the sales revenue of new products as the variables of innovation output. Of all the estimation results seen in Table 9.1, the coefficient estimates of PRI and FOR are the ones that are positive and highly significant statistically no matter which indicator is used to measure the innovation output, indicating a higher degree of innovative efficiency on the part of NGEs and FFEs than that of SOEs. In other empirical studies using different data samples, different researchers have similarly concluded a lower level of innovative efficiency for SOEs (Zhang et al. 2003; Jefferson et al. 2006; Wu Yanbing 2006b). Thus their conclusions and our estimation results are mutually verifiable. SOEs are generally low in terms of both production efficiency and innovation efficiency, which results from their serious principal-agent problem, as well as the lack of effective incentive, supervisory, and manager-selection mechanisms.

Note that the estimation results of enterprise ownership are sensitive to the representational methods of innovation efficiency. When innovation efficiency is measured by the number of patents/R&D expenditures and the number of new products/R&D expenditures (Columns (1) and (3) in Table 9.1), NGEs score higher than FFEs in terms of innovation efficiency; when it is measured by the number of patents/R&D personnel and the number of new products/R&D personnel (Columns (2) and (4) in Table 9.1), FFEs rank higher than NGEs in innovation efficiency. When the innovation output is measured by the sales revenue of new products, however, FFEs are always higher than NGEs in innovation efficiency according to the estimation results, no matter which indicator is used to measure innovation

[2]The eastern region includes 11 provinces/municipalities: Beijing, Tianjin, Hebei, Liaoning, Shanghai, Jiangsu, Zhejiang, Shandong, Guangdong, and Hainan; the central region includes 8 provinces: Shanxi, Jilin, Heilongjiang, Anhui, Jiangxi, Henan, Hubei, and Hunan; and the western region includes 10 provinces/regions: Inner Mongolia, Guangxi, Sichuan, Guizhou, Yunnan, Shaanxi, Gansu, Qinghai, Ningxia, and Xinjiang.

Table 9.1 Regression results of the single-factor model of innovation efficiency

	(1) Ln(P/R)	(2) Ln(P/L)	(3) Ln(N/R)	(4) Ln(N/L)	(5) Ln(S/R)	(6) Ln(S/L)
Constant term	−9.441*	−7.452*	−6.821*	−5.073*	−1.672*	0.133
	(−17.512)	(−14.702)	(−18.199)	(−16.648)	(−3.177)	(0.280)
PRI	0.935*	0.835*	0.414*	0.358*	0.464*	0.397*
	(8.732)	(8.262)	(5.426)	(5.746)	(4.374)	(4.133)
FOR	0.779*	1.135*	0.253*	0.604*	0.774*	1.112*
	(6.917)	(10.709)	(3.25)	(9.555)	(7.154)	(11.356)
NSOE	0.946	1.133***	1.381*	1.824*	1.711*	2.131*
	(1.495)	(1.905)	(3.124)	(5.08)	(2.759)	(3.809)
OPEN	0.159	0.479*	−0.181	0.197**	0.409**	0.778*
	(0.952)	(3.045)	(−1.534)	(2.048)	(2.488)	(5.229)
TIME	0.102*	0.232*	−0.137*	−0.017	0.023	0.137*
	(3.669)	(8.836)	(−7.016)	(−1.075)	(0.854)	(5.594)
EAST	−0.156	0.280**	−0.261*	0.181**	0.569*	1.009*
	(−1.142)	−2.174	(−2.741)	(2.327)	(4.288)	(8.392)
CENT	−0.395*	−0.367*	−0.164**	−0.088	0.291**	0.360*
	(−3.416)	(−3.369)	(−2.043)	(−1.345)	(2.593)	(3.554)
F value	17.571	46.623	18.183	21.394	17.287	65.732
Adj.R^2	0.188	0.389	0.186	0.213	0.178	0.462
Observed value	501	502	527	529	527	528

Notes: 1. The figures in parentheses are t-values
2. *, ** and ***indicate significant parameter estimates respectively on 1%, 5% and 10% significance levels

efficiency (Columns (5) and (6) in Table 9.1). Thus, we can infer that, compared with FFEs, NGEs are higher in terms of the efficiency of R&D expenditures, but lower in the efficiency of R&D personnel. As the sales revenue of new products reflects, to some degree, the market value of product innovation, our estimation results also indicate that FFEs are more successful than NGEs in terms of market development and the commercialization of new products. This conclusion is by no means isolated. For example, through their study of the data from British, German, and Irish manufacturing enterprises, Love and Roper (2001) found that FFEs are more successful than domestic enterprises in the commercialization of innovation, even though they are smaller in the quantity of innovative ideas produced. With the data available in China, we have also shown here that FFEs are better than domestic enterprises in the commercialization efficiency of new products.

It can also be seen from the estimation results in Table 9.1 that the coefficient estimates of denationalization (NSOE) are positive and statistically significant, which indicates the positive influence of denationalization on innovation efficiency. Since the beginning of China's reform and opening up, the proportion of non-SOEs has been on the rise concurrently with the constant deepening of property right reform of SOEs. A higher degree of denationalization in a given region indicates a more active market economy with less administrative interference on the part of the government, which offers a good incentive environment for an enterprise's innovation. The coefficient estimates of openness (OPEN) are significantly positive in most estimation results. Through the spillover and competitive effects of technology, the economic opening up has optimized the allocation of resources, sped up the technical updating of enterprises, and improved their innovation efficiency. As for the time and regional variables, the estimation results of the models are different, which is mainly caused by the different variables of innovation output. For example, when different indicators of innovation efficiency are adopted, efficiency levels vary between the eastern, central, and western regions. Whatever the indicators, however, both NGEs and FFEs have a higher level of efficiency than SOEs, which reflects a stable relationship between enterprise ownership and innovation efficiency.

9.2.3 The Function Model and Estimation Results of Technological Innovation

9.2.3.1 Model Specifications

As a common practice in the existing literatures, we chose to base our analysis on the Cobb-Douglas Production Function. We took R&D capital and R&D personnel as the input factors of innovation and take into consideration the other factors that might influence innovation efficiency, and then set up the following function model of innovation:

$$LnY_{ijt} = c + \alpha LnK_{it} + \beta LnL_{it} + \gamma_1 PRI_{it} + \gamma_2 FOR_{it} + \eta X_{it} + \varepsilon_{it} \qquad (3)$$

In the function, Kijt and Lijt refer to, respectively, the R&D capital stock and R&D personnel of Enterprise j in Region i in Year t, while α and β, respectively, refer to the output elasticity of R&D capital stock and that of R&D personnel. The other variables denotes the same information as those used in the single-factor models of innovation efficiency. The control variable, X, includes the degrees of denationalization and openness, as well as the dummy variables of time and region.

What is noteworthy in the Innovation Function Model (3) is that R&D expenditure not only affects the innovation output of the present period, but also that seen in a number of later periods, so its influence on innovation output must be examined through the calculation of R&D capital stock. We calculate R&D capital stock by using the Perpetual Inventory Method (PIM). The formula is $K_{it} = R_{it} + (1 - \tau)K_{i,t-1}$, where K stands for R&D capital stock, R for R&D expenditure, and τfor the depreciation rate. The following is a description of the major parameters of R&D capital stock calculation:

1. R&D price index = (Purchases or the construction of fixed assets/R&D expenditures) × Price index of investment in fixed assets + (Raw material cost/R&D

expenditures) × Purchasing price index of raw materials + (Other costs/R&D expenditures) × Price index of other costs. The *China Statistical Yearbook* provides the annual price indexes of investment in fixed assets of the 30 provinces/municipalities/regions surveyed from 1998 to 2003,[3] but of the purchasing price index of raw materials, it only gives the annual national data, rather than the provincial data. We have converted the above two types of indexes into constant prices as expressed in the prices of 1998. As the meaning of "Other costs" as a category is rather vague, we express the "Price index of other costs" as the average of provincial price indexes of investment in fixed assets and the purchasing price indexes of raw materials. We deflate the R&D expenditures with the calculated R&D price index, and in doing so get the real R&D expenditures of each province/municipality/region from 1998 to 2003.

2. We set the depreciation rate τ of R&D stock as 15% (Griliches and Lichtenberg 1984; Hall and Mairesse 1995; Crépon and Duguet 1997; Hu et al. 2005).
3. The R&D stock of the base-period is $K_1 = E_1(1+g)/(\tau+g)$, where g is the average growth rate of R&D expenditure in all the periods prior to sampling. Assume that the average growth rate of R&D expenditure was 5% in all the periods prior to the sampling (Hall and Mairesse 1995), and then $K_1 = R_1(1 + 0.05)/(0.15 + 0.05) = 5.25R_1$, that is, the R&D stock is 5.25 times the R&D expenditure in the base period. When the base-period R&D stock is worked out, we can calculate the R&D capital stock of different types of enterprises in each region by using the Perpetual Inventory Method (PIM).

9.2.3.2 Estimation Results

Compared with the single-factor model of innovation efficiency, the innovation function more reasonably reflects the nature of innovation, as it takes into account the two input factors of R&D capital and R&D personnel, and, therefore, the estimation results are more real and reliable. Table 9.2 shows the estimation results of this model. In the table, Columns (1), (2), and (3) are the results integrating the number of patents, the number of new products, and the sales revenue of new products, respectively, as the variables for measuring innovation efficiency. To further verify the reliability of the estimation results, we remove the dummy variables of the eastern and central regions and add the dummy variables of 29 provinces/municipalities/regions in order to carry out a new regression, the results of which are in Columns (4), (5), and (6) of Table 9.2.

As can be seen in the estimation results shown in Table 9.2, the innovative output of R&D personnel is of a greater elasticity than that of R&D capital,

[3] As there is no available price index of the investment in the fixed assets of Guangdong from 1996 to 2000 and Hainan from 1996 to 1999, we used the national price index of investment in fixed assets in the data of the two provinces. This method is also used in calculating the stock of introduced foreign and domestic technologies, which involves the provincial price indexes of investment in fixed assets.

Table 9.2 Regression results of the innovation function model

	(1)	(2)	(3)	(4)	(5)	(6)
	Ln(P)	Ln(N)	Ln(S)	Ln(P)	Ln(N)	Ln(S)
Constant term	−6.836* (−11.891)	−5.005* (−15.519)	−0.883*** (−1.700)	−7.765* (−3.904)	0.008 (0.007)	0.980 (0.563)
LnK	0.173** (2.163)	0.194* (4.451)	0.276* (3.898)	0.114 (1.365)	0.147* (3.437)	0.223* (3.255)
LnL	0.643* (8.770)	0.714* (16.832)	0.865* (12.993)	0.767* (9.772)	0.642* (14.656)	0.952* (14.447)
PRI	0.733* (7.224)	0.309* (5.060)	0.505* (5.332)	0.746* (7.749)	0.233* (4.149)	0.523* (6.202)
FOR	0.611* (4.529)	0.300* (3.741)	1.404* (11.321)	0.755* (4.942)	−0.039 (−0.440)	1.458* (10.908)
NSOE	1.937* (3.221)	2.213* (6.089)	1.125** (1.996)	3.449 (1.525)	−1.488 (−1.124)	−0.823 (−0.416)
OPEN	0.613* (3.808)	0.232** (2.367)	0.494* (3.248)	0.683 (1.133)	−0.346 (−0.966)	−0.156 (−0.292)
TIME	0.202* (7.452)	−0.042* (−2.604)	0.118* (4.711)	0.199* (5.727)	0.022 (1.095)	0.160* (5.277)
EAST	0.363* (2.662)	0.169** (2.115)	0.752* (6.048)			
CENT	−0.194*** (−1.745)	−0.013 (−0.197)	0.178*** (1.721)			
PRO				YES	YES	YES
F value	148.063	474.876	293.909	47.100	152.889	104.765
Adj.R^2	0.726	0.890	0.834	0.768	0.912	0.877
Observed value	501	527	527	501	527	527

Notes: 1. The figures in parentheses are t-values
2. *, ** and *** indicate significant parameter estimates on, respectively, 1%, 5%, and 10% significance levels
3. With the data of Shandong Province as the reference variable, and a total of 29 dummy variables

indicating a greater contribution of R&D personnel to innovation than that of R&D capital. The coefficient estimates of the explanatory variable NGEs, which are our principal concern, are all positive and significant at a level above 1%. This indicates that, according to the regression results, NGEs still have a higher innovative efficiency than SOEs, even when the two input factors of R&D capital and R&D personnel are taken into account. As to which is of a higher innovation efficiency—NGEs or FFEs—the answer depends on the variable of innovation output. But using the model of new-product sales revenue, FFEs still have a higher efficiency than NGEs in the commercialization of new products (Columns (3) and (6) in Table 9.2), which is consistent with the estimation result of the single-factor model of innovation efficiency seen in Table 9.1.

Of the estimation results in Columns (1)–(3) of the table, the coefficient estimates of the two variables, denationalization (NSOE)—representing the degree of ownership reform and the proportion of importexporttrade—and (OPEN)—

representing the degree of openness—are both significantly positive, which indicates that the deeper the degree of ownership reform and the greater the degree of openness, the greater their contribution to the improvement of enterprise innovation efficiency. The coefficient estimates of the dummy variables of the eastern region are also quite positive, indicating a higher innovation efficiency than those of other regions. Interestingly, however, these results are different from what we find in Columns (4)–(6) of Table 9.2, where the coefficient estimates of NSOE and OPEN are no longer significant. It is likely that this is mainly because the degrees of NSOE and OPEN of a region are closely related to the regional features and can be largely explained by the provincial dummy variables under control, which comprehensively reflect the features of the region in question. Thus, once the provincial dummy variables are under control in the regression model, such variables as denationalization and openness—which reflect specific regional features—are no longer statistically significant.

9.2.4 *The DEA Two-Step Model and Estimation Results*

9.2.4.1 Model Specifications

First, we calculate the efficiency of technological innovation for the three types of enterprises in each region by using the Data Envelopment Analysis (DEA) method, and then study the influence of ownership on overall enterprise innovation efficiency.

DEA is a data-oriented evaluation method used to assess the performance and relative efficiency of a group of decision-making units (DMU) with multiple inputs and outputs. The calculation of technical efficiency by DEA can be based on either input or output.[4] We adopt the input-based approach defined by Fare et al. in 1994. Suppose DMUkth (k = 1, . . ., K) uses Input $x_{k,n}^t$ of Type n (n = 1, . . ., N) in Period t (t = 1, . . ., T), and gets Output $y_{k,m}^t$ of Type m (m = 1, . . ., M). Under the constant returns to scale (C) and strong disposability of inputs (S), the input possibility set (reference technology) is defined as:

$$L^t(y^t|C,S) = \left\{ \left(x_1^t,\cdots,x_N^t\right) : y_m^t \leq \sum_{k=1}^K z_k^t y_{k,m}^t, m = 1,\cdots,M; \\ x_n^t \geq \sum_{k=1}^K z_k^t x_{k,n}^t, n = 1,\cdots,N; z_k^t \geq 0, k = 1,\cdots,K \right\}$$

In this equation, Z represents the weight of the observed values of each DMU. When the reference technology is specified, the non-parametric programming

[4]From different angles of analysis, a reference technology or its advanced practice can be expressed in three equivalent ways—an input-demand set, an output possibility set, and a curve graph. Under the constant returns to scale and strong disposability of inputs, no matter which of the three methods used, all will lead to the same result.

model for the Farrell input-Oriented Measure of Technical Efficiency of DMUk[th] is as follows:

$$
\begin{aligned}
&F_i^t\left(y_{k'}^t, x_{k'}^t \mid C, S\right) = \min \theta_{k'} \\
&s.t.\ y_{k',m}^t \le \sum_{k=1}^{K} z_k^t y_{k,m}^t, m = 1, \cdots, M \\
&\sum_{k=1}^{K} z_k^t x_{k,n}^t \le \theta_{k'} x_{k',n}^t, n = 1, \cdots, N \\
&z_k^t \ge 0, k = 1, \cdots, K
\end{aligned}
$$

The values of Technical Efficiency are between 0 and 1. The technical efficiency of DMUs at the technological frontier is 1, and less than 1 of those elsewhere. In the calculation of innovative efficiency by DEA, the input factors of innovation are R&D capital stock and R&D personnel. R&D capital stock is measured in the same way as in the Innovation Function Model; innovation output is measured by the number of patents, the number of new products, and the sales revenue of new products. As the innovative efficiency of each DMU is calculated, the influence of enterprise ownership on innovation efficiency can be assessed in the following way:

$$F_{ijt} = d + \lambda_1 PRI_{ij} + \lambda_2 FOR_{ij} + \eta X_{it} + \varepsilon_{ijt}$$

In this equation, F is the indicator of innovation efficiency measured by DEA. With the three indicators of innovation output, i.e., the number of patents, the number of new products, and the sales revenue of new products, we can get three indicators of innovation efficiency, respectively marked as F_P, F_N, and F_S. We will later make a regression analysis of all three.

9.2.4.2 Estimation Results

Table 9.3 shows the regression results of the above model, in which innovation efficiency measured by DEA is the explained variable. F_P, F_N, and F_S are the indicators of innovation efficiency based on the number of patents, the number of new products, and the sales revenue of new products, respectively. Similar to those seen in Table 9.2, Columns (1)–(3) in Table 9.3 are the regression results with controlled dummy variables for the eastern and central regions, and Columns (4)–(6) are the regression results with controlled dummy variables of the 29 provinces/municipalities/regions. We can find that, in Table 9.3, when the innovative efficiency measured by DEA is taken as the explained variable, the degree of denationalization (NSOE) and openness (OPEN) are no longer significant in most of the subsequent estimation results. This indicates that ownership reform and economic opening are sensitive to the calculating method used to establish innovative efficiency.

Once again, the coefficient estimates of NGEs and FFEs are significantly positive among all estimation results. Moreover, the coefficient estimates of FFEs are higher than those of NGEs. These results tell us that FFEs are the highest in terms of innovation efficiency, followed by NGEs, while SOEs are the lowest. As

Table 9.3 DEA regression results with innovation efficiency as the explained variable

	(1)	(2)	(3)	(4)	(5)	(6)
	F_P	F_N	F_S	F_P	F_N	F_S
Constant term	−0.019 (−0.206)	0.089 (0.924)	0.274* (3.073)	−0.617 (−1.598)	0.226 (0.563)	0.259 (0.712)
LnK	0.086* (4.463)	0.092* (4.659)	0.035*** (1.901)	0.084* (4.493)	0.092* (4.797)	0.035** (1.991)
LnL	0.116* (5.884)	0.150* (7.500)	0.167* (8.994)	0.112* (5.872)	0.146* (7.471)	0.165* (9.277)
PRI	0.065 (0.590)	0.185 (1.642)	−0.149 (−1.422)	0.775*** (1.683)	−0.001 (−0.003)	−0.113 (−0.260)
FOR	0.012 (0.390)	−0.021 (−0.689)	0.058** (2.062)	0.026 (0.206)	−0.208 (−1.604)	−0.063 (−0.537)
NSOE	0.010** (2.041)	−0.006 (−1.206)	−0.026* (−5.551)	0.003 (0.373)	0.000 (0.015)	−0.024* (−3.703)
OPEN	−0.006 (−0.267)	−0.026 (−1.065)	0.077* (3.355)			
TIME	−0.063* (−3.074)	−0.060* (−2.913)	0.002 (0.084)			
EAST				YES	YES	YES
CENT	7.973	10.416	27.215	3.742	3.715	8.436
PRO	0.086	0.111	0.258	0.152	0.149	0.323
F value	522	530	530	522	530	530

Notes: 1. The figures in parentheses are t-values
2. *, ** and *** indicate significant parameter estimates on, respectively, 1%, 5%, and 10% significance levels

we have seen, in the estimation results of both the single-factor model of innovation efficiency and the innovation function model, NGEs are more efficient in the development of patents and new products but less efficient in the commercialization of new products. The estimation results here, however, show that NGEs have fallen behind FFEs in all aspects of innovation efficiency. To some degree, this difference highlights the influence of research methods on the estimation results, as well as the importance of investigating the same issue by different methods to ensure the reliability of testing conclusions. Through different methods of analysis, we have come to certain robust conclusions. That is, on the one hand, both NGEs and FFEs are higher than SOEs in innovation efficiency, and on the other hand, the innovation efficiency of NGEs and FFEs is determined by the innovation output variables and the research methods used.

9.3 Conclusions

The above analysis of the current status of NGEs' technological innovation indicates that their overall capacity for technological innovation is constantly increasing. In different regions, however, NGEs' technological innovation capacities vary greatly; their models of technological innovation also sharply differ from industry to industry; and their returns on innovation are relatively small. Moreover, NGEs are still faced with many difficulties in their pursuit of technological innovation, such as the lack of a complete mechanism for technological innovation, an unsound legal environment, financing difficulties, and a shortage of talents. In this chapter, we have focused on NGEs' efficiency in terms of technological innovation. Based on the panel data of large- and medium-sized industrial enterprises in 30 provinces/municipalities/regions across China from 1998 to 2003, and with the controlled variables of denationalization and openness in each region, we have conducted an empirical study by using the single-factor model of technological innovation efficiency, the function model of technological innovation, and the DEA method. We have discovered that NGEs score higher than SOEs in innovation efficiency, which indicates that a clear ownership structure is an important condition for the stimulation of innovation and promotion of efficiency.

Despite their greater efficiency of technological innovation than that of SOEs (which is due to the advantage they hold in property rights), China's NGEs are generally small in size and, at present, suffer from a shortage of both R&D funds and talent; furthermore, most of them do not have the capacity to sustain technological innovation. Therefore, in order to cultivate technological innovation entities that are adaptable to the market economy, it is necessary to deepen the reform of SOEs and implement modernizing systemic reforms, keeping in mind, however, that the focus should be on the cultivation of large and strong NGEs through market competition. Besides, SOEs and NGEs must focus on different fields of technological innovation. The former must concentrate on the type of fundamental innovation that concerns national security and strategy, while the latter must be more inclined towards practical technological innovation. We must further deepen these reform processes and perfect the policies outlining them so as to create a better market environment for NGEs' development. We must establish a modern enterprise system, rely on the modern market service system, and guarantee NGEs' further growth and development within a modern factors market, which involves the marketization of relevant interests such as the labor force, capital, technology, land, and other natural resources.

In the face of increasingly fierce market competition, NGEs must strengthen their concept of innovation, discard outdated methods of thinking and codes of conduct, ceaselessly move beyond existing concepts, improve their innovative ideas and systems for innovation, and accelerate their technological modernization. The operators of NGEs must consolidate their belief in promoting enterprise development through technological innovation, encourage competition and innovation, actively absorb new information from external sources, and improve their risk-bearing capacity. They must give top priority to the long-term development of their enterprise and regard technological innovation as the focus of enterprise strategies throughout the process of development. Only in this way can NGEs improve the foundation of their technological innovation and develop technological achievements with independent intellectual property rights or products with high competitiveness, which will benefit their long-term development.

Based on existing laws and regulations, we must sort out, classify, amend, supplement, and perfect those policies related to technological innovation and the protection of innovation achievements, while also working out more detailed rules. In particular, we must establish corresponding legal norms for such issues relating to NGEs' technological innovation as the monetary price accorded to scientific achievements, technical royalties, shareholding and stock options with technologies, the ownership of employee-developed technologies, the service management of technological agents, and the industrialization of scientific and technological achievements. As the situation requires, we must consider the promulgation of more laws and regulations, such as rules on encouraging NGEs' technological innovation and regulations on the protection of NGEs' intellectual property rights, and more. We should also strengthen the enforcement of existing laws and provide a relatively complete legal safeguard for NGEs' technological innovation. In addition, the government should also increase the subsidies for those technologies that are easy to imitate and enhance the protection of intellectual property rights.

We should better solve NGEs' financing difficulties insofar as they are related to technological innovation. The governmental decision-makers must square up to the market rules, rectify the goals and purposes of the stock market establishment, and provide NGEs with a fair and healthy capital market environment. The government must facilitate NGEs' fundraising by means of equity financing, project financing, and more. The government must establish a sound mechanism for innovation investment; allow eligible NGEs to issue corporate bonds in accordance with related state stipulations; encourage financial institutions to start such businesses as financial leasing, corporate finance, and account trusts; improve the means of service and means of insurance institutions; implement product innovation and service innovation that is oriented towards NGEs; and encourage conditional regions to establish credit guarantee funds as well as regional credit re-guarantee institutions for NGEs. Only in this way can we provide increased financial security for NGEs' technological innovation.

Bibliography

Australian Industry Commission (1995) Research and development, Report no. 44. Government Publishing Service, Canberra

Crépon B, Duguet E (1997) Estimating the innovation function from patent numbers: GMM on count panel data. J Appl Econ 12(3):243–263

Economics Division of All-China Federation of Industry & Commerce (ACFIC) (2010) Report on analysis of 500 Chinese NGEs 2010. All-China Federation of Industry & Commerce (ACFIC), Beijing

Fare R, Grosskopf S, Lovell CAK (1994) Production frontiers. Cambridge University Press, Cambridge

Griliches Z (1964) Research expenditures, education, and the aggregate production function. Am Econ Rev 54(6):961–974

Griliches Z (1979) Issues in assessing the contribution of research and development to productivity growth. Bell J Econ 10:92–116

Griliches Z, Lichtenberg F (1984) R&D and productivity growth at the industry level: is there still a relationship? In: Griliches Z (ed) R&D patents and productivity. University of Chicago Press, Chicago, pp 465–496

Hall BH, Mairesse J (1995) Exploring the relationship between R&D and productivity in French manufacturing firms. J Econ 65:263–293

Hu AGZ (2001) Ownership, government R&D, private R&D, and productivity in Chinese industry. J Comp Econ 29(1):136–157

Hu AGZ, Jefferson GH (2008) A great wall of patents: what is behind China's recent patent explosion? J Dev Econ 90:57–68

Hu AGZ, Jefferson GH, Qian J (2005) R&D and technology transfer: firm-level evidence from Chinese industry. Rev Econ Stat 87(4):780–786

Huang M (2009) Report on the development of China's NGEs (no. 6), 2008–2009. Social Sciences Academic Press, Beijing

Jefferson GH, Bai H, Guan X, Yu X (2006) R&D performance in Chinese industry. Econ Innov New Technol 15(4/5):345–366

Liu Y, Xu Z (2006) Report on Chinese non-governmental enterprise competitiveness (no. 3). Social Sciences Academic Press, Beijing

Love JH, Roper S (2001) Location and network effects on innovation success: evidence for UK, German and Irish manufacturing plants. Res Policy 30:643–661

Mansfield E (1965) Rates of return from industrial research and development. Am Econ Rev 55:110–122

Wu Y (2006a) R&D and productivity: an empirical study on Chinese manufacturing industry. Econ Res J 11:60–70

Wu Y (2006b) R&D stock, knowledge function and productive efficiency. China Econ Q 5(4):1129

Zhang A, Zhang Y, Zhao R (2003) A study of the R&D efficiency and productivity of Chinese firms. J Comp Econ 31:444–464

Chapter 10
Community Banks and SME Financing: The Financing Environment of NGEs' Growth and Development

Hongling Wang

10.1 "Ownership Discrimination": An Outdated Interpretation

For commercial banks, it is also risky to make loans to SOEs. But once such loans turn sour, the government will usually mediate and seek "excuses" in order to extricate the debtors. This is one of the most important reasons why state-owned commercial banks continue to make loans to SOEs even when they hold large losses.[1] On the contrary, it is very difficult for NSOEs, especially NGEs, to obtain loans from state-owned commercial banks. It is all the more so when China's commercial banking system is still strongly informed by the planned economy. This phenomenon is summarized as "ownership discrimination" in academia.[2] In December of 1993, the State Council announced the *Decision on Reform of the Financial System* and proposed to turn the state-owned specialized banks into real

[1]When SOEs run into financial troubles, their usual recourse would be to argue their case to the government, the thrust of which is that their survival concerns the livelihood of many employees and if they go bankrupt, personnel placement would become a sensitive issue of public concern. Therefore, they would ask the government for help. To save such enterprises, the government will usually mediate on their behalf with the banks, who will offer loans to these enterprises, namely the so-called "loans for stability and unity."

[2]According to Fan Gang, the current banking system of China is dominated by state-owned banks. They are unwilling to offer loans to SMEs, most of which are non-public enterprises, as they are afraid to take responsibility for possible loss of state-owned assets. Brandit and Li discovered through an analysis of the Chinese data that NGEs have more difficulty getting bank loans and are usually required to have higher guarantee conditions even if they succeed in getting loans (which are usually very small amounts). This verifies the ownership discrimination in China's state-owned banks.

H. Wang (✉)
Chinese Academy of Social Sciences, Beijing, China

Y. Liu (ed.), *New Interpretations on the Development of China's Non-Governmental Enterprises*, Research Series on the Chinese Dream and China's Development Path, DOI 10.1007/978-981-10-3872-3_10

commercial banks. After nearly 20 years of reformation, the former state-owned banks have largely given up the function of policy banks; like ordinary enterprises, their primary goal is the pursuit of profit. That being the case, the ownership of enterprises should have been no longer important when banks offer loans. In fact, however, they are still reluctant to lend money to most NGEs. Their attitude toward NGEs has not changed after the banking reform, but the reasons are fundamentally different. Should we still attribute NGEs' difficulty in getting loans to the concept of "ownership discrimination," it would not beat all persuasive.

As a matter of fact, nowadays in China, large-sized NGEs have much less difficulty in getting indirect financing from banks, and the best of them have even become gold-standard clients of the banks. Figure 10.1 shows the short-term bank loans in 2007 and 2008 made to 57 small-cap companies listed on the Shanghai and Shenzhen Stock Exchanges. These 57 companies are typical representatives of NGEs, where the top ten shareholders are natural persons with total shareholdings of between 62.31% and 79.25%. Their annual reports show that the Agricultural Bank of China, joint-stock banks, and city commercial banks are constantly providing them with short-term loans, and more than one third of these loans are credit loans without charges on assets or other items. The most important reason why these NGEs have won the favor of the banks is their considerable size—they are the giants of NGEs.

In the following analysis, either with the term "NGEs" or "SMEs," we are indeed discussing their bank financing from the perspective of enterprise size. Whether a given enterprise can successfully get bank loans is not necessarily related to whether they are state-owned or private. The only relevant fact is that, in present-day China, large enterprises are basically SOEs, while most SMEs are NGEs. Through the reform of "invigorating large enterprises and relaxing control over small ones," the government has long privatized most small- and medium-sized SOEs. It is certain that, if there were still small- and medium-sized SOEs, they

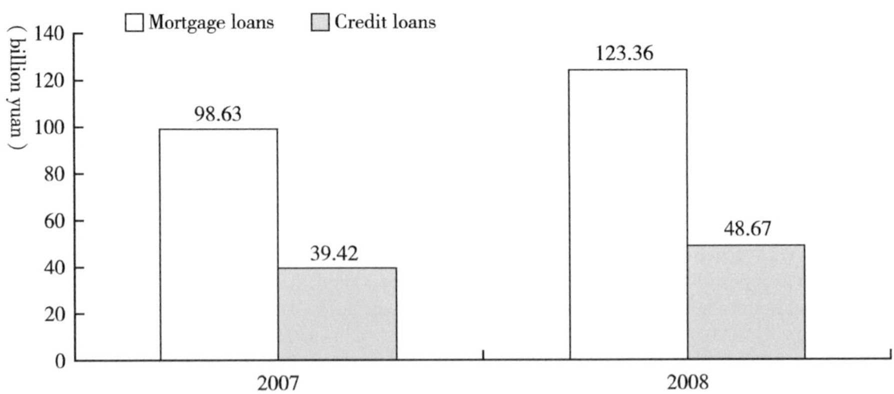

Fig. 10.1 Short-term bank loans to 57 listed NGEs 2007–2008 (billion RMB) (Source: Information disclosure of listed companies on CSRC website; Hongyuan Securities; Great Wisdom Infoport)

would have no less difficulty in getting bank loans than NGEs. As the property right of enterprises can no longer explain their difficulty in getting loans, people have resorted to the property rights of banks for explanation.

10.2 The Privatization of Banks: A Plausible Premise

In the discussion on how to solve NGEs' (or more precisely, SMEs') difficulty in getting loans, there is another misunderstanding in academia, i.e., the attempt to replace state-owned banks with private ones so as to solve NGEs' loan difficulty. The reason for this misconception is that China's banking industry has long been highly monopolized by state-owned banks.

Why should banks be privatized? On this issue, the focus is quite different between scholars at home and abroad. Most foreign economic literatures give reasons for the privatization of banks from the perspective of efficiency. For example, it is believed that, in the traditional theory of property rights, that private commercial banks are more efficient in operation than state-owned and cooperative banks. La Porta et al.[3] gathered material on the governmental ownership of banks in many countries and found the phenomenon is universal. The proportion of the governmental ownership [of banks] is even higher in those countries with a low efficiency and per capita income, where the financial system is undeveloped, the government pursues interventionism, and intellectual property rights are not adequately protected. It is noteworthy that those countries with a high proportion of governmental share of banks in the 1970s usually corresponded to a slow financial and economic rate of development, as well as a correspondingly low output efficiency in the 1990s. Bonin, Hasan, Wachtel, and Paul[4] studied the relationship between the ownership structure and operation efficiency of banks in six transitional countries (Bulgaria, Croatia, the Czech Republic, Hungary, Poland, and Russia) in 1999 and 2000, and found the efficiency-based rankings from top to bottom were foreign banks, private banks, and state-owned banks when their operations were measured by assets and returns on capital.

Since the 1990s, however, Chinese academia has been criticizing the financial monopoly left over by the traditional planned economy. The most immediate cause for this is the difficulty facing NGEs in financing—they are provided with only 1% of the total amount of domestic banks' loans when they already account for over 25% of China's GDP and over 50% of China's industrial output (during the Ninth Five-Year Plan). It has also directly triggered academic appeals for breaking financial monopolies and developing private banks. SOEs' monopoly of the

[3]La Porta, R., Lopez-de-silanes, F., Shleifer, A. (2002). Government Ownership of Banks. *Journal of Finance*, LVII (1),265–302.

[4]Bonin, J. P., Hasan, I., Wachtel, Paul. (2003). *Bank Privatization and Performance: Evidence from Transition Countries*. Presented at World Bank Conference on Bank Privatization, 20–21.

Table 10.1 Credit structure of Minsheng and state-owned banks (%)

Item	Bank	2006	2007	2008
Loan proportion of single biggest borrower	Minsheng Bank	5.45	4.95	3.41
Loan proportion of 10 biggest borrowers		45.31	35.40	26.45
Loan proportion of single biggest borrower		3.10	3.10	2.90
Loan proportion of 10 biggest borrowers	Industrial and Commercial Bank of China	21.70	21.10	20.40
Loan proportion of single biggest borrower	Bank of China	2.20	3.40	3.40
Loan proportion of 10 biggest borrowers		15.70	16.10	17.60
Loan proportion of single biggest borrower		5.82	4.70	3.68
Loan proportion of 10 biggest borrowers	China Construction Bank	23.40	19.86	20.72

Source: CSRC website; information disclosure of listed companies

financial industry is hindering the development of the private sectors of economy. Therefore, innovation is urgently needed in this industry and priority should be given to the privatization of financial institutions, without which NGEs' development will remain crippled—one foot in private ownership while the other remains in state ownership. The lack of coordination between the 2 ft has disabled NGEs' development. An effective way to solve NGEs' financing difficulty is to develop private banks. It is imperative that private banks be established and developed as soon as possible.[5]

In China, it is an indisputable fact that both state-owned commercial banks and joint-stock commercial banks emerging after the country's financial reform are unwilling to make loans to SMEs. In order to solve NGEs' financing problem, appeals from all sides finally led to the birth of Minsheng Bank, the first private bank in China. Unfortunately, it, too, is unwilling to give loans to small and medium-sized NGEs. Evidence shows Minsheng Bank is even worse than the state-owned banks in financing services for small and medium-sized NGEs. Table 10.1 is a comparison of the loan structure of Minsheng Bank and three major state-owned banks from 2006 to 2008.[6] According to the data presented

[5]Dong Fureng. (Nov. 5, 2002). *China Business Times*.

[6]For example, China Minsheng Bank was established after many years of public appeals. Academia had expected it to kick off the privatization of China's banking industry and therefore settle SMEs' difficulties in getting loans. Minsheng has disappointed the scholars, however. In SME lending, it has even been doing worse than the state-owned Agricultural Bank; in capital scale, it has actually gone beyond the scope of small- and medium-sized private banks; in business models, it is approximating the four major state-owned banks; and in target clients, it has already been assimilated by the state-owned banks.

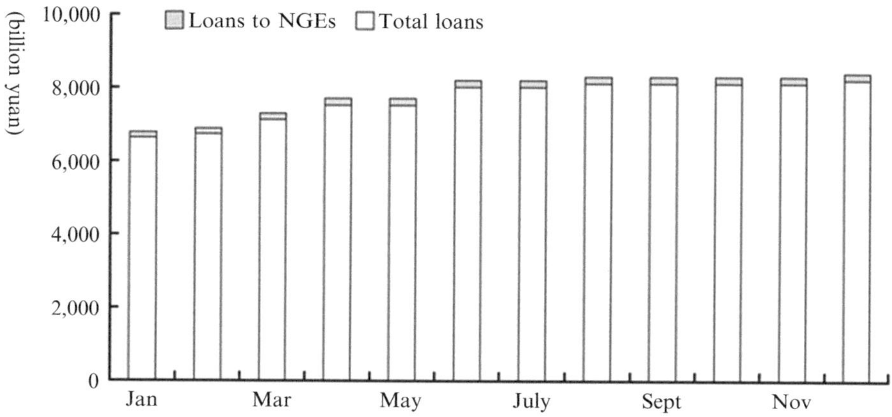

Fig. 10.2 Loan structure of joint-stock commercial banks in 2009 (Source: Statistics in 2009, People's Bank of China)

below, compared with state-owned banks, Minsheng Bank seems to be more inclined to lend to large enterprises.

In Fig. 10.2 above, we can see the statistics of loans to private enterprises and individual businesses in 2009 made by the Bank of Communications, Citic Bank, China Everbright Bank, Huaxia Bank, China Minsheng Bank, Guangdong Development Bank, Shenzhen Development Bank, China Merchants Bank, Shanghai Pudong Development Bank, Industrial Bank, Hengfeng Bank, China Zheshang Bank, Bohai Bank, and Sino-German Bausparkasse. In this period, their monthly loans to these economic entities fluctuated around 2% and no more than 2.57% of the total. It must be pointed out that "private enterprises" here include large-sized NGEs. That is to say, if we just examine the loans granted to non-governmental SMEs, the proportion would be lower.

When considering public opinion, state-owned banks are far from satisfactory in terms of their credit services to non-governmental SMEs. But what confuses people is that the joint stock banks and city commercial banks, which are not state-owned, are also unwilling to offer loans to small- and medium-sized NGEs. Even the long-awaited establishment of private banks has failed to solve this difficult problem. What kind of banks, then, can really increase the financing rate of SMEs? This is our major concern in the following section. In the planned economy, it is true that state-owned banks did have a serious "ownership-based credit discrimination" against NSOEs. But if people conclude from it that the privatization of banks will overcome NGEs' loan trouble, they will be moving towards the wrong direction. From an economic point of view, the reason for this mistake is that they have mixed up the concepts of ownership and size. They are bound to fail if they attempt to solve those loan difficulties that rooted in enterprise size through the ownership reform of banks.

10.3 Community Banks and Relationship Lending

10.3.1 Experience and Practice Abroad

The concept of a "community bank" was introduced to China from the U.S. and other Western countries with developed financial systems. The word "community" here is not a strict geographical concept, rather, it is different from the "urban community" in Chinese. It can refer to a city, a county, or even a populated area in either urban or rural areas. Accordingly, community banks are called local banks in Japan or regional banks in Germany.

Foreign scholars usually define this type of bank in the easiest way. For example, a community bank is an independent banking institution with its assets of less than USD 1 billion. Some scholars believe that the assets of a community bank should vary with the level of national development. For example, the standard could be less than USD 1 billion in developed countries or, rather, USD 100 million in developing countries.[7] The assets-based definition of community banks is accepted by the Federal Deposit Insurance Corporation (FDIC), whose bank reports have themselves classified institutions in this way. On its website, the Independent Community Bankers of America (ICBA) defines the term as, "community banks are independent, locally owned and operated institutions with assets ranging from less than 10 million to multi-billion dollars." The size of the institution's assets can be a simple indicator of community banks, but it is difficult to precisely define community banks—a complex economic phenomenon—with one single indicator. So, while still regarding the size of the assets as central to the definition of this type of institution, some scholars have tried to define community banks from the perspective of relationship banking. For example, Emmons proposed standard community banks as small banks in concentrated areas and with an advantage in relationship lending. The Federal Reserve Bank of Chicago has four criteria for what constitutes a community bank: first, small in size; second, operated regionally; third, in traditional models of banking services; and fourth, relationship finance as the heart of banking.

In fact, it is not hard to grasp the basic characteristics of community banks. Compared with other banks, community banks are basically characterized by their close human relations with the economic entities and residents in their localities, as their shareholders are mainly from these communities. It is exactly in such close humanistic exchanges that they provide community members with customized financial services. In sum, community banks can be defined as "small- or medium-sized banks based on human relations and characterized by relationship banking." Their target clients are mainly industrial and commercial SMEs and

[7]Berger, A., Miller, Nathan., Petersen, Mitchell., Rajan, Raghuram., Stein, Jeremy. (2002). Does Function Follow Organizational Form? Evidence from the Lending Practices of Large and Small Banks. *NBER Working Paper No. 8752*, February.

individual residents. From the perspective of relationship lending, Berger[8] came to the conclusion that medium- and small-sized banks are SMEs' best financing partners. Similarly, Strahan and Weston[9] concluded it is the inherent assets' size that makes medium- and small-sized banks SMEs' ideal financing partners. In their study, *Further Evidence on the Link Between Finance and Growth: an International Analysis of Community Banking and Economic Performance*, Berger, Hasan, and Klapperd analyzed the data of 21 developed countries/regions and 28 developing countries from 1994 to 2000. They took community banks' market shares, their average degree of efficiency (measured by costs or benefits), and several more dummy variables as the external variables, and used GDP, employment in SMEs, and the proportion of total bank loans to GDP as internal variables. They concluded that the following were features of the countries with developed community banking: a high proportion of employment in SMEs, high GDP growth, the promotion of competition to improve the efficiency of the banking industry and the generation of a large flow of credit. In their study, *The Role of Community Banks in the American Economy*, Keeton, Harvey, and Wiuis conducted an empirical test on community banks' contribution to the development of specific industries in 2002. According to their test results, in loans to small businesses, community banks had a 33% market share of loans under USD 1 million, much higher than their market share of deposits (19%) and their share of bank assets (15%); in agricultural loans, community banks were responsible for 39% of the commercial loans and 80% of agricultural loans under USD 0.1 million; in retail banking, community banks had 24% of the deposits incorporate accounts of less than USD 0.1 million, and 15% in those above USD 0.1 million, and were lower than large banks in terms of fees for small transactions.

10.3.2 Relationship Lending

Relationship lending is a technique widely used by foreign banks when lending to SMEs, which is designed to minimize the risks of SME loans by means of long-term cooperation as well as comprehensive and detailed relations between banks and enterprises. To economists, it is essentially an institutional arrangement built by the cooperation between SMEs and small- and medium-sized banks to prevent the adverse selection and ethical hazards caused by information asymmetry and to overcome potential market failure in financial transactions.

Compared with large enterprises, SMEs are usually unable to provide transparent financial information or eligible collaterals, and thus become prime candidates

---

[8]Berger, Allen N., Klapper, Leora F., Udell, Gregory F. (2001). The Ability of Banks to Lend to Informationally Opaque Small Business. *Journal of Banking and Finance* 25, 2127–2167.

[9]Strahan, Philip E., & Weston, James P. (1998). Small Business Lending and the Changing Structure of the Banking Industry. *Journal of Banking and Finance*, 22, 821–845.

Table 10.2 A comparison of different types of loans

Type	Loan basis	Features	Scope	Drawbacks
Financial statements lending	Qualified financial information reflected in financial statements	Credit loans requiring no collateral	Large enterprises with transparent information	Unfit for SMEs with inadequate financial information
Mortgage loans	Quantity and quality of valuable collateral	Lower business costs and strong monitoring afterwards	Enterprises with collateral	Tedious procedures and high costs of mortgages
Credit score lending	Credit records from quantitative statistical models	Low-cost loans of high efficiency	Small loans to enterprises	Complex analysis; limited application
Relationship lending	Private information of enterprise reputation and owner's conduct	Convenient information exchange and lasting credit relations	SMEs of all types	Soft budget constraints on enterprises; potential rip-off by banks

Source: Berger and Udell (1995)

of banks' credit rationing. To reduce the probability of the adverse selection and ethical hazard, foreign banks have developed several lending techniques, and relationship lending is the most appropriate for SME financing. American scholars Berger and Udell (1995) categorized four types of western banks' techniques in lending to enterprises (Table 10.2).

The other types of lending usually rely on communication by letter and telephone, so they are also called arm's-length lending. Relationship lending is different in that it mainly relies on "soft information," which is difficult to quantify, verify, or deliver. Such information tends to be highly personified and is rarely available through public channels, but, rather, is collected through loan officers' long-term and multi-channel personal contacts with enterprise owners or their multi-dimensional contacts with their communities as well as the stakeholders (shareholders, creditors, clients, employees, and so forth.) of enterprises. Such soft information can largely replace hard information such as financial data and can partially fill the credit gap resulting from SMEs' inability to provide qualified financial information or eligible collateral.

Relationship lending is an internal system of market transactions. It reflects a long-term, closed, and standardized contractual relationship between an enterprise and a settlement bank (or a few banks). The maintenance of this relationship can help the banks collect information on the prospects for and loan repayment probability of the enterprise and facilitate making loan decisions. Relationship lending is very popular in developed countries such as the U.S. and Germany. According to an empirical research by Harhoff and Körting,[10] most SMEs in Germany have established long-term credit relations with one or two banks, and many have

[10]Harhoff, D., & Köting, T. (1998). Lending Relationships in Germany: Empirical Evidence from Survey Data. *Journal of Banking and Finance*, 22, 1317–1353.

obtained over two-thirds of their loans from one single bank. In the U.S., according to Berger and Udell,[11] SMEs keep their financing relations with their settlement banks for as long as 9.37 years on average, and get over 85% of their loans from these banks.

Relationship lending is widely and successfully applied to SMEs' financing in developed countries primarily because of its unique advantages as follows. Relationship lending is beneficial to the pareto improvement in the information exchange between banks and enterprises. On the one hand, relationship lending has solved the problem of information "free-riding" between a settlement bank and other banks in competition for transactional loans, and thus ensures the settlement bank can reuse the collected information and achieve a scaled economy based on such information. On the other hand, SMEs are willing to disclose to their settlement banks some important information they would never make public in the financial market or leak to other banks. Out of their own interests, those settlement banks entitled to this exclusive access to such private information will not release it. In this way, the banks and enterprises have realized more effective information sharing arrangements. If an enterprise turns to other banks halfway through the process, it will have to pay a high conversion cost for the information. As a result, it tends to maintain the existing credit relationship by strengthening its degree of information disclosure and self-discipline, which can reduce the banks' later costs of monitoring.

Relationship lending has facilitated the formation of long-term implicit contracts between banks and enterprises. In the real economy, explicit written contracts are usually incomplete, so enterprises hope to sign long-term implicit versions with various stakeholders (shareholders, employees, creditors, and so forth.), which can bring a lot of benefits in advance. Experience shows that relationship lending contracts are generally less strict than transactional lending contracts, whereby the banks and enterprises can renegotiate or exercise discretion more flexibly upon unexpected impacts, which facilitates the formation of long-term implicit contracts between them. As such contracts are based on mutual understanding and trust, they can effectively govern potential conflicts of interest between the banks and enterprises, and provide the latter with a long-term, stable channel of financing, as well as a liquidity guarantee in time of crisis.

Relationship lending enables banks to more easily monitor the mortgage assets of enterprises. To accommodate the fact that most SMEs have insufficient property or land for mortgage, foreign banks usually accept their accounts receivables and inventory as collaterals. This improves SMEs' financing environment, but, meanwhile, it also requires banks to improve their competence for dynamically monitoring the collaterals' market values. Usually, SMEs are clearer than banks about the market movements or values of their inventory and receivables. Therefore,

[11]Berger, A. N., & Udell, G. F. (1998). The Economics of Small Business Finance: The Role of Private Equity and Debt Market in the Financial Growth Cycle. *Journal of Banking and Finance* 22, 613–673.

undoubtedly, it would greatly improve the monitoring efficiency and lower monitoring costs if the banks could get strong enterprise support. In Japan, once an enterprise gets loans from several banks, they will jointly hold its shares, but only one of them, i.e., the main bank, will assume the principal responsibility for enterprise supervision. Hence, a main bank generally is the one that has the largest capacity for fund raising and utilization of funds for certain enterprises, and keeps long-term, regular, and comprehensive trading relations with them in terms of enterprise shareholding, personnel dispatch, and so forth. Relationship lending smoothes the inter-temporal interests of both parties by means of long-term contract terms, and the relatively stable symbiotic relationship contributes to the formation of their joint interests. According to Petersen and Rajan,[12] some credit subsidies (e.g., lower loan rates than the equilibrium interest rate) provided by banks in SMEs' initial stage can greatly reduce the chance of their adverse selection and ethically hazardous behavior, and make a success of even seemingly impossible deals. By providing such subsidies, the banks may have failed to profit in these deals, but are endowed with certain "market power" based on long-term relationship with the enterprises. As the interdependent relationship is established, the banks can later make up for their previous loss by implementing loan rates higher than the equilibrium interest rate. As we can see, the "market power" has actually brought them the capacity and space to adjust credit prices and policies in different stages of SMEs' development. As their "market power" increases, SMEs with lower credit ratings will also be able to get loans from them.

Plenty of literature abroad has proven that long-term relationship banking with concentrated transaction objects helps SMEs improve their loan availability and meet loan requirements. For example, the duration of the credit relations between banks and a given enterprise is positively correlated with its loan availability; the number of banks providing loans to an enterprise is negatively correlated to its loan availability[13]; the strengthening of long-term cooperation helps lower the interest rate of SMEs' loans,[14] soften the impact of interest rate fluctuation on SMEs' loan interest rate, and reduce the demand on their loan guarantees and collaterals. Obviously, relationship lending is of great economic prudence in considering SMEs' financing.

In foreign countries, it is true that relationship lending has already become an established approach to external financing for SMEs, but in practice, it also causes additional costs to both parties. For banks, such long-term relations can lead to soft budget constraints on enterprises themselves. As the implicit contracts between banks and SMEs are flexible in relationship lending, the possibility of renegotiation may encourage some enterprises to change their motivations after borrowing. For example,

---

[12]Petersen, M., & Rajan, R. (1995). The Effect of Credit Market Competition on Lending Relationships. *Quarterly Journal of Economics,* 110, 407–443.

[13]Harhoff, D., & Köting, T. (1998). Lending Relationships in Germany: Empirical Evidence from Survey Data. *Journal of Banking and Finance* 22, 1317–1353.

[14]Scott, J., & Dunkelberg, W. (1999). Bank Consolidation and Small Business Lending: a Small Firm Perspective. In R. Lang (Ed.), *Business Access to Capital and Credit*, 328–361.

they may be tempted to overinvest or to invest in high-risk projects, which may hold up the lending banks. Once such enterprises are confronted with a severe financial crisis, the banks will have to make additional loans to them for nothing but to collect on earlier loans. For enterprises, such a dilemma is the "hold-up" of banks. As the study by Boot shows, an information monopoly can take place when much private information about an enterprise is possessed by one bank, who may make profits by setting a higher price for loans. If the enterprise has realized the risk of "lock-in," it may refuse to borrow from the bank, which may then result in underinvestment. If the enterprise chooses to build transactional relations with more banks to avoid being "held-up," however, it may lead to information "free-riding" between the banks. Therefore, it is urgent that research be done on the new field of relationship lending as to how to avoid soft-budget constraints on enterprises and the "hold-up" of the banks.

As research literatures suggest, the best way to solve a soft-budget constraint is to entitle banks to priority claims on enterprises' debts or to increase subsidiary conditions on credit contracts, which will reinforce the position of bank representatives in renegotiations and enable them to make timely interventions. As to the "hold-up" problem, it is necessary for enterprises to introduce competition, so as to reduce the two-way monopoly of information by banks. But the construction of long-term relations with several banks lowers the output value of this information and, in doing so, throws cold water on banks' enthusiasm for lending to young enterprises.

10.3.3 Community Banks Taking Shape in China

In China, people have very different definitions of a community bank. Some think it is essentially a private bank that specifically serves SMEs in a community[15]; some believe that rural or urban credit cooperatives are community banks[16]; some even assume that community banks are the business outlets of state-owned commercial banks in communities that provide humanized and customized financial services. Admittedly, more domestic scholars define a community bank from the perspectives of assets size and target clients. For example, some maintain that small- and medium-sized banks that have been independently established and are operated in accordance with the market-oriented principle within communities in certain areas are community banks, which mainly serve SMEs and individual clients.[17]

[15]Xu Dianqing. (2001). *200 Questions on Non-Governmental Banks*. Beijing: Peking University Press, p. 3.

[16]Ying Yixun. (June 3, 2005). SMEs Loan Practice of Tailong Urban Credit Cooperative in Taizhou City. *Southern Weekly*.

[17]Ba Shusong. (2002). The Active Community Financing in the U.S. *Finance & Trade*, (9), 132–133. Liu Wei., & Zhu Yushun. (2004). On Development of China's Rural Credit Cooperatives in Light of Community Banks in U.S. *Rural Finance Forum*, (3), 63–65. Wang Aijian. (2006). *Development Models of China's Community Banks*. Beijing: China Financial Publishing House, pp. 3–7.

Whether in China or countries with developed market economies, it is not so much that community banks function as financial entities within an economic system, rather, researchers categorize them as being involved in certain types of credit-based financial institutions. At least, the term is nowhere to be found in industrial and commercial registrations. This is not enough to stop economists from accurately defining a community bank, however. Focusing on both bank size and specialized divisions within the banking industry, we are now able to define it briefly but precisely: a community bank is a financial institution based on human relationships and mainly engaged in relationship banking. In this definition, the ownership structure of banks is neglected. As long as they are based on human relationships and mainly engaged in relationship banking, they are regarded as community banks, be they state-owned, privately controlled, or joint stock banks.

Such financial institutions may be located in either cities or rural areas—their location has no effect on whether they are community banks. There is no strict requirement as to their size, but financial institutions will no longer engage in relationship lending when they have grown past a certain size; otherwise they would go against the basic principle of specialized division in the banking industry.

The business radius of financial institutions is an important factor in our identification of community banks. As the credit businesses of community banks are based on human relationships, the spatial distance in relation to their clients is very important. The theoretical model of Hauswald and Marquez (2000) reveals that relationship lending is conversely proportionate to informational distance,[18] which is further proven by the following cases.

10.4 Taizhou Commercial Bank: No Small Loans Offered to Enterprises Outside the City

The province of Zhejiang is very developed insofar as informal finance. If there is one particular area where non-state financial institutions outrun the state-owned banks in the proportion of deposits, it is Luqiao District of Taizhou City in Zhejiang Province. At the beginning of this century, there were a total of nine urban credit cooperatives in this district, the largest of which had accepted deposits of over RMB 3 billion. In September of 2001, when a bank run occurred on several credit cooperatives in Taizhou, one of them failed to cope with the crisis, and the Chairman and Managing Director absconded with money. In March of 2002, when the state reorganized the credit cooperatives in Taizhou, Taizhou Commercial Bank was jointly founded by Ginza Credit Cooperative in coordination with other cooperatives, with the result that 95% of its capital was private. One year later, its

[18]Hauswald, R., & Marquez, R. (2000). Relationship Banking, Loan Specialization and Competition. *Indiana University Working Paper*.

total amount of loans had increased from RMB 3.5 billion to 6.2 billion, up by 78%; its loan balance had also soared to over RMB 4 billion, up by 40%, while its bad loans had dropped by 8.23%. In Taizhou, there are more than 43,000 enterprises with independent legal status, but only 3689 of them are enterprises of any notable scale. In other words, it is very developed in small businesses. Currently in Taizhou Commercial Bank, loans of less than RMB 1 million account for about 94% of total loans, and the balance of these loans is about 60% of the total loan balance. According to its chairman, Chen Xiaojun, clients requiring loans of around one million are preferred, while those requiring more than five million are not accepted as clients. In this bank, the proportion of business managers to employees is much higher than that of state-owned or other joint-stock banks. The large team of business managers has ensured that the bank retains close human relations with its clients. These managers may inquire of their clients issues pertaining to the operation and power consumption of their enterprises, how often they live at home, whether they have any substance addictions, and so on; they may also observe its clients' management by how they place things, judge their character and habits by how they dresses themselves and whether they are careless spenders by their hobbies and spending practices, and so forth. In turn, the clients communicate to a significant degree with their managers. For example, they may turn to their managers should there be any difficulty in the family. As to the bank's radius of business, Chen Xiaojun spoke by way of analogy. When a taxi is running in the city, the driver charges at the metered price because it is a small transaction, but if it is a long journey, the driver will charge by hundreds or even thousands, as it is a big deal. So once its radius goes beyond the city, Taizhou Commercial Bank offers no small loans. The above example, though not perfect, has revealed that it is difficult for managers to keep close human relations with their clients when the credit business goes beyond a certain geographic range.

We can also define a community bank from the employee composition of a given financial institution. As a community bank is mainly engaged in relationship lending, it must be equipped with plenty of lending officers (often referred to as client managers) with specialized knowledge for human exchanges and the collection of "soft information." The following case further illustrates this point.

10.5 Tyrone Bank: More Client Managers Required for Small Loans

As SMEs are generally short of the "hard information" required by big banks, Tyrone Bank invented a new credit model for SMEs' financing. The model is based on the products, collateral, and owner's personality of a given enterprise, as well as the information collected from its water and electric meters and customs declaration forms. For example, Tiandi Air Conditioning and Refrigeration Fittings Co., Ltd. in Taizhou of Zhejiang Province exports more than 70% of its air conditioning accessories abroad. Affected by the global financial crisis, the company—with what was then its fixed assets of RMB 3 million—was faced with a capital chain rupture. General Manager Zhang Maibo resorted to bank lending but was rejected by seven banks as the company did not meet their requirements. Later, when he learned from a friend that Tyrone Bank had a lower threshold, he applied for a loan of RMB 450,000. The bank immediately assigned two client managers to make a credit review and found him to be honest and on good terms with his neighbors and friends, and without bad habits like gambling. They also found that the air conditioning accessories produced by his company were daily necessities and that the decline in the company's existing orders was only a temporary market adjustment. More importantly, Zhang was a man of substance—he had a house in the city and a car. In addition, though the readings of the water and electric meters and the figures on his customs declaration forms had declined to various degrees, they still remained within the scope of control. Hence, in consideration of his repayment willingness, capability, and guarantee, the Bank provided him with an unsecured loan of RMB 500,000. Since its founding in 1993, Tyrone Bank has been focusing on SMEs using this new model of financing. By 2009, it had made over 130,000 loans, over 93%of which were guaranteed credit loans; its loan balances totaled RMB 66 billion, and the average loan balance was RMB 555,700.

According to our investigation, by investigating a potential customer's "personality," Tyrone Bank intends to make sure that a customer is trustworthy, for an individual's good morality and reputation is the guarantee for repayment; by "products," it intends to make sure that they sell well, for well-sold products with higher added values can guarantee the good fundamentals of an enterprise; and by "collateral," it intends to make sure that they are reliable, for tangible assets like houses and cars can effectively counter balance and constraint the clients. The above three measures are considered soft information, which may not be easy to control. So in its regular analysis of risk prevention and control, Tyrone Bank pays more attention to the hard information of enterprises collected from their water and electric meters and customs declaration forms. As the meters are right there and tell no lies, readings are able to give the production information and its changes over time, while customs declaration forms reflect whether foreign trade enterprises have sold their products either at home or abroad.

On a post-loan visit to a dyeing and printing enterprise, a client manager of Tyrone Bank found a sharp decline in its water and power consumption for that month, and made a decisive and timely change in terms of preservation of its assets, due to the fact that that industry is closely related to water and electricity use. But the enterprise had provided very nice data in its financial statements and everything seemed normal during the loan review. Later, it was proven to be in great trouble and about to close down. In post-loan inspections, in addition to face-to-face conversations with the clients, the managers of Tyrone Bank often make in-depth front-line investigations as to enterprise operation and production, so as to acquire more comprehensive and accurate information. To some degree, they are much like detectives, and it is through their efforts that the bank is able to effectively control for risks. In 2008, its return on assets was 1.62%, its return on capital was 32.86%, and its provision coverage was 160%, which were respectively 0.6%, 17.04%, and 27% higher than the average of listed banks. Over the past 5 years, its non-performing loan ratio has been controlled below 1.5%. Especially in 2008, the figure was only 0.79%, nearly two times lower than the average of listed banks.

In terms of staff composition, Tyrone Bank is clearly different from state-owned or joint-stock banks in that 40% of its employees are client managers.

From the above two cases, we can presume that the two variables—the radius of credit business and the proportion of client managers to bank employees—are helpful for defining a community bank. We believe that, if we are able to make a large-scale investigation to test these variables, they will benefit the advancement of further empirical research in this field.

As previously defined, a community bank is a financial institution based on human relationships and mainly engaged in relationship banking. Note that the term "financial institution" is used in the definition, rather than "bank." The reason is that a "financial institution" in this sense can either be a publicly-registered bank or some financial institution engaged in relationship lending but without the legal status of a bank, such as a small loan company or a pawnshop. Such institutions are not called banks by law, because the current financial management system does not allow them to take deposits as banks do. But they do, in fact, take deposits like banks, with the only difference being that they do so secretly.[19] If we ignore the sources of their funding, however, their behavior on the credit market completely accords with the features of community banks. According to a study by the CASS Economic Research Institute, the credit business of small loan companies and pawnshops is itself based on human relations, or, in other words, these institutions are engaged in relationship lending. This will be made clearer with a brief introduction to the operation of small loan companies in Pingyao of Shanxi province (Table 10.3).

These financial institutions make small and short-term loans to dispersed customers. The terms of such loans may be 1–3 months, or 6 months, but no longer than 12 months. In actual interviews, we have found that these financial institutions are extremely familiar with their clients and know almost everything about their operations, personalities, habits, hobbies, and even their family life. It is the gathering of such "soft information" that enables these financial institutions to maintain a non-performing loan ratio far below that of big banks.

Very similar to small loan companies are pawnshops, which have been in China for more than 1800 years (according to the records in *The History of the Later Han*

[19]In our field investigation, we have found that some small loan companies and pawn guilds privately absorb large deposits from some special groups, which may not be called deposits but financial products, instead. For example, some people, owing to their special status, have high and stable incomes, or plenty of high-quality assets, so they can receive a larger amount of credit loans from the state-owned banks in accordance with the legal interest rate. Afterwards, they can give the money to small loan companies or pawnshops for financial management, which promises them a far higher interest income than that of bank loans.

Table 10.3 Operation of small loan companies in Pingyao, Shanxi

Year	Loan amount (mn RMB)	Loan clients	Peasants' loans (%)	Enterprise loans (%)	Average interest rate (%)	Operating profit (mn RMB)
2006	69.5662	770	81.5	18.2	19.67	2.7912
2007	179.2328	811	79.12	20.88	19.56	8.9501
2008	339.9134	875	71.29	28.71	19.12	8.2631
2009	383.4557	858	67.92	32.08	17.96	1.5286

Notes: 1. The highest loan interest rate is 23.256% and the lowest 15.66%
2. In 2007, the proportion of loans under RMB 50 thousand was 76.24%
3. In the data of all the years, the shortest term of loans is 1 month, and the longest 12 months
Source: A field survey in 2009 by Microeconomic Research Office, CASS Economic Research Institute

Dynasty). Though pawn broking started later in other countries, it was already a commercial activity in Europe in the early middle ages, when some Jews in exile were making a living in it. Throughout the history of pawn broking at home and abroad, it is in essence a marginal financial activity in which pledge loans are made for the charge of interest. Due to particular historical reasons, pawn broking once perished in China. Since China entered the orbit of the market economy, the private sectors of the economy have been developing rapidly. Limited by their economic strength, credit, and even the market, however, many private SMEs have no access to bank credit as a form of support. But they do have raw materials, finished products, machines, factories, or commodities in stock. Thus, when they are in urgent need of capital, pawning is the best method of financing. By pawning their assets, they can get pawn loans for immediate relief, revitalize stock funds, sustain their reproduction, accelerate the circulation of commodities, and motivate the participation of enterprise funds in the capital circulation of society as a whole.

Like small loan companies, the target clients of pawnshops are numerous SMEs and individual operators.[20] The only difference is that pawn shops are more inclined to mortgage loans than to credit and guarantee loans. But mortgage loans also accord with our definition of a community bank—that is, relationship lending based on human relationships. Besides, the two variables of pawn shops—the radius of credit business and the proportion of client managers to employees—agree with the basic characteristics of a community bank.

In conclusion, community banks are currently taking shape in China, with embryonic forms found in city commercial banks like Taizhou Commercial Bank and Tyrone Bank, the scattered village banks, and numerous small loan companies and pawnshops. If the government provides them with the necessary policy support, broadens their business scope, and at the same time strengthens their risk control, it will benefit the development of community banks in China in a real sense. It is worthwhile to learn from certain practices in the U.S., which is well-developed in

[20]For example, in 2009, Baoruitong Pawn Shop made over 30,000 deals and loans of over RMB 3 billion, with more than 90% of its borrowers being SME owners or individual operators.

terms of community banking.[21] In the development of community banks in China, it is necessary to prevent the blind tendency to "grow big" in small- and medium-sized banks.[22] It is also necessary to limit the business radius of community banks through legislation, so as to limit them from outgrowing the scope of what can be feasibly considered a community bank.

Bibliography

Ba S (2002) The active community financing in the U.S. Financ Trade (9)

Banerjee AV, Besley T, Guinnane TW (1994) Thy neighbor's keeper: the design of a credit cooperative with theory and a test. Q J Econ 109:491–515

Berger AN, Udell GF (1995) Relationship lending and lines of credit in small firm finance. J Bus 68:351–382

Berger AN, Udell GF (1998) The economics of small business finance: the role of private equity and debt market in the financial growth cycle. J Bank Financ 22:613–673

Berger AN, Udell GF (2002) Small business credit availability and relationship lending: the importance of bank organizational structure. Econ J 112:32–53

Berger AN, Saunders A, Scalise JM, Udell GF (1998) The effects of mergers and acquisitions on small business lending. J Financ Econ 50:187–229

Berger AN, Klapper LF, Udell GF (2001) The ability of banks to lend to informationally opaque small business. J Bank Financ 25:2127–2167

Berger AN, Miller N, Petersen M, Rajan R, Stein J (2002, February) Does function follow organizational form? Evidence from the lending practices of large and small banks, NBER working paper no. 8752. National Bureau of Economic Research, Cambridge

Bonin JP, Hasan I, Wachtel P (2003) Bank privatization and performance: evidence from transition countries. In: Presented at World Bank Conference on Bank Privatization, p 20–21

Cole RA, Goldberg LG, White LJ (2004) Cookie cutter vs. character: the microstructure of small business lending by large and small banks. J Financ Quant Anal 39(2):227–251

Harhoff D, Köting T (1998) Lending relationships in Germany: empirical evidence from survey data. J Bank Financ 22:1317–1353

Hauswald R, Marquez R (2000) Relationship banking, loan specialization and competition. Indiana University working paper

---

[21]The American National Banking Act issued in 1864 stipulated that banks should operate only within a certain administrative region, and restrictions on banks' inter-state operations officially became a federal law in 1927 in the form of *McFadden-Pepper Act*. The inter-state business regulation has limited the expansion of big banks and objectively provided legal support for the development of community banks. *The Community Reinvestment Act* released in 1977 in the United States requires that financial regulatory authorities regularly assess whether financial institutions within their jurisdiction meet the financial needs of local communities, and publish on a regular basis the contributions of financial institutions to their communities. The evaluation results will become an important factor to be considered by the government when a financial institution applies for new deposit branches or new forms of business.

[22]Under the pressure of competition and the influence of relevant policies, there is currently a tendency among small- and medium-sized banks in China to blindly "make it bigger." Regional joint-stock banks of small and medium sizes are competing against each other in their attempt to be listed on the stock market and developing themselves into large national banks.

Jayaratne J, Wolken J (1999) How important are small banks to small business lending? J Bank Financ 23:427–458
La Porta R, Lopez-de-silanes F, Shleifer A (2002) Government ownership of banks. J Financ LVII (1):265–302
Levonian ME, Soller J (1995, December) Small banks, small loans, small business. Mimeo. Federal Reserve Bank of San Francisco, San Francisco
Lin Y, Sun X (2008) Banking structure and economic growth: evidence from Chinese provincial panel data. Econ Res J (9)
Liu W, Zhu Y (2004) On development of China's rural credit cooperatives in light of community banks in U.S. Rural Financ Forum (3)
Meyer LH (1998) The present and future roles of banks in small business finance. J Bank Financ 22:1109–1116
Petersen M, Rajan R (1995) The effect of credit market competition on lending relationships. Q J Econ 110:407–443
Scott J, Dunkelberg W (1999) Bank consolidation and small business lending: a small firm perspective. In: Lang R (ed) Business access to capital and credit, pp 328–361
Strahan PE, Weston JP (1998) Small business lending and the changing structure of the banking industry. J Bank Financ 22:821–845
Wang Z (2004) On the credit market for small- and medium-sized enterprises. J Financ (1)
Wang A (2006) Development models of China's community banks. China Financial Publishing House, Beijing
Xu D (2001) 200 questions on non-governmental banks. Peking University Press, Beijing
Ying Y (2005) SMEs loan practice of tailong urban credit cooperative in Taizhou City. Southern Weekly, 3 June.
Zhang J (2002) Relationship-based lending to small business and banks' organizational structure. Econ Res J (6)

Chapter 11
High-Tech Industries: New Space and Opportunities for NGEs' Growth and Development in the New Stage

Qiang Gu and Ruiqing Dong

11.1 China's Private High-Tech Industries: Developments and Achievements

11.1.1 NGEs as an Important Force in the Development of High-Tech Industries

In recent years, supported and guided by a series of scientific and technological programs, as well as by the reform of the country's scientific and technological system and related policies, China's high-tech industries have made rapid progress. Many enterprises, however, are still weak in independent innovation and the industrialization of scientific and technical achievements. Meanwhile, China's NGEs are on the rise and gaining in strength, and have become an important force for leading the innovation and development of China's high-tech industries.

First and foremost, NGEs are ceaselessly expanding their scale among high-tech industries. Although FFEs still dominate China's high-tech industries, with the support of national policies, NGEs' output values in these industries have been steadily increasing in recent years. As Fig. 11.1 shows, in China's high-tech industries, the industrial added value of NGEs accounted for 13.6% in 2003, but by 2007, it had increased to 24.4%, while the proportion of FFEs and SOEs were 62.7% and 12.9%, respectively. According to ACFIC's report of 500 Chinese NGEs in 2011, China's private high-tech enterprises are developing steadily and their technological levels and R&D capacities continue to improve. Of the top 500 NGEs, 240 were recognized as high-tech enterprises, 360 had their key technologies developed through independent innovation, 89 had constructed "National Enterprise Technical Centers," and 127 had established post-doctoral

Q. Gu (✉) • R. Dong
Ministry of Industry and Information Technology of China, China

Y. Liu (ed.), *New Interpretations on the Development of China's Non-Governmental Enterprises*, Research Series on the Chinese Dream and China's Development Path, DOI 10.1007/978-981-10-3872-3_11

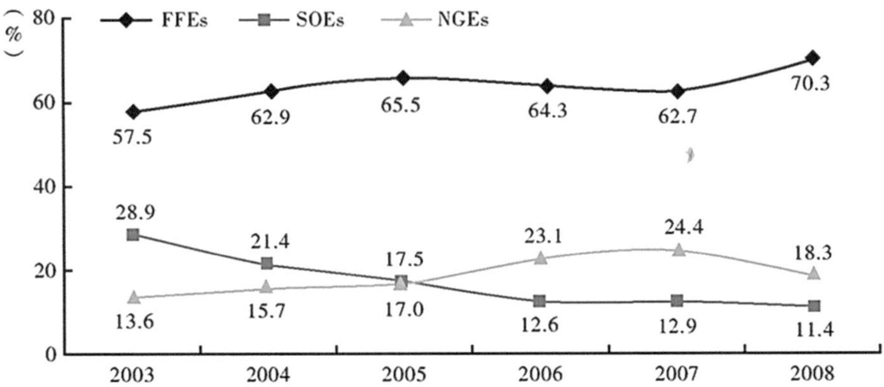

Fig. 11.1 Proportions of FFEs, SOEs, and NGEs in China's high-tech industries 2003–2008
Note: The data from 2008 were the respective proportions of the output values of FFEs, SOEs, and NGEs in the overall output value of the high-tech industries. In the previous years, the data were the proportions of the industrial added values of the three types of enterprises in the overall added value of the high-tech industries. But we can only find the overall data and those of SOEs and FFEs in *China Statistics Yearbook on High Technology Industry* of each year. For the convenience of calculation, we have presumed three forms of enterprise ownership in China's high-tech industries, namely SOEs, FFEs, and NGEs, and get the data of NGEs by subtracting those of SOEs and FFEs from the overall
Source: NBS. *China Statistics Yearbook on High Technology Industry* (2003–2009)

workstations. NGEs also showed sustained growth in patent results. Of the 500 NGEs, 322 claimed 47,120 patents, of which invention patents accounted for 43.8%. NGEs have been actively leading or participating in the formulation of national industry standards. A number of large, high-tech NGEs with a considerable voice in their industries have already risen, as well.[1]

Secondly, NGEs are continuously optimizing their distribution among high-tech industries. Structurally, China's NGEs in high-tech industries are mainly engaged in pharmaceutical manufacturing, electronic components manufacturing, communications equipment manufacturing, medical instrument and equipment manufacturing, and computer manufacturing. According to the database created by CASS Center for Private Economic Studies, from 2006 to 2008, NGEs above a designated size continued to increase in the above-mentioned high-tech industries and fields. From 2006 to 2008, the average annual growth rate was 22.5%; the three industries with the greatest numbers of NGEs were pharmaceutical manufacturing, electronic components manufacturing, and electronics manufacturing (See Table 11.1). According to ACFIC's report of 500 Chinese NGEs in 2010, there were 37 NGEs in electrical machinery, equipment, and cable manufacturing, and 27 in smelting and the pressing of ferrous and non-ferrous metals, making them the top two industries insofar as the number of high-tech NGEs. What's more, 13 NGEs

[1]Economics Division of ACFIC. (2011). *Report on the Study of Top 500 Chinese NGEs*, p. 44.

Table 11.1 The distribution of NGES above a designated size in high-tech industries 2006–2008

Industry	NGE numbers			Average annual growth rate (%)
	2006	2007	2008	
Pharmaceutical manufacturing	4052	4409	5187	13.1
Medical instrument and equipment manufacturing	493	581	775	25.4
Communications equipment manufacturing	599	685	860	19.8
Computer manufacturing	342	403	574	29.6
Electronics manufacturing	556	687	1094	40.3
Electronic components manufacturing	1813	2264	3305	35.0
Total	7855	9029	11,795	22.5

Note: NGEs here are used in the narrow sense and do not include those with investment from Hong Kong, Macao, Taiwan, and foreign countries. Mentioned elsewhere in this chapter are NGEs in the broad sense, namely, a general term that covers enterprises of different ownerships except state-owned and state-holding enterprises, including individual businesses, private enterprises, collective enterprises, Hong Kong, Macao, and Taiwan investment enterprises and FFEs
Source: Database of NGEs above the designated size from 2006 to 2008, CASS Center for Private Economic Studies

were engaged in pharmaceutical manufacturing and 10 in communications equipment, computers, and other electronic equipment manufacturing.

Third and finally, NGEs in high-tech industries are gradually increasing their input in science and technology. Figure 11.2 shows an increasing trend of new-product development expenses and R&D expenditures among China's NGEs in high-tech industries, which has become more evident since 2006. In 1995, NGEs' new product development expenses and R&D expenditures were only RMB 465 million and 186 million, respectively; by 2008, they had increased to RMB 20.889 billion and 18.573 billion, respectively. On the other hand, with the improvement of both the knowledge content of products and the intensification of international competition, patents not only represent certain technologies to NGEs, but also stand for their comprehensive competitive power and developmental potential. In recent years, NGEs in China's high-tech industries have become increasingly aware of the protection of intellectual property rights, and their application for and possession of invention patents are constantly increasing. In 1995, NGEs only applied for 87 patents and owned 45 invention patents, while in 2008, the numbers soared to 16,078 and 8869, respectively—185 and 197 times 1995 (See Table 11.2 below). In addition, according to ACFIC's report on a survey of 500 Chinese NGEs in 2010, China's NGEs have been constantly valuing and enhancing technological innovation, and are continuously achieving innovative products. Of the Top 500 NGEs in 2009, 32 won National Prizes for Progress in Science and Technology, 149 won Provincial Scientific Progress Prizes, and four won the ACFIC Science and Technology Award, with the great majority of the winners being high-tech enterprises.

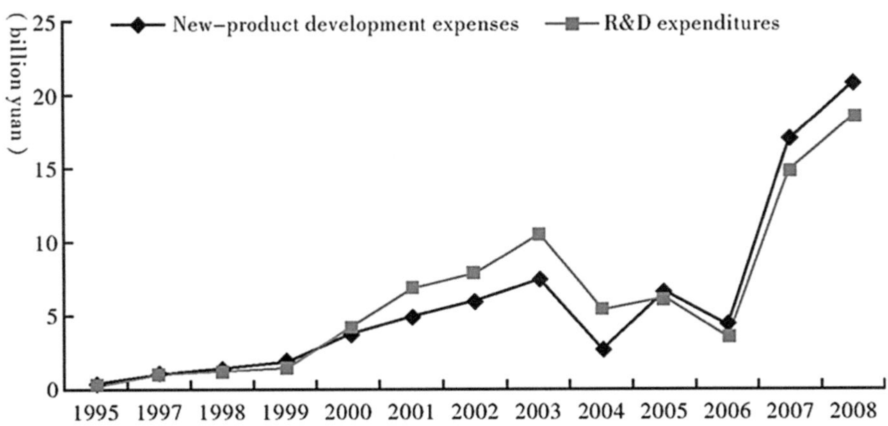

Fig. 11.2 Variations in new-product development expenses and the R&D expenditures of NGEs in China's high-tech industries
Note: We can only find the overall data and those of SOEs and FFEs in *China Statistics Yearbook on High Technology Industry* of each year. For the convenience of calculation, we presume three forms of enterprise ownership in China's high-tech industries, namely SOEs, FFEs, and NGEs, and get the data of NGEs by subtracting those of SOEs and FFEs from the overall
Source: NBS. *China Statistics Yearbook on High Technology Industry* (1996–2009)

Table 11.2 Science and technology input of NGEs in high-tech industries 1995–2008

Year	New-product development expenses (bn RMB)	R&D expenditures (bn RMB)	Invention patents	Patent applications
1995	0.465	0.186	45	87
1997	1.050	1.015	80	233
1998	1.388	1.290	200	380
1999	1.803	1.497	321	556
2000	3.713	4.056	392	929
2001	5.063	6.900	957	2009
2002	5.944	7.936	1129	3087
2003	7.441	10.444	1710	4047
2004	2.795	5.362	1204	3464
2005	6.542	6.237	3095	5313
2006	4.365	3.629	1349	2546
2007	16.934	14.760	4412	18,029
2008	20.889	18.573	8869	16,078

Note: We can only find the overall data and those of SOEs and FFEs in *China Statistics Yearbook on High Technology Industry* of each year. For the convenience of calculation, we presume three forms of enterprise ownership in China's high-tech industries, namely SOEs, FFEs, and NGEs, and get the data of NGEs by subtracting those of SOEs and FFEs from the overall
Source: NBS. *China Statistics Yearbook on High Technology Industry* (1996–2009)

11.1.2 A Feasible Mechanism for NGEs' Entry into High-Tech Industries

NGEs are the corporate form of the highest degree of marketization in present-day China, and the fundamental objective of their entry into high-tech industries is to obtain incremental benefits and high added values. High-tech industries are enterprise collections based on high and new technologies that are engaged in the research, development, production, and technical services of one or more high and new technologies as well as their products, which are characterized by high growth, high input, high output, high returns, and high risks. At present, China's NGEs are rising rapidly in power and have already become an important force in the development of high-tech industries. Why are they able to enter the high-tech industries and develop so rapidly? In this section, we will analyze the feasibility of NGEs' entry into and development in high-tech industries from both the microscopic perspective (the growth mechanisms of NGEs and high-tech industries) and the macroscopic perspective (the appropriate environment for high-tech industries).

11.1.2.1 Highly Coupled Growth Mechanisms of NGEs and High-Tech Industries

Laws reflect the inevitability of development. Under certain conditions, it is internal factors that determine the direction and trends of development. The "high risk, high input, and high returns" features characterizing high-tech industries originate from internal and irresistible laws of development. New technologies have to face and overcome all kinds of unknown risks, from technological birth to application and diffusion; the application market of new technologies has to grow from small to large; and there must be some contractual mechanism related to the protection of intellectual property rights and incentives for scientific and technical personnel, which can ensure that the most deserving innovator wins and gets his or her due returns. China's NGEs have some inherent advantages that follow the laws governing the development of high-tech industries, which are mainly manifested in the following aspects.

Firstly, in the face of various unpredictable risks to their development, NGEs have all the power of production and operations; they typify independent operations, independent development, self-financing, and self-restraint, and are therefore free from the phenomenon of "virtual owners." No matter whether their decisions turn out to be successful or not, there can be no confusion between operational and moral risks. At the same time, NGEs' production and operations are market-oriented, their production factors are regulated by the market, and their economic behaviors and activities are restricted by market rules. It is through continuous innovation and new-product development that they are able to seize the market. They therefore experience "the survival of the fittest" in market competition. In addition, all their production activities are closely related to their operators' interests, so both the operators and owners, driven by material benefits, will aim at profit maximization and fully mobilize their enthusiasm and creativity in the pursuit of such.[2] It is the above mechanistic advantages, which are strongly coupled to the laws governing high-tech industries' development, that have given NGEs such strong vitality and enabled them to gradually develop into an effective force in high-tech industries.

Secondly, it is through their painstaking efforts and self-development rather than government dispensations that NGEs are able to win potential market shares. Additionally, it is the innovative and entrepreneurial activities of numerous NGEs that have facilitated the gradual maturity of the application market of new technologies and have resulted in many large high-tech NGEs with international competitiveness. Many world famous high-tech companies have developed from small firms into large transnational corporations, such as Microsoft, Intel, Apple, and Yahoo. In the development of China's NGEs, the state has not constructed any corresponding mechanism for their venture investment in new technologies. Rather, they have to venture into the market at their own risk, but with the result that a number of them have developed into large-scale groups, such as Lenovo in Zhongguancun, the Founder Group of Peking University, and Huawei in Shenzhen. Meanwhile, the enterprising culture of NGEs, especially scientific and technological NGEs, is an inspiring one that encourages further innovation. Such cultural soil is conducive to the innovation and transformation of scientific and technological achievements, as well as to the overall growth of high-tech industries.

Thirdly, embroiled in market competition since their birth, NGEs—especially those scientific and technological NGEs committed to the application and development of new knowledge and new technologies—are clear and definite in their application of property rights and fully reflect the principles of distribution of work, capital, management, and technology. All of this contributes to the capitalization and demutualization of knowledge and encourages the joint promotion of technological innovation by technology and capital owners, management personnel, and entrepreneurs. In addition, NGEs are economically vital and full of impetus for technological innovation, and, for their part, private entrepreneurs are fairly perceptive about market reaction. This makes it easier to boost financial innovations and the development of venture investment as well as the integration of financial capital and high-tech industries, which will promote the coordinated development of NGEs and high-tech industries. According to data released by the Statistics Center of Shenzhen Securities Information Co., Ltd., of the 123 companies formally listed on the Growth Enterprises Market (GEM) by September 30, 2010, about 92% are NGEs. With its capacity to accumulate financial capital, GEM has been providing sufficient funds for the rapid growth of these "Little Giants" in the private sectors of economy.

[2]Gu Shengzu. (2000). Reflections on the Strategic Significance and Measures of Developing Technological NGEs. *Wuhan Economic Research*, (1), 1–9.

11.1.2.2 The Industrialization of High and New Technologies: A New Impetus to NGEs' Entry

Following more than 10 years of rapid development, China's high-tech industries have been steadily increasing their overall strength and capacity for independent development while constantly optimizing and upgrading their industrial structure, and there have emerged a large number of innovative and competitive high-tech enterprises as a result. As the growth mechanisms of NGEs and high-tech industries are highly correlated, the rapid growth of these industries is bound to attract and drive NGEs to enter and develop therein.

First, high-tech industries are the fastest growing section of China's national economy. From 1998 to 2009, the total industrial output value of these industries increased from RMB 711.1 billion to 6043.1 billion, up by 19.5% annually; the proportion of their industrial added value in GDP rose from 2.11% in 1998 to 4.33% in 2009; the export of high-tech products increased from USD 20.3 billion to 376.9 billion, up by 27.6% annually; the proportion of high-tech products in the total volume of foreign trade increased from 15.3% in 1998 to 31.1% in 2009. This rapid growth has attracted a large number of NGEs—especially private scientific and technological enterprises—into China's high-tech industries, which have already become an important force in the development of these industries.

Secondly, high-tech industrial zones have provided a superior platform for NGEs' growth. Currently, such zones have already taken shape in China and are undergoing fruitful development. They have effectively integrated high and new technologies, high-tech enterprises, technology markets, and related service factors within certain areas, constructed a working platform for the development of China's high-tech enterprises, and created a beneficial environment for technological innovation. It is exactly the environment, opportunities, and excellent resources—like access to technologies and information—that have attracted many NGEs into the high-tech industries, where they have methodically developed and grown. There are plenty of examples of such private high-tech enterprises having grown up in these special zones, e.g., Lenovo and Founder in the Haidian Science & Technology Park, Zhongguancun, Beijing, and Huawei in Shenzhen High-Tech Park.

Finally, the development of high-tech industries enjoys many national supporting policies. To promote their development, the state has released various supportive policies concerning taxation, finance, intellectual property protection, and talent, all of which have become important driving forces behind NGEs' entry into the high-tech industries. Take the country's taxation policies, for example. Currently, China has implemented 37 preferential tax policies in nine classes regarding science and technology. These policies have covered every aspect of the high-tech industries, including tax policies in support of high-tech enterprises (e.g., key enterprises concerned with national support are entitled to a 15% reduction in their income tax rate), policies encouraging R&D input, tax policies encouraging investment, tax policies encouraging technical-equipment upgrading and technology import, and tax policies encouraging the development of science and technology services. Moreover, the country continues to increase investment in high-tech industries. For example, following the founding of the Innovation Fund for Small Technology-Based Firms (科技型中小企业技术创新基金, kēJìxíng zhōngxiǎo qǐyè jìshù chuàngxīn jījīn) in 1999, the central government had, by 2008, invested a total of RMB 8.338 billion in 13,488 innovative projects.[3]

11.1.3 Prominent Problems in NGEs' Entry into High-Tech Industries

Although China's NGEs have made rapid development in high-tech industries, as we will see, they are still faced with numerous prominent problems.

First, NGEs' low level of research and development. Generally limited in strength and scale, China's NGEs are still not able to meet the investment demands of "high input, high risk, and high output" required in high-tech industries, and they are very limited in their R&D input for high and new technologies. In terms of investment models, NGEs usually prefer to "capture market opportunities" with "small investment" and expect "quick and secured returns." They generally lack the experience of investment in the "three-high" (i.e., high input, high risk, and high output) technological industries, as well as the ability to understand the input mechanisms and to appropriately grasp project chances. Very few NGEs have independent intellectual property rights, and still fewer have high-level scientific achievements regarding independent intellectual property rights. Compared with FFEs, China's NGEs are relatively low in asset efficiency (i.e., sales revenue created by unit assets) and competitiveness, and therefore are divided and locked at the low-end links of the global value chain. Meanwhile, the localized production of many international enterprises are gradually offsetting the cost advantages of domestic enterprises and further squeezing the domestic market. Internationally, many low-cost rivals have arisen, including India, Vietnam, Thailand, and Malaysia in Asia, Mexico in North America, and Turkey in Europe; the constant upgrading of international technical standards and technical barriers has put the low-cost advantage under the control of technologies. All these factors are gradually weakening the "low-cost advantage" of China's NGEs in high-tech industries. This has intensified the competition in China's high-tech industries and increased the barrier to their entry, to say nothing of high-tech NGEs' upgrading and development or to the investment and entry of those from traditional industries.[4]

---

[3]Department of Development Planning, Ministry of Science and Technology., & Enterprise Department, Ministry of Finance. *Annual Reviews of Innovation Fund for Small Technology-Based Firms 1999–2008*. Available at http://www.innofund.gov.cn/innofile.

[4]Li Weidong & Li Wei. (2008). NGEs' Strategies for Investment in Hi-Tech Industries. *Advanced Materials Industry*, (8), 75–76.

Second, NGEs' insufficient funds for technological innovation. Currently, the average R&D input of China's scientific and technological NGEs is less than 3% of their income, far lower than the internationally accepted proportion of over 10% for sci-tech enterprises. There are several reasons for this. To begin with, most of China's scientific and technological NGEs are low in initial capital and limited in their funds for sustained technological innovation. What's more, although local governments have set up some special funds in order to introduce science and technology projects and talents and to support technological innovation among enterprises, scientific and technological NGEs have to go through tedious procedures before being able to obtain even a small sum. Furthermore, as most scientific and technological NGEs are small in both size and assets and are short of real estate for mortgage, it is rather difficult for them to get loans from banks, a situation which is worsened by certain discriminatory policies with regard to NGEs' credit. Some high-tech NGEs have to turn to informal finance and get the blame for illegal fund-raising; some enterprises even have to resort to usury for development funds. In addition, government-dominated venture investment is limited in its source of funds, single in capital structure, and imperfect in operation, and therefore can hardly support the R&D of high-tech NGEs. And finally, the capital market is undeveloped and short of supportive policies; the initial investment of venture capital, credit guarantees, and investment in high-tech SMEs incubation funds are still in the initial stage, and it is difficult for scientific and technological NGEs to seek financing by listing on the stock market or issuing bonds.[5]

Third, the immature systems, mechanisms, and policy environment of the Chinese economy. Through more than 30 years of reform and opening-up, NGEs' development environment have been consistently improved in China, but there are still some serious problems to NGEs' entry into and development in high-tech industries, such as the insufficient, unsystematic, and even mismatched support of tax policies, the imperfect exit mechanisms of venture investment, and the backward governmental services supporting NGEs' investment and development in high-tech industries. In addition, the allocation of scientific and technological resources is currently still dominated by universities and research institutes in China, but most of their scientific achievements are technology-oriented, while very few projects are market- or investment-oriented. As a result, the R&D of scientific and technological resources can hardly meet NGEs' needs for industrialization investment, which, in turn, fails to engage them in technical R&D at the national level. At the same time, the intermediary service system has not yet been fully constructed to support NGEs' investment and development in high-tech industries, and its functions—including the capital market, information, and technology services—have not yet been brought into full play. Moreover, as China is still at the low end of the global value chain of high-tech industries, Chinese enterprises mainly participate in processing and manufacturing, while the high-

[5]China Small- & Medium-Sized Enterprise Research Institute. Problems in NGEs' Participation in the Development of High-Tech Industries in China, at http://www.sme2000.com.cn/index.asp.

tech products are generally low in value-added rates. Accordingly, the low ROI (return on investment) is by no means attractive to NGEs. All the above problems seriously restrict NGEs' entry into, as well as their development in, high-tech industries.

11.2 The Coordinated Development of NGEs and High-Tech Industries

11.2.1 A Model of the Degree of Coordination Between Sci-Tech NGEs and High-Tech Industries

11.2.1.1 A Model of System Order Degree

We first define the system order degree. Suppose that the order parameter variables of the sci-tech NGEs' system in development are, $\theta^s = \left(\theta_1^s, \theta_2^s, \cdots, \theta_n^s\right)$, $\wedge\, n \geq 2$, $\beta_i^s \leq \theta_i^s \leq \alpha_{i,}^s i \in [1, n]$ in which the greater the value of $\left(\theta_1^s, \theta_2^s, \cdots, \theta_n^s\right)$, the higher the system order degree, and vice versa; on the contrary, the greater the value of $\left(\theta_{k+1}^s, \theta_{k+2}^s, \cdots, \theta_n^s\right)$, the lower the system order degree, and vice versa. Thus we get the following definitions.

Definition 1: The order degree of the sci-tech NGEs' system with the order parameter component θ_i^s.

$$\mu\left(\theta_i^s\right) = \begin{cases} \left(\theta_i^s - \beta_i^s\right)\left(\alpha_i^s - \beta_i^s\right)^{-1}, i \in [1, k], \\ \left(\alpha_i^s - \theta_i^s\right)\left(\alpha_i^s - \beta_i^s\right)^{-1}, i \in [k+1, n]. \end{cases}$$

We can know from the above definition that $\mu\left(\theta_i^s\right) \in [0, 1]$, and that the bigger $\mu\left(\theta_i^s\right)$, the larger the contribution of θ_i^s to the order degree of the sci-tech NGEs' system. In general, "the total contribution" of the order parameter variables to the order degree of the sci-tech NGEs' system can be measured through the integration of $\mu\left(\theta_i^s\right)$. A common method in practice is the linear weighted sum method, namely,

$$\overline{\mu}(\theta^s) = \sum_{i=1}^{n} \omega_i \mu\left(\theta_i^s\right), \omega_i \geq 0, \quad \sum_{i=1}^{n} \omega_i = 1.$$

Definition 2: In the above equation, $\overline{\mu}(\theta^s)$ represents the order degree of the sci-tech NGEs' system. We can know that $\overline{\mu}(\theta^s) \in [0, 1]$ and that the bigger $\overline{\mu}(\theta^s)$, the higher the order degree of the sci-tech NGEs system, and vice versa.

Suppose that the order parameter variable of the development quality of the high-tech industries' system is $\theta^e = \left(\theta_1^e, \theta_2^e, \cdots, \theta_n^e\right)$ where $m \geq 2, \beta_j^e \leq \theta_j^e \leq \alpha_j^e, j \in [1, m]$. We can also get $\overline{\mu}(\theta^e) \in [0, 1]$ through an analysis similar to the above.

11.2.1.2 A Model of the Degree of Coordination Between Sci-Tech NGEs and High-Tech Industries' Systems

Definition 3: Suppose that at the initial time (or in a specific time period) t_0, the order degree of the sci-tech NGEs' system is $\overline{\mu}_0(\theta^s)$ and the order degree of the high-tech industries' system is $\overline{\mu}_0(\theta^e)$, and that when the system evolves to Time t_1, the order degree of the sci-tech NGEs' system changes into $\overline{\mu}_1(\theta^e)$, and the order degree of the high-tech industries' system changes into $\overline{\mu}_1(\theta^e)$. If $\overline{\mu}_1(\theta^s) \geq \overline{\mu}_0(\theta^s)$ and $\overline{\mu}_1(\theta^e) \geq \overline{\mu}_0(\theta^e)$ are simultaneously true, the sci-tech NGEs' system and the high-tech industries' system are in coordinated development from t_0 to t_1. The coordination degree model is as follows:

$$C = \operatorname{sig}(\cdot)\sqrt{|\overline{\mu_1}(\theta^s) - \overline{\mu_0}(\theta^s)||\overline{\mu_1}(\theta^e) - \overline{\mu_0}(\theta^e)|}.$$

In the equation, $\operatorname{sig}(\cdot) = \begin{cases} 1, \overline{\mu_1}(\theta^s) - \overline{\mu_0}(\theta^s) \geq 0 \wedge \overline{\mu_1}(\theta^e) - \overline{\mu_0}(\theta^e) \geq 0, \\ -1, \text{otherwise}. \end{cases}$

We can know from the equation that $c \in [-1, 1]$ and that the bigger its value, the higher the degree of system coordination, and vice versa. Meanwhile, this definition also synthesizes the two subsystems. If the order degree of one subsystem increases significantly while that of the other increases little or even decreases, the whole system will be in a state of poor or even no coordination, which manifests as $c \in [-1, 0]$. This definition can be used to measure the trend of the degree of system coordination in the reporting period in comparison with that in the base period, which can thus benefit the dynamic analysis of system coordination degree.

11.2.2 Empirical Tests

11.2.2.1 The Degree of Order of Sci-Tech NGEs' System

Table 11.3 includes the order parameter indicators of the sci-tech NGEs' system, of which, the lower end is the values in China in 1998 and the upper end is those in 2009.

As the different observation units may cause great differences in the observed values, we must first standardize the raw data by using the SAS statistical analysis software, so as to nondimensionalize the indicators. The following is the standardized order parameter matrix of the sci-tech NGEs system:

Table 11.3 Order parameter indicators of the sci-tech NGEs' system

Year	Enterprises	Industrial added value (bn RMB)	Employees (mn)	R&D expenditure (bn RMB)	Technical income (bn RMB)
1998	70,052	115.5	3.97	34.2	42.1
1999	79,477	153.9	4.92	43.1	55.2
2000	86,100	220.2	5.59	40.6	80.4
2001	100,950	262.1	6.44	48.5	88.1
2002	109,384	359.6	7.83	54.4	136.0
2003	124,937	756.2	9.61	79.2	171.9
2004	141,353	994.8	11.30	98.7	236.5
2005	143,991	1296.6	12.12	123.0	275.7
2006	150,595	1599.5	13.89	164.0	351.4
2007	162,337	2095.9	15.88	213.0	521.7
2008	178,392	2605.2	18.18	273.5	693.9
2009	196,035	2891.8	20.81	351.1	923.0

Note: The sci-tech NGEs here are in the broad sense, i.e., a general term that covers enterprises of different ownerships except state-owned and state-holding enterprises, including individual businesses, private enterprises, collective enterprises, Hong Kong, Macao, and Taiwan investment enterprises and FFEs. Besides, as there are no available statistics of China's sci-tech NGEs in 2008 or 2009, the data of both years here are the predicted values by the index smoothing forecasting method

Source: Ministry of Science and Technology. Statistical reports on China's sci-tech NGEs from 1998 to 2007

$$Z = \begin{vmatrix} -1.4545 & -1.0076 & -1.2621 & -0.8951 & -0.9138 \\ -1.2205 & -0.9688 & -1.0886 & -0.8092 & -0.8671 \\ -1.0561 & -0.9018 & -0.9662 & -0.8333 & -0.7771 \\ -0.6874 & -0.8595 & -0.8109 & -0.7570 & -0.7496 \\ -0.4780 & -0.7609 & -0.5569 & -0.7001 & -0.5785 \\ -0.0918 & -0.3602 & -0.2317 & -0.4608 & -0.4503 \\ 0.3158 & -0.1190 & 0.0770 & -0.2726 & -0.2196 \\ 0.3813 & 0.1859 & 0.2269 & -0.0380 & -0.0796 \\ 0.5453 & 0.4920 & 0.5502 & 0.3577 & 0.1907 \\ 0.8368 & 0.9936 & 0.9138 & 0.8306 & 0.7989 \\ 1.2355 & 1.5083 & 1.3340 & 1.4144 & 1.4139 \\ 1.6735 & 1.7979 & 1.8145 & 2.1634 & 2.2320 \end{vmatrix}.$$

As the order parameter indicators have different influences on the system, to reveal this relationship, we must give different weights to different indicators. The procedures are as follows:

First, we must work out the correlation coefficients of any two indicators, as they reflect the mutual influence between the indicators themselves. The following is the correlation coefficient matrix:

$$R = \begin{vmatrix} 1.0000 & 0.9630 & 0.9900 & 0.9295 & 0.9269 \\ 0.9630 & 1.0000 & 0.9898 & 0.9851 & 0.9775 \\ 0.9900 & 0.9898 & 1.0000 & 0.9695 & 0.9653 \\ 0.9295 & 0.9851 & 0.9695 & 1.0000 & 0.9973 \\ 0.9269 & 0.9775 & 0.9653 & 0.9973 & 1.0000 \end{vmatrix}.$$

Second, if an indicator is highly correlated to the others, it has a greater influence on the others as well as a greater role in the system, and should thus be given a relatively larger weight, and vice versa with less correlated indicators. The overall correlation of an indicator to all the others can be calculated as follows:

$$R_i = \sum_{j=1}^{n} |r_{ij}| - 1, (i = 1, 2, \cdots, n).$$

Third, we normalize the R_i in the above formula and get the weight of each indicator:

$$\omega_i = R_i / \sum_{j=1}^{n} R_j, (i = 1, 2, \cdots, n).$$

By using the above formulas, we can work out R_i and ω_i as follows:
$R_1 = 3.8094$, $R_2 = 3.9154$, $R_3 = 3.9146$, $R_4 = 3.8814$, $R_5 = 3.867$.
$\omega_1 = 0.1964$, $\omega_2 = 0.2020$, $\omega_3 = 0.2019$, $\omega_4 = 0.2002$, $\omega_5 = 0.1995$.

When the weight of each indicator is calculated, we can get the order degrees of the sci-tech NGEs' system by using the formulas from Definitions (1) and (2). The results are in Table 11.4.

As we can see in Table 11.4, the order degree of China's sci-tech NGEs' system has been increasing yearly. It was low in 1999 and 2000, but has been growing rapidly since 2005, indicating a more orderly development of sci-tech NGEs in terms of their industrial scale, output values, contribution to sci-tech progress, the construction of qualified talents, and so forth. This mainly results from several important documents released by the State Council: *Opinions on Encouraging, Supporting, and Guiding the Development of Individual, Private, and Other Non-Public Sectors of the Economy* in 2005, the first document on the promotion of non-public sectors of the economy since the founding of the People's Republic of China; *Several Opinions on Furthering the Development of SMEs* in 2009; and *Several Opinions on Encouraging and Guiding the Sound Development of Non-Governmental Investment* in 2010. Encouraged and guided by the above policies and measures, China's sci-tech NGEs have consistently been increasing their overall strength.

Table 11.4 Degrees of order of the sci-tech NGEs' system

Year	$\mu(\theta_1^s)$	$\mu(\theta_2^s)$	$\mu(\theta_3^s)$	$\mu(\theta_4^s)$	$\mu(\theta_5^s)$	Degree of system order
1999	0.075	0.014	0.056	0.028	0.015	0.038
2000	0.127	0.038	0.096	0.020	0.043	0.065
2001	0.245	0.053	0.147	0.045	0.052	0.108
2002	0.312	0.088	0.229	0.064	0.107	0.159
2003	0.436	0.231	0.335	0.142	0.147	0.258
2004	0.566	0.317	0.435	0.204	0.221	0.348
2005	0.587	0.425	0.484	0.280	0.265	0.408
2006	0.639	0.535	0.589	0.410	0.351	0.505
2007	0.733	0.713	0.707	0.564	0.544	0.652
2008	0.860	0.897	0.844	0.755	0.740	0.819
2009	1.000	1.000	1.000	1.000	1.000	1.000

11.2.2.2 The Degree of Order of the High-Tech Industries' System

Table 11.5 includes the order parameter indicators of the high-tech industries' system, of which, the lower end is the values of China in 1998 and the upper end is those in 2009.

The following is the standardized order parameter matrix of the high-tech industries' system:

$$Z = \begin{vmatrix} -1.1058 & -1.1159 & -0.9749 & -1.1242 & -0.9107 & -0.9907 \\ -1.0494 & -1.0456 & -0.9572 & -1.0778 & -0.8870 & -0.9126 \\ -0.9376 & -0.9032 & -0.9305 & -0.8967 & -0.8425 & -0.8312 \\ -0.8433 & -0.8298 & -0.8949 & -0.7030 & -0.7764 & -0.7735 \\ -0.6988 & -0.6826 & -0.7794 & -0.5767 & -0.6474 & -0.6581 \\ -0.4207 & -0.4064 & -0.5439 & -0.4292 & -0.4911 & -0.5257 \\ -0.0532 & -0.1210 & -0.0552 & -0.1344 & -0.3304 & -0.3527 \\ 0.2829 & 0.2692 & 0.2825 & 0.1646 & 0.0077 & 0.1801 \\ 0.6716 & 0.6902 & 0.6424 & 0.5563 & 0.4439 & 0.4992 \\ 1.1029 & 1.0320 & 1.0823 & 0.9311 & 1.0356 & 0.9810 \\ 1.4405 & 1.3958 & 1.5355 & 1.3944 & 1.3394 & 1.4765 \\ 1.6109 & 1.7174 & 1.5933 & 1.8956 & 2.0587 & 1.9075 \end{vmatrix}.$$

The matrix of correlation coefficients between the indicators of high-tech industries is:

Table 11.5 Order parameter indicators of the high-tech industries' system

Year	Total output (bn RMB)	Industrial added value (bn RMB)	Employees (mn)	R&D expenditure (bn RMB)	Patents applied	New-product development expenses (bn RMB)
1998	711.1	178.5	3.80	5.7	1076	7.1
1999	821.7	210.7	3.84	6.8	1482	9.4
2000	1041.1	275.9	3.90	11.1	2245	11.8
2001	1226.3	309.5	3.98	15.7	3379	13.5
2002	1509.9	376.9	4.24	18.7	5590	16.9
2003	2055.6	503.4	4.77	22.2	8270	20.8
2004	2776.9	634.1	5.87	29.2	11,026	25.9
2005	3436.7	812.8	6.63	36.3	16,823	41.6
2006	4199.6	1005.6	7.44	45.6	24,301	51.0
2007	5046.1	1162.1	8.43	54.5	34,446	65.2
2008	5708.7	1328.7	9.45	65.5	39,656	79.8
2009	6043.1	1476.0	9.58	77.4	51,989	92.5

Note: The industrial added value of 2009 is predicted value and the rest data of that year are from *China's Statistics Yearbook 2010*

Source: NBS. *China Statistics Yearbook on High Technology Industry* (1999–2009) and *China Statistical Yearbook 2010*

$$R = \begin{vmatrix} 1.0000 & 0.9988 & 0.9972 & 0.9916 & 0.9770 & 0.9866 \\ 0.9988 & 1.0000 & 0.9952 & 0.9955 & 0.9830 & 0.9909 \\ 0.9972 & 0.9952 & 1.0000 & 0.9868 & 0.9773 & 0.9876 \\ 0.9916 & 0.9955 & 0.9868 & 1.0000 & 0.9902 & 0.9941 \\ 0.9770 & 0.9830 & 0.9773 & 0.9902 & 1.0000 & 0.9961 \\ 0.9866 & 0.9909 & 0.9876 & 0.9941 & 0.9961 & 1.0000 \end{vmatrix}.$$

By using the above formulas, we can work out R_i and ω_i as follows:

$R_1= 4.9512$, $R_2= 4.9634$, $R_3= 4.9441$, $R_4= 4.9582$, $R_5= 4.9236$, $R_6= 4.9553$.
$\omega_1= 0.1667$, $\omega_2= 0.1671$, $\omega_3= 0.1665$, $\omega_4= 0.1670$, $\omega_5= 0.1658$, $\omega_6= 0.1669$.

When the weight of each indicator is calculated, we get the order of degrees of the high-tech industries' system by using the formulas found in Definitions (1) and (2).

As we can see in Table 11.6, the degree order of China's high-tech industries has been constantly improving. It was rather low before 2001, but has been growing rapidly since 2002. This mainly results from the *Decision of the CPC Central Committee and the State Council on Strengthening Technical Innovation, Developing High Technology, and Realizing Industrialization* released in 1999. At that time, China's high-tech industries entered a new period of development, but the degree order of the country's high-tech industries was low still in this period. Since 2001, the state has introduced a series of policies and measures that support the development of high-tech industries, such as *Several Issues on the Support of High-*

Table 11.6 The degrees of order of high-tech industries' systems

Year	$\mu(\theta_1^e)$	$\mu(\theta_2^e)$	$\mu(\theta_3^e)$	$\mu(\theta_4^e)$	$\mu(\theta_5^e)$	$\mu(\theta_6^e)$	Degree of system order
1999	0.021	0.025	0.007	0.015	0.008	0.027	0.017
2000	0.062	0.075	0.017	0.075	0.023	0.055	0.051
2001	0.097	0.101	0.031	0.139	0.045	0.075	0.081
2002	0.150	0.153	0.076	0.181	0.089	0.115	0.127
2003	0.252	0.250	0.168	0.230	0.141	0.160	0.200
2004	0.387	0.351	0.358	0.328	0.195	0.220	0.307
2005	0.511	0.489	0.490	0.427	0.309	0.404	0.438
2006	0.654	0.637	0.630	0.556	0.456	0.514	0.575
2007	0.813	0.758	0.801	0.681	0.655	0.680	0.731
2008	0.937	0.886	0.978	0.834	0.758	0.851	0.874
2009	1.000	1.000	1.000	1.000	1.000	1.000	1.000

Tech Industries' Development in 2001, *Several Opinions on Furthering the Strategy of Rejuvenating Trade through Science and Technology* in 2003, and *China's High-Tech Products Export Directory* (2003 Edition). Since then, China's hi-tech industries have achieved exponential development, and the degree of system order was measurably higher than before.

11.2.2.3 Degree of Coordination Between Sci-Tech NGEs and High-Tech Industries

Following the results above, we take the degree of order of the subsystems as the intermediate variable and the first year as the base year of each period (i.e., Periods 1999–2000, 2000–2001, 2001–2002, 2002–2003, 2003–2004, 2004–2005, 2005–2006, 2006–2007, 2007–2008 and 2008–2009) to get the degree of coordination between the sci-tech NGEs and high-tech industries C by using the coordination degree formula in Definition (3). As can be seen in Table 11.7 and Fig. 11.3, the sci-tech NGEs and high-tech industries' systems of China are generally in coordinated development (positive values of C), but the coordination degree of the composite system is relatively low, fluctuating smoothly between 0.1545 and 0.0303 with an average below 0.10. What's more, according to the trends in variation in Fig. 11.3, the order degree of the high-tech industries' system was clearly lower than that of the sci-tech NGEs' system before 2005, but has been growing much more rapidly and significantly than that of the sci-tech NGEs' system since 2005. This is closely related to China's policy orientation towards the vigorous development of high-tech industries and the promotion of their strength and scale. In contrast, despite the state's active support, sci-tech NGEs have not made significant improvement of their development since 2005.

The above analysis reveals that the composite system of sci-tech NGEs and high-tech industries has been in coordinated development, and that, with NGEs'

Table 11.7 Calculated coordination degrees of the composite system of sci-tech NGEs and high-tech industries

Year	Degree of order of the sci-tech NGEs' system	Degree of order of high-tech industries' system	Degree of order of composite systems (*C*)
1999	0.038	0.017	–
2000	0.065	0.051	0.0303
2001	0.108	0.081	0.0359
2002	0.159	0.127	0.0484
2003	0.258	0.200	0.0850
2004	0.348	0.307	0.0981
2005	0.408	0.438	0.0887
2006	0.505	0.575	0.1153
2007	0.652	0.731	0.1514
2008	0.819	0.874	0.1545
2009	1	1	0.1510

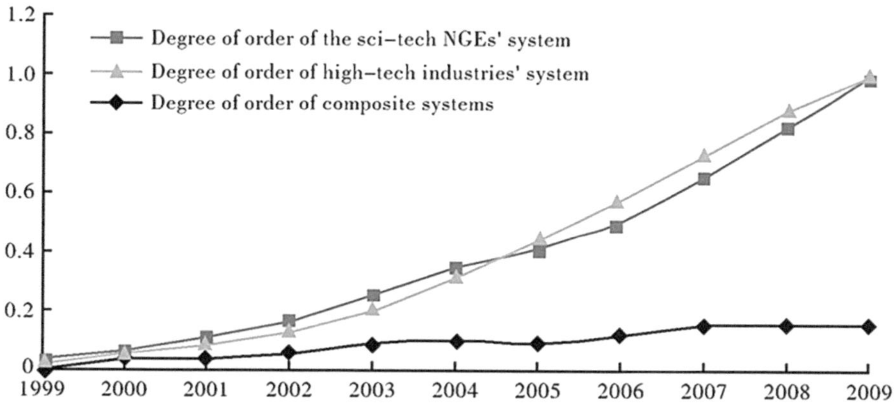

Fig. 11.3 Coordination degree variations of the composite system of sci-tech NGEs and high-tech industries

innate advantages, it is therefore feasible for them to enter high-tech industries The coordinated development of the two subsystems indicates that sci-tech NGEs have already become an important force in the development of China's high-tech industries, which has, in turn, driven the growth of China's sci-tech NGEs. But it should also be noted that the degree of coordination of the composite system in general is relatively low, indicating there are still some barriers to sci-tech NGEs' entry into China's high-tech industries. Despite their rapid development, China's sci-tech NGEs are mostly small in size, weak in the foundations of their capacity for technological innovation, and lack any impetus for innovation; their scientific and technological input is far from sufficient; they are faced with financing difficulties and are short of any mechanisms for venture investment in science and technology industries. Therefore, their role in promoting the development of high-tech industries is limited.

11.3 The Interaction Between the Cultivation of Sci-Tech NGEs, the Development of High-Tech Industries, and NGEs' Growth

11.3.1 A Quantitative Analysis of Ridge Regression

To study the positive effect of high-tech industries and sci-tech NGEs on the development of China's NGEs in general, we must first estimate the regression equation with the econometric method:

$$\ln Y = \alpha + \beta_1 \ln X_1 + \beta_2 \ln X_2 + \varepsilon.$$

In the above equation, $\ln Y$, $\ln X_1$ and $\ln X_2$ respectively stand for the natural logarithms of the total output value of NGEs, the industrial added value of high-tech industries, and the industrial added value of sci-tech NGEs (See Table 11.8).

Why is it necessary to make a natural logarithmic transformation of the total output value of NGEs, the industrial added value of high-tech industries, and the industrial added value of sci-tech NGEs from 1999 to 2009? To answer the question, we must make a residual analysis of the original time series data. If the assumption of the multiple linear regression model (i.e. $\sigma_1^2 = \sigma_2^2 = \cdots = \sigma_n^2$) is true, the scattered points should distribute randomly in a band between −2 and +2 in the residual plot of the predicted values, and their distribution is approximately normal. Such a distribution is called a normal residual plot.

We analyze the residual plot of the original time series data (Fig. 11.4), and find that, with the increase in the predicted value, the absolute value of the studentized residual (i.e., the standardized form of general residuals) varies irregularly and disobeys the normal distribution; the studentized residual exhibited an obvious rising trend from 1999 to 2002 and from 2007 to 2009, and in drastic fluctuation around the X-axis in the remaining years; in 2003, it was even as low as −2.014 and fell outside the band where the scattered points should have been distributed across the residual plot. Therefore, we conclude that there is a quite strong heteroscedasticity in the original time series data, and that the observed values are not independent from each other. As a result, it is highly necessary that we conduct a natural logarithmic transformation of the total output value of NGEs, the industrial added value of high-tech industries, and the industrial added value of sci-tech NGEs from 1999 to 2009. As can be seen in Fig. 11.5 below, after the natural logarithmic transformation of the original time series data, the residual plot approximately obeys the normal distribution (approximate symmetrical distribution on both sides with the residual value of 2004 as the symmetry axis), which proves both the necessity and feasibility of the logarithmic transformation of the original time series data.

Before the ridge regression, we can conclude from the output results in Table 11.9 that: (1) the regression equation is $\ln \widehat{Y} = -1.014 + 1.4117 \ln X_1 - 0.0213 \ln X_2$;

Table 11.8 Relevant values of China's NGEs, high-tech industries, and sci-tech NGEs 1999–2009

	Industrial added value of high-tech industries		Industrial added value of sci-tech NGEs		Total output value of NGEs	
	X_1 (bn RMB)	$\ln X_1$	X_2 (bn RMB)	$\ln X_2$	Y (bn RMB)	$\ln Y$
1999	210.7	7.653	153.9	7.339	1764.2	9.778
2000	275.9	7.923	220.2	7.697	2112.0	9.958
2001	309.5	8.038	262.1	7.871	2531.7	10.139
2002	376.9	8.235	359.6	8.188	3256.2	10.391
2003	503.4	8.524	756.2	8.931	4393.0	10.690
2004	634.1	8.755	994.8	9.205	8407.3	11.339
2005	812.8	9.003	1296.6	9.470	8800.9	11.385
2006	1005.6	9.216	1599.5	9.680	11,666.1	11.667
2007	1162.1	9.361	2095.9	9.950	15,605.4	11.958
2008	1328.7	9.495	2605.2	10.168	21,155.7	12.262
2009	1476.0	9.600	2891.8	10.272	24,656.7	12.415

Note: The total output value of NGEs in each year is calculated in this formula: NGEs = collective-owned enterprises + collective-joint enterprises + joint-stock cooperative enterprises + private enterprises + joint stock limited companies + limited liability companies (excluding state-owned, state-holding, and state-owned joint enterprises)

Source: NBS. *China Statistics Yearbook on High Technology Industry* (1999–2009) and *China Statistical Yearbook 2010*

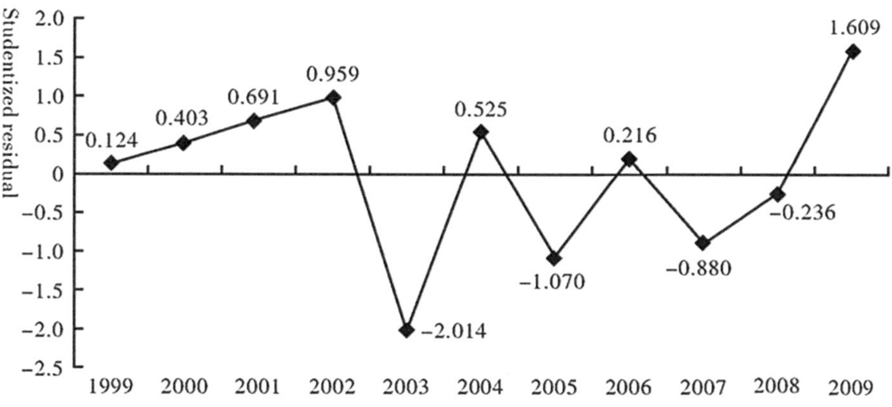

Fig. 11.4 Predicted residual data of the total output value of China's NGEs 1999–2009

(2) the variance inflation factor (VIF) of the two independent variables is 99.722, far more than 10, which indicates a serious multi-collinearity between the variables as well as a close correlation between the growth of China's sci-tech NGEs and the development of high-tech industries; (3) the coefficient of Variable X_2 is negative in the regression equation, which is contrary to reality; the t-values of Variables X_1 and X_2 are small, while all the independent variables have insignificant influence on Dependent Variable Y (the P-value of Independent Variable X_1 is 0.0419, and that of

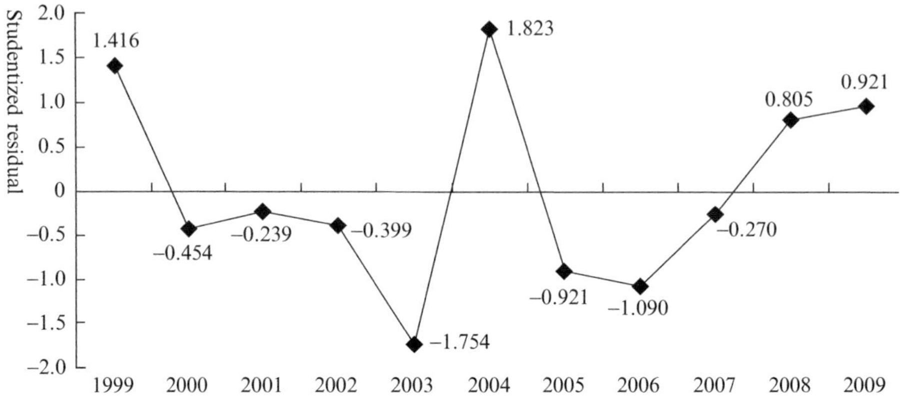

Fig. 11.5 Predicted residual data of the total output value of China's NGEs 1999–2009 after logarithmic transformation

Table 11.9 Analysis results of multiple linear regression (before ridge regression estimation)

Variable	Freedom	Parameter estimation	Standard error	*t*-value	Significance probability (*P*) of *t*-value	Variance inflation factor
Intercept	1	−1.01437	1.73607	−0.58	0.5751	0
X_1	1	1.41170	0.58351	2.42	0.0419	99.72235
X_2	1	−0.02131	0.37832	−0.06	0.9565	99.72235

Table 11.10 Results of collinearity diagnostics

No.	Characteristic root	Condition indicator	Variance proportion		
			Intercept	X_1	X_2
1	2.99359	1.00000	0.00005294	0.00000617	0.00001368
2	0.00637	21.67272	0.04454	0.00020804	0.00733
3	0.00003549	290.41782	0.95541	0.99979	0.99266

X_2 is 0.9565) under the significant level of $\alpha = 0.05$, while the regression equation is highly significant (F-value is 278.48, and the significance probability of P-value is <0.0001), which suggests that the significant influence of the independent variables on the dependent variables has been completely obscured by the multiple correlation between the variables.

From the collinearity diagnostics in Table 11.10, we can further conclude that: (1) the largest condition indicator is $290.42 > 100$, indicating a strong correlation between the two variables, and (2) the variance proportions of the two variables in the same line of the largest condition indicator are larger than 0.5, indicating the two independent variables are in themselves variable sets of strong correlation.

The multiple collinearity between independent variables has led to insignificant regression coefficients in the above model. To solve this problem, we choose to

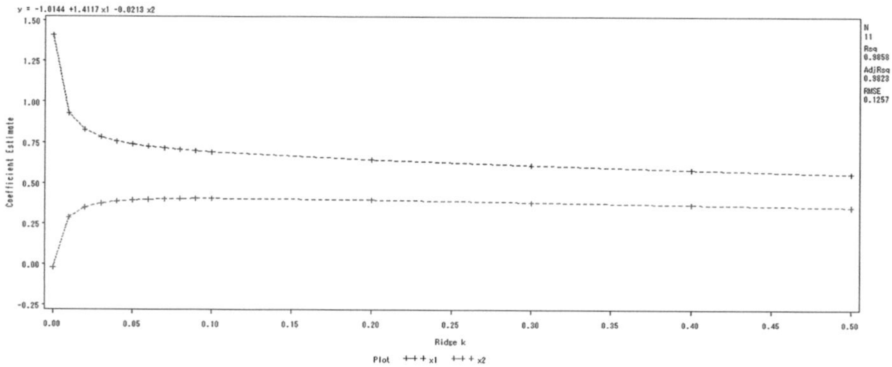

Fig. 11.6 Ridge trace of high-tech industries, sci-tech NGEs, and NGEs' development

eliminate the collinearity by using the ridge regression method and thereby get a more fitting regression equation.

We can see from the ridge trace in Fig. 11.6 that, when $k \geq 0.10$, the ridge track curve tends to be stable. We establish a ridge regression equation by using the ridge regression estimations of $k = 0.10$. According to the values in the output data sets on Line OBS-23 in Table 11.11, we can then write the regression equation as follows:

$$\ln \widehat{Y} = 1.4497 + 0.6911 \ln X_1 + 0.4032 \ln X_2.$$

This requires the constant term of a double logarithmic linear regression model, namely, $\widehat{A} = e^{1.4497} = 4.2618$. Therefore, the ridge regression equation for the total output value of China' NGEs is:

$$\widehat{Y} = 4.2618 {X_1}^{0.6911} X_2^{0.4032}.$$

All the symbols of the regression coefficients in the ridge regression equation are meaningful. All the variance inflation factors of the regression coefficients are less than 3 (0.4551 in Line 22 and Columns X_1 and X_2 in Table 11.11), and the root mean square error is very small (0.1450 in Line 23 and Column "Root mean square error" in Table 11.11). This ridge regression equation is a typical Cobb-Douglas production function. Through the total differentiation of the equation, we get the elastic coefficients of Variables X_1 and X_2:

$$\frac{d\widehat{Y}/Y}{dX_1/X_1} = 0.6911,^{6} \qquad \frac{d\widehat{Y}/Y}{dX_2/X_2} = 0.4032.$$

[6]The derivation of the elastic coefficients: Suppose the general form of the Cobb-Douglas production function is $Y = AL^{\alpha}K^{\beta}$. We take the total differentials on both sides of the equation, and find $\frac{dY}{dL} = \alpha AL^{\alpha-1}K^{\beta} = \frac{\alpha AL^{\alpha}K^{\beta}}{L} = \alpha\frac{Y}{L}$, so $\frac{dY/Y}{dL/L} = \alpha$. Similarly, we can find $\frac{dY/Y}{dK/K} = \beta$.

Table 11.11 Output data sets of high-tech industries, sci-tech NGEs, and NGEs

No.	Value k	Root mean square error	Intercept	X_1	X_2	Y
1		0.1257	−1.0144	1.4117	−0.0213	−1
2	0.00			99.7224	99.7224	−1
3	0.00	0.1257	−1.0144	1.4117	−0.0213	−1
4	0.01			11.3788	11.3788	−1
5	0.01	0.1310	0.4236	0.9276	0.2881	−1
6	0.02			4.2584	4.2584	−1
7	0.02	0.1335	0.7518	0.8276	0.3485	−1
8	0.03			2.2918	2.2918	−1
9	0.03	0.1351	0.9204	0.7829	0.3732	−1
10	0.04			1.4805	1.4805	−1
11	0.04	0.1364	1.0354	0.7565	0.3859	−1
12	0.05			1.0686	1.0686	−1
13	0.05	0.1377	1.1257	0.7385	0.3933	−1
14	0.06			0.8306	0.8306	−1
15	0.06	0.1389	1.2026	0.7251	0.3977	−1
16	0.07			0.6804	0.6804	−1
17	0.07	0.1403	1.2711	0.7144	0.4005	−1
18	0.08			0.5793	0.5793	−1
19	0.08	0.1418	1.3342	0.7055	0.4021	−1
20	0.09			0.5078	0.5078	−1
21	0.09	0.1434	1.3934	0.6979	0.4029	−1
22	0.10			0.4551	0.4551	−1
23	0.10	0.1450	1.4497	0.6911	0.4032	−1
24	0.20			0.2668	0.2668	−1
25	0.20	0.1667	1.9330	0.6443	0.3948	−1
26	0.30			0.2164	0.2164	−1
27	0.30	0.1935	2.3465	0.6112	0.3808	−1
28	0.40			0.1892	0.1892	−1
29	0.40	0.2221	2.7186	0.5832	0.3665	−1
30	0.50			0.1701	0.1701	−1
31	0.50	0.2506	3.0582	0.5584	0.3528	−1

The above elastic coefficients reflect the relative importance of the two variables to NGEs' development. Hence, we can get the interactive relationship between high-tech industries, sci-tech NGEs, and NGEs. That is, when the industrial added value of sci-tech NGEs remains constant, a 1% increase in the industrial added value of high-tech industries corresponds to a 0.6911% increase in the total output value of China's NGEs; when the industrial added value of high-tech industries remains unchanged, a 1% increase in the industrial added value of sci-tech NGEs corresponds to a 0.4032% increase the total output value of China's NGEs. From the above data, the variation of the industrial added value of China's high-tech industries has a significant influence on the total output value of NGEs, which proves empirically that high-tech industries have become a new field for the development of China's NGEs in the new stage.

11.3.2 Summary

In this section, we analyze the regression equation of the relationship between China's high-tech industries, sci-tech NGEs, and NGEs in general by using the ridge regression method of statistical analysis. By observing the elastic coefficients of the two independent variables of high-tech industries and sci-tech NGEs, we clarify the different roles of the two independent variables in the development of China's NGEs. When observing the above data, we interrogate why high-tech industries have a greater influence on the development of China's NGEs than do sci-tech NGEs (i.e., the elastic coefficient [0.6911] of the industrial added value of high-tech industries is larger than that [0.4032] of the industrial added value of sci-tech NGEs). It seems to go against common sense, considering that sci-tech NGEs are an important part of NGEs in general, while high-tech industries are only a new field of NGEs' development in China's new economic period. Accordingly, compared with high-tech industries, sci-tech NGEs should have had a greater influence on NGEs' development. But upon further consideration, this result has its own sense of inevitability. Through more than 10 years' rapid development, China's high-tech industries have been continuously increasing their overall strength and therefore have a greater and greater influence on NGEs' development. On the other hand, although China's sci-tech NGEs have made much progress, their proportion to NGEs overall is too small to have significant influence on the development of China's NGEs at large. This is why the development of China's high-tech industries has a greater influence on NGEs than do sci-tech NGEs.

In addition, in the ridge regression equation, the elastic coefficient of the industrial added value of high-tech industries is 0.6911, which indicates that the development of high-tech industries is a powerful driving force behind NGEs. But is this in line with our conclusion of a low degree of coordinated development between China's high-tech industries and NGEs in Sect. 11.2? It is generally believed that a great leading role of high-tech industries in NGEs' development means a high degree of coordination between the two, and vice versa. This is not the case, however. Our regression equation here is based on the industrial added value of high-tech industries, the industrial added value of sci-tech NGEs, and the total output value of NGEs, while the coordination degree model comprehensively measures the coordinated development between the subsystems as drawn from enterprise numbers, industrial added value, employee numbers, R&D funds, and so on. That is, our conclusion to this section—i.e., that the development of high-tech industries is a powerful driving force of NGEs—only takes into account output values and is thus not complete or systematic. In contrast, the degree of coordination synthesizes all the indicators that can measure industrial development and comprehensively reflects the degree of coordinated development between high-tech industries and NGEs. A low degree of overall coordination, however, does not necessarily mean low single indicators of coordinated development. Therefore, our conclusion here does not contradict the one reached in Sect. 11.2, that China's high-tech industries and NGEs are in a low degree of coordination.

Our conclusion to the empirical research of this section is that the development of high-tech industries is a significant driving force behind NGEs' growth, and that, in China, it is of great referential significance to encourage, guide, and support NGEs' participation in the development of high-tech industries by means of practical and effective policies and measures, especially in such provinces as Zhejiang and Jiangsu with extant developed private economic sectors. In order to better support NGEs' development, China has issued quite a number of supportive policies. Whether at the state or local level, however, no specific policies have been released to encourage NGEs' participation in the development of high-tech industries. Therefore, we suggest that policy makers formulate further guidance in this regard, in order to create a better environment for NGEs' development, constantly strengthen their capacity for independent innovation, establish a sound socialized service system for NGEs, and give full play to the development of China's high-tech industries in order to lead and drive NGEs' growth.

11.4 Conclusions

To begin with, we must actively create a sufficient environment for NGEs' development, improve the system of policies and laws governing NGEs, and support their entry into high-tech industries. We must further ease the burden of NGEs, especially SMEs, and fully rectify the arbitrary administrative conduct concerning NGEs, such as arbitrary fines and charges. We must further broaden the scope of NGEs' market access, lower the threshold to their entry, and create an open and fair market environment. We must actively support the development of those leading enterprises and high-tech industries with independent intellectual property rights, improve the technical resources and innovation capacity of China's high-tech industries, and, further, gradually make them the main goal of NGEs' innovation and development.

Secondly, we must further promote NGEs' capacity for independent innovation. We must support and guide private sci-tech SMEs to participate in key national scientific and technological projects, and treat them in the same way we treat large SOEs in terms of project approval, evaluation, and rewards. We must standardize the legislation of technological taxation, perfect the policy regarding NGEs' income tax, encourage enterprises' investment in research and development, and establish a system of preferential tax policies for venture investment. We must actively promote various forms of cooperation between administration, production, education, and research, and encourage NGEs to establish a technological innovation alliance by way of "the big leading the small," and integrate resources both at home and abroad for the development of NGEs' innovation.

Thirdly, we must further ease NGEs' financing difficulties. We should complete and perfect the financing guarantee system for sci-tech NGEs, and, in doing so, construct a multi-level and multi-modal financing guarantee system for them. We must actively develop a system of "grass-roots financing" to serve micro- and small-sized NGEs and encourage NGEs to develop high-tech industries with bank loans. We must encourage the increased development and aggregation of private funds, industrial capital, and venture investment companies, as well as guide them to further invest in start-up and growth-period private SMEs. We must perfect the mechanism by which we cultivate NGEs into listed companies, and actively support those NGEs possessing good credit and the considerable scale and strength to issue bonds, restructure, and list on the stock market through mergers and acquisitions. We must increase governmental investment in high-tech industries with more supportive funds and form a multi-level investment portfolio with venture capital, so as to attract sci-tech NGEs into high-tech industries.

Fourthly, we must reinforce the protection of NGEs' intellectual property rights, phase out the privileges held by FFEs in terms of intellectual property protection, and create for NGEs an equal environment for market competition by giving equal treatment to domestic and foreign intellectual property rights. We must vigorously cultivate various intermediary organizations of intellectual properties, introduce and train quality personnel for such intermediary services, and establish a sound market order.

Finally, we must establish a sound social service system for NGEs. In the areas in which private sci-tech SMEs are highly concentrated, we must establish product testing centers in a planned way so as to improve enterprises' R&D capacities and reduce their R&D costs. Wherever conditions permit, we must implement governmental guarantee for the financing of private sci-tech SMEs, construct and develop a system of commercial guarantees, and establish policy-based financial institutions in time to support the development of such enterprises. When considering government services, the government should formulate a hierarchical but coordinated service system, speed up the reformation of NGEs' administrative systems and the administrative approval system, foster and promote the clustered development of those high-tech industries capable of innovation, bring into full play all types and levels of development zones in order to attract NGEs' participation in the development of high-tech industries, and reinforce the demonstrative effect of key high-tech projects. We must also improve the intermediary service institutions and bring into full play their functions, such as market discovery, information collection, optimization of resource allocation, and quality and efficient services.

Bibliography

Ahlstrom D, Bruton GD, Yeh KS (2008) Private firms in China: building legitimacy in an emerging economy. J World Bus 43:385–399

Baumol WJ (2008) Small enterprises, large firms, productivity growth and wages. J Policy Model 30:575–589

Cai Q, Wu Z (2006) Barriers to technological NGEs' development and the countermeasures. Pioneering Sci Technol Mon 12

China Small- & Medium-Sized Enterprise Research Institute. Problems in NGEs' participation in the development of high-tech industries in China. http://www.sme2000.com.cn/indicator.asp. Accessed 21 July 2010

Department of Development Planning, Ministry of Science and Technology, and Enterprise Department, Ministry of Finance. Annual reviews of innovation fund for small technology-based firms 1999–2008. http://www.innofund.gov.cn/innofile. Accessed 25 July 2010

Economics Division of All-China Federation of Industry & Commerce (ACFIC) (2011) Report on the study of top 500 Chinese NGEs. All-China Federation of Industry & Commerce (ACFIC), Beijing

Gao H (2001) Applied statistical methods and the SAS system. Peking University Press, Beijing

Gu S (2000) Reflections on the strategic significance and measures of developing technological NGEs. Wuhan Econ Res 1

Himmelberg CP, Petersen BC (1994) R&D and internal finance: a panel study of small firms in high-tech industries. Rev Econ Stat 76(1):38–51

Kolasa M (2008) Productivity, innovation and convergence in Poland. Econ Transit 16 (3):467–501

Kong J (2005) NGEs: new force in high-tech industries. China Ventur Cap High-Tech 6

Li W, Li W (2008) NGEs' strategies for investment in hi-tech industries. Adv Mater Ind 8

Li S, Vertinsky I, Zhou D (2004) The emergence of private ownership in China. J Bus Res 57:1145–1152

Lu F, Li J (2007) The empirical analysis of the coordinating models for the systems of science-technology and economy: 1998–2003. J Taiyuan Univ Technol (Social Sciences Edition) (3)

Meng Q, Han W (2000) Study of the coordinating measurement model with respect to composite system. J Tianjin Univ 33(4):444–446

National Academy of Engineering Staff (1995) Risk and innovation: the role and importance of small, high-tech companies in the U.S. economy. National Academies Press, Washington, DC, pp 7–15

Tsai Y, Lin Y, Kurekovac L (2009) Innovation R&D and optimal investment under uncertainty in high-tech industries: an implication for emerging economies. Res Policy 38:1388–1395

Wang X, Zhao H (2005) Improving innovation ability of privately-owned scientific & technological enterprises. Social Sciences Academic Publishing House, Beijing

Wu Y, Wu Z, Zhang T (2007) Strategic measures analysis of promoting private capital participation in development of high-tech industries. J North China Univ Technol 4

Zhang M (2001) On linkage of high-tech industries with the capital market. Hunan Econ 4

Zhang A, Zhang Y, Zhao R (2003) A study of the R&D efficiency and productivity of Chinese firms. J Comp Econ 31:444–464

Chapter 12
Transnational Operations: New Models and Paths for NGEs' Development in the New Stage

Xianliang Xia

Ever since the global financial crisis, China's NGEs have experienced many changes in their transnational operations and development, such as issues related to the environment, policies, and their own capacities, and have, as a result, entered a new stage of transnational operations and development. As the financial crisis has brought China's NGEs such problems as a shrinking overseas market, an increase in receivable accounts, more difficult financing, and the reoccurrence of international trade protectionism, it has simultaneously provided them with new opportunities to accelerate resource integration, adjust their industrial structure, and improve their comprehensive strength for transnational operations.

12.1 The Motivation and Significance Behind NGEs' Transnational Operations

12.1.1 The Motivation Behind NGEs' Transnational Operations

12.1.1.1 Transnational NGEs' Need for Access to Overseas Resources and Markets

Transnational operations are necessary for the expansion, survival, and development of enterprises. At present, China's economic development is still restricted by a backwards model of production, limited resources, and a lack of independent core technologies. Therefore, the main purpose of the transnational operation of China's

X. Xia (✉)
Chinese Academy of Social Sciences, Beijing, China

Y. Liu (ed.), *New Interpretations on the Development of China's Non-Governmental Enterprises*, Research Series on the Chinese Dream and China's Development Path, DOI 10.1007/978-981-10-3872-3_12

NGEs is still to expand into the international market and obtain international resources, so as to make full use of the "two markets" and "two types of resources" available to them. As surveys have shown, the top two motivations of NGEs' overseas operation are "to expand the overseas market" and "to attain overseas market information," respectively; "to gain higher profits" ranked third; "to accumulate international business experience" ties with "to cultivate internationalized talents" at fourth; and "to obtain advanced technologies" comes in fifth (Li Chaoming 2006). In fact, the first three motivations all center around the market, while the others are oriented towards resource acquisition. In the wake of economic globalization and faced with competition from transnational enterprises that deploy their resources worldwide, China's NGEs can hardly survive or develop if they only stick to the domestic market and resources—transnational operation has become the inevitable choice for their expansion and sustainable development. After China's entry into the WTO, NGEs are faced with the challenge of globalization. To grow larger and stronger, they must integrate themselves into the international market, take advantage of international resources, and actively participate in international competition. Therefore, the transnational operation of China's NGEs is the only rational approach to their sustainable development, the inevitable teleological choice, an irresistible trend of world economic development, an objective demand of national economic development, and a necessary choice for NGEs' survival and development.

12.1.1.2 Transnational NGEs' Obtainment of Intangible Assets and the Need for Improved Capacity and Efficiency

By way of transnational operations worldwide, China's NGEs can integrate their market with their resources and, in doing so, organize their labor divisions. To participate in the division of the global industrial value chain, they will have to build a value chain of their products, increase their market share, and prolong the life cycles of their products, while also optimizing their internal resource allocation, assets structure, and cost structure. By way of transnational operations, China's NGEs can introduce scarce resources from abroad, obtain advanced technologies, talents, and world famous brands to make up for their disadvantages in domestic competition; they are further able to avoid trade barriers and participate in international competition, so as to improve the global integration of resources, markets, and their organizing capability, optimize the global allocation of their resources, and promote their efficiency and international competitiveness. The international financial crisis that erupted in 2008 represented a reshuffling of the global capital market, talent market, resource market, and commodity market. It has provided a good opportunity for China's NGEs to carry out an appropriate globalization strategy, expand onto the international market, obtain international resources, and orient themselves towards greater success.

12.1.1.3 The Necessity of Transnational NGEs to Implement Global and Regional Strategies

The choice of enterprises as to whether they should conduct transnational operations in developed or developing countries is born out of differing purposes. NGEs' investment in developed countries is mainly to occupy the market of these countries, increase the global market share of their products, and win business advantages. Moreover, they can also gain the advantage of production factors by use of their talent pools, advanced technologies, and the famous brands of more developed countries. In contrast, NGEs' investment in developing countries is not simply for the purpose of avoiding domestic market competition and occupying the market. A more important strategic goal of NGEs is to enjoy the preferential policies of the host countries and acquire short-term profits. Based on their own needs, resources and capacities, China's NGEs are making reasonable investment and operational ventures in different countries and regions throughout the world.

12.1.2 The Significance of NGEs' Transnational Operations

12.1.2.1 Improvements to NGEs' Management Ability and International Competitiveness

In the post-financial crisis era, it is impossible to survive and sustain enterprises by merely relying on the domestic market and resources. Not only is international competition getting more fierce and the international market more closely guarded, market segmentation and exclusion have become increasingly serious between different regions, different industries, or through different channels. Under these circumstances, it is difficult for any enterprise to survive by operating within a single country. NGEs' transnational operations not only determine their survival at home, but also their future trajectory. Thus, since the turn of the century, it has already become a new strategic choice for China's NGEs' to pursue greater (Liu Yingqiu 2003). Through their transnational operations, NGEs can optimize the market and resource allocations, as well as expand their market and increase their market share; they can directly obtain foreign economic resources and factors in order to make up for the resource shortages of their parent companies at home; they are able to acquire target market information and advanced technologies, optimize their product structure, and improve the competitive power of their products; they can also transform and optimize their investment and capital structure, improve their governance structure, and make their internal management more scientific and standardized by learning from the management models of other transnational enterprises. Only by making good use of both markets and both types of resources can NGEs better temper their teams, expand their space for development, and survive in the waters of fierce international competition.

12.1.2.2 Improvements to China's Industrial Structure and Development Model Transformation

NGEs' transnational operations promotes the flow and transfer of China's excess production factors and production capacity to the international market, and at the same time brings back those resources that are scarce in China as well as foreign advanced technologies, which are of strategic significance to the transformation of China's economic development model. In terms of its macro economy, China is currently faced with such problems as excessive domestic investment, the overcapacity of traditional industries, insufficient consumer demand, an overdependence on exports, and its extensive model of economic development. By encouraging NGEs to conduct transnational operations, China can expand onto the international market; transfer abroad those industries of excessive capacity, high energy consumption, high pollution, high emissions, or low technical content; adjust and improve its industrial structure; expand its overseas investment returns; and enhance its ability to participate in and influence the world economy.

12.1.2.3 NGEs' Importance as a Symbol of China's Progress Towards a Developed Economy

For developed countries in the West, an important symbol of their developed economy is having a large number of well-known transnational companies, ones which can integrate and optimize worldwide resource allocation and have changed GDP-based growth into a GNP-based economic growth. At present, China is still a developing country with a relatively backwards economy. The transnational operation of China's NGEs is still operating at a small scale and low stage, and is furthermore far from being common. They are still weak in terms of the allocation of global resources. The majority of NGEs survive and develop mainly by relying on the domestic market—that is, their development is still largely confined to the domestic space. Only when NGEs have generally succeeded in transnational operations and their GDP-based growth has changed into a GNP-based growth can we say that China has significantly improved its level of economic development and become an economic power. NGEs' transnational operations are of great strategic significance and are an important symbol of a developed national economy in China. China must actively encourage its NGEs to "go global" and "survive as a winner," and, in doing so, grow into real transnational companies with concrete global strategies.

12.2 NGEs' Transnational Operations and Development in the Post-financial Crisis Era: A New Environment and New Problems

The international financial crisis has brought about profound changes in the economic structure and environment of the world. Following this crisis, China's NGEs have been faced with a new external environment and new internal problems in terms of their international operation, which not only brings many opportunities, but also potential challenges.

12.2.1 A New Environment for NGEs' Transnational Operations and Development

12.2.1.1 The Global Economic Slowdown After the Financial Crisis

The Western countries are still suffering from high unemployment, weak consumer markets, and a lack of new growth drivers of the economy; the damaged international financial system still greatly restricts the real economy; new problems like asset bubbles have begun accumulating before the old ones, like "de-leveraging," have been settled; massive speculating and arbitraging funds have flown into commodity markets, such as that of oil; and commodity prices and the USD exchange rate are likely to fluctuate more drastically in the international market. All this is to say, the recovery of the world economy is bound to be a slow and tortuous process. Due to the global financial crisis, the world economy will remain in a period of slow growth for at least the following 3–5 years. As has been pessimistically predicted by UNCTAD (United Nations Conference on Trade and Development), global economic growth will not exceed 1.6% in 2010. According to the *World Economic Situation and Prospects 2010* report by the UN Department of Economic and Social Affairs, a 2.2% negative growth is expected for the gross world products of 2009, but if the current policies to stimulate economy are sustained, the global economy will grow by 2.4% in 2010. A more optimistic prediction by the IMF is that the world economy can restore growth in 2009 and, furthermore, increase by about 3% by the end of 2010. The U.S., Japan, and some other developed countries in the EU will possibly be subjected to a long period of economic downturn and recession. The UN report predicts that the U.S. will experience a 2.5% negative growth in 2009 but a 2.1% increase in 2010, and that the EU and Japan will grow slowly, by 0.6% and 0.9%, respectively, in 2010. The slowdown of economic growth in the world's major developed economies will affect the growth of international investment demands and consumption demands. Despite the improving indicators of major economies, there are more and more uncertain factors in international trade, such as high unemployment rates, the slow and tortuous recovery of the world economy, the protection of domestic markets, and an increasingly fierce competition for the international market. In addition, as more and more developing countries engage in the process of economic globalization and take part in the international division of labor, some of China's industries tend to overlap those of other developing countries, which intensifies competition and causes trade frictions. Therefore, the economic environment for transnational operations and development is not at all optimistic. For NGEs, economic growth is not only an independent variable but also a dependent variable of their own developmental process.

12.2.1.2 Increase of Foreign Policy Restrictions and the Frequent Occurrence of Trade and Investment Protectionism

NGEs' international development is now faced with greater risks, worse environments, and more international constraints than ever before. There are all kinds of uncertain risks in their overseas operations, such as political policy risks, market risks, financial risks, exchange rate risks, legal risks, and so forth. Despite the general trend of peace in the world, civil strife, wars, and abnormal regime changes are not rare in some regions due to the deterioration of national relations, fights for political power, and ethnic and religious conflicts. NGEs' transnational operations are also likely to meet with some unpredictable risks caused by the differences in consumers' demands, cultures, and preferences, the fluctuations of economic performance and market demands, and changes in interest rates, exchange rates, and other prices. With the rise of China's economy, some countries have adopted unfriendly attitudes towards Chinese enterprises, which manifests as hostility, jealousy, boycotts, reputation damage, and so forth. With these kinds of worsening environments and increasing risks, it is now increasingly difficult for Chinese enterprises to conduct transnational operations. To the NGEs of mainland China, the main challenge for their going global is their ignorance of overseas markets and lack of overseas operational experience. Their international business activities are more or less restricted not only by complex international laws, treaties, and technical regulations (as well as country-specific investment and trade laws and regulations), but also the various laws and regulations on consumer protection, labor protection, and marketing management. In general, NGEs are subject to greater risks in transnational operations and development as most of them are lacking in funds, backward in technologies, short of talents, simple in organizational structure, division, and collaboration, and weak in management and risk tolerance.

Moreover, with trade frictions and investment limits on the rise, the protective measures that were adopted during the crisis may evolve from temporary to long-term policies. According to statistics provided by China's Ministry of Commerce, 20 countries/regions had initiated 81 investigations against China in 2007, concerning anti-dumping, anti-subsidy, and safeguarding and special safeguarding measures, which involved USD 3.6 billion, up by 95.1% over the previous year. In addition, the U.S. had launched 17 "337 Investigations" against China's export

Table 12.1 Trade remedy investigations on China's cargo trade 2004–2009

Year	2004	2005	2006	2007	2008	2009
Total	57.0	63	86.0	81	93.0	116
Amount involved (bn USD)	1.26	2.1	2.05	3.6	6.14	12.7
Anti-dumping	–	–	–	–	70.0	76
Anti-subsidy	–	–	–	–	11.0	13
Safeguard measures	–	–	–	–	10.0	20
Special safeguard measures	–	–	–	–	2.0	7
337 investigations	–	7	13.0	17	11.0	8

Source: Ministry of Commerce. *National Trade and Investment Environment Reports 2005–2010*

products (See Table 12.1). In 2008, China's export products were subject to 93 trade remedy investigations by 21 countries/regions, involving a total of about USD 6.14 billion. Of these investigations, 70 were anti-dumping, 11 were anti-subsidy, ten were safeguarding measures, and two were special safeguarding measures. In that year, the U.S. had launched 11 "337 Investigations" against China's export products. In 2009, trade frictions against China and the amount involved were both at record highs. In that year, China's export products suffered 116 trade remedy investigations involving a total of about USD 12.7 billion, of which, 76 were anti-dumping, 13 were anti-subsidy, 20 were safeguard measures, and seven were special safeguarding measures. On the other hand, intellectual property disputes further increased overseas, and the U.S. had launched eight "337 Investigations" against Chinese products. At the end of 2009, the U.S. imposed anti-subsidy duties of anywhere from 10.36% to 15.78% on the oil well pipes imported from China, which involved USD 2.8 billion.

It is expected that there will be even more severe protectionist measures against China's product exportation, overseas investment, and transnational operations in 2010, and this will create various disadvantages for Chinese enterprises engaged in transnational operation. In particular, the erroneous pursuit of a rebalance in global economy and trade by the U.S. and some European countries will have a negative effect on China's exports and investment, and as a result frictions concerning China's foreign trade and investment will undoubtedly increase. There are all kinds of reasons for foreign governments to resent China's exports or investment, beyond which superficial issue always lies some distrust of Chinese products or capital. Chinese capital is far from integrated into the international market, and this is unlikely to change for the better in the near future. Chinese enterprises must look at the new problems with fresh ideas, fresh strategies, and fresh visions and really integrate into the global capital market by adopting new methods and models of transnational operation and development.

NGEs' transnational operation is subject to the trade and investment protectionism of foreign countries. Influenced by the financial crisis, the overseas business of the vast majority of Chinese merchants has slipped since 2008. What's more, Chinese merchants have suffered losses in many places due to the protectionist policies of trade and investment by the host governments. At the end of June 2009,

Russia suddenly closed down the Cherkizovsky Market in Moscow in the name of "Gray Custom Clearance," which had a tremendous impact on Chinese exporters to Russia. According to available statistics, this incident against Chinese enterprises resulted in a direct economic loss of over RMB 40 billion, and caused direct losses to 20,000 Chinese enterprises and collateral damages to another 30,000 or more. On November 24, 2009, related departments in Bucharest, Romania, began to inspect the Niro Market where Chinese merchants were concentrated, and closed down more than 300 shops. At that time, the entire EU assumed an attitude of boycott towards China's small commodities. Under these circumstances, in Spain, jittery Chinese businessmen frequently suffered groundless blows from the local government, which was pressured to protect local businessmen at a competitive disadvantage. For example, on July 9, 2009, the municipal government of Madrid announced that it had ordered 38 Chinese wholesale shops and "100-yuan stores" to halt their business for rectification, and another 99 to suspend business altogether. The protectionism of such countries damaged businessmen from China's Zhejiang Province the most. A survey shows that 39.1% of Wenzhou's manufacturing SMEs had entirely or partially halted production at the end of 2008; even when Wenzhou's manufacturing industry began to slowly recover at the end of 2009, nearly 20% of its SMEs were still in a state of economic depression. What's more, Wenzhou's manufacturing enterprises above a designated size were beset with various difficulties. In the first 9 months of 2009, 665 such enterprises were running at a loss, an annual increase of 56.5%. At present, a large number of Wenzhou businessmen are still confused about the prospect of investment. They no longer invest in the traditional manufacturing industry, but neither are they able to find new channels for industrial investment. Therefore, it is hard to realize the industrial upgrading or transformation of such types of capital.

12.2.1.3 Excessive Regional Trade Agreements and the Overdevelopment of Free Trade Zones

In recent years, following the fruitless Doha Round Negotiations, many regional economic organizations and free trade zones have emerged that are potential obstacles to free trade and investment for non-members, and their overdevelopment has posed a severe shock to the role of the WTO and other multilateral systems. With the further development of economic globalization, regional economic integration is accelerating and regional trade organizations are emerging one after another, represented by free trade zones. By December of 2008, 421 regional trade organizations had been reported to WTO by their members and 230 regional trade agreements were put into force; by July 31, 2010, the figures were 474 and 283, respectively. Of the regional trade organizations, 90% are free trade areas, while less than 10% are customs unions. The internal trade of all the regional economic groups has accounted half the total amount of global trade. When these regional trade arrangements play a role in promoting trade, they are, to a certain degree, impeding the trade and investment of non-members, and have in doing so thus weakened the function of the multilateral trading system.

12.2.1.4 Great Changes in the International Industrial Structure and Technical Environment

As the U.S.-led western developed economies have gradually switched to high-end manufacturing, services, and knowledge industries, developing economies are now dominating the manufacturing and service sectors at the lower end of the value chain. Western transnationals are deepening their internal division by stripping and eliminating non-profit business while highlighting their core businesses and control over industrial chains. Transnationals play the most significant role in promoting technological innovation; they also promote international industrial shift by making active changes and deepening their internal division. On the other hand, new energy sources and new environmental protection technologies sought after in order to cope with the international financial crisis and global warming will soon bring forth new industries and new divisions of labor. New technologies will bring new products and new standards, give rise to the formation of new industrial and technical structures, and finally change the existing competitive environment.

In the post-crisis era, China' NGEs are faced with new opportunities and challenges in promoting their international competitiveness. Economic globalization and the international financial crisis have brought China a rare chance to expand its global openness, accept international industrial transfers, promote its industrial transformation and upgrading, and speed up the adjustment of its industrial structure and the transformation of the models governing its economic development and foreign trade growth; in short, a chance to bring into full play its advantages and eliminate the bottleneck of its development and a chance to formulate new advantages and sustain stable economic growth. The financial crisis has sped up the process of regional economic integration and the establishment of free trade zones and prompted transnationals to transfer their industries to China, and has thus brought China's NGEs a chance to accept and support such an industrial shift. The international financial crisis has forced some transnationals to eliminate outdated or backward technologies in their home countries, and has thus provided China's NGEs with a chance to obtain fully developed technologies. The global financial crisis has also caused the transnationals of developed countries to accelerate business spinoff and industrial shift, eliminate technically backward equipment, implement industrial and technological innovations, and, furthermore, has aroused the desire to carry out asset acquisition and speed up technology licensing, joint ventures, and cooperation. All these have provided good chances for the transnational operation and development of China's NGEs. During the economic crisis, recurrent sales difficulty has required producers to adjust their product structure to be more in line with the new market demands, and forced enterprises to speed up their technological innovation and shorten their new product launch time for greater market competitiveness. By introducing externally-advanced technologies alongside achieving internal technological innovation, NGEs are stepping up the upgrading and reformation of traditional manufacturing industries and increasing the technical content and quality of their products so as to improve their international competitiveness. With their international technological innovation and industrial upgrading, China's NGEs now have a good chance to introduce new industries or businesses and improve the international competitiveness of their industries, as well as an opportunity to introduce practical new technologies and adjust their production and product structures so as to improve their competitiveness on the international market. China's NGEs must adapt themselves to the changes in the international industrial division, to the industrial structure adjustment, and to the new technical environment, accomplish their own industrial transformation and upgrading, and enhance their international competitiveness.

12.2.1.5 Profound Changes in the International Investment Environment

The international financial crisis has resulted in a serious recession and depression among many developed countries, where investment is sluggish with gloomy prospects, whereas China, with its sustained rapid economic growth, has become a haven for many transnationals from the crisis. Through various channels, a large amount of foreign funds have entered China and flowed into those fields featuring fast asset appreciation and rapid liquidation, such as its stock markets and real estate and assets; meanwhile, some foreign direct investment has entered industrial projects with good returns. This has provided an opportunity for NGEs to introduce foreign investment or to participate in supporting the transnationals while improving their international competitiveness in the process.

Due to the international financial crisis, many transnationals have been forced to divest themselves of some business, and plenty of enterprises are experiencing financial woes or on the verge of bankruptcy, and, consequently, are eager to sell some high quality assets at a relatively low price. For those of China's NGEs "going global," this is a good chance to carry out international mergers and acquisitions or equity investment, which will assuredly increase the channels open to and market chances for transnational operations.

Since the international financial crisis, new forms of trade and investment protectionism have continuously emerged. Endless new technical trade barriers, emerging technical standards and competitive platforms, an uncertain legal framework on climate change and ecological and environmental protection, the ever changing international division and industrial structure, and new and complex restrictions on investment and trade—all these have brought new challenges to China's NGEs and required them to improve their level of transnational operations and development.

Global climate change and the trend of increased importance being attached to a low-carbon economy are having a profound influence on the international investment environment. In recent years, global warming has become an increasingly serious and urgent problem without a ready solution. One of the main causes of global economic imbalance is that the world only focused on economic development, but has neglected environmental protection in the past. As a low-carbon economy centers around technological innovation based on energy saving and emissions reduction, the innovation of industrial structures and institutions, and the fundamental transformation of the survival and development philosophy of human beings, it is bound to have a profound influence on such aspects as the transformation of the global real economy and the adjustment of industrial structures and financial systems; it is an essential requirement if the world economy is to break out the crisis and resume a balanced development. The world needs to construct a new economy, a new civilization, and a new order in order to reach a new equilibrium. The low-carbon economy has gradually become an irresistible trend since it was brought forth. On September 8, 2007, Chinese President Hu Jintao made a speech at the 15th APEC leaders' informal meeting. He pointed out that, with a highly responsible attitude towards both humankind and the future, China has been constantly and consistently attaching great importance to climate change by painstakingly developing a low-carbon economy and a resource-saving and environmentally-friendly society; China has set up a leading group for tackling climate change, issued a series of laws and regulations, and formulated a national plan on climate change; China has made a positive contribution to reducing and curbing global greenhouse gas emission by a series of policies and measures, such as adjusting its economic structure, improving its energy structure, raising its efficiency in terms of energy use, promoting increased forestation, and implementing family planning. The European Union has regarded the low-carbon economy as a "new industrial revolution" and formulated a package of corresponding policies. Japan has formulated the *Action Plan for a Low-Carbon Society* and made a low-carbon society the direction of its future development and the government's long-term developmental goal. In the U.S., the Obama administration put forth a new-energy strategy soon after it came to power, and the Senate has passed the *Low-Carbon Economy Act*, hoping that the new-energy-based low-carbon economy will pull the U.S. out of the economic downturn and help it maintain its leading position in the world economy.

As global warming and the low-carbon economy have caught the eye of the world (especially developed countries like the U.S. and Japan), Western public opinion has exerted unprecedented pressure on China to assume its "responsibility in emissions reduction." China is now faced with many daunting challenges, including the carbon emissions reduction obligations imposed by western developed countries, the potential threat of "green protectionism," and the development of a low-carbon economy. For example, the UN Climate Change Conference in Copenhagen at the end of 2009 was full of blame and conflicts of interest. On December 28, 2009, *The Guardian* online published an article by Martin Khor, entitled: "Blame Denmark, not China, for Copenhagen Failure: The Decision to Override the Multilateral Process and Hold a Secret Meeting of Select Nations Ruined Any Chance of Success." He corrected the mistake of British Climate

Change Secretary Ed Miliband and Mark Lynas, who had accused China of "hijacking" the conference into failure. He pointed out that it had indeed been "hijacked," but by the host Denmark, rather than China, and criticized a few developed countries for attempting to dominate the legitimacy of the solution to climate change. American economists represented by Krugman proposed that carbon tariffs be imposed on imported products from countries taking no emissions reduction commitment (Krugman 2009). Unsupported by any economic, legal, or moral theory, this proposal was of a profound strategic intention and was more of a tool for political hegemony and vested economic interests than a mechanism for carbon emissions reduction. In the future, the world will welcome a greater variety of new economic environment to the solution of global climate change.

12.2.2 New Problems in the Transnational Operations and Development of China's NGEs

12.2.2.1 Ownership Discrimination Sustained Domestically

In China, the general understanding of capital is usually biased. Many people regard it as a pest only for profit. Since China was a semi-feudal and semi-colonial society, its people have been shackled and damaged by foreign compradors and bureaucratic capital. After the founding of the People's Republic of China, everyone, from political figures, experts, and scholars to the general public, had tried to avoid that which is private. At that time, China was a country with a lagging and entrenched selfishness. As private capital had no chance to develop, social and economic development had suffered as a result. In addition, the behavior of public officials abusing public power for private interest had greatly damaged both the economy and society. So people could only expect to replace private capital with state-owned capital and foreign capital, as they always felt that private capital was dirty in origin (indeed, some of it was embezzled from state-owned or collective capital). They generally had a distorted view of private capital and were unwilling to see it grow strong. Those policies and their derivatives, however, born in the context of a national hatred and the elimination of anything private, have turned state-owned capital into national capital that is closely related to governmental interest and even above the national interest, or into bureaucratic capital that does not belong to any individual bureaucrat. They have also turned foreign capital into one that is superior to the national treatment. Some people take for granted that state-owned capital can safeguard public welfare, people's livelihoods, and the national interest, and that it should be given certain special rights as a result. In point of fact, this is a misunderstanding of capital, for it is no longer capital that does not run after profit. There is no good or bad capital—the key lies in how to use and manage it. The best people can expect of state-owned capital is that the government will use it to realize their purposes when necessary, and nothing else. Disbelief in private capital and expectations of monopoly by state-owned capital will bring no true well-being. In fact, private capital is a reflection of people's wealth. In developed Western countries, much wealth resides in the hands of the people, while the state holds but a small part of it; therefore private capital as an institution is developed in these countries. Many citizens hold some degree of shares of an enterprise and have investments in the form of financial assets in the stock market or other capital markets. Such investment is not only the product of accumulated national wealth, but also an important source of people's income. A country can never be strong unless its people are rich. It is necessary to develop non-governmental or private capital so as to make our people rich and the nation strong.

Some policies within China clearly discriminate against private capital, however, as they only accept the entry of state-owned or foreign capital. Some policies are over-sensitive to the political ideology of enterprise ownership, and have too many restrictions on NGEs' development. Consequently, they do not enjoy the same national treatment as is enjoyed by enterprises under other forms of ownerships; neither can they receive governmental support in various forms, like SOEs. As they can hardly get the government-controlled benefits in normal ways, such as through the domestic market, resources, and preferential policies, NGEs have to establish private relations with government officials. Official bribery has become an increased cost necessary to the business development of private capital. Many local officials are so afraid of any association with NGEs, which may bring them trouble, that they seldom regard NGEs as enterprises deserving equal national treatment in project approval and policy making. It is safe to say that constraints on NGEs' development exist among and within every aspect of China's economy and society. According to Feng Lun (2007), private capital has always been an affiliation or complement to state-owned capital, and, therefore, the best way to protect itself is to stay away from the industries and sectors monopolized by state-owned capital, and stay content with some small business and do some good things like building roads and bridges. In face of state-owned capital, only by insisting the stance of cooperation rather than competition, complement rather than replacement, and affiliation rather than arrogation can private capital have room for operation and sustain its development. This is an accurate portrait of non-governmental capital[1] in China's national economy at present.

Currently, some related policies and measures in China seem to be colored with a negation of the practices put into play since the country's reform and opening up—the promotion of the common development of various forms of ownership, the relaxation of control over non-public sectors of the economy, and the facilitation of the "advance of NGEs and retreat of SOEs" and rapid development of the national economy. For example, in present-day China, there are such problems as the "advance of SOEs and retreat of NGEs," the narrow living space of NGEs due to financing difficulties, the existence of many policies restricting NGEs' access to certain industries, the increase of laborers' wages and social benefits, and the rise in

[1]Non-governmental capital is in fact private capital, as different from state-owned capital. The former is used to avoid using the word "private".

production costs caused by the appreciation of the RMB exchange rate. All these are gradually weakening the competitiveness and profit margin of those NGEs engaged in domestic production, processing, and the export trade. The deteriorating domestic market and environment for NGEs' survival and development is likely to shake their foundation at home and weaken their business reputation, brand recognition, and accumulation of capital, knowledge, and technology, all of which will certainly affect their capacity for transnational operations and development. The result would be insufficient strength on the part of NGEs for sustaining exports, as well as a lack of capital and intellectual property advantages in overseas investment.

12.2.2.2 Inhibition of the Global Economic Recession as Imposed on NGEs' Export Growth

The global financial turmoil and real economy depression caused by the international financial crisis has struck a significant blow to the transnational operation and development of China's NGEs. As the crisis swept across the world's most developed countries, market demand among China's major trade partners—such as the U.S., Japan, and the EU—has shrunk. This has directly caused a sharp decline in NGEs' volume of exports, and many export-oriented NGEs are having operational difficulties, with some even on the verge of bankruptcy. Due to the decline in international demand, industrial overcapacity, and fluctuations of raw material prices, China's export-oriented NGEs have generally experienced declining product prices—their higher output no longer brings a higher income, and may even reduce their income. As profit margins decline, a large amount of industrial capital has gradually withdrawn from the real economy. The slump in the export market has caused difficulties for many NGEs in their operations and overseas investment, and some private investors consequently prefer short-term asset speculation on stocks and real estate.

12.2.2.3 The Promotion of NGEs' Transnational Operation Capacity

China's NGEs have advantages insofar as they have clear property rights, flexible mechanisms of control, and efficient decision-making in terms of investment. On the other hand, however, they came to transnational operations late and thus have a relatively weak foundation in this field. They still lack international competitiveness in many aspects, such as advantages of scale, technological innovation, brand power, internal governance structure, human capital, and transnational operational capacity. Between the international financial crisis and the complex economic situation at home, their own problems and shortcomings have been more clearly exposed, mainly in three aspects: first, most NGEs are not competitive in the volatile market environment, as they lack core technologies and independent brands; second, most of them are clearly controlled, as they are at the least significant end of industrial value chains; and third, most of them lack adequate adaptability to the complex economic environment due to their poor management (Huang Mengfu 2009).

At present, most NGEs engaged in transnational operations are small not only in terms of registered capital and the size of their assets, but also in business scale and number of employees, and most of them are in what can be considered a small-scale exploratory stage of transnational operations. Their internal structure and management system can hardly meet the requirements of competition on the international market; their capital is insufficient and their profitability poor; their international trade activities are usually divided and thus can hardly produce a cluster effect (Yi Liqun 2008). For example, among the NGEs of Zhejiang Province, average overseas investment is USD 587,800, and the average overseas sole investment is only USD 96,700 (Li Qian 2008). The transnational investment of China's NGEs is much smaller than the average size of overseas subsidiaries(about USD 6 million) of transnational corporations of developed countries, and smaller still than the average scale(about USD 2.6 million) of those from other developing countries. Without advantages of scale in either investment or operations, China's NGEs will lose many opportunities to enter and develop within the international market, which may increase their operational risks and costs and weaken their capacity for financing and market expansion.

12.2.2.4 Improvement of Policies and Regulations Supporting NGEs' Transnational Operations

In February 2005, the State Council released *Opinions on Encouraging, Supporting, and Guiding the Development of Individual, Private, and Other Non-Public Sectors of the Economy* and made it clear that the government should support NGEs developing domestic and foreign markets, as well as actively provide them with information on both markets; that the government should encourage and support the expansion of exports and going global to invest overseas; that the government should give NGEs the same treatment as other types of enterprises in overseas investment, import and export credit, and export credit insurance; that the government should encourage NGEs to apply for intellectual property rights outside China; and that the government should bring into full play the roles of intermediary organizations—such as industry associations and chambers of commerce—and make good use of the national SMEs' market development funds to support NGEs' development of the international market. In May 2007, in line with the spirit of the CPC Central Committee and the State Council on encouraging, supporting, and guiding NGEs' development, China's Ministry of Commerce, Ministry of Finance, the People's Bank of China, and ACFIC jointly issued *Several Opinions on Encouraging, Supporting, and Guiding NGEs' Foreign Investment and Cooperation*, which encourages, supports, and guides NGEs' participation in international competition and cooperation by means of overseas investment, contracted projects, and labor service cooperation, and so forth., and the formation of a number of transnational enterprises with strong international competitiveness. The document proposes to give NGEs policy support in administrative examination and approval, taxation, finance, foreign exchange, and insurance, as well as extensive support and encouragement in overseas investment direction and services, and also to support NGEs' development on the domestic and international markets, which has given impetus to their transnational operation. Although these policies have played a positive role in the transnational operation and development of China's NGEs, however, the actual effect is by no means obvious. It is true that the 14th CPC National Congress established the orientation of China's economic system reform towards a socialist market economy as well as the scientific connotation of China's basic economic system, and that the State Council has issued a series of policies and guidelines that encourage, support, and guide NGEs' development. But, in general, the phenomena of "glass door" and "swing door" are still common, which not only restrict NGEs' entry into domestic industries and sectors, but also constrain the foreign investment and project and labor contracting of NGEs "going global." Many administrative problems still exist, such as the tedious, complex, and inefficient procedures of examination and approval through too many departments, which seriously hinders NGEs' normal and legal entry into and participation in overseas investment and operations.

China is still young in terms of the development of transnational operations, and its NGEs have little basis for engaging in overseas operations and development. The state has not yet included NGEs' transnational operations in its mainstream macro management, which is basically in a *laissez-faire* state. The government has not yet made enough preparation in providing information services, legal guidance and business direction for NGEs, which can hardly get adequate help for their transnational operation (Liu Yingqiu 2003). There is neither a governmental/social services system for NGEs' "going global," nor a supervisory system on the implementation of encouraging and supporting policies. Neither has the government transformed itself into a service-oriented one, nor has it acquired enough experience in the macroscopic management of enterprises' transnational operations, from whom NGEs cannot get appropriate services such as information services, legal services, or consultation services on international investment and trade. Meanwhile, NGEs' risks of overseas operations are increased by China's incomplete intermediary services system, as well as by the shortage of intermediary institutions capable of supporting NGEs' entry into the international market by providing them with effective overseas market information or such services as market surveys, the strategic layout and planning of transnational operations, and/or legal services.

Under the conditions of soaring transnational investment in various forms throughout the world and the rapid development of China's own transnational operation, there is no valid law in China to promote, protect, and manage investment, which has seriously lagged behind the situation and demands of both domestic and overseas investment. So far, China has not formulated any basic laws or norms on the protection of overseas investment and financing and transnational business activities, like *The Transnational Corporations Law*, *The Overseas*

Investment Law, or *The Overseas Financing and Guarantee Law*. At present, the governmental macro management of enterprises' transnational operations mainly depends on a series of policies and regulations formulated by related departments. Although they are playing some role in transnational operational management, these policies are less systematic, consistent, persistent, stable, and transparent than laws, and some of them are even biased, which restrict the transnational operation and development of enterprises, especially that of NGEs.

In their transnational operations, NGEs going global are faced with many problems, such as difficulties in indirect financing and guarantees, the lack of access to finance, high financing costs, and the high threshold of direct financing. Currently, NGEs generally lack guarantees for their credits and thus cannot win strong financing support from financial institutions. It is true that policies have been issued outlining NGEs' loan guarantees in many places, but their support for NGEs' transnational operations, specifically, is quite limited, as the guaranteed funds are relatively small in size. The difficulty in getting loans from financial institutions has forced NGEs to seek financing in the high-interest and high-risk underground or in private lending markets, which increases their costs of financing and weakens their competitiveness in the international market. In China's state-owned commercial banks, some financial businesses (such as export credits and buyers' loans) are mainly targeted at SOEs and FFEs. On the other hand, NGEs engaged in transnational operations usually suffer from ownership discrimination by these financial institutions, and can hardly receive due financial support in credits, insurances, or guarantees. As a result, some of them cannot help but watch development chances slip away, and many NGEs can no longer sustain their development even when they are already participating in the international market. In addition, China's current management system exercises strict control over the foreign exchange of enterprises, especially that of NGEs. This constrains their transnational investment, as their self-retained amount of foreign exchange is very limited and the application for foreign exchange is quite complex and tedious.

China's NGEs are heavily burdened with taxes and fees. The heavy tax expenses incurred in the domestic market have led to a shortage of funds for NGEs' innovation and their "going global," and the arbitrary charges have further increased enterprise burdens. In some places, local governments usually deem NGEs as "cash cows" for their expenses ,and they often solve their own financial hardships by adding items of charges and increasing apportioned fees. The poorer the place, the more serious the problem. In the national tax policies, NGEs generally do not enjoy equal national treatment. For example, they are subjected to double taxation on their income. That is, not only must they pay corporate income tax like SOEs, they also have to pay an individual income tax upon their after-tax profit. For private limited liability companies, they have to pay individual income taxes for the conversion of stockholders' equity into increased enterprise capital. In contrast, FFEs are entitled to a return of a certain percentage of their corporate income tax if they reinvest their profits. China's tax policies for NGEs are still less stable, specific, and normative, and the tax preference for NGEs is monotonous and limited (Xiao Shaoping 2006). When export-oriented SMEs and those engaged in overseas investment are severely damaged in the international financial crisis and are really in need of national assistance, they can expect anything but the support of the national relief funds. This once again reveals the insignificant effect of China's supportive fiscal and tax policies on private SMEs' technological innovation, structural adjustment, and employment expansion, and above all the necessity of improving them.

12.3 Changes in NGEs' Modes of Transnational Operation in the New Economic Stage

Based on the traditional models of transnational operation, China's NGEs have to face new problems, new challenges, and new tasks as the financial crisis continues. They must adapt to the general trend of globalization and localized development, as well as to the new environment and characteristics following the international financial crisis. They must discover new opportunities and create new approaches and models of transnational operation, which manifest specifically as new methods, new courses, new paths, and new levels of NGEs' transnational operation in the new economic stage.

12.3.1 Changes to NGEs' Foreign Trade in Recent Years

In recent years, China's NGEs have been rapidly expanding their foreign trade and their proportion of overall foreign trade has been increasing yearly. In 2004, of China's total exported goods of USD 593.37 billion, 11.7% (USD 69.25 billion) was by NGEs[2]; of the total imported goods of USD 561.42 billion, only 7.5% (USD 41.98 billion) was by NGEs from 2004 to 2009, NGEs' goods exports and imports were increasing yearly, and their proportions of overall export and import were also on rise (See Table 12.2). In 2008, NGEs' exported goods (USD 326.03 billion) accounted for 22.8% of China's total exported goods (USD 1.42854 trillion), and their imported goods (USD 130.44 billion) accounted for 11.5% of China's total imported goods (USD 1.13308 trillion). In 2009, NGEs' exported goods (USD 297.92 billion) accounted for 24.8% of China's total exported goods (USD 1.20166 trillion), and their imported goods (USD 145.35 billion) accounted for 14.4% of China's total imported goods (USD 1.00555 trillion).

Import and export trade makes up a significant proportion of NGEs' international business. With the significant promotion of their strength and their capacity for international trade, NGEs are already equipped with the ability and experience necessary for their going global and transnational operations. NGEs' contributions

[2]Here NGEs refer to private enterprises, as different from SOEs, collective enterprises, and FFEs.

Table 12.2 Proportions of NGEs' goods imports and exports 2004–2009 (%)

Year	2004	2005	2006	2007	2008	2009
Export share	11.7	14.7	17.6	20.3	22.8	24.8
Import share	7.5	8.2	9.2	10.5	11.5	14.4

Source: General Administration of Customs of People's Republic of China. http://www.chinacustomsstat.com/aspx/1/NewData/Stat_Data.aspx?state=2&month=12&year=2010

to China's exports increased from 2.22% in 1999 to 11.7% in 2004, a growth of 9% over 5 years. From 2004 to 2009, the figure had further increased to 24.8%, a growth of 13% over another 5 years. There was an obvious acceleration in the speed of growth. The same was true of their imports. Through imports, NGEs have not only acquired raw materials, machinery, and the equipment needed for their production and operation, but also greatly improved their product quality and strengthened the competitiveness of their products on the international market (You Hongbing 2009).

Although China's NGEs began international operations relatively late, they are developing very quickly. In particular, some large NGEs have made remarkable achievements in foreign trade and transnational operations in recent years, and some have gradually established their international marketing networks and developed their own international brands. Most NGEs, however, have made very little R&D investment. Therefore, they are generally weak in independent innovation and have few technical patents or famous brands, and without remarkable advantages in competition, they are usually weak in international competitiveness. The export trade of China' NGEs is not correlated with their R&D input and number of patents; the major source of their competitiveness in export trade is not their capability for independent innovation (Xia Xianliang 2006). According to a survey on the independent innovation of China's manufacturing NGEs by the CASS Center for Private Economic Studies in 2006, of the 822 enterprises surveyed, only 275 were owners of patents (which had an average of 28 patents), while the other 547 were without patents, accounting for two-thirds of the total; 14 enterprises (1.7%) were owners of PCT international patents and had an average of only 4.8 international patents; 18 were applying for an average of 3.5 PCT international patents. Due to their insufficient capacity for innovation, NGEs' international competitiveness is being weakened by the rising costs of production and export marketing. The majority of them are still engaged mainly in the labor-intensive processing and manufacturing industries of low technical content and remain at the lower end of industrial value chains. Without their own international patents or brands, NGEs are faced with the deterioration of their trade conditions year by year, as the international competition grows more intense and export prices keep declining.

Currently, China's NGEs still lack influential brands that are able to dominate the international market, while the brands they have are low in added value and weak in international competitiveness. Of China's overall exports, branded products account for less than 10%, much lower than that of developed countries (over

25%). China's NGEs are behind the times in terms of brand building and strategies. They usually have no long-term objectives in regards to brand building but only seek instant benefits and quick success (Wang Haiying 2008). For example, less than 10% of the lighter producers of Wenzhou have registered their own brands, and the rest mainly operate in the pattern of ordering, sampling, and brand designating or OEM. Japanese enterprises simply stick their own trademarks on Wenzhou lighters and sell them as their own products in the international market. Most products of China's NGEs are low in technical content and without independent brands; they are at the low end of the industrial value chain and of little international competitiveness except for their low prices.

In addition to the traditional import and export trade, there are various forms taken by NGEs' international operations. The prevailing forms include licensed trade, compensation trade, contractual cooperative production, the international processing and assembling trade, and project contracting (Li Na 2009). By increasing their outward foreign direct investment (OFDI) and engaging in transnational investment and operation activities such as project contracting, designing, and consultation services, NGEs can gradually transform their models of development and improve their globalization levels.

12.3.2 Changes in NGEs' OFDI in Recent Years

In recent years, NGEs have achieved certain developments in both the scale and number of OFDI, whereas SOEs and collective enterprises are on the decline in terms of both OFDI stock and enterprise numbers, which reflects the fact that NGEs are gradually increasing OFDI in their transnational development.

At the end of 2007, SOEs accounted for 71% of China's OFDI stock, down 10% from the previous year; limited liability companies accounted for 20.3%; limited stock corporations accounted for 5.1%; private enterprises and joint-stock cooperative enterprises accounted for 1.2%, respectively; FFEs and enterprises with investment from Taiwan, Hong Kong, and Macao accounted for 0.8%; collective enterprises accounted for 0.4% (See Table 12.3). If we regard enterprises other than SOEs, collective enterprises, FFEs and those with investment from Taiwan, Hong Kong, and Macao as NGEs, they had already accounted for 27.8% of the overall OFDI stock of 2007.

At the end of 2007, SOEs accounted for 19.7% of China's domestic OFDI entities, limited liability companies for 43.3%, private enterprises for 11%, limited stock corporations for 10.2%, joint-stock cooperative enterprises for 7.8%, FFEs for 3.7%, enterprises with investment from Taiwan, Hong Kong, and Macao for 1.8%, collective enterprises for 1.8%, and enterprises of other types for 0.7%. By the same definition used with NGEs, they accounted for 73% of the domestic OFDI entities at the end of 2007.

By the end of 2008, over 8500 domestic Chinese OFDI entities had established 12,000 enterprises with direct investment at home and abroad, China's OFDI stock

Table 12.3 Proportions of stocks and quantities of domestic OFDI entities 2007–2009 (%)

Registered type	Stock proportions of domestic OFDI entities			Quantity proportions of domestic OFDI entities		
	2007	2008	2009	2007	2008	2009
SOEs	71.0	69.6	69.2	19.7	16.1	13.4
Limited liability companies	20.3	20.1	22.0	43.3	50.2	57.7
Limited stock corporations	5.1	6.6	5.6	10.2	8.8	7.2
Joint-stock cooperative enterprises	1.2	1.2	1.0	7.8	6.5	4.9
Private enterprises	1.2	1.0	1.0	11.0	9.4	7.5
Collective enterprises	0.4	0.4	0.3	1.8	1.5	1.2
Enterprises with investment from Taiwan, Hong Kong and Macao	0.8	0.1	0.1	1.8	1.8	1.8
FFEs	–	0.8	0.5	3.7	3.5	3.1
Others	–	0.2	0.3	0.7	2.2	3.2

Note: As some enterprises have not reported their going global; their data are not included in the bulletins. The real OFDI size is much larger the statistics listed here
Source: Ministry of Commerce. *China's OFDI Statistical Bulletins 2007–2009*

had reached USD 183.97 billion, and the overseas enterprise assets totaled over USD 1 trillion. By the end of 2008, SOEs accounted for 69.6% of China's OFDI stock, down 1.4% from the previous year; limited liability companies for 20.1%; limited stock corporations for 6.6%; joint-stock cooperative enterprises for 1.2%; private enterprises for 1%; FFEs for 0.8%; collective enterprises for 0.4%; enterprises with investment from Taiwan, Hong Kong, and Macao for 0.1%; and enterprises of other types for 0.2%. The OFDI stock of China's NGEs accounted for 29.1% of the total, which was 1.3% higher than the same figure for 2007.

In 2008, limited liability companies accounted for 50.2% of all domestic OFDI enterprises, an increase of almost 7% over the previous year; SOEs accounted for 16.1%; private enterprises for 9.4%; limited stock corporations for 8.8%; joint-stock cooperative enterprises for 6.5%; FFEs for 3.5%; enterprises with investment from Taiwan, Hong Kong, and Macao for 1.8%; collective enterprises for 1.5%; and enterprises of other types for 2.2%. By the end of 2008, NGEs accounted for 77.1% of China's domestic OFDI enterprises, 4.1% higher than the figure in the previous year.

At the end of 2009, SOEs accounted for 69.2% of overall OFDI stock, down by 0.4% from the previous year; limited liability companies for 22%, up by 1.9%; limited stock corporations for 5.6%; joint-stock cooperative enterprises for 1%; private enterprises for 1%; FFEs for 0.5%; collective enterprises for 0.3%; enterprises with investment from Taiwan, Hong Kong, and Macao for 0.1%; and enterprises of other types for 0.3%. By the end of 2009, China's NGEs with foreign direct investment stock accounted for 29.9% of the overall OFDI stock, 0.8% higher than the figure in the previous year.

By the end of 2009, 12,000 domestic enterprises had made direct investment in over 13,000 enterprises abroad. Of these domestic OFDI enterprises, 57.7% were limited liability companies; 13.4% were SOEs; 7.5% were private enterprises; 7.2% were limited stock corporations; 4.9% were joint-stock cooperative enterprises; 3.1% were FFEs; 1.8% were enterprises with investment from Taiwan, Hong Kong, and Macao; 1.2% were collective enterprises; and 3.2% were enterprises of other types. NGEs accounted for 80.5% of the domestic OFDI entities, 3.4% higher than the figure in the previous year.

12.3.3 Changes in NGEs' Modes of Overseas Investment and Entry

Traditionally, China's NGEs have carried out their international operations mainly through proprietary or agent services regarding imports and exports, border trade, foreign capital or technology introduction, supporting FFEs and establishing strategic alliances with them, business outsourcing, and direct investment, including Greenfield Investment, mergers, and acquisitions. Compared with the enterprises of developed countries, China's NGEs are small in terms of the size of their overseas investment and primitive in their motives of transnational operation; as unitary investment subjects, they mainly enter overseas markets by means of sole or joint investment. (Li Na 2009). At present, the traditional Greenfield Investment model is still the major form of overseas investment for China's NGEs, supplemented by transnational mergers and acquisitions, equity replacement, venture investment and strategic alliances; at the same time, some new forms of investment are being increasingly adopted, such as license contracting of non-equity investment, outsourcing, and BOT management contracting.

According to the *Report on an Analysis of 500 Chinese NGEs 2010* released by the Economics Division of ACFIC and China Financial Consultancy Co., Ltd. in August of 2010, 117 (23.4%) had made overseas investments by 2009, up 4.4% over 2008; they possessed a total of 481 enterprises and projects abroad, up 57.19%; their overseas investment totaled USD 2.25274 billion, up by 47.59% over 2008.

Of the 500 NGEs in 2009, the major mode of overseas investment was wholly-owned new enterprises, which was adopted by 103 (20.6%), an increase of 33 and up 47% over 2008. The second-most popular mode was joint-venture new enterprises, adopted by 82 (16.4%); a few NGEs had entered overseas markets through mergers or joint stock, adopted by 22 (4.4%) and 37 (7.4%), respectively (See Table 12.4).

The investment and entry modes of those NGEs planning to expand overseas in the following 3 years are somehow different from those adopted by enterprises that already have overseas investment. Of the 500 NGEs, 112 (22.4%) have adopted joint-venture new enterprises, while 98 (19.6%) have chosen wholly-owned new enterprises. Obviously, Greenfield Investment (or investment in new establishments) is

Table 12.4 Trend of overseas investment modes of 500 NGEs surveyed in 2009

Modes of investment		Overseas investment made		Overseas investment in 3 years	
		Enterprises	Proportion	Enterprises	Proportion
New enterprises	Wholly-owned	103	20.6	98	19.6
	Joint-ventures	82	16.4	112	22.4
Mergers		22	4.4	49	9.8
Joint stock		37	7.4	63	12.6

Sources: Economics Division of ACFIC., & China Financial Consultancy Co., Ltd. (2010). *Report on Analysis of 500 Chinese NGEs 2010*

still the most common mode or method of NGEs' overseas investment and entry, with strategic alliances like joint ventures being their favorite. Besides, 49 (9.8%) NGEs have chosen a mode of mergers and acquisitions that transfers control rights, and a slightly larger number of NGEs (63) have adopted joint-stock investment, accounting for 12.6%. For China's NGEs, it is comparatively scientific to invest in wholly-owned and joint-venture new establishments, as they are still weak in the management, capability, and strength of transnational investment, and have very slight advantages in this respect.

In face of the increasingly strong labor unions in Western countries, it is not desirable for Chinese enterprises without enough control to enter overseas market by means of mergers or wholly-owned investment models, as these types of investment are likely to be constrained by labor unions and trapped in cultural dilemmas and the difficulty in integrating management models. Comparatively, joint-venture and joint-stock investment can take advantage of the power of local capital and avoid cultural shocks and the adverse impact of labor unions. Accordingly, we make the following suggestions as to the overseas investment of China's NGEs.

12.3.3.1 Active Formation of Transnational Strategic Alliances

The transnational strategic alliance is an important form of organization in the internationalization and transnational operation and development of enterprises. Over 90% of large transnational corporations of western developed countries have established various forms of strategic alliances. Strategic alliances can take the form of non-agreement cooperation, agreement cooperation, joint ventures or cross shareholding. For example, agreement-based strategic alliances are usually formed in foreign outsourcing or the contracting outsourcing of foreign companies, which establishes a long-term relationship between supply and demand. For China's NGEs, the formation of transnational strategic alliances—especially the establishment of joint-venture companies with foreign partners—is an important approach to the international market and the enhancement of their competitive advantages.

China's NGEs must follow the principle of methodically increasing their level of cooperation and begin to rely on their own information, trust, and such recognition as is accumulated through long-term cooperation. Only in this way can they establish strategic alliances of in-depth cooperation with their foreign partners. Generally, both parties within such a strategic alliance already have some level of mutual recognition and trust as well as a good knowledge of each other's resources, capabilities, governance, and cultures, and have considerable faith in the performance integrity of the partner. The gradual improvement of cooperation levels can reduce business costs and cooperation risks, as well as lay a solid foundation for the formation of higher-level strategic alliances. Meanwhile, China's NGEs should strengthen their communication and coordination in these strategic alliances, sustain the dynamic adaptability of the alliances, and prevent the overflow of core resources or any crisis of confidence in the alliances. What's more, they must learn from their partners the knowledge of management, marketing, production, and operations, as well as the way and art of managing both intangible and tangible assets.

12.3.3.2 The Vigorous Expansion of International Indirect Investment

Affected by the international financial crisis, many host countries have suffered a slowdown of their economic growth, tightened their credit, and even implemented capital project control. As a result, the performance of NGEs engaged in overseas investment is not at all optimistic. Such impacts have directly caused a serious shortage of confidence among China's NGEs in overseas investment and a decline in their impulse to invest in new projects. Many of them have even delayed or suspended projects already in motion. Moreover, the financial crisis has also triggered a downturn of the global stock market, which has affected the major target countries of overseas listings and made it more difficult for NGEs to seek direct financing by that means (Zhao Yonghua and Lin Qingbing 2009; Zhan Biying 2009).

Traditional OFDI usually requires joint-venture investors to negotiate with their partners on joint investment and cooperation or for solely-funded investors to expand the market independently, which is greatly limited by the partners' will or the investors' own capabilities. On the other hand, due to their small capital and weak investment capacity, NGEs are generally unable to conduct transnational equity mergers and acquisitions, which are purchase with a larger proportion of equity. If they intend to enter the international market and operate transnationally, NGEs can directly make equity investments in foreign stock markets, which is also a method of transnational capital operation. By this method, rather than mergers and acquisitions, NGEs are able to acquire a smaller proportion of equity through securities trading, obtain joint-stock investment gains, and avoid investment risks by optimizing their investment portfolios. China's NGEs can make overseas investments by purchasing securities or bonds in foreign stock markets or by making loans to foreign clients in credit markets. Such indirect foreign investment mainly aims for capital appreciation by means of higher stock dividends, interest, or price spread arbitrage. But in such investment, investors only receive the benefits of their financial assets. They will not have appreciable control over the investment objects or the direct ownership of the investees' movable or immovable properties, or participate directly in the operations and management of the target enterprises.

Now, some of China's NGEs that are engaged in international investment have not only invested in virtual assets like stocks and bonds, but have also begun investing in those immovable properties of a stronger assets nature, such as city commercial real estate, mineral resources, and land. What China's NGEs make in buying foreign securities or in offering loans is virtual investment, through which they can collect regular dividends and interest, or gain price differences through securities trading. Certainly, investors will weigh the benefits and risks of direct and indirect investment, and constantly adjust the modes, projects, and markets of their investment accordingly. Through constant shifts between international real industries and virtual capital and between international direct and indirect investments, China's NGEs can develop into transnational corporations that are well adapted to the international commodity market, factor market, and capital market, and thus make China a strong country for both direct and indirect overseas investment.

12.3.3.3 The Establishment of Chinese Images by Listing and Financing Overseas

In the past, NGEs usually made OFDI with their own capital, technologies, brands, and equipment. Now, however, they can register shell companies in countries featuring developed and open capital markets by investing locally or in free ports, and raise funds by listing in the stock market. In this way, they are able to conduct localized transnational operations with local funds, personnel, means of production, and resources, and remedy the bottlenecks of their development in these aspects.

For transnational listings and operations, what NGEs need is nothing but a team of talents capable of international capital operation, which is a new approach to transnational operation for those NGEs short of funds. The main approaches to overseas listing include formal Initial Public Offerings (IPO), the purchase of shell corporations, and back-door listings, among others. China's NGEs can also directly apply to overseas securities authorities for registration and public offerings as Chinese domestic companies and apply for listed transactions on foreign stock exchanges.

Many of China's NGEs have excellent assets and are standardized in internal governance, with outstanding performances, lucrative profits, and high growth potential. They can seek overseas listings and financing through the services of foreign financial institutions and consultants, such as listing and financing packages, reports for approval, and stock issuance.

For China's NGEs, formal domestic IPO takes quite some time and money, but once they succeed in listing and financing in overseas markets, they cannot only export their capital and expand their OFDI, but also reform their internal governance structure, improve their management levels, develop their financing channels, and bring in plenty of capital. All this will contribute to the formulation of their strategies for localized development and a higher-level, longer-term, and more standardized development.

12.3.4 Changes in NGEs' Modes/Methods of Transnational Operation

Transnational operational modes that accord with the current productivity of China's NGEs mainly include lower-end sales, production and processing, R&D designing, representative offices, project contracting, resource development, and border trade and business. However, different NGEs may adopt different transnational operational methods with their own focuses.

From the data of 2008 and 2009 as published in the *Report on the Analysis of 500 Chinese NGEs* by the Economics Division of ACFIC and China Financial Consultancy Co. Ltd., we have found changes in the modes of both their current and planned transnational operations. In the current modes of transnational operation, the proportion of sales network building, overseas processing factory building, resource developing, and project contracting in 2009 are slightly higher than those in 2008, indicating an increase in the amount of attention granted to these modes; meanwhile the proportion of R&D institute establishing has dropped from 5.8% in 2008 to 5.4% in 2009 (See Table 12.5). Sales difficulties due to the financial crisis have forced NGEs to put more emphasis on the layout of their global sales networks; increase the adjustment of overseas industrial structures; avoid the risk of rising raw material prices, increasing production and operation costs, and shrinking international markets; expand capacity transfer to overseas markets; and increase investment in new factories closer to their overseas markets. At the same time, NGEs have been practical and attached great importance to overseas project contracting and resource developing.

Of all the intended transnational operational modes of the 500 NGEs surveyed, sales network building, factory building, and representative agency establishing were given greater emphasis than the others in 2009, which respectively accounted for 40.6%, 40.6%, and 26%, up by 7.8%, 11%, and 1.6% from 2008. The largest number and proportion of the surveyed NGEs had planned to build overseas sales networks, which received the highest degree of attention. Since the financial crisis, NGEs have begun attaching greater importance to building factories overseas, so as to shift their industrial capacity and adjust their industrial structure. There was a sharp rise in the number of NGEs inclined to build factories overseas as well as the proportion of such enterprises overall (up by 11%). Representative offices are usually the windows into NGEs' overseas investment and transnational operation. For China's private SMEs, it is an important and practicable mode of transnational development to establish such overseas offices.

Table 12.5 Changes in the transnational operational modes of 500 NGEs surveyed between 2008 and 2009

Mode	Current transnational operations				Planned transnational operations			
	2008		2009		2008		2009	
	NGEs	Proportion(%)	NGEs	Proportion(%)	NGEs	Proportion(%)	NGEs	Proportion(%)
Sales network building	106	21.2	112	22.4	164	32.8	203	40.6
Factory building	41	8.2	44	8.8	75	15.0	130	26.0
Representative office establishing	–	–	–	–	121	24.2	129	25.8
R&D institute establishing	29	5.8	27	5.4	45	9.0	72	14.4
Project contracting	29	5.8	45	9.0	52	10.4	69	13.8
Resource developing	25	5.0	26	5.2	46	9.2	71	14.2
Border trade cooperating	–	–	–	–	54	10.8	60	12.0

Sources: Economics Division of ACFIC & China Financial Consultancy Co., Ltd. (2010). *Report on Analysis of 500 Chinese NGEs 2010*

In 2009, with the growth of their capabilities and strength, an increasing number of NGEs had planned to engage in transnational operations, and there was an increase in both their overall number and proportion to the whole, both of which were higher than the same figures from 2008, indicating a promising increase in the degree of NGEs' transnational operations. In 2009, NGEs intending to establish R&D institutes, conduct project contracting, undertake resource development, and carry out border trading cooperatives accounted for 14.4%, 13.8%, 14.2%, and 12%, respectively, higher than the same figures in 2008, which were 9%, 10.4%, 9.2%, and 9%, respectively. This reflects the fact that greater attention has been paid to R&D and resource development after the crisis. As NGEs have very slight advantages in the ownership of OFDI projects, they cannot win significant advantages through productive OFDI. They must increase their overseas R&D investment so as to promote their domestic R&D capacity and product designing, strengthen their investment in resources, trade, and services, and improve the degree of their investment. Accordingly, we make the following suggestions as to the transnational operation and investment of China's NGEs.

12.3.4.1 The Vigorous Establishment of Overseas Sales Networks

Currently, China's NGEs are quite strong in the area of domestic manufacturing industries, but are experiencing a bottleneck in the expansion of their export sales. Over many years, NGEs' exports have relied mainly on self-exporting or export agencies. Strictly speaking, China's foreign trade is merely "foreign" trade and has not yet developed into international or global trade, as its business development is still under the control of foreign importers. Along with their rapid growth and the corresponding expansion of business, China's NGEs have come to realize that transnational operations based on imports and exports through dealers are no longer adequate for their development, as they are unable to master the direction of the international market and are short of both technical support and storage cooperation in their target countries. They must enter the international market directly, set up their own sales companies overseas, and enhance the competitiveness of their product. Chinese NGEs investing in overseas productions and operations are just at the initial stage of international trade, but once they establish an international foundation, they will enter the stage of global trade. The setup of overseas sales companies is the turning point from foreign trade to international and global trade. In the past, China's foreign trade companies usually set up foreign trade "windows" abroad and looked for local agents, and only then established joint ventures with local partners. Now, however, they can set up sales subsidiaries as necessary, usually in cities with convenient transportation and logistics close to the sales markets. According to their development strategies, NGEs should project the "points," "lines," and "areas" of their marketing channels worldwide on the basis of location advantages, the cost efficiency of channels, and the penetration effect of marketing publicity, and in doing so perfect the layout of their marketing channels.

NGEs must prepare to establish their overseas sales networks so as to be strategically equipped for their development into global companies in the future.

12.3.4.2 The Bold Exploration and Development of Online International Trade

Two-thirds of U.S. retailers now require that their suppliers be able to handle the entire transaction, from start to finish, in the electronic data interchange (EDI) system. In EDI-based commercial sales, from the moment a consumer pays for a commodity and the barcode is scanned, retailers are able to find accumulated information in the database about the sales, stocks, and earnings of that commodity, as well as the suppliers' commodity catalogues on the platform. Based on such information, they can decide from which supplier to buy and then send out their electronics accordingly. China's NGEs have the option to adopt different patterns or compositions of online international trade according to their products, marketing capacities, and informatization capabilities. They should build their own e-commerce platforms, equip themselves with advanced concepts for online sales, establish better brands with lower costs but higher efficiencies, and give full play to the flow of economic and trade informatization, so as to win their proper share in the international market. On the other hand, they should promptly deal with all traces of logistics, provide perfect customer service, receive and appropriately handle customer feedback, strengthen their product innovation and quality control, and reduce credit sales so as to cut down on bad debts. They should not only familiarize themselves with the demands of customers in different countries and regions, but also arrange transnational production, transportation, and after-sales services accordingly, all of which have set higher requirements on enterprises in the internet age. China's NGEs must adapt themselves to the changes that have occurred in their target markets, customer characteristics, and product categories; they must overcome geographical, cultural, and temporal differences; they must rebuild customer relationships oriented to individualized demands and increase customer trust in online products, brand reputation, and network sales. To this end, NGEs should adjust their organizational structures, shorten their supply channels, change the mode of internal operations, expand virtual malls and further develop their distributors, reduce online sellers and organization levels, highlight their brands and individualized websites, and balance the relationship between brand globalization and the localization/regionalization of brand identities, so as to effectively meet individualized demands and provide different commodities for different customers. Meanwhile, they must provide effective and prompt return and exchange services and secure the safety of customers' property. China's NGEs should actively advertise and pursue cross-cultural publicity on large foreign portals, professional websites, and entertainment websites, set up online stores on high-traffic websites, and strengthen business cooperation and even form alliances with both domestic and foreign e-commerce websites.

12.3.4.3 Active and Innovative Methods for Financing Exports

In commodity trading, the use of short-term structural financing tools based on such assets as inventory, advance payment, and accounts receivable can facilitate trade; in relevant international settlements links, settlement-based financial intermediation can promote international trade. The types and procedures of trade financing are determined directly by the settlement methods chosen by importers and exporters, who can accelerate capital turnover by way of settlement financing and by solving funding difficulties concerning accounts receivable or payable. Sometimes, the importer's bank may cut credit to the importer, who would require the exporter to change the originally decided settlement by letter of credit (L/C) into sales on account (O/A) or documents against payment after sight (D/P). In this case, the exporter would have his or her funds tied up and have to accept the importer's credit risks, and, consequently, many Chinese exporters are unwilling or afraid to accept such orders. In 2009, China's short-term export credit insurance reached USD 90.27 billion, a yearly growth of 122.6%, and directly pulled in high-risk business worth USD 64 billion, a 5% growth for China's export and a 9% growth in general export trade. By September 15, 2010, the short-term export credit insurance by China Export and Credit Insurance Company had reached USD 104.39 billion, a yearly increase of 107.2%, which strongly supported the development of China's foreign trade. In its national policies, China encourages commercial banks to increase trade financing, which is critical to the steady development of its foreign trade and the stable growth of its economy, as well as to the expansion of emerging export markets and the consolidation and promotion of China's status in the international trade system. Compared with traditional modes of trade financing and the foreign trade mode of importers' purchasing with cash, financing trade is a worthwhile method of transnational operations during marketing difficulties in the economic crisis. This mode of trade brings a high risk of bad accounts receivable or messy debts, however, and will tie up much of a company's liquidity and slow down capital turnover. Therefore, such financing trade agreements should only be signed between long-term clients with considerable tolerance for or controllability of risks.

12.3.4.4 Going Global in Industrial Clusters

In the past, the OFDI of NGEs' going global was usually made single-handedly, without industrial support or services, which resulted in many difficulties for transnational operations. With their small size and weak capacity for international operations, individual NGEs are never as capable of investment as transnational corporations and international consortia. If they join together to form a complete industrial chain, however, they will be able to make an integral internal market and expand their international competitiveness and influence. Hence, it can be regarded as a new method for going global and engaging in overseas investment. Industrial clusters are grouped within large-scale agglomerations of manufacturers of similar products and related institutions in specific geographical areas. Based on the share of such resources as infrastructures, information, technologies, and labor forces, they are able to form huge supporting systems of division and collaboration, flexible manufacturing, and industrial innovation. The rise and development of industrial clusters has already become a distinct characteristic of the industrial economy in Jiangsu and Zhejiang as well as a strong supporting factor in the creation of economic miracles in this area. In China's eastern coastal areas, township NGEs exhibit a high degree of division and collaboration, so industrial clusters are able to boost the internationalization of specialized markets in the area (You Beilei and Rui Baojuan 2009). For example, the development of industrial clusters in Zhejiang Province is highly correlated with its export mode, which is dominated by general trade and electromechanical, clothing, and textile production (Zhu Xiwei and Jin Xiangrong 2007). By going global in industrial clusters, China's NGEs gain many advantages—they are able to achieve new economies of scale, improve their overall productivity, make use of the cluster effect and cluster brands, share market and technical information, cultivate characteristic industries or product lines, build their core competitiveness, and increase their capacity for risk resistance. At present, some leading export-oriented enterprises of Zhejiang are attracting international funds, technologies, and talents by means of overseas listings, the import of internationally-advanced production equipment, and the flexible introduction of foreign R&D and design talents, and as a result have gradually formed international leading R&D capabilities and technological advantages while establishing internationally famous brands. Following the transnational development of such leading enterprises, many clusters from Jiangsu and Zhejiang are going global in the wild goose lineup model based on an internationalized and specialized division of marketing and production, technical research, and development and brand-building. Those of China's NGEs that are going global in industrial clusters can form industrial chains and build industrial parks in foreign countries. They can enjoy various preferential policies and are free to trade and make investment in these countries. They are able to properly handle their orders and avoid trade barriers and the risks of exchange rate fluctuations even in a time of financial crisis, and thus improve their general risk tolerance. Meanwhile, their overseas operations contribute to the optimization of China's industrial structure and to reducing the resource and environmental pressure of China, as well as to the utilization of the eliminated or idle machinery and equipment at home. On the other hand, the going global of such industrial clusters also requires proper coordination and service work by intermediary organizations such as industrial associations, chambers of commerce, and so forth.

12.4 The Internationalization of the RMB for NGEs' Transnational Development

The transnational operation of enterprise is closely related to exchange risks. The internationalization of China's RMB is an objective requirement of the modernization and internationalization of China's national economy. Currently, as the conditions are basically mature, the state has already taken measures to strategically push forward the internationalization of the RMB. The course of RMB internationalization and the transnational operation of Chinese NGEs are closely correlated and promote each other. The internationalization of the RMB has already become a new and important prerequisite for the international operation of China's NGEs.

12.4.1 The Expansion of RMB Settlements in International Trade to Promote NGEs' Transnational Operations

The global financial crisis has brought China's NGEs a historic opportunity to promote the internationalization of the RMB. Under the current international monetary system dominated by the US dollar, the import capacity of many poor countries is limited by the hard constraint of their international payment capabilities, and as such they are unable to import Chinese goods due to the inability to pay in US dollars, no matter how attractive the products are in price and quality. The financial crisis has prompted China to steadily pilot and practice RMB settlements in international trade and to push forward the internationalization of the RMB.

China has carried out currency swaps with some of its trade and economic partners, which contributes to the trade settlement in each other's currency and the aversion of exchange risks of dollar-dominated settlements in bilateral trade. The internationalization of the RMB can also reduce the influence of exchange rate fluctuation on trade.

As the US dollar is currently dominating the pricing, settlement, and payment in international trade, the occurrence of certain exchange risks is almost impossible to avoid, as there is always some fluctuation of the exchange rate between USD and RMB from the moment an international trade negotiation is made and the agreement is signed to when the bank receives the dollar settlement. Though such fluctuations can be predicted and lessened by hedging tools, they can never be completely eliminated. But the internationalization of the RMB and RMB settlements in international trade can eliminate such risks caused by currency changes and exchange rate fluctuations, as RMB settlement makes the trade predictable and thus promotes the steady growth of international trade.

By expanding the import of its trade partners, China can basically maintain a certain level of trade surplus with them and enable the RMB to go abroad on a larger scale. It will also enable its partners to afford more Chinese products, as they can receive RMB in their trade with China and purchase Chinese commodities in RMB. RMB settlement should not only be encouraged in border trade. In negotiations between China's NGEs and their partners on the settlement of general trade, RMB settlement should also be encouraged as the primary means of import and export payment.

The policies of China should benefit both parties of foreign trade who fix prices and settle their trade in RMB and use and hold RMB in international trade. Only in this way can the RMB be widely used in international trade and NGEs' transnational operations will increase the proportion of RMB settlements in international trade, which, in turn, can promote NGEs' transnational operation and development overall.

12.4.2 Reform of the RMB Exchange Rate Formation Mechanism to Stimulate NGEs' Transnational Operations

The internationalization of the RMB means the establishment of a mechanism of the marketized formation of exchange rates and the system of free settlement and exchanges, as well as the liberalization of the RMB trade and currency exchange, which will have a complex influence on related trade and investment. The internationalization, marketization, and liberalization of the RMB will promote the marketized formation of the RMB's exchange rate and gradually improve its value. The appreciation of the RMB may have a certain amount of negative impact on NGEs' competitiveness in the export trade, but it can facilitate their OFDI and import trading. The exchange rate of the RMB is a strategic game between great powers, which not only affects Sino-US trade and investments but also the relationship between China and the world economy as a whole.

The expansion of RMB supply and circulation in the international market, as a result of the international operation of China's NGEs, will gradually change the trend of its appreciation into a balanced demand and supply on the market. The increasing proportion of RMB in transnational operations will gradually lower the proportion of USD in China's foreign reserve and reduce the pressure of a dollar supply increase, leading to a balanced exchange rate between the two currencies in the market, which will contribute to the marketization of an RMB exchange rate formation mechanism.

The internationalization of RMB is also conducive to NGEs' foreign investment and international cooperation. The free convertibility and exchange of RMB can greatly reduce the restriction of foreign exchange control on the foreign investment and cooperation of small- and medium-sized NGEs and thus promote NGEs' transnational investment and cooperation, as they can freely exchange RMB and other currencies in the market and freely make international remittances and capital flow. On the other hand, NGEs' massive transnational operations can promote the wide use of RMB in international trade, investment, and project cooperation, and increase the circulation, holding, using, trading, and storage of RMB on the international market.

The appreciation of RMB is the objective trend unless great risks should arise in China's economy. It objectively reflects the formation of market rates of exchange and the free-market mechanism. Under the expected appreciation of the RMB, many NGEs will have a hard time in exports when they can, at best, only maintain their existing market share and receive less surplus income in US dollars. For labor-intensive NGEs, the depreciation of the RMB is crucial to their export expansion, but China will not undertake that in the current crisis lest there should be a currency devaluation race in the neighboring countries. In addition to the pressure of RMB appreciation, these NGEs have to face another austere pressure, namely, the upgrading of their technologies and industries and the adjustment of their product structure, which will in turn accelerate the appreciation of the RMB, increase export costs, weaken export motivations, and reduce foreign exchange income and the impetus for increases to the exchange rate.

12.4.3 The Internationalization of RMB Financial Businesses to Facilitate NGEs' Transnational Operation

To push forward the internationalization of the RMB, China encourages Chinese-funded financial institutions to set up overseas branches and RMB offshore financial centers, so as to promote exchange liberalization and international currency exchange, as well as to carry out foreign aid and financial cooperation. The use of the RMB in border trade pricing and settlement by Chinese enterprises has accelerated the entry and circulation of large amounts of RMB into neighboring countries. Citizens of these neighboring countries, however, may have difficulty converting RMB into their own currencies as they do not house enough Chinese-funded banks, which impedes its circulation in these countries. Encouraging Chinese-funded banks to set up overseas branches is therefore of great importance for promoting NGEs' transnational operations and the internationalization of the RMB. At the same time, providing trade partners with RMB financing is not only an important measure necessary to strengthening their directional import capability, but also an opportunity for China's financial institutions to expand their credit business overseas and to gain overseas loan markets for China's massive savings. Chinese-funded banks should provide appropriate amounts of mid- and short-term RMB export credit for the governmental agencies and enterprises of their neighboring countries, so as to expand the use and regional influence of the RMB. As cash transactions are usually high in costs and risks and may have carriable problems—even resulting in counterfeiting, tax evasion, and smuggling—Chinese banks should be encouraged to set up more financial outlets for easy non-cash transactions in bills of exchange, checks, or credit cards. Therefore, China's encouragement for more overseas branches of Chinese-funded banks is not only a demand for RMB internationalization, but also a demand on the foreign trade and overseas investment of Chinese enterprises. It can not only increase RMB-based international financing, but also the use of the RMB in international payment and exchange as well as in foreigners' purchase of Chinese products. This is very important for the expansion of financial services needed for the transnational operations of China's NGEs, and beneficial for cash payment, remittances, and other services needed for NGEs' international trade and investment.

China must also speed up the establishment of an RMB offshore financial center in Hong Kong so as to facilitate the formation of RMB free exchange mechanisms and market exchange rate mechanisms, which will contribute to an upsurge of foreign investment and the transnational operation of Chinese enterprises in the process of RMB internationalization and the creation of an excellent financial environment for their transnational operations. While the global financial crisis has posed many difficulties to the national and corporate finances of many countries, China is contributing to the relief of such fiscal and financial hardships by means of international development aid and debt relief, which, in return, has also expanded the international market and developed international relations for China's export and labor cooperation. On the other hand, China's foreign aid in RMB has not only expanded the international scope of its use, but also promoted trade with the recipient countries and the diversification of the import and export markets. By expanding its foreign aid in RMB, China is enabling its enterprises to obtain an advantageous position in their trading with the host countries, as well as in project contracting and international investment in these countries. In addition, the currency swaps and financial cooperation between China and its trade partners are also facilitating NGEs' transnational operations in many ways.

Bibliography

Braun S, Huelsbeck M (2007) Enforcing intellectual property rights through organizational measures: the case of German companies in China. In: Preliminary draft submitted to the 2nd Annual Conference of the EPIP Association

Feng L (2007) Across the river of history. China Entrep (2)

Han X (2004) Status and strategies of transnational operation of China's NGEs. North Econ Trade (2)

Huang M (2009) NGEs faced with both challenges and opportunities. Rural Work Commun (3)

Jiao F (2009) Analysis of the internationalization of China's NGEs. Int Econ Trade Res (5)

Khor M (2009) Blame Denmark, not China, for Copenhagen failure: the decision to override the multilateral process and hold a secret meeting of select nations ruined any chance of success. http://www.guardian.co.uk/commentisfree/cif-green/2009/dec/28/copenhagen-denmark-china. Accessed 10 Sept 2010

Kolstad I, Wiig A (2009) What determines Chinese outward FDI? CMI working paper, WP 3. Chr. Michelsen Institute, Bergen

Krugman P (2009) The WTO is making sense. Published in his column blog *The conscience of a liberal*. The New York Times, 26 June

Li C (2006) An empirical study of transnational operation of China's NGEs. Econ Theory Bus Manag (7)

Li Q (2008) Analysis on status and barriers of NGEs' transnational operation. China Township Enterp Account (12)

Li N (2009) Analysis on status and barriers of the transnational operation of China's NGEs. Sci Technol Inf (14)

Liu Y (2003) Transnational operation: a new strategic choice for non-public enterprises to gain rapid development. Mod Econ Sci 3:15

Liu Y, Zhang L, Wei Z (2009) Analysis of "going global" of 50 most competitive Chinese NGEs. China Ind Econ (2)
Quan X, Chesbrough H (2010) Hierarchical segmentation of R&D process and intellectual property protection: evidence from transnational R&D labs in China. IEE Trans Eng Manag 57(1):9–21. Based on Quan X (2005) Transnational research and development labs in China: local and global innovation. Ph.D dissertation, University of California, Berkeley
Wang H (2008) NGEs' internationalization: status & paths. Int Econ Coop (12)
Xia X (2006) Independent innovation and international development of China's NGEs. In: Liu Y, Xu Z (eds) Report on Chinese non-governmental enterprise competitiveness (no. 3). Social Sciences Academic Press, Beijing
Xiao S (2006) Revenue policy support for development of non state-owned economy. J Jiangsu Vocat Tech Inst Econ Commer 2:7
Yi L (2008) Reflecting the problems in NGEs' transnational operation and the countermeasures. Mod Bus Trade Ind (3)
You H (2009) Approaches to promotion of NGEs' international competitiveness. Enterp Vitality (2)
You B, Rui B (2009) How to promote the internationalization of specialized markets relying on industrial clusters. Commercial Times (15)
Zhan B (2009) Thoughts on influence of global financial crisis on private enterprises and countermeasures. J Cent Inst Social 1(2):20
Zhao Y, Lin Q (2009) NGEs under the influence of international financial crisis: challenges and countermeasures. SMEs Manag Sci-Tech (22)
Zhu X, Jin X (2007) Industrial clusters of Zhejiang Province in the process of internationalization. Zhejiang Econ (17)

Epilogue to the Chinese Edition

This book reports research findings from "China's NGEs: Development, Environment, and Policies," a Chinese Academy of Social Sciences Key Research Project approved in 2009, which was also sponsored as a general program by the National Social Science Foundation in the same year (Program No. 09BJY045). Upon the conclusion of the project, however, we decided to rename it *New Interpretations on the Development of China's Non-Governmental Enterprises* (Referred to as *New Interpretations* hereinafter). There are two reasons for this change: first of all, we had already systematically reviewed, summarized, researched, and interpreted the birth, development, and reform of China's private economic sectors in the earlier "Research on Thirty Years of Reform and Development of China's NSOEs," a subprogram of a 2008 CASS Key Research Project, and, as such, found it undesirable to repeat the previous achievements. On the other hand, the beginning of the twenty-first century had witnessed a great event, that is, China's entry into the WTO. This had urged us to shift our research to the development of China's NGEs in the post-WTO era and make new and more in-depth empirical analysis and theoretical generalization of the new situation, new phenomena, new problems, new trends and new progress of NGEs' development in the new stage.

As stated, *New Interpretations* focuses on what is "new." Since the country's reform and opening up, China's NGEs have progressed rapidly, but their development has never been smooth. Especially in the twenty-first century—when the socialist economic market system (with Chinese features) was initially established–the historical mission of institutional transformation and transition has not yet been accomplished, and such problems as the unsound, incomplete, and even low-efficient systems and mechanisms have not been reduced with the deepening of reform, but have instead become more numerous and complicated, requiring further painstaking efforts to overcome. Under such circumstances, NGEs are inevitably faced with new difficulties, conflicts, and problems. In addition to the constant difficulty of getting loans and financing that impedes their development, they are troubled with new problems in market access and development as well as

Y. Liu (ed.), *New Interpretations on the Development of China's Non-Governmental Enterprises*, Research Series on the Chinese Dream and China's Development Path, DOI 10.1007/978-981-10-3872-3

their migrant employees' difficulties in housing and children's urban education. All these difficulties, conflicts, and problems are directly related to the imperfect external environment of enterprise development, including the obvious constraints of unsystematic and ill-matching governmental policies, but are also due to sluggish institutional transformation and transition as well as imperfect mechanisms and policies. Since the beginning of the twenty-first century, many great changes have taken place in the systems and mechanisms governing the development of NGEs, while at the same time, the institutional and policy-related problems impeding NGEs' sustainable and healthy development have also changed significantly. In this case, it is of an extremely important and newly-practical significance to investigate, interpret, and solve the latest problems and contradictions in NGEs' development in light of a new era, new conditions, and new developments, by using new logic and new methods, and to further explore NGEs' development in this new stage from the perspectives of systems, mechanisms, and policies. This is the first "new" aspect of *New Interpretations*.

The second "new" aspect of the book lies in the fact that it is based on the new conditions and new problems facing both China's reform and opening-up and the country's economic development after its entry into the WTO. It is aimed at exploring the further improvement and development of the basic economic system of socialism with Chinese characteristics and the mechanism of the socialist market economy system. Furthermore, it focuses on exploring and clarifying the logic and principles as to how NGEs can achieve industrial upgrading while simultaneously sustaining sound and rapid development under the new historical conditions under which China's systemic transformation and institutional transition has entered a new and critical stage, so as to better promote the sustained, healthy, and rapid development of China's national economy and the great rejuvenation of the Chinese nation as a whole.

The *Interpretations* are *new* particularly because our research is grounded on "new" empirical evidence and particularly emphasize the surveying and investigations of the real performance and development of China's NGEs. Therefore, over the course of this study, we have demanded that our group members exercise all available means by which to carry out research and come to new conclusions using first-hand information while deepening their theoretical studies.为 To reach this goal, we have particularly valued the full use of the empirical data in China's NGEs Competitiveness Database (created in the above-mentioned investigation and survey), in addition to the best of what we had achieved previously in this field. To pursue in-depth research, we have given equal weight to those mass statistical data and survey materials relevant to the development of NGEs provided by authoritative organizations like NBS and ACFIC.

One more important "new" aspect of the *New Interpretations* is that we have paid special attention to the new stage, new situation, new problems, and new requirements of the development of NGEs in the twenty-first century, and made new interpretations, summaries, and generalizations of their development from this new perspective. How best to facilitate the sustained and healthy development of China's NGEs by improving their institutions and policies, methods for boosting rapid and qualitative development by coordinating their internal governance and industrial restructuring, and how to accelerate their development by consolidating and improving China's basic economic system—they are exactly the focuses of the *New Interpretations*.

Another important "new" aspect of the *New Interpretations* is that we have not only respected the academic vision and individuality of each researcher and author, but also stressed their integration within the broader group consensus. As this research is highly practical and covers many aspects of development, it requires both a collective tackling and individual research, as well as theoretical exploration from a new perspective. We are therefore inevitably faced with various difficulties and challenges. Nevertheless, we have tried our best to achieve a proper balance between respect for individual work and the unity of collective views when proofreading, modifying, and finalizing the book. On one hand, we have emphasized the consistency of the main line of argument and the substantive agreement of primary concepts throughout the book. On the other hand, we have shown enough respect for the achievements of individual researchers and the theoretical insights of each member, without demanding uniformity or an absolute consistency of theoretical viewpoints presented here.

Ultimately, the *New Interpretations* is new scientific research accomplished through the cooperative brainstorming and common effort of the research group. The members are mainly experts from the Graduate School and related institutes of CASS and the Ministry of Industry and Information Technology (MIIT). The team leader, Liu Yingqiu, is Dean of the CASS Graduate School, Director of the CASS Center for Private Economic Studies, and a doctoral supervisor. The deputy leader, Wang Hongling, is a researcher with the CASS Institute of Economics and a doctoral supervisor. Liu Yingqiu was charged with the design and formulation of the general idea and framework outlining the research and chaired many meetings of the research group—where the members conducted thorough and in-depth discussions regarding the outline, basic ideas, and structure of the book—and ultimately made the final decisions about the framework for research and writing of 13 chapters. Chapter 1 was written by Researcher Zhang Jun of the CASS Rural Development Institute, and modified and supplemented by Liu Yingqiu; Chap. 2 was written by Researcher Liu Xiahui of the CASS Institute of Economics; Chap. 3 by Dr. Li Mengjuan of MIIT Electronic Information Institute; Chap. 4 by Researcher Ju Jinwen, the CASS Institute of Economics; Chap. 5 by Dr. Lü Fengyong, Assistant Researcher with the CASS Institute of Finance and Trade Economics; Chap. 6 was written by Xue Bai, Ph.D. student in the Department of Government Policy and Public Management, CASS Graduate School; Chap. 7 was jointly written by Dr. Xu Haoqing, Lecturer, and Zhao Lei, Ph.D. student, both in the Department of Government Policy and Public Management, CASS Graduate School; Chap. 8 was jointly written by Dr. Liu Jianxiong, Lecturer in the Department of Government Policy and Public Management, CASS Graduate School, and Zhu Xiongbing, Ph.D. student in the School of Economics and Management, Tsinghua University; Chap. 9 was written by Dr. Wu Yanbing, Associate Researcher with the CASS Institute of Economics; Chap. 10 by Researcher Wang

Hongling with the CASS Institute of Economics; Chap. 11 was jointly written by Gu Qiang, Deputy Director of the MIIT Planning Division, and Engineer Dong Ruiqing of the MIIT Electronic Science and Technology Information Institute; and, finally, Chap. 12 was written by Dr. Xia Xianliang, Associate Researcher with the CASS Institute of Finance and Trade Economics. When the first draft was completed, it was proofread by Wang Hongling and returned to the writers who further revised the chapters.

The research and writing followed four stages:

1. Preparation. Following a preliminary framework for research and the division of labor, group members collected and sorted out relevant literatures and materials and formulated relevant research ideas for each thematic study.
2. In-depth research. The research group held quite a few thematic meetings and determined the outline for and basic principles of research through collective group discussion. Subsequently, the author(s) of each chapter conducted their research and wrote their first drafts.
3. Formation of the manuscript and approval through group discussion. Based on the first drafts, the research group held a seminar at which the members reported their individual achievements in order to stimulate collective discussion and advice on improving and complementing their research and manuscript. Afterwards, each author polished their writing according to the suggestions provided.
4. Compilation and finalization. Wang Hongling first complied and proofread the book and Liu Yingqiu further reviewed, revised, and finalized it. Additionally, during this stage, Group Secretaries Zhang Liang and Zhao Sanying assisted with the technical treatment of the full text and translated the Table of Contents into English.

At this moment, when the *New Interpretations* is finalized and about to be published, I would like to thank all the group members for their responsible and positive efforts. We would like to thank the CASS Bureau of Scientific Research Management and the General Office of Academic Divisions for the care, support, and aid they gave this program. Our thanks also go to Director Han Chaohua of the Bureau of Scientific Research Management and the General Office of Academic Divisions, to Professor Tian Chun-sheng with China Youth University of Political Studies, to Inspector Huang Wenfu with the ACFIC Department of Research, and to Department Head Guan Mingjun with the CASS Bureau of Finance, Capital Construction, and Planning, all of whom spared time to attend the briefing, granted full recognition to the project, and offered valuable suggestions after carefully listening to our report We would like to express special thanks to the Planning Office of the National Social Science Fund of China and the CASS Bureau of Scientific Research Management, as well as to the anonymous evaluation experts organized therein. Both groups of experts spoke highly of our achievements and offered many important pieces of advice towards further improvement. Our achievement was rated “Excellent” by the experts organized by the CASS Bureau of Scientific Research Management. Under the strict review of the experts with the Planning Office of the National Social Science Fund of China, it was submitted for approval to the Leading Group for National Planning of Philosophy and Social Sciences and was selected with honors by *National Library of Philosophy and Social Science Achievements* in 2011 (Approval No. 11KJY001). Immediately after it was selected, we revised the work in earnest according to the requirements of the above experts and the Planning Office of the National Social Science Fund of China.

Despite our best efforts, this book is far from perfect in terms of empirical analysis, normative studies, and policy recommendations. We would cordially welcome criticism and advice from other scholars and people concerned with this subject and hope further in-depth analysis and research can be made to the series of theoretical or practical issues we have touched on in the *New Interpretations*. We also sincerely hope its publication can not only set the ball rolling, but also play a positive role in promoting the sustained, healthy, and smooth development of China's NGEs and in accelerating the great rejuvenation of the Chinese nation.

Finally, our heart-felt gratitude goes to this authoritative publisher and its editors, appointed by the Planning Office of the National Social Science Fund of China, on the principle of "unified logo, unified cover, unified format, and unified standard," for their painstaking efforts and the hard work that made this project a success. Meanwhile, we would also like to show our special thanks to Researcher Xie Shouguang, President of the Social Sciences Academic Press (SSAP), and Executive Editor Ms. Fan Ying with SSAP, without whose endeavors this book could not have been published so soon.

Liu Yingqiu
Beijing
May 12, 2011.
Rewritten on October 12, 2011.

Postscript to the English Edition

This book—*New Interpretations on the Development of China's Non-Governmental Enterprises,* presented to readers both at home and abroad—is a full adaptation of the original work published by China's Social Sciences Academic Press (SSAP) in early 2012, as required by the large cooperative project, *Chinese Dream and China's Development Path Research Series* (English version), between SSAP and Springer International Publishing AG. In 2011, the Chinese version was inducted into the second installment of the *National Library of Philosophy and Social Science Achievements*, in which it remains the only academic monograph on the development process and logical underpinnings of China's NGEs.

The English version's abridgment and adaptation has followed the principle of faithfulness to the source text while highlighting certain interpretations on the practice of the development of NGEs in China's market-oriented reform. The literature reviews and comments regarding certain thematic research, as well as some overly academic mathematical and statistical analyses, are duly abridged, and Chap. 12 from the Chinese version has been omitted As the primary author, I shall take full responsibility for possible oversights and errors in this adaptation and hope my co-authors can understand if anything should go against their wishes or original intent.

In the abridgement and adaptation, Zhang Liang, who served as academic secretary of the research group and also one of the authors, went through the entire manuscript to ensure format and style consistency in both the text and tables.

Y. Liu (ed.), *New Interpretations on the Development of China's Non-Governmental Enterprises*, Research Series on the Chinese Dream and China's Development Path, DOI 10.1007/978-981-10-3872-3

On behalf of all the authors, I would like to thank SSAP and Springer, as well as the Editorial Board of *Chinese Dream and China's Development Path Research Series*, for their trust and support.

Thanks also go to the translators of the book for their great efforts.

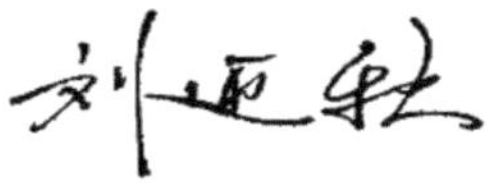

Liu Yingqiu
Hangzhou, China
July 2, 2014.

MIX
Papier aus verantwortungsvollen Quellen
Paper from responsible sources
FSC® C105338

If you have any concerns about our products,
you can contact us on
ProductSafety@springernature.com

In case Publisher is established outside the EU,
the EU authorized representative is:
Springer Nature Customer Service Center GmbH
Europaplatz 3, 69115 Heidelberg, Germany

Printed by Libri Plureos GmbH
in Hamburg, Germany